Robert Black

The Jockey Club and its Founders

In Three Periods

Robert Black

The Jockey Club and its Founders
In Three Periods

ISBN/EAN: 9783744661805

Printed in Europe, USA, Canada, Australia, Japan

Cover: Foto ©ninafisch / pixelio.de

More available books at **www.hansebooks.com**

THE JOCKEY CLUB

AND

ITS FOUNDERS

IN THREE PERIODS

BY

ROBERT BLACK, M.A.

AUTHOR OF 'HORSE-RACING IN FRANCE' ETC.

LONDON
SMITH, ELDER, & CO., 15 WATERLOO PLACE
1891

[All rights reserved]

Inscribed to

THE KINDEST OF FRIENDS

MR AND MRS HENLEY GROSE-SMITH

(OF THE PRIORY, ST HELEN'S, ISLE OF WIGHT)

IN MEMORY OF

NEWMINSTER, NUNNYKIRK, WARLOCK, AND THE WIZARD

PREFACE

HORACE WALPOLE in his 'Letters' tells an amusing story which shows how a denouncer, unless he be sufficiently careful to put the saddle on the right horse, may have the tables turned upon him. Two highly connected Members of Parliament, Messrs. Theobald Taaffe (of the family made illustrious by several Counts Taaffe before the present famous Austrian statesman) and Edward Wortley Montagu (son of the celebrated Lady Mary), being on a visit in Paris in 1747, and being both of them addicted to gambling and rioting, had been thrown into prison there for 'cheating and robbing a Jew' at play, as Walpole bluntly puts it. This was, of course, a matter of great trouble and concern to 'Mr. Speaker,' who, in consequence, vigorously denounced White's Club, which was regarded as the nursing-mother of aristocratic gamblers and reprobates, and addressed himself especially to Lord Coke, whom he apparently considered to be the arch-priest of the Club, and who quietly replied that 'neither of the gentlemen who had given occasion for Mr. Speaker's violent denunciation was a member of White's, but both, he believed, were members of the House of Commons.' To avoid any similar mistake I have been at great pains; not that I have dealt in denunciation, but that I was anxious, on general grounds, to be as sure as I could be of my statements. I have, therefore, thought it incumbent upon me to offer as indisputable evidence as I could discover that the persons to whom I have attributed membership of the Jockey Club before 1835 (which, I believe, was the first year of the now annually published list of members) were really entitled to the distinction thus conferred upon them.

There is no occasion to refer in detail to the matters which within the last few years have made the Jockey Club an object of unusual interest to the public; but they suggested to me the notion that a favourable opportunity had offered itself for presenting a sketch, historical and biographical, of the Club and its members, its acquisition and exercise of authority, and its principal legislative work, from its foundation to the present day, so that an opinion may be formed as to how far that Club is entitled, from its original constitution and its uninterrupted development, to the supremacy which it has partly had thrust upon it and has partly acquired, and how far, if at all, the time has arrived for a modification of its earliest characteristics, maintained now for some 150 years, in round numbers.

Most readers, unless blinded by prejudice, are likely to be convinced that a body better fitted—by its composition, as regards the members, by the reputation it has won, and by what it has done for horse-racing and horse-breeding, which latter requires to be followed by the former as education by examination—to preside over and govern the affairs of the Turf, it would be almost impossible to imagine; and that any alteration in its composition, such as it has been from the first, would destroy its prestige and proportionately lessen its authority and utility. Nor, indeed, would it be reasonable that a Club should be called upon to lower its social qualification and accept uncongenial associates, simply because circumstances have given to it a control over certain matters wholly extraneous to the main purpose of the original institution. All that can be demanded fairly is that, as regards those extraneous matters, some scheme shall be adopted, if any change at all should seem desirable, for giving to the persons concerned a voice and a share in the administration of affairs which are purely external.

At the same time it will appear very clearly that the Club, like any other miserable sinners, have done what they ought not to have done, and have left undone what they ought to have done.

My chief *authorities* (necessarily so interwoven with the work that it would be impossible to give special references) are:—' Calendar of State Papers '; Horace Walpole's 'Letters'; Wraxall's 'Historical Memoirs'; 'Histories of the British Turf'; Admiral Rous's 'Horse-Racing'; Hore's 'History of Newmarket'; the Badminton Library; the Racing Calendars of Cheney, Heber, Pond, Tuting and Fawconer, B. Walker, and Weatherby; Cobbett's 'Parliamentary History,' and Hansard's 'Debates'; 'The Sporting Magazine'; 'Baily's Magazine'; works by 'The Druid'; Obituaries; and the works of Burke, Debrett, Lodge, &c., as well as a scurrilous publication called 'The Jockey Club,' by Charles Pigott (*alias* 'Louse' Pigott), an ex-member of the Club.—R. B.

CONTENTS

THE FIRST PERIOD
1750–1773

CHAPTER		PAGE
I.	FIRST PERIOD	3
II.	THE DUKES	18
III.	THE LORDS	38
IV.	THE SIRS	71
V.	THE MISTERS	98
VI.	FIRST PERIOD (*concluded*)	152

THE SECOND PERIOD
1773–1835

VII.	THE PRINCE OF WALES AND THE DUKES	171
VIII.	THE LORDS	196
IX.	THE COMMONERS	214
X.	A BIRD'S-EYE VIEW	245

THE THIRD PERIOD
1835–1891

XI.	DEPARTED MEMBERS	263
XII.	,, ,, (*continued*)	281
XIII.	PRESENT MEMBERS	306
XIV.	A BRIEF REVIEW	317

CONCLUSION

XV.	CONCLUSION	343

APPENDIX 369

INDEX 381

THE FIRST PERIOD

1750—1773

CHAPTER I

FIRST PERIOD

SIR JOHN CARLETON, an ancestor very likely of the present Lord Dorchester (himself a member of the Jockey Club), appears to have been about the first person who ever exercised against frequenters of Newmarket Heath that somewhat mysterious power of 'warning off,' which seems to invest the Jockey Club in the eyes of the public with a majesty beyond that of all other clubs consisting of noblemen and gentlemen. But it was not 'touts' and defaulters and impertinent writers in the newspapers, under the style and title of 'Argus,' or 'Hotspur,' or 'Craven,' or 'Pavo,' or 'The Devil on Two Sticks,' or the like or the unlike, that Sir John warned off, but noblemen and gentlemen themselves, of whom many, not to say most, were progenitors of the very noblemen and gentlemen upon whom, collectively as a Club, that mysterious power has devolved. Sir John, single-handed, did not, of course, issue his edict on his own account: he was merely the mouthpiece of his Most Gracious Sovereign, who, as we learn from the annals of State Papers

(1636), having observed that 'divers lords and others are accustomed to give their meeting within the King's hunt-grounds of Newmarket, in those places which the King reserves for his own sport,' gave instructions to Sir John Carleton (who was probably the ranger, or whatever may have been his official designation) to 'warn off' the noble and gentle intruders. We have changed all that, and it is now for the descendants of those 'divers lords' to 'warn off' whosoever may have given offence, and they are aided and abetted by a descendant of the very Sovereign who had 'warned off' their forefathers. Nay, it is just a hundred years since the heir to that Sovereign's throne, though he plumed himself even more upon being 'the first gentleman of Europe,' was himself virtually 'warned off' —for a reason, however, which was rather to his credit than not—by the Club which he had delighted to honour by becoming a member of it.

Into the origin, constitution, personality, development, and gubernatorial competency of that Club it is proposed to make some inquiry in the following pages.

Be it premised that no official list of members was published before 1835. It will be necessary, then, or at any rate proper, that some proof of membership should be offered in respect of all the noblemen and gentlemen who are written down members of the Club before that date. The proof will be derived from various sources; from records of races (such as the two Jockey Club Plates at Newmarket in the very earliest days of the Club, and the Jockey Club Challenge Cup, and the Eclipse Foot) in which none but members of the Club could run horses; from documents issued by the Club and signed by certain of its members; from obituaries, in which membership of the Club is specified; and from various more or less trustworthy publications which bear witness to membership either expressly or inferentially, with a probability amounting almost to certainty. Be it premised also that a list thus made up cannot pretend to be exhaustive, since many members would be, as is now and always has been the case, sleeping partners; but that the list, indisputably, will contain the names of all who were most prominent and most active, whether to the advantage or the disadvantage of the Turf, and of that horse-breeding for the improvement of which the Turf is, or should be, in the main an indispensable auxiliary.

Now we may proceed to say a few words about the foundation and the original founders of the Club.

The existence of the Club first received public notice in the 'Sporting Kalendar,' published by Mr. John Pond, a sporting auctioneer (whose daughter's equestrian prowess is mentioned in Dr. Johnson's 'Idler'), of Newmarket and of James Street, Covent Garden, London, at the end of 1751 or the beginning of 1752. In that publication it is announced that there will be run for, at Newmarket, on Wednesday, April 1, 1752, 'A Contribution Free Plate, by horses the property of the noblemen and gentlemen belonging to the Jockey Club, at the Star and Garter in Pall Mall.' Whether it was that the date of April 1 struck somebody as being of ill-omen, or for some other reason, the race did not come off at the date announced, but was postponed until the Newmarket Meeting in May 1753, at which *two* 'Jockey Club Plates,' both for horses belonging to members of the Jockey Club, were run for, and became the precursors of the two Jockey Club Plates thenceforward run for, under like conditions as regards ownership, for many successive years at the Second Spring Meeting, until the Plates fell into the desuetude and oblivion which seem to await, sooner or later, all exclusive institutions.

It is plain, however, from what has been said, that the Jockey Club must have been in existence as early as 1751, and probably as early as 1750, and that its place of meeting was in Pall Mall, at that Star and Garter which was the favourite meeting-house of many clubs, was celebrated for its choice cookery and wines, was notorious for its expensiveness, and was, some few years after the foundation of the Jockey Club, the scene of the tragic quarrel in which Mr. Chaworth was killed by Lord Byron (who, as well as Mr. Chaworth, may have been a member of the Jockey Club, for both, and especially the noble lord, were 'horsey,' but there is no proof of membership in either case). At the Star and Garter, too, it is recorded that ' the laws of cricket were revised, on February 25, 1774, by a committee of noblemen and gentlemen.' But the Jockey Club did not, either in the early days or afterwards, meet always at the Star and Garter as their head-quarters in London; they met sometimes at the Thatched House, sometimes at the Clarendon, and for some years (even after Messrs. Weatherby removed to Old Burlington Street, where the head-quarters of the Club eventually became fixed) at what was known as 'The Corner' (Hyde Park), with a coffee-room and a cook, it is said, provided by the obliging Mr. Richard Tattersall. They also, of course, met, as they still meet, occasionally in one another's houses.

How the Club came to be founded, and at whose initiative, is a mere matter of conjecture. One thing only appears to be pretty certain. Unlike the French Jockey Club (Société d'Encouragement), they (thank goodness) published no 'manifesto'; they (thank goodness again) had no occasion (as the French had) to complain of the sorry condition to which the native breed of horses had been reduced; and there is nothing to show that they harboured the idea of becoming legislators and reformers. The fact is that, as we know from Walpole's 'Letters,' from Jesse's 'Selwyn,' and other similar or dissimilar sources, it was an age of clubs, which were springing up like mushrooms on all sides. What more natural than that the noblemen and gentlemen who frequented Newmarket, where ruffians and blacklegs were wont to congregate, should conceive the notion of forming themselves into a body apart, so that they might gain that strength which union gives, and have at Newmarket, as well as in London and elsewhere, a place of their own, to which not every blackguard who could pay a certain sum of money would have as much right as they to claim entrance?

And, then, it has been reasonably conjectured that they were influenced by another consideration. Since the advent or accession of the Hanoverian kings, a sort of vacancy had been created at Newmarket. It is true that George the First had paid a visit to Newmarket on October 4, 1717, and perhaps at some other time or times; and it is true that King George the Second had kept a 'one-eyed grey Arabian' at Hampton Court, at the service of his loyal and disloyal subjects, for the usual 'consideration'; but, as a rule, the Hanoverian kings had not given that countenance to horse-racing and to Newmarket which had been vouchsafed by the Merry Monarch and his immediate successors, the austere William even, and the good Queen Anne, of whom the latter would run her horses not only at Ascot also but at so distant a race-ground as York. Indeed, it has been propounded that in the days of 'Old Rowley,' whose name is perpetuated by the R. M. (Rowley's mile) at Newmarket, there had been, to all intents and purposes, a Jockey Club of which the King was himself the head and front, and of which his horse-loving and horse-riding courtiers, comrades, rivals in horsemanship (for Charles himself, as well as his son, the unfortunate Monmouth, would 'perform in the pigskin'), and boon companions, were members, and to which he entrusted the keeping of that once famous 'Challenge Whip' (if, indeed, he had anything at all to do with it, which is extremely doubtful), formerly so coveted and now so neglected. Not, of course, that there had been any titular Jockey Club in those rollicking days, else the name could scarcely have failed to be recorded over and over again in the pages of Pepys and Evelyn; but it seems reasonable to assume that there had been an untitular society of the kind, so that traditions of a governing body, with the King for president or patron, and with nobles and gentles for constituents, would be lingering among the frequenters of Newmarket in the latter years of George the Second's reign, when the want of kingly patronage and authority at Newmarket would very naturally suggest to the founders of the Jockey Club the idea of establishing themselves in the place left vacant, with a royal duke, at least, if they could not have a king, at their head. There is sufficient evidence that Charles the Second would not only run but ride his horses in matches, and would decide disputes referred to him, either on his own authority or with the assistance of such a personage as the Hon. Bernard Howard (ancestor, it is said, of the present Earl of Suffolk and Berkshire), who has the reputation of having been the 'Admiral Rous' of that distant period. And so it would happen that to ride their own or one another's or anybody's horses would be one of the new Club's main purposes. This is the more notable and curious because the Club subsequently found it advisable to discourage the practice, and to confine the riding in public races to professional jockeys as far as possible. This too, no doubt, gave rise to the conjecture (for it is apparently no more than conjecture) that the Club originally had a special costume (like that of the Bibury Club), which included 'boots and spurs.' Not even the stewards nowadays seem to adopt any distinguishing dress, though some years ago, if memory may be trusted, they would wear a cut-away brown coat with gilt and 'lettered' buttons, a distinction which probably all the members were entitled to sport if they pleased. It has been surmised that this coat suggested that of the 'Pickwick Club,' in that famous work which, it is well known, was intended originally to be of the sporting order.

However that may be, it has been shown that the Club was started, or, at any rate, first made itself evident, about 1750, and that by 1753 it was in activity at Newmarket.

Let us now see what manner of men its earliest members were, so far as we can discover, and what were the objects which they seem to have had in view (for by their works ye shall know them), that we may form an opinion how far they may be considered to have represented the interests of the persons most intimately connected with the business of the Turf; to have been likely to promote the cause of horse-breeding; to have had the convenience and advantage of the public at heart; and to have been fitted for the discharge of functions which by degrees they partly assumed and partly had thrust upon them, and for transmitting to their successors a sound policy in respect of the Turf and its management.

The Club has now been in existence for nearly a hundred and fifty years. If, therefore, we take the names or titles of such persons as can be proved to have been more or less active members of it for the first twenty years, from 1753 (the year of the Club's first appearance with its two exclusive Plates at Newmarket) to 1773 (a very convenient date at which to halt, because then the long connection between the Club and Messrs. Weatherby and their 'Calendar' commenced), we may be sure that the group will be fairly representative of the noblemen and gentlemen who may be styled the original founders.

It should be remarked, before we proceed any farther, that a name or title, especially the latter, very often covers two or three different individualities, successive holders having been elected successively to the Club, and fathers and sons, brothers and homonymous cousins, having sometimes been members at the same time.

Among the members from 1753 to 1773, then, we

find (to the number of more than 100) persons bearing the following titles or names:

Dukes.—Cumberland [Gloucester], [York], Ancaster, Bridgewater, Devonshire, Grafton, Hamilton, Kingston, Marlborough, Northumberland, Richmond.

Lords. — Abingdon, Ashburnham, Barrymore, Bolingbroke, Carlisle, Cavendish (Marquis of Hartington; Duke of Devonshire), Chedworth, Clermont, Craven, Eglinton, Farnham, Gower, Grosvenor, Spencer Hamilton, Hartington, William Manners, March and Ruglen (Duke of Queensberry), Molyneux, Orford, Ossory (Upper), Pigot, Portmore, Rockingham, Sondes, Strange (self-styled, heir to the earldom of Derby, but never succeeded), Waldegrave.

Sirs.—John Armytage, Thomas Charles Bunbury, Nathaniel Curzon, Lau[w]rance Dundas, Matthew Featherstonhaugh, Thomas Gascoigne, Henry Grey, John [Lister] Kaye, James Lowther, William Middleton, John Moore, Thomas Saunders Sebright, Charles Sedley, John Shelley, Simeon Stuart, Charles Turner, William Wolseley.

Messrs. (whether Hon. or not, whether with military or naval 'handles' or not).—Anderson, †Bladen, Blake, Boothby (Scrymsher), †Boswell (Dr. Johnson's biographer), Brand, Burlton, Calvert, †Cell, *Codrington, Compton, Conolly, Coxe (or Cox), Croft (or Crofts), Duncombe, Fenton, Fenwick, Fettyplace, Foley, Fox (the famous orator), Gardiner, Gorges, Greville, Holmes (or Holme), Hutchinson, Jennison (or Jenison), March, Meynell (the celebrated 'father of fox-hunting'), Naylor, Norris, Offley, Ogilvy, *Ottley, Panton, Parker, Pigott, Pratt, Read, Scott, *Selwyn, Shafto, Shirley, [Sk[c]rymsher or S[c]krymshire *v.* Boothby], Smith, Smith-Barry, Stapleton, Strode, Swinburne, *Swymmer, Varey, Vernon, Warde, Warren, Wastell, Wentworth, Wilbraham.

The reason for the obelisk and the asterisk in certain cases will be explained hereafter.

Before we enter upon the little sketches which will be necessary for a proper understanding of what sort of personages they were to whom these titles and names belonged, and of what they did to the advantage or disadvantage of the Turf and of horse-breeding, it will be well to say a few words about the moral atmosphere which prevailed in the circle from which the members of the Club would, for the most part, be selected. Hear the sober historian, Mr. J. R. Green, discoursing of the period in which the fall of Sir Robert Walpole in 1742 may be considered the central event: 'Of the prominent statesmen of the time,' says he, 'the greater part were unbelievers in any form of Christianity, and distinguished for the grossness and immorality of their lives. Drunkenness and foul talk were thought no discredit to Walpole. A later prime minister, the Duke of Grafton, was in the habit of appearing with his mistress [the notorious Nancy Parsons] at the play. Purity and fidelity to the marriage vow were sneered out of fashion; and

Lord Chesterfield, in his letters to his son [? godson], instructs him in the art of seduction as part of a polite education.' It was the period during which Horace Walpole wrote that 'a quarter of our peeresses will soon have been the wives of half of our living peers,' and during which (as we know from the same Horace Walpole, who tells the sad story of the suicide of Sir John Bland, the Yorkshire baronet, in consequence of losses by gambling, and from many other sources, such as the 'betting-book' at Brookes's and elsewhere) the 'bloods' laid heavy wagers about anything in heaven or earth or the waters under the earth (and down the window-pane), and outrageous gaming was the order of the day, but scrupulousness was not. Read, too, what 'Gilly' Williams wrote, in 1768, to George Selwyn about one of the most conspicuous and, for a time, the most successful, among the early members of the Jockey Club: 'What a turbulent life does that wicked boy [Lord Bolingbroke, familiarly called "Bully"] lead with profligates and rogues of all descriptions.' Read, moreover, the pretty sketch (to be given more fully hereafter) drawn so ingenuously by Lady Sarah Bunbury (in a letter to the aforesaid George Selwyn), of noble and gentle members of the Jockey Club 'playing cards *in the morning* at the coffee-house,' and being denounced (falsely, no doubt) as 'cheats' by somebody who was standing by and betting on the play. Altogether the candid mind will reject as absurd the modern notion (which is so often made the text of a sermon) that the Jockey Club was founded with any purpose of reforming and purifying either the Turf or anything or anybody else, or of legislating for anything or anybody in the sense in which such terms are now understood, and that, in so far as the Club does not give complete satisfaction in those respects, it has derogated from its original position and programme. For all that appears, it had no particular programme, and its main purpose, so far as one can see, was to have a good time, as the Americans say, at Newmarket, by enabling its members to hold their own against the rabble there, without more intrusion than was absolutely unavoidable on the part of the profane vulgar, and with as much clearance of the chaotic confusion which had hitherto prevailed as union, which is strength, could effect. For this purpose it was necessary for the Club to gain the ascendency, which its rank, wealth, and influence soon enabled it to do. Another object, of course, was to win one another's or anybody else's money by acquiring, whether for a price or from breeding, the best horses in creation. And a further object, which cannot be too highly commended, was apparently to knit together the horse-loving, horse-breeding, and horse-racing nobility and gentry of North and South; for we find that, from the very first, representatives of the Northern Turf were among the members of the Southern Club. If we find also, as we probably shall, that in pursuing their own pur-

poses, without any lofty views, and perhaps with but
small regard for the public advantage, the earliest
members of the Club, beyond all other men, before or
since, promoted the improvement of the thoroughbred
and the prosperity of the Turf, good cause will have
been discovered why the institution which they founded
should be considered the sole legitimate depositary of
the extraordinary powers gradually acquired by it.
Whether, under the altered conditions of things in
general, some modification (differing somewhat from
that which was proposed many years ago by the late
Sir Joseph Hawley, and only the other day by the
present Earl of Durham) might not be introduced
with advantage into the Club's procedure (not into
its constitution), so that, while the prestige and
supreme authority of the Club should remain intact,
the voices of other persons deeply interested in the
affairs of the Turf and of horse-breeding might be
heard, and a portion of the Club's authority delegated
for special purposes to a sort of Lower House, or
House of Intermediaries, is a question which will
some day no doubt have to be decided, but need not
be considered here.

As for the process of election to the Club, it has
varied very little for about a hundred years, whatever
it may have been at first; candidates to be proposed
by members (number not specified at first, but in
course of time declared at two) and to be elected by
ballot, nine members forming a quorum and two

black balls excluding. The rule for the election of members of the Coffee-room dates from 1767, when a Mr. Brereton made himself unpleasant, and it was resolved that nobody should be admitted but on the proposal of a member of the Jockey Club and after a ballot; and when the New Rooms were added there was a similar rule for admission to them. So that, after a while, membership of the Jockey Club Rooms by no means meant membership of the Jockey Club.

CHAPTER II

THE DUKES

ACCORDING to the practice which still prevails in some (perhaps benighted) countries of paying respect to Royalty (which is but dust and ashes), precedence has been given, in defiance of the alphabet, to the titles of Cumberland and [York].

We have to deal with two DUKES of CUMBERLAND.

The first is William (second son of George the Second and uncle of George the Third), the 'Hero' or the 'Butcher' of Culloden, according to individual taste and political proclivity.

To prove his membership of the Jockey Club it is sufficient to state that in 1754 he won a Jockey Club Plate with the celebrated Marske (sire of the more celebrated Eclipse), and ran unsuccessfully for another with his grey horse Crab. He was the first Royal member of the Jockey Club, which from that day to this has never lacked a royalty of some kind, if we except some half a dozen years in the first half of Queen Victoria's reign, after which the Royal House of Holland came to the rescue, in memory, perhaps, of the exiled Charles the Second and of 'Dutch' William, of whom the former most certainly, and the latter most probably, would have given countenance to the Jockey Club had it existed in their day. Thus the 'Hero' or the 'Butcher' almost redeemed the Hanoverian dynasty from the reproach which it had incurred for its disregard of horse-racing. The Duke, as is well known, was excluded by political hostility from affairs of State, as far as possible, and so he devoted his undoubtedly great abilities to the Turf and to gambling *faute de mieux*. That he was so inveterate a gambler as to 'throw mains' with a nobleman of like sentiments, when he was out hunting and a check gave an opportunity for a short halt under a tree, cannot perhaps be denied; but it must be remembered that, as has been pointed out, he lived in a gambling age. He is also said to have fallen among thieves, otherwise 'blacklegs,' at Newmarket; but neither Charles the Second with his 'Royal mares,' nor Lord Montagu, of Cawdry, Sussex, with his famous 'Montagu mares,' did more than he for the Turf and for horse-breeding. He was Ranger of Windsor Great Park, and may be said to have been the Father of Ascot races (though Queen Anne had raced there) as truly as Chrysippus was said to have been 'the Father of the Porch.' He is set down in Weatherby's 'Calendar' as the earliest recorded winner of the Challenge Whip (with Dumplin in 1764), though, of course, it had often been won before, and the Duke of Devonshire's Dimple (as early as about 1722) and Mr. Fenton's Matchem (in 1756) are specified in old works as winners of that trophy. However, the Duke's chief claim to be regarded as a benefactor to the cause of the Turf and of horse-breeding is that he became the owner of both Cypron (dam of King Herod) and of Spiletta (dam of Eclipse); that is to say, he bred the two most predominant sires in the genealogy of English race-horses. Moreover, he had his 'Arabian,' like the other great breeders, at a time when the 'Arab' was not quite played out, though the 'Cumberland Arabian' was not of much account. It has been mentioned already that he owned Marske, the sire of Eclipse, as well as Spiletta (or Spilletta) the dam. Cypron was bred by Sir W. St. Quintin, from whom she appears to have been purchased by the Duke about 1755.

The second DUKE of CUMBERLAND with whom we have to do is Henry Frederick (brother of George the Third), born 1744, died 1790, who won the Jockey Club Challenge Cup in 1771 with Juniper (by Snap), not to be confounded with Mr. Gorges' much earlier Juniper (by Babram), winner of a Jockey Club Plate in 1760. This was the Duke of Cumberland who gave his kingly brother so much trouble by marrying the exceedingly fair Mrs. Horton (not the notorious Nancy Parsons, who, oddly enough, was also a Mrs. Horton, but a lady whose maiden name was Luttrell, sister of the memorable Colonel Luttrell, political rival of 'Wilkes and Liberty '), and by the scandal he caused when he had to pay 10,000*l*. damages for disturbing the conjugal affairs of the Earl and Countess of Grosvenor, though the Earl (another member of the Jockey Club) could not obtain a divorce for the reason—so characteristic of the age—that he had done unto others, or at any rate unto one other, as the Royal Duke had done unto him. This Duke and his brother, the Duke of Gloucester (who married the Dowager-Countess of Waldegrave, Horace Walpole's niece Maria), were responsible for the Royal Marriage Act. This Duke of Cumberland succeeded his uncle, 'the Butcher,' as Ranger of Windsor Great Park, and as patron of Ascot races, as well as of horse-racing in general, until his star began to pale before that of the young Prince of Wales (afterwards George IV.). The Duke lived well into 'Derby' times, of course, and ran candidates for the Derby in 1780-1-2-4, and for the Oaks in 1780-1-2-3-4. He owned and bred a great many good horses, though, when his stud was sold, December 10, 1792, there was in it no yearling comparable to his uncle's Eclipse, purchased by the astute meat-salesman, Mr. Wildman, for a mere song. This Duke seems to have stood name-father to the Cumberland Stakes for two-year-olds (1782), whereof the conditions tend to show that the Jockey Club, or some of its members, were already suspicious of the immediate 'Arab' strain, and were convinced that the beneficial influence which it undoubtedly had exercised for a time was, from some mysterious cause, quite played out, and had even become detrimental, for the immediate produce of 'Arabians' were 'allowed 3 lb.'

The name of the DUKE of GLOUCESTER is placed in a bracket, because no unimpeachable proof of his membership is forthcoming. Certainly he is included among the personages abused in a scurrilous publication (of which more hereafter) called 'The Jockey Club' (published about 1790); but the author of that work (who had himself been a member of the Jockey Club, and should therefore have been well-informed), by his own confession includes among the personages whom he abuses some who, though their rank and other qualifications fitted them for membership, were not actually members of the Club. On the other hand, he sometimes mentions (and we may therefore conclude that he would generally mention) the fact, when he has taken this little liberty; so that there is, at any rate, a fair probability of the Duke of Gloucester's real membership.

The name of the DUKE of YORK (Edward Augustus, born 1739, died 1767, brother of George the Third) is placed in a bracket because there is no actual proof that he was a member of the Club, but it is extremely probable that he was, because Boswell dedicates to him 'The Cub at Newmarket,' which looks very much as if the Duke had some personal connection with the Jockey Club. As the Duke was only twenty-three when Boswell was introduced into the Club, only twenty-eight altogether in 1767 (when H.R.H. died at the Prince of Monaco's), and at sea during a part of his life, it is not surprising that proofs of his membership should not be forthcoming, though strong enough is the probability, strengthened by the fact that his younger brother, the Duke of Cumberland, became a member at an early age. This Duke of York is said to have been married to Lady Mary Coke as legitimately as his brothers of Cumberland and Gloucester to Mrs. Horton and Lady Waldegrave.

The DUKE of ANCASTER of the list is the third Duke, who succeeded in 1742 and died in 1778, and whose membership is established by many proofs, among which may be mentioned the fact that his name appears among the subscribers to the Jockey Club Challenge Cup in 1768. He was Master of the Horse to George III., at whose coronation he assisted as (hereditary) Lord Chamberlain. He was twice married: first to a widow, Lady Nicolls, daughter and sole heiress of Mr. W. Blundell, of Basingstoke; and, secondly, to Mary, whom Horace Walpole (a prig and a coxcomb, whose sayings about sportsmen must be taken with more than a grain of salt) describes as 'the natural daughter of a disreputable horse-jockey named Panton.' At any rate, the lady's father, like the memorable Mr. Tregonwell Frampton (a gentleman of good family and position), was 'Keeper of the

King's running-horses' at Newmarket by style and title, and her brother, the 'polite' Tommy Panton (himself a member of the Jockey Club), appears to have been an equerry to the King, and the lady herself became Mistress of the Robes to the virtuous Queen Charlotte. But Horace Walpole was very hard upon all the Ancasters, declaring that 'the last three Duchesses were never sober.' However that may have been, the third Duke worked as manfully as any member of the Jockey Club for the improvement of the English thoroughbred (whether in single-heartedness for that express purpose, or rather, perhaps, for his own amusement and profit by means of bets, is not the main question here), and his name has remained honourably prominent in the 'Calendars' and in the 'Stud Book' in connection with 'Ancaster Starling,' &c. He was also the owner of 'the Ancaster Egyptian' and 'the Ancaster Bay Arabian' (which ran in the 'Arab race' at Newmarket in 1771), though these two horses had little or no effect upon the pedigrees.

As the Ancasters, so far as their ducal title is concerned, belong to the 'extinct animals,' and as the title has an unfamiliar and uncanny look at the present day, the following little sketch may be acceptable. On the very day on which Queen Anne died, in 1714, Her Majesty's Gold Cup was run for at York, and three days before that, at the same place, Her Majesty's horse Star had beaten Her Majesty's Lord Chamberlain's horse Merlin for a paltry Plate (*credite, posteri*) of 14*l*. That Lord Chamberlain is understood to have been Robert Bertie, fourth Earl and first Marquess of Lindsey, and fourteenth Baron Willoughby d'Eresby, who the very next year was created by George the First Duke of Ancaster and Kesteven. He, as we have seen, was a racing man, and sufficiently courtier-like withal to run second to his Queen; and at his death in 1723 he was succeeded by his son and heir Peregrine, who became a noted horse-racer and horse-breeder (as the manes of the 'Ancaster' Gentleman, foaled in 1723, and of the 'Ancaster' Driver, foaled in 1727, and of many another excellent horse might be summoned by a Glendower from the vasty deep to testify) in his day, and was succeeded at his death in 1742 by his son and heir Peregrine, the third Duke, already dealt with. The third Duke was succeeded at his death in 1778 by his son and heir Robert, who at his very early death in 1779 (charitably attributed by Horace Walpole to 'a scarlet fever brought on by drunkenness and rioting'), when he was but twenty-three, was succeeded by his uncle Brownlow Bertie, at whose death in 1809 the dukedom of Ancaster and Kesteven became extinct, though the family name of Bertie still lurks beneath the titles of the Earls of Abingdon and Lindsey, and there is a *Lord* Kesteven (a Trollope, not a Bertie) not unknown upon the Turf. As for the fourth Duke of Ancaster, who died but eleven months after his succession, he may have been, and probably was, a member of the Jockey Club, though he hardly lived long enough to leave proofs of his membership.

He was undoubtedly a scapegrace; and it is recorded that he left an annuity to a dwarf, whom he used to take about with him and 'shy' about like a ball, as fancy prompted him in his cups. Still he must have had his good points (though Horace Walpole would be blind to them), for he had gone in his twenty-first year as a volunteer to North America, whence he was recalled by his father's death in 1778.

The DUKE of BRIDGEWATER of the list is Francis, the third Duke, who was born in 1736 and died unmarried in 1803, having succeeded his (also unmarried) brother in 1748. So that he was just twenty-two when he appended his signature to the first public document issued by the Jockey Club. This was in 1758. He was also one of the subscribers to the Jockey Club Challenge Cup in 1768, and he ran Vampire for a Jockey Club Plate in 1764, &c., proving himself to have been an active member of the Club. He also bred a famous Cullen Arabian mare, dam of Stripling, Grasshopper, Glancer, Spectre, and of the filly which became the dam of Punch (imported by Mr. Powers into America in 1799); but it was his father, Duke Scroop, who possessed the famous Ball (Mr. Astridge's), about the best horse of his day (1716-8). Duke Francis was probably of more account in other lines than in horse-racing, for he it was who was the 'Father of Canals,' and endowed the 'Bridgewater Treatises.' He is said to have been 'highly respected,' as he may well have been, if only for the fact, if it be a fact, that he paid 110,000*l.* a year income-tax. Yet he is said to have been reduced to his last penny during the construction of his great work. In the obituary notice ('Gent. Mag.') of this Duke there is so curious a statement as to his reason for remaining a bachelor all his life that it deserves mention here, if only for the purpose of vindicating his memory. The statement is that the Duke, having gone to stay with a friend, in whose house was also staying the lady engaged to be married to that friend, found the lady so very ready to 'fall' that he became suspicious of the whole sex, and made up his mind that celibacy was the better part of discretion. Of the Duke's behaviour towards his friend (according to the story) there is fortunately the less reason to say anything, inasmuch as there is a weak point in the statement; for the Duke, it appears, proposed to and was refused by the Dowager-Duchess of Hamilton (the 'beautiful Gunning'), and whether that refusal came before or after the incident mentioned in the obituary, such an experience would be as likely as any other to account for his lifelong celibacy. Compare the case of another member of the Jockey Club, the Earl of March and Ruglen (afterwards Duke of Queensberry, better or worse known as 'Old Q.'), who was refused not so much by Miss Pelham as by Miss Pelham's family, for reasons which nobody could or would give, and who (in consequence, it is supposed) remained unmarried all his life (as also Miss Pelham herself).

The DUKE of DEVONSHIRE of the list is a title which covers two different persons, the fourth and the fifth Dukes, whose family name of Cavendish has been connected with the history of horse-flesh and horsemanship most honourably from the earliest times of the English Turf; for it was a Cavendish (but then a Duke of Newcastle), who taught our Charles the Second (the true Father of our Turf) to ride, and wrote the celebrated treatise entitled 'Méthode et Invention nouvelle de dresser les Chevaux'; and another Cavendish (but this time a Duke of Devonshire) is mentioned in the old records as running at Newmarket against 'Mr. Comptroller,' Lord Wharton, Mr. Tregonwell Frampton, and others, in the reign of William the Third, the dukedom of Devonshire dating from 1694.

The fourth Duke, called up to the House of Lords in 1751, during his father's lifetime, as Baron Cavendish, succeeded to the ducal title in 1755, and died in 1764, so that he appears among the members of the Jockey Club as Marquess of Hartington (his title of courtesy), as Lord Cavendish, and as Duke of Devonshire, though it is all one single gentleman wrapped up in three titles. He came, as we have seen, of a horse-loving and racing line, and to a progenitor of his (whether father or other), belonged the famous 'Devonshire' Childers, better known as Flying Childers (bred by Colonel Childers, of Carr House, near Doncaster), the celebrated Basto, the distinguished Plasto, and a whole galaxy of winners, to say nothing of 'Devonshire Arabians' either imported by the family or purchased by them after importation. It was apparently the third Duke whose Dimple is the first winner of the Newmarket Challenge Whip mentioned in the records (about 1722-4). The fourth Duke appears among those members of the Jockey Club who adopted more or less permanent 'colours' in 1762 (as published in the 'Calendars'), and he chose the 'straw,' which the present Lord Hartington has 'illustrated' by means of Morion and others before him, but not, as some of us may think, with such success as may be considered his hereditary as well as personal due. The fourth Duke was Master of the Horse, and won, as Marquess of Hartington (or Lord Cavendish), a Jockey Club Plate with Antelope (formerly Sir M. Wyvill's) in 1754, and, as Duke of Devonshire, another with Atlas in 1759.

The fifth Duke had the reputation of being a scholar rather than a 'jockey,' but his membership of the Jockey Club is proved (to mention nothing else) by his running Dromo for a Jockey Club Plate in 1773. His wife, the 'beautiful Georgiana' (to whom Coleridge addressed the once well-known ode, and who died in 1806), was herself, it is interesting to note, among the horse-racers; for she ran her horse Le Beau, at Newmarket in 1786, against her sister, Lady Duncannon (afterwards Countess of Bessborough), and the exceedingly philippic (and, shall we say, notorious ?) Earl of Clermont; but it cannot be discovered that either she or any other lady was ever a member of the Jockey Club. The fifth Duke died in 1811.

The DUKE of GRAFTON of the list is Augustus Henry FITZ-ROY, the third Duke, born 1735, succeeded 1757, died 1811. To prove his membership of the Jockey Club it is unnecessary to do more than state that he presided over the foundation (at his country-seat, Euston, Norfolk), of the Jockey Club Challenge Cup, which Beau Brummell's valet might have described (had he been valet to the Jockey Club) as 'one of our failures,' for it has been almost *vox et præterea nihil* since 1774. By the way, the number of subscribers to that Cup (at five guineas each) is now (and has been for many years) given as twenty-five in Weatherby's 'Calendar,' whereas it was in the earlier volumes of that work given as twenty-seven (more correctly, as will appear hereafter). This is the Duke to whom allusion is made in Jesse's 'Selwyn,' where we read (1764): 'The Duke [" Culloden "] of Cumberland goes from Newmarket to Euston, and all the sporting Court follows him.' Whence it appears that Euston was a regular rendezvous for members of the Jockey Club. This is the Duke who, as prime minister, was so roughly handled by 'Junius,' and who is so bitterly lashed in the already mentioned 'Jockey Club.' He was 'Lord

Keeper' to the notorious Nancy Parsons (who, by the way, is said to have married Lord Maynard, having previously been Mrs. Horton, as was mentioned in another passage). As a patron of the Turf, however, and as a breeder and runner of racehorses, he deserves the most honourable and respectful notice. His brood-mares, Prunella, and her daughters, Penelope and Parasol, are among the marvels of the 'Stud Book'; and he lived to win the Derby three times (with Tyrant in 1802, with 'Waxy' Pope in 1809, and with Whalebone in 1810), and the Oaks twice (with Pelisse in 1804, and with Morel in 1808). He was divorced, of course, for divorce was the fashion of the age, and a member of the Jockey Club would not fail to be in the fashion; and his ex-Duchess married the Earl of Upper Ossory (another member of the Jockey Club). The Duke, in fact, was true to his descent from the 'Merry Monarch' as regards both Nancy Parsons and Newmarket.

The DUKE of HAMILTON of the list is the sixth, James by name, who married one of the two 'lovely Gunnings.' He was a great gentleman-jockey, insomuch that he could hold his own against the celebrated or notorious Earl of March (afterwards 'Old Q.,' or the 'Star of Piccadilly'). He succeeded to the title in 1723 and died in 1758; and for proof of his membership of the Jockey Club it is sufficient to say that he ran a brown colt, by Babram, for a Jockey Club Plate in 1757. He appears in Horace Walpole's

'Letters,' and in Jesse's 'Selwyn,' in the character of a very 'fast' man; and the story of his hurried marriage, when a ring of the bed-curtains is said to have been utilised for the purpose, is well known. Though he raced and rode in person, he is not prominent among the improvers of the thoroughbred, and seems, in fact, to have inclined towards the 'cocktail'; but, whatever may have been his shortcomings in that respect, they have been amply atoned for by two of his successors—the Duke who was better known as Lord Archibald Hamilton (and who most unexpectedly succeeded his two nephews), and the present Duke.

Our DUKE of KINGSTON is Evelyn PIERREPONT, who succeeded to the title in 1726 and died in 1773, when the dukedom became extinct. He certainly qualified most thoroughly for the Jockey Club so far as the looseness of his domestic screw (a looseness characteristic, as has been said, not of the Club only but of the society to which the earliest members of the Jockey Club would belong for the most part) was concerned; for he married the lady known to history, or, rather, to scandalous chronicle, as the 'notorious Miss Chudleigh,' or the 'infamous Duchess of Kingston.' She had been his mistress for years before he married her; but it is by no means certain that he was privy to the bigamy which she committed in marrying him. He, at any rate, bred, owned, and ran several excellent horses; and a certain filly called Marie Antoine ran in the name of the 'infamous Duchess' herself in 1772 and 1773 at Newmarket Spring Meetings. Scaramouch (by Snap), purchased at the sale of the Duke's stud in July 1774 at Newmarket by the astute Mr. Dennis O'Kelly, and Cronie (by Careless), were among the notabilities bred by the Duke. He was one of the subscribers to the Jockey Club Challenge Cup in 1768.

The DUKE of MARLBOROUGH of our list is the fourth holder of the ducal title (the second having been a Duchess, Henrietta), who was born in 1739, succeeded 1758, died 1817. He ran his colt Pero (by Janus) for a Jockey Club Plate in 1763, but he cannot be regarded as one of the great lights of the Turf, nor did he ever win—or, for all that can be discovered, try to win—a Derby or an Oaks, though he lived well into the time of them. His descendant, Lord Randolph Churchill, bids fair to make up for ancestral indifference.

The DUKE of NORTHUMBERLAND was originally Sir Hugh SMITHSON, who was created Earl of Northumberland on the death of his father-in-law, Algernon, Duke of Somerset, son of the sixth or 'proud' Duke (son-in-law, having married Lady Elizabeth Percy, of Jocelyn, last 'Percy' Earl of Northumberland). Sir Hugh married Lady Elizabeth Seymour, Algernon Duke of Somerset's daughter; and he and his marriage are sneered at by Horace Walpole, who writes about 'the blood of the Seymours and Percies'

D

mingling with 'the blood of a man [Sir Hugh's grandfather] who let or drove coaches.' The descendant of Walpole's hackney-coach driver was Viceroy of Ireland, and Walpole describes how 'her Vice-Majesty of Ireland sailed to Newmarket with her legs out at the foreglass' (in consequence of flooded roads); for both Earl and Countess were extremely 'horsey.' In 1766 the Earl was made a Duke, and succeeded the Duke of Ancaster as Master of the Horse—the right man in the right place, if the many 'Northumberland Arabians' he imported, regardless of cost, may be taken as proof of his zeal in the cause of the thoroughbred. These were the Northumberland Bay Arabian, the Northumberland Brown Arabian (also called Leedes's Arabian), the Northumberland Grey Arabian, the Northumberland Golden Arabian, the Northumberland Chestnut Arabian, &c.; and if their influence is less discernible than that of many others in the pedigrees, the fault does not lie with their importer certainly, and perhaps not any more with his agent, Mr. Phillips. At the time of adopting 'colours,' the Duke with instinctive appropriateness chose 'deep yellow' (as of the guinea), converted afterwards into the still more significant 'all gold.' The Duke died in 1786, but never ran for either Oaks, or Derby, or St. Leger apparently, which were of small account, however, compared with the position they afterwards assumed. The Duke was one of the subscribers to the Jockey Club Challenge Cup in 1768; and he won a Jockey Club Plate with Cæsario (the first 'Matchem' that ran) in 1764, and with Narcissus (by Wilson's Arabian) in 1765.

The DUKE of RICHMOND of the list is the third, who was born 1734, succeeded 1750, died *s.p.* in 1806, when his nephew reigned in his stead. It was he who carried the sceptre at the coronation of George the Third; who, having been ambassador to France, was principal Secretary of State in 1766, and of whom Horace Walpole writes in 1774: 'No man living has a higher opinion of the Duke of Richmond's honour and integrity than I have: I respect his abilities, and am as sure as I can be of anything that he is incapable of an unworthy action.' It was not he, but the second Duke, who, as became the Master of the Horse to King George the Second, imported or at any rate owned the 'Richmond Turk,' sire of 'Dale's Horse.' But it was the third Duke under whose auspices (though Lord George Bentinck, 'managing man' to a subsequent Duke, deserves the name of second founder) Goodwood began to have races of its own. There may have been desultory racing at Goodwood before 1802, but it was not until an opening was made about that time, by the determination of Lord Egremont to give up the races which had been held in his park at Petworth, that the first foundations were laid of a meeting destined in course of years to postpone its season from April to July or August, and by degrees to take the gilt off the gingerbread of Brighthelmstone (now Brighton). The third Duke ran Bounce for a Jockey Club Plate in 1761, Lardon in 1762, &c., &c., and well represented his grandfather, Charles Lennox, first Duke, who was Master of the Horse 1681-2.

It would be expected, naturally, that among the Dukes would be found the name of Rutland, the family which, to use the inversion of terms that is usual among the 'horsey' vulgar, 'belonged to' Bonny Black, the Cyprus Arabian, &c., &c.; but there is no actual proof forthcoming, however strong the probability is, that he who was Duke of Rutland (the third) at the period with which we are dealing, and who, as a Master of the Horse at one time, certainly might have been expected to belong to the Jockey Club, was ever a member of the Club. Nor is there any certain proof (though, again, there is strong probability) that this Duke's eldest son, the popular and gallant Marquess of Granby (who did not live to be Duke), though he brought into the family by marriage with the daughter of the 'proud' Duke of Somerset (to whom the estates had come from the Alingtons [whence the present Lord Alington's title] *par les femmes*) certain manors, including Cheveley, in the neighbourhood of Newmarket, was ever a member of the Jockey Club, as he might be expected to have been, and probably, but not certainly, was. Still the family was represented, as presently will appear, very conspicuously indeed, by Lord W.

Manners, among the members of the Club. The fourth (grandson of the third) is the first Duke of Rutland whose membership of the Jockey Club appears to be established by indisputable and accessible evidence.

CHAPTER III

THE LORDS

THE EARL of ABINGDON must have been Willoughby BERTIE, the fourth Earl, who was born 1740, succeeded 1760, died 1799. For his membership of the Jockey Club, it is enough to say that he won a Jockey Club Plate in 1774 with Transit (by Marske), and in 1777 with Leviathan (by Marske), and would naturally have belonged to the Club before the earlier of those dates. He was a great breeder, a great racer, and a great bettor; but, though he lived well into the days of the Oaks, the Derby, and the St. Leger, he apparently ran for none of them but the Oaks just once in 1779, the first year of running for it. The great feather in his cap was that he bred the famous Pot8os, the best son of Eclipse, and the sire of Waxy (sire of Whalebone and Whisker); but he was so ill-advised, or so 'straitened,' as to sell the horse to Lord Grosvenor at the Newmarket First Spring Meeting, 1778, for 1,500 guineas, the purchaser to have the chance of a race (worth 700 guineas) which the horse was about to run, and which he won, thus costing only 800 guineas. Lord Abingdon, however, on another occa-

sion, had very much the best of the deal with Lord
Grosvenor at the First Spring Meeting in 1779. The
story has so often been wrongly told (as it is by Mr.
Christie Whyte in his 'History of the British Turf,'
an authority greatly and, for the most part, deservedly
followed) that it must be repeated. It appears, then,
that Lords Abingdon and Grosvenor had arranged to
run a match at the said meeting, the former to run
Cardinal York, 4 years, 8 stone, and the latter a filly
by Dux out of Curiosity, 4 years, 7 stone 11 lb., B.C.,
for 1,000 guineas a side, and a 'bye,' or additional bet
of 6,000 guineas (laid by Lord Grosvenor) against
3,000 guineas, the match and bet or bets having, of
course, been made some time before. When the time
for the match to be run came on, the story goes that
Lord Grosvenor called upon Lord Abingdon to 'make
stakes' (in default of which, the rule was that bets
were void, and the match too, of course), which Lord
Abingdon was not prepared to do, and was only saved
by the interposition of the noted 'miser,' Mr. Elwes,
who, though a 'miser,' was nothing if not a sportsman,
and offered to lend the money without ado or security.
The offer was accepted, 7 to 4 was laid *on* Lord Abingdon's horse, and Lord Abingdon won both the original
stakes or bet and the 'bye' as well. Mr. Whyte's
version, adopted by others, makes the sporting 'miser'
lend the money to Lord Grosvenor, which seems to be
absurd, for Cardinal York was backed at 7 to 4 *on*,
and the demand to 'make stakes' was clearly a happy

thought, or a desperate resource, for getting out of an unpleasant position. At any rate, the best authorities give the story as it has been told here. Besides, Mr. Elwes was M.P. for Berkshire and Lord Abingdon's neighbour, as it were, and would be far more likely to back his county and his acquaintance than to help Lord Grosvenor, who may have been a perfect stranger to him. No wonder Lord Grosvenor named his mare Misfortune; but so strange are the ways of Nature that the said Misfortune, though she never won a race (of any importance, if at all), became the dam of the celebrated Buzzard, sire of Castrel, Selim, Bronze, and Rubens, and one of the 'crack' American importations (imported into Virginia by Col. Hoomes; died in Kentucky in 1811), so that there seems to have been something in her to account for Lord Grosvenor's expensive belief in her.

The fourth Lord Abingdon married the daughter and co-heir of Admiral Sir P. Warren (buried in Westminster Abbey); and perhaps his memory is still cherished by the Corporation of Oxford, to which immortal body he presented the handsome Cup won at Oxford (when there were races there) in 1775 by his mare Takamahaka. His titular name, at any rate, is well preserved at Oxford by the familiar Abingdon lasher.

LORD ASHBURNHAM must have been John, the second Earl, LL.D., whose active membership of the Jockey Club is attested by his signature appended to two documents issued by the Club in 1767, though there remain few, if any, memorials of his horse-racing or horse-breeding. He was born 1724, succeeded to the title (which was created in 1730 only) 1736, and died 1812, having married, in 1756, the daughter and co-heir of Ambrose Crawley, Esq. (perhaps an ancestor of Mr. J. S. Crawley, a member of the Jockey Club at the present time), alderman of London. This noble lord is mentioned by Horace Walpole among the millionaires of his day, and as a munificent patron of art. He was a great purchaser of pictures, and perhaps they were more in his line than racehorses. He was at one time First Lord of the Bedchamber and Groom of the Stole, but he was not conspicuous among the personages (such as Lord Clermont, Lord William Manners, Mr. 'Jockey' Vernon, and others) whom Horace Walpole superciliously describes as 'grooms.'

The LORD BARRYMORE of the list appears to have been the sixth Earl, who died in 1773, and who was either a brother, or at any rate a near relative, of the Hon. John Smith-Barry (of whom more hereafter), himself a member of the Jockey Club. This Earl was among the subscribers (1768) to the Jockey Club Challenge Cup, and owned and ran several good horses, including Senlis (by Bajazet), purchased out of the 'Culloden' Duke of Cumberland's stud. The title became extinct in 1823, and it may, therefore, be well to deal at once with the sixth Earl's successors (brothers), of whom one certainly, and two probably, belonged to the Jockey Club.

There is some confusion about the actual successors of the sixth Earl; but what is certain about them seems to be that there were three brothers, who either succeeded the sixth Earl one after the other, or, but for premature decease, might have become Earls one after the other. Two of them, undoubtedly, became respectively the seventh and eighth Earl; as to the third, obituaries and other accounts are misleading and bewildering. However, the three brothers (Richard, Henry, and Augustus) are said to have been popularly known by the nicknames of 'Cripplegate,' 'Newgate,' and 'Hellgate' (this last nickname having been conferred upon the youngest brother, Augustus, to emphasise the fact, presumably, that he was in holy orders, as he was). 'Cripplegate,' the eldest, the immediate successor of the sixth Earl, died in 1793, at the early age of twenty-four, shot accidentally or intentionally by his own hand whilst he was discharging a part of his military duties. His membership of the Jockey Club is amply proved by all sorts of evidence, notably by his winning a Jockey Club Plate in 1788 with Rockingham (*alias* Camden). He was the young gentleman who 'went the pace' so awfully as to become, like Pope's Duke of Wharton, 'the scorn and wonder of the age.' He was the young gentleman whose freaks at Newmarket and elsewhere fill page upon page in books devoted to 'sporting

anecdotes.' Of him it is related that he uncarted a
blind stag for his friends to hunt; that he took the
town-crier's bell and perambulated the High Street
at Newmarket, shouting, 'Oh yes! oh yes! Who
wants to buy a horse that can walk five miles an
hour, trot eighteen, and gallop twenty?' and, when
some unsophisticated hearer among the collected
crowd cried eagerly, '*I* do!' replied demurely, 'Then
I'll let you know when I come across one;' and that
he undertook for a wager to find a man who would
eat a live cat. It is only fair to add that he always
denied the truth of this disgusting story; but it
appears in certain newspapers at or near the time,
with the circumstantial information that he actually
won the wager, and that the worse than cannibal who
enabled him to win it was 'a Harpenden man.' This
Lord Barrymore ran in 1788 (when he was only nineteen years of age) Feenow (purchased from Dr. Johnson's young friend, Sir J. Lade), by Tandem, for the
Derby. That the young lord, for all his wildness,
had his good points we know from Horace Walpole
(not too well-disposed towards members of the Jockey
Club, or towards any kind of sportsmen), who tells us
that he was as clever and droll in the drawing-room
as he was wild and eccentric on the Turf, and that,
with the assistance of Delpini (a male opera dancer,
after whom a famous racehorse and sire of racehorses
was called), he would get up entertainments which
not only set society on a roar but were distinguished

for their elegance. 'Cripplegate' is said to have been succeeded by his brother 'Newgate' (Henry), who seems to have been an inferior edition of himself (and ran third for the Oaks with Miranda in 1808, though there is no proof that he was a member of the Jockey Club), and died in 1823, in which year the title is said to have become extinct, so that 'Hellgate' (Augustus), the other brother, must either have died previously and never succeeded to the earldom at all, or must have come between 'Cripplegate' and 'Newgate,' instead of after the latter.

It was characteristic of 'Cripplegate' that he seemed, according to report, to have been quite disposed to admit the claim, when he was told that the notorious Madame du Barry (Barri) pretended to be connected (through her husband, of course) with the noble family of Barrymore; for, even had he objected to her and her character and her genealogy, he was shrewd enough to know that she personally counted for absolutely nothing in the connection, such as it was, and that her part in the said connection was only nominal.

The LORD BOLINGBROKE of the list is the second Viscount, who succeeded his celebrated uncle (Henry St. John, created Viscount Bolingbroke in 1712) in 1751, and died in 1787. His membership of the Jockey Club (of which, by his horse-racing, his betting, and his divorce from the lady who had been Lady Diana Spencer, and afterwards became the more familiar sounding Lady Di Beauclerc, wife of Dr. Johnson's fashionable friend Topham Beauclerc, he was one of the most typical among the early Fathers) is abundantly testified. Suffice it to say that he was among the subscribers to the Jockey Club Challenge Cup, and he won Jockey Club Plates in 1769 and 1770. He is the 'Bully' (as has been mentioned already) so often spoken of in Jesse's 'Selwyn,' who was 'thought to be too much in the graces of the beautiful Coventry.' He owned the celebrated Paymaster (son of Blank), and the still more celebrated Highflyer (son of Herod). The latter was bred by Sir Charles Bunbury and sold by him to Lord Bolingbroke, who gave the name which has become so famous, and sold the horse in 1779 to Mr. Tattersall, who thus acquired a four-legged gold-mine. Lord Bolingbroke, whilst in partnership with the Hon. Mr. Compton (a member of the Jockey Club, a great gentleman-rider, and owner of the noted Compton Barb, otherwise called the Sedley Grey Arabian) had considerable success upon the Turf, but it is to be feared that, on the whole, he found it ruinous. He owned the useful sire called indifferently the Coombe Arabian, the Pigot Grey Arabian, and the Bolingbroke Grey Arabian; and he owned, if he did not actually import, the Bolingbroke Bay Arabian, which won an interesting race, injudiciously omitted from some of the abbreviated 'Calendars.' The race was run at the Second October Meeting, Newmarket, in 1771. It was 'for African and Arabian horses'; B.C.; 8 stone, 7 lbs. Three ran, and they came in as follows: Lord Bolingbroke's Bay Horse, 1; Mr. Vernon's Jerusalem, 2; Duke of Ancaster's Bay Horse (not the 'Ancaster Egyptian'), 3. However, none of these horses became very noted at the stud. Altogether, Lord Bolingbroke seems to have been one of those members which the Club, especially in these latter days, is better without; brilliant, no doubt, and energetic, but flighty, and disposed to use the race-horse, however good he may be, as a mere instrument of gambling; ready to buy him or sell him, but not caring much to keep him and breed from him.

The LORD CARLISLE of the list is Frederick HOWARD, the fifth Earl, born 1748, succeeded to the title 1758, died 1825. His membership of the Jockey Club is easily proved, if only from the fact that he appears in 1770 (when he was but two-and-twenty) among those members of the Club who agreed to adopt 'colours.' He was one of the most worshipful of all the personages who have ever been members of the Club. For although he had been, up to the age of twenty-nine or thirty, a great gambler and 'macaroni,' insomuch that he became grievously crippled in his pecuniary affairs, he then began to mend his ways, and to think of retrieving his fortunes. As is well known, he was nearly allied in blood to the illustrious poet Lord Byron, whose talents he shared; for he, too, was a poet and letter-writer of no mean order, and he was not undistinguished in the senate. He was also a patron of art. It was a proof of the high estimation in which his abilities and character were held that he was sent on a mission to America at the time of the rebellion of the colonies; and it was probably not his fault, but that of others and of the times, that the mission was fruitless. Moreover, he was at one time Viceroy or Lord-Lieutenant of Ireland. That he should have had a hereditary tendency towards horse-racing, and should have been a member of the Jockey Club, was only in the nature of things; for not only has there always been even more connection between Howard and horse (at any rate since the days of Charles the Second and the great Turfite Bernard Howard, hereinbefore mentioned) than between Macedon and Monmouth, but his own family had introduced into this country, or at any rate owned, the Carlisle Turk and the Carlisle Barb (otherwise called 'a foreign horse of Sir C. W. Strickland's'), and had bred the Wharton mare and the celebrated Buckhunter, better known as the Carlisle gelding, a horse which must have been running until he was eighteen years of age, if, as the records say, he was foaled in 1713, and the following account of him is correct: 'When running for a Plate at Salterley Common, Buckhunter broke a leg (after winning the first heat), which deprived him of his life, and he was buried near to the Pails [palings] of Stilton Churchyard, where he happened his misfortune, in the year 1731.' It must not be concluded—as it well might—from this that the race was run in the churchyard; but the writer, like Thucydides and other high authorities, gives his readers an opportunity for the exercise of that common sense which Mr. Washington Moon and other low authorities will not employ or allow to be employed in dealing with the Queen's English. The said writer adds: 'Though Buckhunter was in a very high form, yet there were horses of his time that would beat him; but he had rarely an equal, and hardly ever a superior, with relation to those principal points of being capable of running with all degrees of weight, of supporting repeated heats, of travelling and running often, and continuing the whole for so great a number of years, and to the age that he did. The excessive spirits of his youth rendered him almost ungovernable, and caused him to be castrated, which lost to breeders a promising English stallion.' But for this the Howards of Carlisle, perhaps, might have bred a race of horses whereof the descendants at the present day would 'whip creation,' including Ormonde, St. Simon, Barcaldine, and *hoc genus omne*.

The LORD CHEDWORTH of the list was John Thynne Howe, second Baron, who succeeded to the title in 1742, died *s.p.* in 1762, and was succeeded by his brother, H. F. Howe, who died unmarried in 1781, and was succeeded by his nephew, at whose death, in 1804, the title became extinct. This Lord Chedworth (whose father had bred the famous Regulus, sold at the breeder's death to Mr. Martindale, the saddler, of St. James's Street) won a Jockey Club Plate in 1757, and was owner and breeder of many good horses, including Moses (foaled 1746, sire of Otho) and Aaron (foaled 1747, the famous rival of the equally famous Little Driver), a little horse, 'generally measuring under 14 hands,' and the (never trained) Godolphin Arabian mare that was dam of the celebrated Coquette (by Mr. Compton's Barb), and was the only sister to the famous Regulus. This Lord Chedworth, therefore, certainly did a member of the Jockey Club's duty to the Turf and to horse-breeding.

LORD CLERMONT (first and last Earl, though his barony and viscounty were continued in another branch) was William Henry FORTESCUE, who was born in 1722, and died *s.p.* in October 1806, at the Steyne, Brighton, on which occasion it was announced in the newspapers that 'the deceased Lord was the Father of the Turf, and ranked among the most intimate friends of the Prince' (of Wales, of course). He was described, not altogether untruthfully, it is to be feared, some years before his death (by an enemy, it is true, but '*fas est et ab hoste doceri*'), as a 'hoary profligate'; and it is not impossible that he was the original of Thackeray's 'Marquis of Steyne,' though a certain Marquess of Hertford runs him close, and is preferred by some authorities or conjecturers. The Earl was very intimate with the French Royal Family in the days of Marie Antoinette and old 'Égalité';

and the latter nominated (if he did not actually run, as owner) Lord Clermont's Cantator for the Derby of 1784. The Earl was the somewhat dangerous 'guide, philosopher, and friend' of the 'First Gentleman,' and when they drove out together in the bleak air of Newmarket Heath, would so carefully protect his old bones with wraps that he was frequently mistaken for the Prince's aunt Amelia (herself of 'horsey' proclivities), and the Prince won golden opinions for his supposed affectionate solicitude for his aged relative. The Earl is sneered at by Horace Walpole, who met him in society now and then, and tells us how on one occasion he spoke of having read in Livy, or some other 'classic,' that 'Scipio introduced toothpicks from Spain.' Upon which, the fastidious Horace expresses surprise that 'my Lord Clermont should ever have heard of any Scipio but a racehorse of that name.' And certainly the Earl was great upon the Turf and in the breeding of racehorses, whether alone or in confederacy with Lord Farnham. He bred the great Trumpator, buried at the end of the Clermont course (now almost forgotten) at Newmarket; he was owner of the still greater Conductor, and of Marc Antony; he was an active administrator of the Jockey Club (as his signatures bear witness in 1770 and 1771); he won the Derby in 1785 with Aimwell (by Marc Antony), the only descendant in the male line of the Alcock Arabian among the great winners; and the Oaks in the same year with Trifle (by Justice); and the Oaks in 1792 with Volante (by Highflyer), *not* Volanté, as it is generally given, when he was also second with Trumpetta (by Trumpator).

The LORD CRAVEN with whom we are concerned here was the sixth Baron, nephew of the fifth (who was much addicted to horse-racing, but does not appear to have been a member of the Jockey Club, though he may very well have belonged to it). He succeeded to the title in 1769, and died in 1791, when his title descended to his son, the seventh Baron, the distinguished soldier, who was created Viscount Uffington and first Earl of Craven, in 1801. The sixth Baron is described (by an enemy) as a 'sot,' which may have accounted for the conduct of his wife, Lady Craven, the notorious personage whose 'works' were 'printed and published by Horace Walpole' at his private press, Strawberry Hill, and who, at her husband's death, became by regular marriage the Margravine of Anspach she is supposed to have been virtually (rather than virtuously) before. The sixth Lord Craven's name is appended to various resolutions passed by the Jockey Club in 1771, and he seems to have been name-father of the Craven Stakes, first run for in 1771, and the first public race (bar matches) in which two-year-olds were admitted to run, whether against their seniors or against one another, under the auspices of the Jockey Club, at what thenceforward became known as the Newmarket Craven Meeting.

LORD EGLINTON of the list is made out to have been Alexander MONTGOMERY (MONTGOMERIE), the tenth Earl, who succeeded to the title in 1729, and was killed in a scuffle in 1769 by Mungo Campbell, an excise officer, with whom a dispute had arisen about a question of trespassing upon the Earl's property with fire-arms. Lord Eglinton's name appears in the very earliest published list of members who (in 1758) signed a resolution of the Jockey Club. He was not so famous on the Turf as his descendant of 'Tournament' memory, but he bred and ran some good horses, and was the owner of the untrained Omar (by Lord Godolphin's Arabian), sire of Sir C. Bunbury's Nobody, Mr. O'Kelly's Miss Spindleshanks (dam of Soldier, Corporal, Gunpowder, &c.), and at one time owned Cripple, sire of the celebrated Gimcrack (not bred, however, by Lord Eglinton). This was the Lord Eglinton who introduced 'Bozzy' (Dr. Johnson's biographer) to the Jockey Club in 1762, as will appear hereafter. It is, of course, from the second title of this earldom that the celebrated horse Ardrossan received its name.

The LORD FARNHAM of the list is Robert MAXWELL, the second Baron, who succeeded to that title in 1759, was created Viscount in 1761 and Earl in 1763, and died in 1779, when he was succeeded in the barony by his brother Barry, who was created Viscount in 1781 and Earl in 1785, and died in 1800. The title became extinct in 1823.

The first Earl's membership of the Jockey Club is handsomely proved (to mention no other evidence) by his winning a Jockey Club Plate in 1773 with the celebrated Conductor (son of Matchem, and one of the 'cracks' of the 'Stud Book' as well as of the Turf); and, whether he raced alone or in partnership with Lord Clermont, he was great both at post and paddock (especially as owner of Miss Osmer [dam of the Duke of Cumberland's Blunderer and Sir H. Fetherstone's Tortoise] and of the Shepherd's Crab mare, that was the dam of Charon, Leonidas, Premier, Velocity, Jerker, and Bacchanal). The Earl's family supplied not only the Turf with horses but the Church with bishops (notably a Bishop of Dromore and subsequently of Meath).

Of LORDS GOWER there are two on the list; both the first Earl (the original owner of the famous Gower stallion, a son of the Godolphin Arabian, and inferior to few, if any, sires of his own or any other time), and the second Earl, Granville, first Marquess of Stafford, grandfather of the late Earl Granville. The first Earl of Gower won the very first Jockey Club Plate in 1753 with Beau Clincher, and died in 1754. The second (born 1721, died 1802), who sat in the House of Commons as Viscount Trentham, and was afterwards Lord Privy Seal, Lord Chamberlain, and Lord President of the Council, and some time Master of the Horse, came into possession of his father's (the first Earl's) horses and ran Clio, by the Gower stallion, for a Jockey Club Plate in 1755, and her own brother Sweepstakes for a Jockey Club Plate in 1756, &c., &c. His grandson, the late popular Earl Granville, though unknown among the winners of horse-races, even if he ever ran a horse for a public race of importance (though he is said to have been sleeping partner in more than one), was himself for very many years a member of the Jockey Club, and at his death was probably its *doyen*, as he was elected a member about half a century ago, in 1846 or thereabouts, the very year in which he succeeded to the title.

We now come to the greatest racer and the greatest bettor (who, like the famous Colonel Mellish, seldom or never 'opened his mouth under 500 guineas') of the whole lot, namely LORD GROSVENOR, the first Earl, who was born 1731, created a Baron 1761, Viscount and Earl 1784, and died August 5, 1802, and after whom Earl's Court, Kensington, is named, from the house in which he lived there. He was originally Sir Richard Grosvenor (about the seventh baronet), and how devoted he was to the Turf may be inferred from a remark of Horace Walpole's : 'Sir R. Grosvenor is made a Lord, Viscount, or Baron, I don't know which, nor does he, for yesterday [March 17, 1761], when he should have kissed hands, he was gone to Newmarket to see the trial of a racehorse.' He was one of the subscribers to the Jockey Club Challenge Cup in 1768. He married in 1764 Henrietta Vernon (probably a sister of Horace Walpole's Mr. 'Jockey'

Vernon), from whom he could not get a divorce for the reason already mentioned. He is said to have lost 300,000*l.* by a thirty years' connection with the Turf; but his family do not appear to have come to the workhouse in consequence, to judge from the figure made upon the Turf and elsewhere by his descendants, the Marquesses and the present Duke of Westminster. Lord Grosvenor won the Derby in 1790, 1792, and 1794, with Rhadamanthus (when he was also second with Asparagus), with John Bull, and with Dædalus (own brother to Rhadamanthus); the Oaks in 1781, 1782, 1783, 1797, and 1799 with Faith, Ceres, Maid of the Oaks, Niké, and Bellina; several Jockey Club Plates, the Jockey Club Cup and the Newmarket Challenge Whip, two or three times each of them; and besides the horses mentioned (to say nothing of a Grosvenor Arabian and Barb) he either bred or owned at one time or another such celebrities as Violante (so called after a famous dancer of the day, and bred before the Earl's death in 1802), Mambrino (sire of Messenger, the 'father of American trotters'), Trajan, Cardinal Puff, Pot8os, Gimcrack, Sweet William, Sweet Briar, &c. When the members of the Jockey Club chose 'colours' in 1762 (and 1770) he selected the 'orange and black cap,' which, in the modified hue of 'yellow and black cap,' we identify with the Grosvenors (unless a Mostyn or a Merry intervene) to this day.

LORD SPENCER HAMILTON is made out to have been

a brother of Archibald, ninth Duke of Hamilton (who succeeded to the dukedom contrary to all reasonable odds), to have been born in 1742, to have been an officer in the Guards, to have had his signature appended to a resolution of the Jockey Club in 1771, when he was but twenty-nine years of age, to have been a noted 'gentleman jockey' (like others of his family), to have been tolerably conspicuous on the Turf, though completely overshadowed by the victorious Lord Archibald, and to have died unmarried in 1791.

LORD WILLIAM MANNERS, brother of the third Duke of Rutland, seems to have been born about 1697, and to have died in 1772, and, according to Horace Walpole, to have been 'better known in the groom-porters' annals than in the annals of Europe.' He is certainly very well known in the annals of the Turf, if that is what the disdainful Horace means, and he ran Fop (a gelding) for a Jockey Club Plate in 1755. He owned, and probably bred, the brothers Chuff and Poppet, by (Flying) Childers; and he bred Tawney (son of Mr. Panton's celebrated Crab and a Cyprus Arabian mare), that was near leader in Lord March's famous 'carriage-match' at Newmarket in 1750.

LORD MARCH is, of course, James Douglas, EARL of MARCH and RUGLEN (born 1725, died 1810), whose name appears in all the earliest transactions of the Jockey Club (of which he was a most active member), and who is almost too well known as 'Old Q.' (the last Duke of Queensberry, successor to the Duke whose Duchess was so kind to Gay). How he bred, and owned, and raced, and rode, and betted; and how ingenious he was in his carriage-match (a four-wheeled carriage, drawn by four horses, with a person in or upon it, to do nineteen miles in an hour), and in his wager about transmitting a letter fifty miles in an hour (by enclosing it in a cricket ball, which twenty-four cricketers passed one to another), everybody probably remembers. But it may not be so well remembered that he was disappointed in love, having proposed to Miss Pelham, niece of the prime minister, Duke of Newcastle, and been rejected by her family, after which both he and she remained unmarried for life (cf. the case of the Duke of Bridgewater), which may have accounted for some of his subsequent career; and that he is said to have disputed with George Selwyn the paternity of Maria Fagniani, whom the third Marquess of Hertford married, and to whom, it is said, both 'Old Q.' and Selwyn left a fortune. It is curious that so great a racer and so 'knowing' a 'hand' never won the Derby or the Oaks, though he tried for both—for the former frequently; but, as his 'knowingness' has been turned into a weapon against his memory (which has many other more vulnerable points), it may be well to record what was said of him by one of his so-called victims, the unfortunate 'Chillaby' Jennings (a member of the Jockey Club, of whom more hereafter).

'Queensberry,' said he, 'was always honourable in his bets, only he was a far better jockey than any of us.' In fact 'Old Q.' was, no doubt, a fair specimen of what the authors of 'Guesses at Truth' call 'the Devil's gentleman'; that is, the conventional 'man of honour.' It is to be feared, however, that neither as Lord March nor as 'Old Q.' did he regard the racehorse as much more than 'an instrument of gambling.' In 1766 he writes to Selwyn: 'Bully [Bolingbroke], Wilmington, and myself are left here [at Newmarket] to reflect coolly on our losses and the *nonsense of keeping running-horses.* . . . Scott has lost three thousand.'

LORD MOLYNEUX is the Charles William MOLYNEUX, ninth VISCOUNT MOLYNEUX and first EARL of SEFTON, who apparently stepped into the shoes of his uncle (a Jesuit, incapable of holding titles) in 1759, conformed to the Established Church in 1768, was created Earl of Sefton in 1771, and died in 1795. He appears among the subscribers to the Jockey Club Challenge Cup in 1768. He lived well into the times of the Derby; and, though he does not seem to have run either for it or for the Oaks, his name is closely connected with the great Epsom race by memories of Sefton (Mr. W. S. Crawfurd's), the winner of it in 1878, and with Newmarket by Sefton House.

LORD ORFORD (who appears among the signatories of the earliest extant published 'Order' of the Jockey Club in 1758) is, of course, George WALPOLE, the third Earl (of the first creation), grandson of the famous Sir Robert Walpole, and the 'mad' nephew of Horace Walpole (who succeeded him and adopted the style and title of 'uncle to the late Earl of Orford'). The third Earl succeeded to the title in 1751, and died in 1791, and with him, it has been said, the good old English sport of 'hawking' virtually expired. He is best remembered for the havoc which he brought upon a fine estate, and for the sale of his grandfather's splendid collection of pictures, which he sold to the Empress of Russia. How he hawked, how he (and the Marquess of Rockingham) raced geese (the feathered variety) at Newmarket, and how he insisted upon driving red-deer instead of horses, four-in-hand, and got hunted by a pack of hounds, may be read in the chronicles of sport. It is not improbable that he did as much as anybody (as will be shown hereafter) to bring two-year-old racing (the introduction of which has been attributed, without satisfactory proof, to Sir Charles Bunbury) into fashion at Newmarket; and it is by no means certain that the fashion is a bad one. As for his madness, he was 'only mad nor-nor-west'; he not only knew a 'hawk' from a 'handsaw,' but 'a horse from a donkey,' as the saying is. He owned and bred many excellent horses: he bred, for instance, the famous Firetail (by Squirrel), said (and by the Jew Apella, the late Sir Francis Hastings Doyle, and the marines, but not the sailors, believed) to have run the Rowley Mile at Newmarket in one minute four seconds and a half at the First Spring Meeting of 1773; and he owned the Orford Barb mare (dam of Piper, by Captain; Houghton, by Squirrel; Spitfire, by Eclipse), &c. All this looks like a benefactor of the Turf; but the Earl seems to have been a confirmed and reckless gambler, and altogether such a member of the Jockey Club as the Club and the Turf are better without.

LORD [UPPER] OSSORY is John FITZPATRICK, second and last Earl, one of the subscribers in 1768 to the Jockey Club Challenge Cup, which he won in 1772 with Circe (by Matchem), and in 1777 with Dorimant (by Otho), bred by himself, and one of the best horses ever foaled. He is the Lord Ossory of whom David Hume spoke so highly and prophesied such good things (a prophecy which lacked complete fulfilment); and he was the 'Proculeian' brother of the 'Admirable Crichton' Colonel Fitzpatrick, and the husband (as already remarked) of the divorced Duchess of Grafton. He was noticeably successful in his career upon the Turf, his retirement from which was attributed (even by so scurrilous a writer as Mr. Pigott, author of 'The Jockey Club') to his disgust at the people and the practices encountered upon it. He bred and owned and ran a number of good horses, many of them sons and daughters of the celebrated Otho (purchased by him from Mr. 'Jockey' Vernon, as Horace Walpole calls him). Among them may be mentioned Comus (a runner in France, and one of the first English horses that stood at the stud there), Saturn, Spot, Turnus, and Otheothea (a brood mare of some repute, though a bad racer). His Coxcomb (own brother to Dorimant), after a short but distinguished career upon the race-course, went to the stud, but even then was frequently hunted, and in 1789, at the advanced age of *eighteen*, took part in a 'remarkable fox-chase,' at the conclusion of which, we are told, 'the few who were in it was (*sic*) from 25 to 30 miles distance from home. *Coxcomb*, aged eighteen, was up to the hounds the whole time, and was rode by a gentleman who weighed upwards of 12 stone.' Lord Ossory owned, if he did not import, the Ossory chestnut Arabian which stood at Ampthill, Bedfordshire, and which was the sire of Lord Grosvenor's Selima (daughter of Snapdragon), foaled 1772. Altogether, Lord Upper Ossory seems to have been the sort of member that would do honour as well as excellent service both to the Jockey Club and to the Turf. The title became extinct in 1818, though Lord Ossory is understood to be a sub-title of the Marquess of Ormonde.

The LORD PIGOT of the list is a historical and a tragical character; for he must be the unfortunate Sir George Pigot who was created Baron Pigot of Patshull, near Wolverhampton, in 1766, was Governor of Fort George, Madras, and for whose treatment (including deprivation of government and imprisonment, which seems to have caused his death), certain persons (*v.* 'State Trials') named George Stratton, Henry Brooke, Charles Flayer, and George Mackay, and perhaps others, were called to account and fined 1,000*l.* apiece. His membership of the Jockey Club is proved from the fact that he ran an unnamed bay colt for a Jockey Club Plate in 1773, which was won by Mr. Vernon's Giantess. At his death the peerage apparently became extinct, as he left no legitimate male children. He, however, had a natural son, who became Sir Hugh Pigot, K.C.B., Admiral of the White (died in 1875, aged eighty-two), and two brothers, Hugh (who, curiously enough, was also an admiral), and (the eldest of the three) General Sir Robert, Bart., whose son, General Sir George, was also a light of the Turf. Sir George, who was born in 1766 and died in 1841, raised the 130th Regiment, with which he served in the Peninsula, and was father of the late Sir Robert Pigot, of Patshull, who died in June 1891, at ninety years of age, and had owned some successful race-horses, including Essedarius, with which horse he challenged for the Newmarket Whip in 1851, having run second with him for the Cesarewitch the year before. It was probably Sir George (*v.* 'Stud Book,' vol. ii. p. 53) who owned the Patshull Arabian which stood at Patshull about 1800-1, and he was very likely himself a member of the Jockey Club.

LORD PORTMORE must have been Charles COLYER, the second Earl, who succeeded unexpectedly to the title (which became extinct in 1835) in 1729: his elder brother Viscount Milsington or Milsintown (for it is variously spelt, according to the wont of the age, which was more addicted to gambling than to orthography), having previously died and having had children who also died previously. The second Earl's membership of the Jockey Club is attested by his signature appended to the Jockey Club 'Order' of 1758. He (as well as the Viscount Milsington who was apparently his eldest son, and who ran Scarf for the Derby of 1781) was a great racer and breeder. He won the first (1751) of all the Great Subscriptions at York, with Skim (by the Bolton Starling); and he bred Mr. Grisewood's Partner (sire of the famous Gimcrack's dam), the celebrated Cartouch mare (dam of Sir J. Moore's Miss South, South-West, &c.), and the renowned little Highlander (14 hands, 1 inch), by Victorious. He was also one of the owners of the famous Othello (Black-and-All-Black), by Crab. He died in 1785, having done his duty to the Turf.

LORD ROCKINGHAM, the second and last Marquess, is the popular Charles Watson WENTWORTH, who gave its name to the Doncaster St. Leger (in 1778) from his friend and neighbour Colonel (afterwards General) St. Leger, of Park Hill (whence the Park Hill Stakes), near Doncaster. He belonged rather to the northern than to the southern members of the Jockey Club, whereof his membership is attested, if any attestation of so great a certainty be required, by his signature appended to the first document published by the Jockey Club in 1758. He was one of those persons who may be said to have greatness thrust upon them, for he was summoned—not exactly like Cincinnatus from the plough, but like himself and others of his day, if not of our own—from the race-course to the post of prime minister, in which capacity he and his colleagues so acquitted themselves that his political opponents delighted to quote the doggerel of the day to the effect that 'The Ministry sleeps, and the Minister's Rocking'em.' He appears to have been strongly of Horace's opinion that '*dulce est desipere in loco*'; and his favourite 'locus,' when he was not in the north, was Newmarket, where he would indulge in desipience so far, it is said, as to back his goose (feathered) against my Lord Orford's, as well as his horse or horses against anybody else's. He was not a very 'clayver' man, perhaps, as Shakespeare is said to have been, but he was an honest man, the creature once considered to be 'the noblest work of God,' but now very lightly esteemed (because, let us hope, he has become so common). He was a most liberal patron of the Turf, both north and south, and he did his part in the improvement of horse-flesh. He owned at one time or another, but did not breed, the famous Sampson (Mr. Robinson's, but bred by Mr. Preston, 15·2 hands high, considered gigantic for his time, when combined with such bone as he had), Whistle-jacket (bred by Sir W. Middleton), and Bay Malton (bred by *Mrs.*

Ayrton, of Malton, to whom, at her *wedding-dinner*, his dam was lent by her father Mr. Fenton, leading to a pointed rather than delicate proposition, after the fashion of the time, on the part of one of the guests, Mr. Preston, then owner of the stud-horse Sampson), by Sampson; and he bred as well as owned the celebrated Solon (by Sampson out of Emma, by the Godolphin Arabian), by whose match with Lord Bolingbroke's Paymaster (3 to 1 *on* the latter, October 1770, at Newmarket) he won 4,000 guineas. Oddly enough, Solon, after leaving the race-course, was used as a charger by Lord Rockingham. *Autres temps, autres mœurs*; in these latter days such a horse would be either sold for a small fortune to 'furrin parts,' or hurried to his owner's own stud to be 'coined' as soon as possible. Lord Rockingham, singular to relate, never won the St. Leger after he had named it, but he won what was the first unnamed edition of it with an unnamed filly, afterwards called Alabaculia. He was among the subscribers to the Jockey Club Challenge Cup, and he won the Newmarket Challenge Whip, in the very year (1768) in which that Cup was instituted, with Bay Malton, beating Cardinal Puff easily. That there was a mixture of eccentricity (illustrated by the goose-race) and shrewdness in the family is probable from the marriage contracted by the Marquess's sister, Lady Henrietta Alicia Wentworth, with her groom (who has acquired posthumous gentility in 'peerages'

F

and similar publications as W. Sturgeon, 'esquire'), and from the care and prudence with which she had her property tied up and settled on herself and her children (if there should be any little grooms or groomesses), with just 100*l.* a year for the 'esquire,' if he should survive her. After this, it is said that it was considered almost a personal matter to have a sturgeon (which was a very favourite fish at the time) at dinner, if the Marquess of Rockingham had accepted an invitation to it. The Marquess had no (legitimate) children, if, indeed, he had a wife (and apparently he had abstained from that expensive luxury for reasons, according to Sir N. W. Wraxall, which the great surgeon John Hunter would have commended highly), so that with him, who died in July 1782, the title became extinct and his estates (on the principle that 'he that hath to him shall be given') passed to his nephew, Lord Fitzwilliam. The Jockey Club would be well off with many more members like the second Marquess of Rockingham. He betted freely, it is true; but it is a question whether he would ever have sent out 'commissions,' even if there had been any organised 'ring' in his day.

LORD SONDES of the list is apparently that Lewis MONSON who is understood to have taken the additional name of Watson in compliance with the desire of his benefactor, the third Lord (second Marquess of) Rockingham. He was born in 1727, created Baron

Sondes, of Lees Court, Kent, in 1760, and died in 1795. In 1764, soon after he began to air his title, he is found running second with an unnamed bay colt (by Tarquin) to Lord Northumberland's Cæsario (by Matchem), for a Jockey Club Plate, which sufficiently establishes his membership; but for all that, and though he married a niece of the Duke of Newcastle (whose family name suggests the Pelham Barb, the Curwen Bay Barb, Alcock's Arabian, *alias* Pelham's Grey Arab, and the Brocklesby Stakes at Lincoln), he is not among the most prominent Fathers of the Jockey Club, or improvers of the thoroughbred.

The LORD STRANGE of the list is James STANLEY, son and heir of the eleventh, and father of the wonderfully popular twelfth Earl of Derby, and he died before his father (so that he never succeeded to the earldom) in 1771, having established his membership of the Jockey Club, as early as 1754, by running the celebrated Sportsman (winner of five King's Plates) unsuccessfully for a Jockey Club Plate. He raced likewise with Jenny, Kitty, Gift, &c., and well seconded his father (who had run Brown Betty for the King's Plate for five-year-old mares as long before as 1723), as well as paved the way, as it were, for his son, who was to 'belong' to the never-to-be-forgotten Sir Peter (Teazle). Lord Strange insisted upon bearing that title (if not from the cradle to the grave, at any rate, as soon after leaving the cradle as could be expected),

F 2

although his right to it was disputed, and it now appears to go with the dukedom of Athole, whereof the holder 'sits as Earl Strange.' It was this insistent Lord Strange, according to the authorities, who introduced the name and personality of the Smiths into the perhaps equally well known but certainly less prolific family of the Stanleys, by marrying one of the daughters and co-heiresses (Mr. John Barry, of the Earls of Barrymore's family marrying the other or an other) of a certain Hugh Smith, millionaire by trade, of Weald House, Essex. He thus prudently prepared the way for the profuse extravagance of his son, heir and successor, the twelfth Earl of Derby, by becoming the sire of whom he did scarcely less for the Turf, and a great deal more for cock-fighting, than if he had been the sire of the great Sir Peter (Teazle) himself.

LORD WALDEGRAVE is James WALDEGRAVE, second Earl, born 1714 (or 1715), succeeded to the title 1741, and died (of small-pox) 1763. His name is appended to the first public document issued by the Jockey Club in 1758; and he ran for Jockey Club Plates in 1760 and 1761. He was not one of the most prominent owners and breeders, though he owned some very fair horses, and in his stud, for a while, was the famous mare (Regulus) Mixbury. He left at his death a literary contribution in the form of 'Historical Memoirs' (1754-7). He was in many respects a very estimable personage, who, in spite of his protesting that he was 'only an inoffensive man of pleasure and fashion, and did not want to be bothered' (just like Lord Rockingham), was, much to his annoyance, advanced to high honour, and was made 'governour' to two Royal Princes, of whom one was afterwards George III. The second Earl of Waldegrave married Horace Walpole's niece, Maria (natural daughter of Sir Edward Walpole), who became Duchess of Gloucester, and was mother of the Maria Waldegrave who, according to Horace Walpole, was very shabbily treated by the Earl of Egremont, and, in fact, jilted by him, but she afterwards married the fourth Duke of Grafton for better or worse. Lord Waldegrave, having no male issue, was succeeded by his brother John (died 1784), who as a Master of the Horse might very well have been a member of the Jockey Club, but proofs of his membership are not forthcoming. The second Earl must be reckoned one of the most distinguished and most creditable among the Fathers of the Jockey Club.

As in the case of the dukes it is surprising to find no Rutland among the ducal members of the Jockey Club, so, in the case of the lords, one is inclined to be astonished at the conspicuous absence of the second Lord Godolphin's name. He was racing at Newmarket at the time of the Jockey Club's foundation; but no certain proof of his membership can be discovered. It must be remembered, however, that he was very old at the Club's first appearance at Newmarket in 1753, at which time he was seventy-five (he died in 1766). He may even have grown too groomish for so fashionable a body; but it certainly is strange that the founders of the Jockey Club should not have included—if they did not include—the owner of the Godolphin Arabian.

CHAPTER IV

THE SIRS

SIR JOHN ARMYTAGE, whose membership of the Jockey Club is attested by his signature appended to the first public document issued by the Club (March 1758), must have been the gallant young baronet who left his home in the North, his friends in the South, and his sport and pleasure on the Knavesmire and the Heath, to serve as a volunteer under General Blythe in those dark days which followed the convention of Closterseven, in 1757, when Lord Chesterfield, the imperturbable, was sufficiently moved to declare that we were 'no longer a nation,' and apparently fell on the field in the September of that very same year in which he had signed the 'Order' of the Jockey Club. He was succeeded by his brother Sir George; the very same baronet, no doubt, who won the Doncaster Gold Cup with Stargazer (dam of Teddy-the-Grinder), in 1787, who was among the 'quality' invited to meet the 'First Gentleman' and the Duke of York at the Mansion House, York, on the occasion of their memorable visit to the North in 1789, and who was himself very likely a member of the Jockey Club, though no proof can be advanced of his membership. Sir John was no more than twenty-seven at the time of his death, and it is, therefore, not surprising that he should have left few marks of his individuality on the history of the Turf and of the stud.

Sir THOMAS CHARLES BUNBURY, who was steward, and received the subscriptions for the Jockey Club Plate in 1768, and became a sort of 'Perpetual President,' as he is sneeringly called by an enemy, of the Jockey Club (something like Admiral Rous in later times), is perhaps the most familiar by name to the world of all the men who have ever been members of the Jockey Club. He was born in 1740, succeeded to the Baronetcy in 1764, first appeared (as Mr. Bunbury) on the Turf in 1763, and by 1768, as has already been observed, was steward of the Jockey Club. No doubt his proximity to Newmarket, as a resident upon his estate at Great Barton, near Mildenhall, Suffolk, which he represented in Parliament for many years, would be enough, combined with a 'strict attention to business' (that is, to horse-racing), to account to a considerable extent for the control which he obtained over affairs at 'head-quarters'; but that there was 'something about him' personally is abundantly evident, if only from the mention of him in the 'Receipt to make a Jockey,' and from the more creditable fact that he was preferred above all rivals for the hand of the lovely Lady Sarah Lennox, whom the King would gladly have made Mrs. George the

Third, had there been no obstacle in the way. It is true that Lady Sarah afterwards brought upon him the greatest grief and dishonour which a wife can bring upon a husband, and it is true that there is no accounting for woman's eccentricities in matrimonial matters; but there is reason to suppose that in this case the chosen husband was really a superior person. Divorce, however, was his fate, as it was that of many another brother-member of the Jockey Club. It was mainly owing to one Lord William Gordon that the divorce (in 1776) took place; and, 'as that was a duelling age' (to quote the gifted author of 'The Gay Cavalier'), surprise has sometimes been expressed that it did not 'lead to human gore' (to borrow the words of the immortal Sim Tappertit). The explanation is unique, and worthy of the period. When Sir Charles was about to take the usual steps, it was objected that he was bound to take the known poachers upon his manor in proper alphabetical order, in which case Lord William's turn would not come on for some time, as he stood about tenth on a list so constructed. Strange to say, however, like the filly Misfortune, that was so worthless in her early years and yet became the dam of the great Buzzard, the divorced Lady Sarah became some years afterwards the wife of the Hon. Colonel Napier, and was the mother of the famous Sir Charles and Sir William Napier, *duo fulmina belli.* Sir Charles Bunbury himself married a second time late in life somebody who was nobody, but he left no issue, and died at the great age of eighty-one in 1821. He was elder brother of the famous caricaturist, Henry Bunbury ('H. B.,' preferred by Horace Walpole to the great Hogarth himself), who, as will appear hereafter, is also included by a certain authority among the members of the Jockey Club. The most notable, or, at any rate, the most amusing, incident of Sir Charles's career in Parliament, was probably during the delivery of his maiden speech, when, being overcome by a sudden diffidence (in which he resembled great men like Addison, and even orators commended by Cicero), he sank hurriedly down into his seat in such fashion as to elicit from 'the late ingenious Charles Townshend' such a pun as that humourist would have been sure to make with the substitution of an *m* for an *n* in the name of Bunbury.

The successes of Sir Charles upon the racecourse and at the stud were very notable rather than numerous. He won the very first Derby (with Diomed in 1780); he was the first to win both Derby and Oaks in one and the same year (with Eleanor in 1801, enthusiastically described as 'a hell of a mare'); he was the first to win both Derby and Two Thousand in one and the same year (with Smolensko in 1813, a great horse, preserved by an ingenious device from being seized for a 'heriot'); and he bred but sold to Lord Bolingbroke (who gave the name) the celebrated Highflyer, the 'luck of Tattersall Hall.'

On Sir Charles, as one of the stewards in conjunction with Mr. Ralph Dutton and the 'polite' Mr. Thomas Panton, devolved the unpleasant duty of virtually 'warning off' the Prince of Wales (in connection with Escape, and Chifney's riding of him, when the Prince behaved like the 'First Gentleman'); and to him has been attributed, from the days of Mr. Christie Whyte to those of Sir Francis Hastings Doyle (writing in the 'Fortnightly' of June 1881), and even later still, the 'invention of two-year-old races,' and attributed generally as if it were discreditable to him.

But creditable or discreditable, let the saddle be put on the right horse.

Was it, then, Sir Charles Bunbury who 'invented' two-year-old racing? Mr. John Orton, of the well-known 'Annals,' a great authority, and others, assert that two-year-old racing originated in a match run at York between two youngsters of that age, belonging respectively to the Rev. Henry Goodricke (a Prebendary of York Minster, owner of the celebrated 'Old England mare,' and winner, generally under somebody else's name, whether Mr. G. Crompton's or another, of the Doncaster St. Leger on several occasions) and a Mr. John Hutchinson (originally a stableboy, and afterwards John Hutchinson, 'esquire,' of Shipton, near York, a man of substance and a breeder of famous racehorses, including Beningbrough and Hambletonian, winners of the St. Leger, and Oberon, by Highflyer). Unfortunately the date of the match is not given, nor is any account of it to be found in the public records, so that it was apparently (as would be likely) a private match at a time when there was no public racing going on at York. Moreover, according to the public records there was two-year-old public racing at Newmarket several years before it was in vogue, either for general racing or for matches, in the North. For the Craven Stakes, in which two-year-olds were first officially admitted to run among competitors of all ages (though two-year-olds had run matches there, either one against another or against older horses, as early as 1769), dates from 1771; whereas no earlier case of two-year-old running in public in the North is to be discovered by diligent search of public records than the match at Hambleton in 1779, when Mr. Coates's or Mr. Burdon's 'Czarina, 8 stone 7 lb., beat Mr. Hutchinson's bay colt (by Turk), bred by Mr. Passman, 8 stone both two-year-olds,' over the cruel distance of 'two miles,' the Mr. Hutchinson being the John Hutchinson to whom, in conjunction with the Rev. Henry Goodricke, the invention of two-year-old racing has been attributed. However, we know from other sources that Mr. Garforth, another great northern breeder and runner of racehorses, used to speak of two-year-old racing as 'the parson's new plan.' We know, further, that nobody would be likely to teach a Yorkshireman anything new about horses, and we know that it was at York in 1788 that a condemnable novelty was introduced, when a notorious match was run between a horse and a mare carrying *thirty* stone each. We know, besides, that Sir Charles Bunbury attended York races when he was a very young man (for he purchased Dux at York in 1766, when he was only twenty-six), where he would certainly meet both the Rev. H. Goodricke and Mr. John Hutchinson, both older than he (one a little and the other a great deal), and more experienced in horseflesh (for Hutchinson, the junior of the pair, already had charge of the famous Miss Western in 1751, when he was but fifteen, and when Sir Charles was but eleven), and he would rather have learned a 'wrinkle' from them than have been able to show them anything. On the whole, then, even if Sir Charles did introduce two-year-old racing at Newmarket, and though in Mr. Orton's own 'Annals' (of York and Doncaster) the earliest instance recorded of such racing in public is the epigrammatic match between Sir W. Vavasour's Hope and Sir C. Turner's Despair, at Doncaster in 1790, there is some reason to believe that Mr. Orton's statement as to the origin of two-year-old racing is correct—that it originated in a private match between two noted horse-breeders in the North, and that it was imported (whether by Sir Charles Bunbury or by somebody else) from the North to the South. For there is no evidence, so far as diligent search can discover, that either the Rev.

H. Goodricke or John Hutchinson (until this latter went South to look after Hambletonian on the eve of the great match with Diamond in 1799) ever visited Newmarket, so that they, or either of them, might have carried home thence the idea of the 'parson's new plan.'

But in any case, whether two-year-old racing was introduced at Newmarket from the North, or in the North from Newmarket, the evidence which can be collected goes to show that the invention or introduction of it cannot be assigned with probability to Sir Charles Bunbury, unless it be probable that a man would be conspicuously absent from among the earliest practisers of what he himself invented or introduced. And what are the facts? Investigation has revealed no earlier case of an undoubted two-year-old run by Sir Charles than Parthian for the Craven Stakes in 1774, though two-year-olds had been run at Newmarket since 1769 by Mr. South (who ran Precarious, 'rising three,' in February), by the 'mad' Lord Orford, by Lord Clermont, by Messrs. Blake and Foley, and others, Sir Charles having run against them, indeed, but with an older horse, and invariably over a very short course (from a quarter to three-quarters of a mile). Sir Charles, in fact, as Mr. W. Day remarks in his 'Racehorse in Training' (first edition, p. 78), was proverbial for his gentle usage of horses, at any rate in training; and it may be that the bad name which he has earned as a promoter of 'short distance races' he owes to his humanity. It is noticeable, too, that his name has survived to this day in connection with Bunbury's Mile at Newmarket, not, as might have been expected had he been the accepted inventor of two-year-old racing, with a T.Y.C. He shares, of course, with the rest of the Jockey Club the blame for having allowed yearlings to run at Newmarket, and for having established a regular Y.C.; but he is again conspicuously absent from among the runners of yearlings, the prominent innovators being Mr. 'Jockey' Vernon, my Lords Grosvenor, Foley, Clermont, Egremont, Derby, Barrymore, Messrs. C. J. Fox (the distinguished orator), Panton, and Ladbroke, and H.R.H. the Prince of Wales. So much it has been thought right to say, because Sir Charles's memory has incurred a great deal of odium on the ground that he was a promoter of 'young' as well as of 'short' races. There is no intention here, however, of condemning two-year-old racing, if kept within due limits. The youngsters are said by very high, if not the highest, authorities to be all the better for an early training; and, if they are to be trained, they must be exercised, and the exercise may as well take the form of a public race (if exertion be not overdone), on the principle on which the old trainer John Osborne decided that 'if horses must sweat, they might as well sweat for the brass,' that is, for public stakes. Sir Charles was a Father, not only to the English Turf but also to the American, for to

America went his Derby winner Diomed, and there the horse died in 1808, aged thirty-one, having begotten the famous American sire, Sir Archie, or Sir Archy, sire of Timoleon, sire of Boston, sire of Lexington. Of course, Sir Charles had his Bunbury Arabian, but it did not do much for the pedigrees.

Sir NATHANIEL CURZON (and previously Mr. CURZON in the annals of the Turf), of Kiddlestone, Derbyshire, is he who, having previously been M.P. for Derbyshire, was created Baron Scarsdale in 1761, and his membership of the Jockey Club is attested in many ways, and among them by his running for a Jockey Club Plate in 1757. He was a noted breeder, owner, runner, and rider; and the name of himself or of his father, who seems to have set him a racing and breeding example, or of one of his family, was attached to at least one of the 'Sons of the Desert' imported to improve the breed of the English horse, under the style and title of 'the Curzon Grey Barb.' As for his title of Scarsdale, there was an Earl of Scarsdale (probably not a Curzon, however), who ran for the Newmarket Town Plate in 1695, and was beaten by the famous or notorious Mr. Tregonwell Frampton with 'the King's horse.' He or his father was at one time owner of the Beaufort Arabian mare that was the dam of Jason (by Standard) and Y. Jason (by Y. Standard).

Sir LAWRANCE DUNDAS (who is, no doubt properly, included in the more trustworthy lists of subscribers to the Jockey Challenge Cup in 1768), of Aske, Yorkshire, is presumed to have been the gentleman who was created a Baronet in 1762, died in 1781, and was succeeded by Sir Thomas (created Baron Dundas, of Aske, in 1794), progenitor of the Earls of Zetland, of whom and their 'spots' and their connection with the Jockey Club more will have to be said hereafter. Sir Lawrance, who, as Mr. Dundas, is believed to have been Commissary-General, owned Bay Richmond, *alias* Sarpedon (under which name he ran in Jamaica), by Feather, and, being confederated with the famous Mr. Peregrine Wentworth, ran Carabineer (a name, in the form of Carbineer, borne in recent times by a celebrity of the Zetland stud), brother to the celebrated Yorkshire Jenny, in 1774 and 1775. Sir Lawrance bred Pontac, sire of Sir Thomas (*i.e.*, Sir T. [Dundas]), with which horse the Prince of Wales won the Derby in 1788.

Sir M. FEATHERSTONEHAUGH or FETHERSTONHAUGH, which seems to be the more correct form, ran for the Jockey Club Plates won by Lord Chedworth's chestnut filly in 1757, and by Mr. Francis Naylor's Sally in 1759 respectively, and had a stud-farm at Uppark, Sussex, where his son Sir Henry (of whom more anon) was born. He likewise possessed the estates of Haringbrook, Essex, and Fetherstonhaugh Castle, Northumberland. He was, moreover, F.R.S., and M.P. for Portsmouth, and altogether a great personage. The name is commonly met with in the abbreviated form, Fetherston, and it might naturally be supposed that the other was found too long for life, οἷοι νῦν βροτοί εἰσι, and accordingly curtailed. But Fetherston is really the right form; for there were originally two brothers, who divided the family property between them, part of which (in Northumberland) lay low, and part (in Durham) lay high; so the two brothers agreed to distinguish themselves by adding 'haugh' for the 'low,' and 'halge' for the 'high,' to their name, according to the site of their domain. Ultimately the lean kine swallowed up the fat; in other words, the property of both the 'haugh' and the 'halge' branch merged in the representative of the former, Sir Matthew, whose father, plain Mr. Matthew, had been twice Mayor of Newcastle, and had married a rich Miss Brown, and whose uncle, become Sir Henry, wished both his property and his title to be continued in his nephew. And so it was. Sir Matthew's son, born at Uppark, December 22, 1754, 'rose,' as we shall see, to be a sort of 'gentleman-jockey to the Prince of Wales,' just as Dr. Johnson's young friend, Sir John Lade, became 'coachman' to the same Royal Highness. Sir Matthew died in 1761, and therefore had no chance of winning St. Leger, Oaks, or Derby; but he owned Sog, by Cade; Henricus, by Othello (Black and All Black), &c.; and he bred Proserpine and her sister, by Henricus, &c., &c. Uppark, in Sussex, had its race-meeting under the auspices of the old Fetherstons, but of very brief existence.

Sir THOMAS GASCOIGNE, of Barnbow, Lasingcroft, and Parlington, Yorkshire, was one of those great Northern lights of the Turf whom the founders of the Jockey Club, much to the credit of their wisdom and their national sentiments, cordially admitted from the very first to the association whose headquarters and principal arena were in the South at Newmarket. He was born in 1743 and died in 1810; and though there is no actual proof that he belonged to the Jockey Club before 1778, when he is gazetted as the winner of a Jockey Club Plate with his unfortunate horse Magog (the joint property of himself and Mr. Stapleton, another member of the Jockey Club), there is reason to suppose that his membership would date from some years before. That he was a member of the Club scarcely admits of a doubt, else, as Jockey Club Plates could be run for by members of the Club only, Magog would have appeared in the name of the other half-owner, Mr. Stapleton, whose membership is proved as early as 1768 by the fact of his being one of the subscribers to the Jockey Club Plate. Sir Thomas, whose surname must not be confounded with that of Mr. Gascoyne (another member of the Jockey Club), is said to have been descended from the family of which a shining historical light is the famous Chief Justice Gascoigne, by whom (according to legend) Prince 'Hal' (afterwards Henry V.) was committed to prison. With Sir Thomas the baronetcy became extinct, for he had the misfortune to lose his only son by an accident out hunting, and a very touching epitaph shows how keenly the poor father felt the blow. Indeed, it is said to have shortened his life, though he lived to the age of sixty-seven, which is only three years short of the average span allotted by the Psalmist. Sir Thomas was succeeded by a connection of the family, Mr. Richard Oliver, who, apparently, had married one of the baronet's daughters, took the baronet's family name, and is the Mr. Gascoigne who won the St. Leger in 1811 with Soothsayer, by Sorcerer, and in 1824 with Jerry, by Smolensko. Sir Thomas had married the widow of Sir C. Turner, another great light of the Northern Turf, and a member also of the Jockey Club, so that there was quite a plethora of horsiness in the family. Sir Thomas and his 'frequent friend and pardner,' Mr. Stapleton, won between them a vast number of great races, including the St. Leger in 1778, 1779, and 1798, with Hollandaise, by Matchem; with Tommy, by Wildair, and with Symmetry, by Delpini; and the Oaks in 1803 with Theophania, by Delpini. And in the pedigrees (v. Mambrino in the 'Stud Book,' for example) we come upon mention of ' a Foreign Horse of Sir T. Gascoigne's,' though that Sir Thomas must have been a predecessor, probably the father, of our immediate Sir Thomas. As for the Gascoigne-Stapleton Magog, he has been termed 'unfortunate,' because he is one of the earliest recorded instances of barbarous 'nobbling'; for we read that, on the eve of the race for the Gold Cup at Doncaster in 1778, 'when he was backed at high odds . . . the night before running some villains broke two locks and got into the stable to Magog, and, by cutting his tongue nearly off and giving him something inwardly, rendered him at that time incapable of starting.' Unfortunately we do not read that the atrocious scoundrels were caught and received as nearly their meed as Judge Lynch, a tree, and a rope, or calmer justice, a trial, a gallows, and a hangman, could give it them, or that any sort of judgment befell them; but, fortunately, on the other hand, we do read that the horse recovered, won more races, and was a good sire. It is curious in these days to note that he got his name from standing 16 hands high (a very common height in aftertimes, when the name of Magog was given to a horse that is said to have stood 18 hands high, and, be it observed, to have been unable to 'go' for more than half a mile); but that was then considered gigantic. Sir Thomas, or one of his family, be it further remarked, is reported to have possessed at one time a famous black mare, which had belonged to one Nevison, a highwayman, whom fancy has identified with the 'Dick Turpin' of criminal romance, conferring, of course, the name of Black Bess upon the mare.

Sir H. GREY is undoubtedly the Sir Henry Grey, of Howick, Northumberland, who died unmarried in

1808, whereby it is said that 37,000*l.* a year fell to his nephew, the newly-created Earl Grey. That Sir Henry was a member of the Jockey Club appears from his signature to the Jockey Club resolution of 1758 (signed by thirty-one members); and that he raced occasionally is attested by Fox, winner in his name of a Royal Plate as early as 1755 at Ipswich, &c., but he is not among the most prominent racing members of the Jockey Club.

Sir JOHN KAYE, another among the signatories of the Jockey Club document in 1758, is the Baronet (descended, says heraldic tradition, from Sir Kaye or Kay, a knight of the Round Table) who was high sheriff for the County of York in 1761 and died unmarried in 1789, of Denby Grange, seven miles from Wakefield, six from Huddersfield, and thirty-seven from York. He was succeeded in the baronetcy by his brother, Dean of Lincoln, the Very Rev. Sir Richard, who died *s.p.* in 1809, when the baronetcy expired, and in the estates by his kinsman Lister Kaye, Esquire, who was created a Baronet in 1812, and became Sir John P. Lister Kaye. So it is made out, but the genealogical cooks appear to have spoilt the genealogical broth a little in some of the obituaries. At any rate Sir John Kaye was one of the great Northern lights of the Turf and of the Jockey Club. He bred Frenzy and her son Phænomenon (winner of the St. Leger in 1783); and he bred and owned for a time the famous mare Perdita (by Herod), dam of the still more famous Yellow Filly or Yellow Mare (bred by Mr. Tattersall) that won the Oaks for Sir F. Standish in 1786. As for Phænomenon, he was imported into America some time between 1798 and 1803 (in the latter year, according to Bruce's 'American Stud Book'), and died (in 1803, according to the same authority) 'soon after landing' in New York.

Sir J. LOWTHER, if there be no mistake, is the Sir James who was called 'the little tyrant of the North' by 'Junius,' and was afterwards better known by the flattering title of 'the bad Lord Lonsdale.' At any rate Sir James was created Earl of Lonsdale in 1784. He was one of the 'West Indian' members (of whom we shall see more) of the Jockey Club; that is to say, he was the son of Robert Lowther, Governor of Barbadoes. He was 'horsey' by hereditary right, paternally and maternally; for his mother appears to have been Catherine, daughter of the very 'horsey' Sir Joseph Pennington and of Margaret Lowther (daughter of the first Viscount Lonsdale, whose family were all 'horsey' and imported or owned the 'Lonsdale Bay Arabian,' the 'white-legged Lowther Barb' [chestnut], &c.). Sir James, who was M.P. for Cumberland and Westmoreland before he became a peer (and is said to have put the great William Pitt in for Appleby), is understood to have inherited the estates of his granduncle, the third Viscount, who died in 1750. In 1761, it seems, Sir James married a daughter of the Earl of Bute, but had no children, and at his death, in 1802, the barony, viscounty, and estates appear to have passed to his cousin, the Rev. Sir W. Lowther, of Swillington. Sir James is said to have been satirised by 'Peter Pindar,' and to have fought a duel with a Captain Cuthbert. His unpopularity appears to have been connected with the 'eviction of tenants' (just as if he had been an Irish landlord of our day); but he was allowed by common consent to have left an admirable will, and he is mentioned by Horace Walpole as a munificent patron of art. He was, at any rate, a munificent patron of the Turf and the thoroughbred; and he is said to have had in his stud at one time six stallions whose aggregate age was 144 years. Among them were Pleader (died at thirty-one, all but a fortnight, in April 1801) and Ajax (died in November, 1800, at twenty-nine), and we are told that the two old horses stood together in the same stable for several years, agreed together, and walked out together in the Park, at Lowther, Westmoreland, when 'Ajax affected his youthful vigour, and Pleader tottled after him.' A pleasant glimpse this of the wicked ways of the 'bad Lord Lonsdale,' who seems at least to have been careful of his old and decrepit horses. Sir James appears in the list (1762) of those members of the Jockey Club who agreed to adopt 'colours,' but seems not to have made up his mind what they should be, and in the list of 1770 does not appear at all. He won, however, a Jockey Club Plate with Jason in 1757 and with

Ascham in 1763. He is credited with having done a very sporting thing in 1758, when he bought Mirza (after winning one of the Jockey Club Plates) for 1,500 guineas from Mr. Fulke Greville and offered to back the horse for 10,000 guineas (and allow 4 lb.) against the redoubtable Snap (sire of Goldfinder, Angelica, &c.); but the latter 'being on his way to the North,' where he was to retire to the stud, 'the challenge was not accepted' by the 'Northumberland confederacy' (Messrs. Swinburne and Shafto, brothers, all members of the Jockey Club).

Sir WILLIAM MIDDLETON, Baronet, of Belsay Castle, Northumberland, was one of the great 'Northern lights' of the Turf, though he was beaten with the famous Whistlejacket (bred by him, but sold in 1756 to Lord Rockingham) by the Duke of Ancaster with Spectator for a Jockey Club Plate in 1756. Sir William is understood to have died *s.p.* in 1757, and to have been succeeded by his brother (John Lambert), who died in 1768, and was succeeded by his son (the hero of Minden, where he was desperately wounded). Sir William is said to have been M.P. for Northumberland from 1722 to 1757, the year of his death. He owned the Bartlet's Childers mare that bred Squirrel (*alias* Surly), Midge, Thwackum (*alias* Scipio), and Camilla, all by a son of Bay Bolton, and Miss Belsea (Belsay). The Bartlet's Childers mare's dam was sister to the two famous True Blues.

Sir JOHN MOORE, Baronet, of Fawley Court, Berks,

is made out to have succeeded his brother, who died unmarried in 1738; to have himself died *s.p.* at eighty years of age or more in 1799, and to have been succeeded by his brother, at whose death *s.p.* in 1807 the title became extinct. Sir John appears to have sold Fawley Manor to the Vansittarts (who sold it to a Mr. Tipping, whose niece and heiress married the Rev. Philip Wroughton, and brought the property into that family), and to have migrated into Suffolk, near Bury St. Edmunds, where he died. He 'went ahead' in his youth, according to George Selwyn and his correspondents; but he was a great breeder, owner, and runner of racehorses. He was one of the subscribers to the Jockey Club Challenge Cup in 1768; and at the death of the 'Culloden' Duke of Cumberland in 1765, he had purchased the illustrious (King) Herod. He refused 2,000 guineas offered by the King of Poland for the horse; but, nevertheless the great sire is stated by some authorities to have died at Sir John's stud-farm in such a terrible state of dirt, neglect, and disease that, if the story be true, nothing 'bonum' can be said for Sir John, though he is dead. Perhaps Herod had turned so savage that the only grooming he could receive consisted in 'intermittent dashes with a broom,' as has been related of another horse that had lost his temper; otherwise one would think that self-interest, if no better feeling, would ensure proper attention for a valuable animal of that description.

Sir T. SEBRIGHT (who ran the *dun* colt Creampot for a Jockey Club Plate in 1759, when dun was not at all an uncommon colour for a racehorse) was apparently Sir Thomas Saunders Sebright, the fifth Baronet, who died unmarried in 1761 at the early age of thirty-eight, and was succeeded by his brother, Lieutenant-General Sir John Saunders Sebright, which accounts for the fact that Creampot is assigned in the 'Stud Book' to Sir John, though Heber distinctly states that the colt was run by ' Sir *Thomas* Seabright.' The name of Saunders came from the heiress who brought the property of Beechwood, Herts, into the family by her marriage with Sir Thomas (the fourth Baronet, who died at the early age of forty-four in 1736, and whose younger brother was murdered, whilst travelling in France, at the still earlier age of twenty-five). The family contributed to the common cause of the Turf a ' Sebright Arabian,' whose influence appears in the pedigree of the aforesaid Creampot, which horse became the property of Mr. ' Jockey' Vernon, the oracle of Newmarket.

Sir CHARLES SEDLEY (or SIDLEY, for this seems to have been the old original form), whose membership of the Jockey Club is attested in many ways, notably by the mention made of him (as one of the kindest and most genial members of the Club) by ' Jemmy' Boswell in ' The Cub at Newmarket,' and by the fact that he won a Jockey Club Plate in 1776 (with the famous Trentham, then *ten years old*, purchased in 1773 of Sir J. Moore), and with Molecatcher in 1777, came of the family whose name was rendered rather notorious than famous by the witty but undeniably disreputable Sir Charles Sedley, whose daughter was James II.'s witty but brazen mistress, created (even to her shameless father's creditable indignation) Countess of Dorchester. The Sir Charles with whom we are dealing here was the son of the Sir Charles Sedley, of Southfleet, who was created a Knight in 1688 and a Baronet in 1702; and having married the daughter and heiress of a Mr. Collinge, of Nuttall, Notts., died in 1727. The Sir Charles his son, member of the Jockey Club, exchanged Southfleet (and Northfleet) with the Reverend T. Sanderson for Kirkby Baber, Leicestershire, and obtained the manors of Hayford and Harleigh by marriage with a Miss Frith. He also, of course, possessed the estate of Nuttall, Nottinghamshire, where he appears to have lived principally. At any rate, he was for many years M.P. for Nottingham. He died in 1778, leaving a daughter, who married Lord Vernon, and the title became extinct. Sir Charles promoted the cause of the Turf and of horse-breeding on a very extensive scale as breeder, owner, and runner of almost countless thoroughbreds, first-rate, second-rate, and third-rate. He became the owner of Mr. Compton's Barb (sire of Lord Bolingbroke's celebrated Coquette), which is so favourably prominent in the pedigrees, and is called indifferently the Compton Barb and the Sedley Grey Arabian. As Sir Charles died in 1778, of course he had no chance of winning either the Derby or the Oaks; nor does he seem to have run for the race which, ever since 1778 (included), has been known as the Doncaster St. Leger.

Sir JOHN SHELLEY, of Michel Grove and Maresfield Park, Sussex, is the fifth Baronet, whose membership of the Jockey Club is proved by his running for a Jockey Club Plate in 1774 and (with the bay filly Everlasting, bred by him, dam of the famous Skyscraper, that won the Derby of 1789 for the youthful Duke of Bedford) in 1779. He succeeded his father in 1771. He was M.P., P.C., Clerk of the Pipe, &c., and died in 1783. He came of a racing strain maternally (for his father had married first a Scawen and then a Pelham); he it was who brought (by marriage) the Maresfield property into the family; and he must have been the 'Jack' Shelley of whom we read in Jesse's 'Selwyn' and who (about 1763, when there seems to have been more of the sporting spirit about than there is now) is said to have won a foot-race-match (at Oatlands or Newmarket), for 20 guineas a side, 'with his hands tied behind his back.' Michel Grove has become a household word, or two household words, among lovers of horse-racing; but the sixth Baronet (son and namesake of the fifth), to whom we shall come anon, was the great horse-racer, winner of the Derby with Phantom and Cedric.

Sir SIMEON STUART (or STEUART, or STEWART), whose name appears among the signatories of a Jockey Club 'agreement' of February 10, 1771, must have been the third Baronet of Hartley Mauduit, Hants. He was M.P. for Hampshire, and he is apparently the (then Mr.) Stuart who ran the indicative grey colt Hartley (telling of the above-mentioned place in Hampshire) at Odiham in 1758. He bred both the said Hartley and a filly (by Babraham, son of Whirligig, by Bajazet) from the Crab mare that was the dam of Lord Bolingbroke's (afterwards Mr. Quick's) Charlotte (by Blank), and the same Lord's Doge (by Regulus). Sir Simeon, however, was not among the most prominent racing and breeding members of the Jockey Club, and seems to have inclined (though to say so may be a breach of the 'de mortuis nil nisi bonum' precept) towards 'schedule g' and the 'cocktail.' But his were days when members of the Jockey Club delighted to ride their own hunters, even on the race-course, where, nowadays, it is a rare sight to see a member of the Jockey Club in the pigskin, the exhibition not being encouraged by the Club.

Sir CHARLES TURNER of the list must have been a simple 'Mister' at the time his signature was appended to five resolutions of the Jockey Club in 1771, of Kirkleatham, Yorkshire. He was created a Baronet in 1782 and died in 1783. He represented York City in Parliament from 1768 to the day of his death, was one of the great 'Northern lights' of the Turf, and a great sportsman altogether. It is recorded that he 'sported freely' when he matched his Brutus against Lord Rockingham's Remus at Newmarket in 1757 for 500 guineas, B.C., 8 stone 7 lb. against 8 stone 11 lb., and won; and he was the hero of the leaping-match in 1752 or 1753, when he performed with ease in 36 minutes, for a wager of 1,000 guineas, the task of riding ten miles and taking forty leaps, for which he was allowed at least 45 minutes, if not longer. He was also the hero of a run with his hounds, in 1775, after 'the noted old fox Cæsar, who made an extraordinary chace . . . upwards of 50 miles.' It was his son (also perhaps a member of the Jockey Club) who in 1796 married the daughter (or a daughter) of the rich banker Sir W. Newcomen (who eventually seems to have blossomed into a noble lord), of Carrickglass, and it is published abroad that he had to relinquish horse-racing as part of the settlement or marriage-agreement. The relinquishment, however, can only have been 'over the left,' or, at any rate, temporary (whether the promise were cancelled by mutual consent or merely broken like pie-crust), for he was evidently 'on the Turf' when he died, at the early age of thirty-eight, in 1810, though no proof has been discovered that he was (as he most likely was) a member of the Jockey Club. It was this young Sir Charles who at York August races in 1795 had purchased in a lump from Mr. John Hutchinson (first stable-boy and then 'esquire') for

3,000 guineas the famous horses Boningbrough, Hambletonian (winner of the then imminent St. Leger), and Oberon. It is noticeable that this Sir Charles's widow (who seems to have become reconciled to horse-racing, if it were she and not—as is more likely—her father who had objected to it) married another horse-racer (and member of the Jockey Club), Mr. H. Vansittart; just as the elder Sir Charles's (we have already seen) married the great Northern light of the Turf (and also member of the Jockey Club), Sir T. Gascoigne.

Sir W. WOLSELEY, whose membership of the Jockey Club is established as early as 1755, when Countess ran in his name for a Jockey Club Plate, was one of the Wolseleys of Staffordshire (and of Mt. Wolseley, Ireland, from which Irish branch the gallant Lord Wolseley, of Cairo, is understood to be descended), and is made out to have been Sir William, fifth in succession from Sir Charles (created a Baronet by Charles the First in 1628), whose son (Sir Charles) was a Cromwellite and M.P. for Staffordshire (1654–1656). Sir William seems to have succeeded his uncle (Sir Henry, fourth Baronet), to have married a daughter of W. Pigott, Esquire, of Doddeshall, Bucks, a very 'racing' connection (if names go for anything), and to have died in 1779. Sir William Wolseley's Barb (whether imported by him or not) testifies to the Baronet's services as a breeder, not only to the English but to the French Turf; for that Barb was the sire of Lord Grosvenor's Riddle, that was the dam (in 1771) of Lord Grosvenor's celebrated horse Barbary (sold to Comte d'Artois in 1775-6, before the great 'deluge' prophesied by Madame de Pompadour, and by him imported into France and raced there at Sablons, and afterwards sent to the Count's stud, after winning several stakes and matches on French soil).

CHAPTER V

THE MISTERS

WE have now come to the plain 'Misters,' whom, having no particular 'scent,' such as a ducal, baronial, or similar title, for us to follow, it is sometimes a little difficult to run to earth, as naval and military 'handles' and the courtesy-prefix of 'honourable' are very often omitted, and would not be sufficient guide, even if they were not. Be it premised that the asterisk denotes that the bearers of the names so distinguished were connected with the West Indies, where, when slavery was not yet abolished and planters had large fortunes, energetic efforts were made to introduce and propagate the thoroughbred, and to establish horse-racing (to such purpose, indeed, that some of our early 'Calendars' give the results of races held in Jamaica, &c.); and the election of such gentlemen as members of the Jockey Club in its early days tends to emphasise what has been said about the wise and liberal spirit displayed by the Club in welcoming, if only the qualifications of social rank and of property were satisfactory, representatives of the

Turf and the Stud from north, south, east, or west, home-born, home-bred, home-resident, or colonial.

Mr. ANDERSON, whose membership of the Jockey Club is ascertained from the fact that his name is appended to a Rule of the Jockey Club dated April 19, 1769, appears to have been identical with the Captain Francis Anderson who was a great 'gentleman-jock' in his day, riding both in the North and in the South, at York and at Newmarket, against such well-known riders and members of the Jockey Club as Messrs. Vernon, Shafto, Compton, Lord Orford, &c. He probably belonged to the northern family of Andersons, of whom the head (at the foundation of the Jockey Club) was Sir Edmund Anderson, Bart., who died in 1765. But as Mr. Anderson is not conspicuous among the owners and breeders, he cannot be said to have done much for 'the cause.'

†Mr. BLADEN (whose membership rests upon the slender foundation of what is remembered of a statement in an 'obituary,' and upon inference drawn from the proverb *noscitur a sociis*, and from various other indications) is he who ran against three other gentlemen, all members of the Jockey Club, for the Weights and Scales Plate of 1759; but as that race, though the Jockey Club found the money for it, may not have been then (its first year), and certainly was not afterwards, confined to members of the Jockey Club, his running for it on the occasion mentioned is no evidence whatever of membership of the Club. It

is more in favour of his membership, perhaps, that he and his two daughters (of whom one married the Earl of Essex and the other Colonel St. John, brother of the 'Bully' Lord Bolingbroke, a very 'horsey' and Jockey-Club-like connection) are mentioned as constant visitors at Newmarket and as intimate friends of 'Old Q.,' who was the 'Star' not only 'of Piccadilly,' but also of the Jockey Club. At least, this Mr. Bladen seems to have been identical with the Colonel Thomas Bladen, or Thomas Bladen, Esq., a Commissioner of Forests and Plantations, whom we meet with in Walpole's 'Letters' and Jesse's 'Selwyn,' who was M.P. at various times for Old Sarum, Steyning, &c., and died in 1780 at the age of eighty-two. He ran races with Aristotle, Essex Lady, and other horses of more or less note (whereof Aristotle, by the Cullen Arabian, was imported into Virginia, and died there in 1775), probably half-bred; and there was a Bladen stallion, to which he very likely 'belonged.'

The name of BLAKE covers three separate gentlemen, Messrs. Andrew, Patrick (afterwards Sir Patrick), and Christopher, who were all probably one happy family, whether father and sons, or brothers, or otherwise related, for they all belonged to the Blakes (originally of Ballyglasmin Park, Galway), of Langham Hall, Suffolk. Their membership of the Jockey Club in each case is undoubted, for Andrew (who seems to have died about 1761) ran for a Jockey Club Plate in 1757 and 1758; the other two (of whom Patrick was created a Baronet in 1772) were signatories of documents issued by the Jockey Club in 1770 and 1771, and Patrick was a subscriber to the Jockey Club Cup in 1768. It is pretty certain that Patrick and Christopher Blake were brothers, and they were among the most memorable breeders, owners, and runners of racehorses. To Mr. Christopher belonged the legendary Firetail (bred, however, by the 'mad' Lord Orford, by Squirrel), when that descendant of the flying Pegasus won the match with the equally legendary Pumpkin (belonging to the Hon. Mr. Foley, but bred by the celebrated Mr. John Pratt, of Askrigg, a member of the Jockey Club), when the pair are said to have covered the R.M. (which should have been a distance of one mile and one yard at that time) in 'one minute four seconds and a half' (perhaps arising out of the misprinting of the figures, 1 $41\frac{1}{2}$); a fact which, if it were really accomplished, would go far to render probable the 'mile in a minute' once attributed to Flying Childers (but never authenticated, and, in modern times, relegated to the domain of fiction and 'seven-league boots'), and would put the performances of Prince Charlie, the roaring 'King of the T.Y.C.,' and of all our modern 'flyers' (though bred, it is a common complaint, for mere speed at the risk of inferior stamina) into impenetrable shade. This match, after which Firetail was purchased by Mr. Foley, led to the promulgation of the Order of the Jockey Club (1773), 'that all Betts between

Pumpkin and Firetail are null and void, those horses being now the property of the same gentleman,' together with a 'Rider' to the effect that 'all Betts between two [? or more] horses become null and void if the horses subsequently become the property of one and the same person or his avowed confederate.'

The quickest authenticated modern time for the Rowley Mile is that of Diophantus, in the Two Thousand of 1861 (when the Rowley Mile distance was a mile and seventeen yards, instead of a mile and one yard, which would make a very slight difference—between two and three strides, in fact), when it was run in 1 min. 45 secs. It must be remembered, however, that Firetail and Pumpkin were 'rising four,' and very nearly quite four years old on April 14, 1773 (when racehorses took their ages from May 1, instead of, as now, January 1), and carried half a stone less than Diophantus (a true three-year-old in April 1861, carrying 8 stone 7 lb.), and that the match was more likely than the general race to be a test of utmost possible speed. The question is, to what extent an advantage of both weight and age can be reckoned upon to augment speed over a given distance, and it is obvious that the extent is not unlimited (for speed must depend upon a combination of length of stride and quickness of recovery, and these again depend upon faculties which no advantage of weight and age can render illimitable). Can that advantage, then, ever be equivalent in point of time, in a mile, to some 30 seconds or 40 seconds? It certainly seems impossible; for 30 seconds (to suppose that Diophantus could have gone at the rate of 15 seconds faster at a pinch) would be equivalent to a third of a mile, and 25 seconds to nearly 500 yards. Altogether, then, the time attributed to Pumpkin and Firetail for a mile seems to be utterly incredible.

Sir Patrick Blake was evidently a fine old typical member of the Jockey Club, for he married (in 1760) Annabella Bunbury (sister of the celebrated Sir Charles, himself, as we have seen, divorced), from whom he was divorced (at her suit) in 1778, and died in 1784, having served his country as M.P. for Sudbury. The divorced lady married George Boscawen, Esq., of St. Peter's, Isle of Thanet; and that is a name redolent of the Turf, and of the late Viscount Falmouth, a conspicuous member of the Jockey Club. As regards Mr. Christopher Blake, there is not so much that is interesting to be recorded; at least research has not revealed it. There is every reason to believe, however, that even he was mortal, though he did win his match by means of the redoubtable Firetail, though he won a Jockey Club Plate with Quill in 1771, and though he was a very notable member of the Jockey Club as a staunch patron of the Turf and promoter of horse-racing and horse-breeding. R.I.P.

Mr. BOOTHBY, who naturally (as will appear farther on) signed the Jockey Club ordinance of 1767 touching the exclusion of unauthorised persons from the Coffee Room, was a remarkable person in many ways. He seems to have called himself sometimes Boothby and sometimes Scrymsher (or Scrymshire), and sometimes Clopton, or Charles Scrymsher Boothby, or Charles Boothby Scrymsher, or Charles Boothby Scrymsher Clopton (for pardonable reasons connected with property, no doubt), but the worst of it is that there appears to have been no agreement about the orthography of the word beginning with Scr— or Skr—. Perhaps he did not know how to spell it himself (as seems to have been commonly the case with gentlemen and their names in the 'good old times'), but certainly it is found in print in the forms Scrymsher, Scrymshire, Scrimshire, and Scrimsher. He was commonly known as 'Prince' Boothby, for the reason (says an enemy) of his inordinate regard for rank and titles (so that the 'exclusive' resolution of 1767 would be sure of his signature); and he is said to have carried this feeling so far that he would drop an Earl for a Duke without a moment's hesitation. It is even related of him (or of somebody like him) that he went home incontinently and cut off his 'pigtail' one day, because he had met an illustrious personage, who, being fond of a joke, had readily agreed to hide his own 'pigtail' under his coat-collar to see what would be the effect upon the 'Prince.' But, though he might cut off his hair, he stuck to his hat, that is, to his form of hat; for it is said that he had worn the same sort of hat (not the same hat, as some authorities have it, not being careful to make their meaning clear) for twenty years, without any change of shape (a 'fad' which one would have a difficulty in gratifying nowadays, when we are at the mercy of imperious firms and have to wear what we can get, not what we should like). He, however, made up for his dogged persistency in this little matter by changing his name, as we have seen, frequently—for substantial considerations, however, of property. At last, having inherited several estates and worn but one (style of) hat, the poor gentleman (rather than live any longer among a hat-changing generation) shot himself, in the year 1800. He was brother to the wife of Mr. Hugo Meynell (also a member of the Jockey Club), the 'Father of Fox-hunting'; and he was probably related to a Mr. Robert Boothby who ran racehorses in the early days of the Jockey Club (1758, for instance), but he himself is said (by an enemy again) to have inclined rather towards the 'Board of Green Cloth' than towards the Turf, and to have preferred the impoverishment attainable by the 'bones' at Spa and elsewhere. At any rate, he has left no signs of having contributed to the improvement of the English thoroughbred.

†Mr. Boswell is 'Jemmy' Boswell, the Laird of Auchinlech, the admirer and biographer of Dr. Johnson (whose young friend Sir John Lade was also a member of the Jockey Club, as we shall see hereafter).

'Bozzy' was probably not a substantive member, but he is included here (with an obelisk, denoting doubt) because he expressly declares in his preface to 'The Cub at Newmarket' that the verses were 'written in the Newmarket Coffee Room, in which the author, *being elected a member of the Jockey Club*, had the happiness of spending several sprightly good-humoured evenings.' The date of this statement is 1762, five years before the rule about admission to the Coffee Room, and very likely means no more than that Boswell was made free of the Rooms, for the time of his remaining at Newmarket, on the introduction of Lord Eglinton, a sort of neighbour of Boswell's in Scotland. Boswell's verses begin thus :

> 'Lord E[glintou]n, who has, you know,
> A little dash of whim or so,
> Who thro' a thousand scenes will range
> To pick up anything that's strange,
> By chance a curious Cub had got,
> On Scotia's mountains newly caught,
> And, after driving him about
> Thro' London, many a different rout . . .
> Newmarket Meeting being near,
> He thought 'twas best to have him there,' &c.

From this it is clear that Boswell was not a serious candidate for substantive membership.

Mr. BRAND, whose membership of the Club is conveniently established by the fact that he ran Glowworm (by Eclipse) for a Jockey Club Plate in 1776, is undoubtedly the Thomas Brand (first cousin to the

Duke of Kingston), Esq., of The Hoo, Hertfordshire, one of whose family is mentioned in Walpole's 'Letters' as among the founders of the Dilettanti Club, and another of whose family was classed with Lord Wilton, Mr. Delmé-Radcliffe, and others, as a great 'gentleman-jockey' in the first half of this century. The Mr. Brand here in question is a particularly interesting member of the Jockey Club, because by his marriage with the Hon. Gertrude Roper (who succeeded her brother and became Baroness Dacre in 1794—after Mr. Brand's death, however, in the very same year) he transmitted the blood of the famous 'patriot' John Hampden to his descendant, the present H. B. W. Brand, the first Viscount Hampden and twenty-third Baron Dacre, who was formerly the distinguished Speaker of the House of Commons. Mr. Brand in his horse-racing was aided and abetted by his wife, then the Hon. Mrs. Brand, who, for instance, won a match for 100 guineas with her, or her husband's, bay mare Baccelli (so called after a famous ballet-dancer of those times), at Newmarket First October Meeting, 1776, against Lady Bampfylde (ancestress of the Lords Poltimore) with Fortune-hunter. As for Glow-worm, with whom Mr. Brand ran second for a Jockey Club Plate in 1776, he was a very notable horse, and was sold by Mr. Brand to the popular French Marquis de Conflans, by whom he was imported into France, where he was distinguished both on the race-course (beating King Pepin, Barbary, and Cadet, at Fontainebleau) and at the stud (as the sire of the 'Égalité' Duke of Orleans' Rouge, Vert, and other French-bred animals which ran in England, some of them at two years of age). So that Mr. Brand was a member of the Jockey Club who deserved well both of the English and the French supporters of the Turf.

Mr. BURLTON, whose name is incorrectly given as 'Burton' in many 'Guides,' and whose membership of the Jockey Club is established in many ways, especially by his signature appended to Jockey Club documents of 1767 and 1769, can be almost certainly identified as the Philip Burlton, Esq., of Wickham Mills, Essex, who was 'Inspector of Hospitals' in Germany during the wars of his day, and is, no doubt, he of whom Horace Walpole writes as 'my friend, Mr. Burlton.' He married Frances Marston, a widow, whose stepfather (Henry Parsons, brother of Alderman Humphrey Parsons, of London) left her the property at Wickham Mills; and identity of the persons seems to be bewrayed by the appellations of 'Wickham' and 'Maid of the Mill,' given to a colt and a filly both 'bred by Mr. Burlton,' and by the 'Burlton' Arabian which stood at 'Wickham Mills,' 1767-9. He bred, owned, and ran Stella (by Plunder), winner of the Oaks in 1784, and she was the dam of Statira, the dam of Harpham Lass, dam of the Tramp mare (imported into France in 1827), that was the dam (in France) of Odine (by Tigris), that was the dam of Belle-de-Nuit (by Y. Emilius), that was the dam of the celebrated French sire Ventre-Saint-Gris. All this is stated because the dam of Ventre-Saint-Gris has been confounded very often with an 'Arabian' Belle-de-Nuit (in a French stud), and Ventre-Saint-Gris himself has consequently, but erroneously, been called 'more than half an Arab.'

Mr. CALVERT is the John Calvert whose name is appended to a Resolution of the Jockey Club in 1767, and had already run Fly (by Merlin) for a Jockey Club Plate in 1764. He bred the three grey sisters, Hermione in 1753 (sold to Mr. Vernon), Young Hermione in 1759 (sold to Lord March, 'Old Q.'), and again Hermione in 1763 (sold to Mr. Vernon). He may or may not have been the 'John Calvert, Esq., junior, secretary to the Lord Chamberlain's Office,' of that date or thereabouts; but he was, no doubt, a cadet of the family of the Lords Baltimore, whose title is closely connected with horse-racing, travelling, colonising (witness Baltimore, Maryland), fisticuffs, immorality, and eccentricity in general.

†Mr. CELL, whose name has been obelisked in order to bring posthumous obloquy upon him, may have been the pearl of the Jockey Club, whereof his membership is attested by attachment to the document of 1758, but whether he has been the victim of a misprint or of something worse, his identification defies detection. Let him be *anathema maranatha*.

*Mr. CODRINGTON, whose membership of the Jockey Club is attested by the fact that he ran Augur for a Jockey Club Plate in 1774, is the gentleman who (as we shall see more fully hereafter) varied the racing and betting at Newmarket by 'backing his father's life' against the like-minded Mr. Robert Pigott's father's. The said father was Sir W. Codrington, second Baronet, of Doddington Hall, Gloucestershire, and the family was of West Indian connection; for it was a member of it, Colonel Codrington, of Barbados, who, as we read in Walpole's 'Letters,' founded the library at All Souls, Oxford, and, dying at Barbados in 1710, 'left a large estate for the propagation of the Gospel' (not, as young Mr. Codrington would have preferred, for the propagation of the racehorse), 'and ordered' (with delightfully ingenuous unconsciousness) 'that three hundred negroes' (at that time slaves) 'should always be employed upon it' ('it,' no doubt, being the estate, not the propagation of the Gospel, though grammatically applicable to either). The Colonel was evidently a scholar and a man of letters; he wrote Latin verses, which were published in 'Musæ Anglicanæ,' and he must have differed in many respects from the young Mr. Codrington who betted paternal lives with Mr. Robert Pigott, jun. It seems not improbable, moreover, that Sir William (the father of the filial but speculative young Mr. Codrington) did not approve altogether of his son's views complimentary as they were to Sir

William's vital prospects and powers; for the Baronet is said to have disinherited his son, and to have left his property to a nephew, Bethel Codrington (whose Christian name has a decided smack of 'Little Bethel' and 'Dissent'), in 1792. On the whole one would be inclined to conclude that young Mr. Codrington belonged less to the bright ornaments of the Jockey Club than to the category of 'shocking examples,' which comprised the scurrilous Mr. 'Louse' Pigott, the unfortunate Mr. 'Chillaby' Jennings, and some others, and in more modern times the reckless Lord Courtenay (afterwards Earl of Devon), and the memorable young Marquess of Hastings, who 'belonged' to Lady Elizabeth and The Earl.

Mr. COMPTON is the (? Hon.) Mr. Henry Compton, whose name is appended to the earliest published Resolution of the Jockey Club in 1758, and he was apparently identical with the gentleman of whom 'Gilly' Williams writes to Selwyn, in 1764: 'Bully's [Lord Bolingbroke's] affairs thrive in the hands of Compton; he wins so much at Newmarket,' &c. He was one of the noted 'gentlemen-jocks' of his day, and is found riding in 1758 against Mr. Anderson, the Duke of Grafton, Mr. Vernon, Mr. Shafto, and Lord Orford for a Sweepstakes at Newmarket, 'to be rode by the owners or other gentlemen.' He was evidently of Hampshire, how nearly related to the Earls of Northampton or to the Comptons of Minstead Manor does not signify. He was apparently the owner or importer (or both) of the 'Compton Arabian,' or 'Compton Barb,' afterwards known as the 'Sedley Grey Arabian.' So that he was a memorable member of the Jockey Club.

Mr. CONOLLY (signatory to an agreement of the Jockey Club in 1771) was the Hon. and Right Hon. Thomas, whose wife was Lady Louisa (sister of Lady Sarah Bunbury and Lady Holland). He belonged to the family of the Earls of Longford (before the new creation of 1785), and had a seat at Castletown, Ireland. He was at the very head of the Irish Turf in his day, winning Royal Plates beyond ordinary powers of calculation with Horatius, Banker, Thumper, Huncamunca, Aimwell, Richmond, Arachne, Jolly Bacchus, Courtezan, Demirep (a chestnut mare, foaled 1772, by Horatius), Fanny, Lenox, Medea, Miss Fortune, St. Patrick, Shoemaker, Stumbler, Surveyor, Tigress, &c., including the elegantly named Bumbrusher. A very notable member of the Jockey Club.

Mr. COXE (or Cox, for the orthography even in 'Hansard' is unsettled), one of the signatories to a Jockey Club Resolution of 1767, is evidently Richard Hippisley Coxe, Esq., M.P., of the Somersetshire Hippisley Coxes, of whom three at least would appear to have been at one time among the encouragers of the local races. He is no doubt the 'Dick Cox' (or Coxe) of 'Gilly' Williams and George Selwyn. Though he owned and ran a great many horses, some of considerable note, he is not commemorated among the great 'Fathers of the Turf.' It would seem that Coxe Hippisley and Hippisley Coxe are at least as identical as a horse-chestnut and a chestnut horse, if J. Coxe Hippisley, member for Sudbury at one time, was one of them.

Mr. CROFT (or CROFTS, for the name is spelt both ways, according to the loose orthography of the day), whose membership is established by reference to the runners for the Jockey Club Plates of 1756 and 1768, in which years he ran second with Brilliant and Cato (by Regulus) to the Duke of Ancaster, must have been William Croft (or Crofts), Esq., of West Harling, Norfolk, who died in 1770. He is a very notable member of the Jockey Club, not only as an owner and breeder of horses, but as the reputed 'coach' upon the Turf of the celebrated Sir T. C. Bunbury, whose neighbour he was, so far as Norfolk and Suffolk are neighbouring counties. He is sometimes confounded with the still more famous Northern light, Mr. John Croft (or Crofts) of Barforth, Yorkshire, of Bloody Buttocks notoriety, proprietor of the famous Vintner mare of unknown pedigree; but Mr. Croft (or Crofts), of Barforth, cannot be found among the members of the Jockey Club, even if he survived into the days of the Club.

Mr. DUNCOMBE, who ran for a Jockey Club Plate (won by the Duke of Ancaster's Myrtle) in 1755, and, being a great 'gentleman-jockey,' had figured in a match (owners up) at York in 1745 against Lord

I

March (afterwards 'Old Q.') at that young nobleman's first appearance on the Turf, when the commoner (on Oroonoko) was beaten by the lord (on the gelding Whipper-In), was Thomas Duncombe, Esq., of Helmsley, or Duncombe Park, York. His patronymic had originally been Browne, exchanged for Duncombe, in consequence of a marriage into the family of the Fevershams of Downton. He, of course, belonged to the family at which Pope sneered when he wrote:

> And Helmsley, once proud Buckingham's delight,
> Slides to a Scrivener or a City knight.

Not that the origin of 'proud Buckingham' himself was much to boast of, if the Villiers (favourite of James I.), and not the Bohun, as seems likely, is referred to; but Pope would have his sneer, in which perhaps there is more point than is apparent at a glance. For it has sometimes been asked, 'Why Scrivener, as there is no proof that the worthy Mr. Browne followed the vocation of a scrivener?' But genealogists make out that Thomas Duncombe, M.P. (whose second son, Charles Slingsby Duncombe, of Duncombe Park, Helmsley, York, was grandfather of the first Baron Feversham, of Duncombe Park, born 1784, created Baron 1826), married Miss Sarah Slingsby, maid of honour to Queen Anne and daughter of Sir T. Slingsby, of *Scriven* (whence the malignant innuendo). However, the Mr. Duncombe with whom we have here to deal was one of the great breeders as well as owners and riders, as witness Red Rose (by the Devonshire Blacklegs), Ceres, Rosebud (dam of Mr. Wentworth's Myrtle), Indicus, Patch-Buttocks, &c.; and his membership of the Jockey Club is hereditarily reflected in the person of his descendant, the present (first) Earl of Feversham, who is by no means an indifferent or inactive member of the Club, notwithstanding his advancing age and the unconspicuousness of his colours upon the Turf.

Mr. FENTON, whose membership of the Jockey Club was established at least as early as 1763, when his great horse Engineer (son of Sampson) was beaten by Mr. Fulke Greville's Dorrimond for a Jockey Club Plate, was William Fenton, Esq., of Glasshouse, Leeds, Yorkshire, who would be immortal among breeders of horses if he had done no more for the cause than he did when he bred Engineer; for that horse was not only a great runner and a greater sire (of Mambrino, and a host besides) in this country, but in America his name is treasured as the grandsire of Messenger (son of Mambrino), the 'father of American trotters.'

Mr. FENWICK (one of the subscribers to the Jockey Club Challenge Cup in 1768) was William Fenwick, Esq., of Bywell, Northumberland, and was, like Mr. Fenton, one of the great Northern lights of the Turf and of the Jockey Club. He owned (but did not breed) the celebrated Matchem (by whose services he is said to have cleared 17,000*l*., a huge sum in those days), and the celebrated brood-mare Duchess (dam of Le Sang, Dux, &c.); and his name was one to conjure with upon the Turf from the days of his ancestor, Sir John Fenwick, a great Turf-man in the reigns of James I. and Charles I.

Mr. FETTYPLACE (whose name is appended to a rule of the Jockey Club in 1770) was Robert Fettyplace, Esq., of Earl's Court, Lambourne, Berkshire; and Lambourne is almost as redolent as Newmarket of the Turf. He was aided and abetted in his Turfishness by his wife, the Hon. Mrs. Fettyplace (who was Charlotte Howe, daughter of Lord Chedworth, a very horsey and racing strain, as we have seen), but they have not left very notable traces either in the Calendar or in the Stud Book, though their horse Nabob (? *alias* Flambé, *alias* Young Drudge) is pilloried for all time in the records as running for and coming in first for the Silver Bowl at Salisbury, in 1770, contrary to his Worship the Mayor's express ruling, who refused to hand over the 'objet d'art' on the ground that Mr. or the Hon. Mrs. Fettyplace had not entered their horse in time. What was the end of the dispute—whether *adhuc sub judice lis est*, or whether Æacus, Rhadamanthus, Minos, and the rest of the 'Infernal Bench' have settled the case is not to be discovered.

Messrs. FOLEY and FOX (of whom the former won a Jockey Club Plate with Trentham in 1772, and of whom the latter's membership of the Jockey Club, though notorious, is less self-evident, because he raced chiefly in the name of his friend and partner, Mr.

Foley) were confederates upon the Turf, and were, respectively, the Hon. Thomas Foley (afterwards Lord Foley) and the Hon. and Rt. Hon. Charles James Fox (prince of orators and gamblers).

Lord Foley (second Baron of the second creation) was one of the 'shocking examples' of the Jockey Club. He is said to have begun his career upon the Turf with about 20,000*l.* a year, and 100,000*l.* in ready money; and before his death (at the age of 51, in July, 1793) he had been obliged to retire with no ready money, with his estates dreadfully encumbered, and with his constitution shattered. He was the Foley of whom George Selwyn, the wit, remarked, that 'when he crossed over to France (as he would do to avoid his creditors) it was a pass-over not at all to the liking of the Jews.' He was, as it were, the prototype among members of the Jockey Club of the late unfortunate Marquess of Hastings, even to the closest similitude of dire humiliation; for it is reported that both noble Lords, at the conclusion of their career, were insolently requested to 'stake down' if they desired to have a bet with the public 'layers of odds.'

Mr. Fox (who was born in 1749 and died in 1806, in the same year as Pitt, and just a dozen, or round dozen, of years after his confederate) is well known to have been ruined by gambling two or three times during his life, and, though his splendid political career is inconsistent with the appellation of 'shocking example' in his case, yet he was undoubtedly as bad a confederate as a gambling young Turfite could have, and both he and Lord Foley were such members as the Jockey Club would have been, and always would be, the better without. The pair, however, had some excellent horses at various times (including the famous Pyrrhus as well as the already-mentioned Trentham), but seem to have regarded them almost entirely as instruments of gaming. It was, of course, another Lord Foley who won the Derby in 1806; we shall come to him hereafter.

Mr. GARDINER, whose membership is established by the fact that he is among the signatories of the first Jockey Club document (in 1758), is difficult of identification; but there is some reason to think that he belonged to the family of the Gardiners of Roche Court, and of Beaurepair, Southampton. As, however, he is not among the great owners, breeders, and runners of the Jockey Club, identification is of little consequence.

Mr. GORGES, whose membership is established by the horse Juniper (by Babram, son of the Godolphin Arabian), winner of a Jockey Club Plate in 1760, is no doubt to be identified with Richard Gorges (misspelt Gorge, sometimes), Esquire, of Eye Court, Herefordshire, who was High Sheriff for the county and M.P. for Leominster, and died about the beginning of this century. Mr. Gorges was also the first owner, if not the breeder, of Sourface (by Lord Cullen's Arabian), a noted horse, foaled 1753; but he was not among the most memorable members of the Jockey Club. Juniper, by the way, was imported into Virginia by Colonel Symme.

Mr. GREVILLE (one of the Jockey Club signatories in 1758) was the Hon. Fulke Greville, or Fulke Greville, Esquire, a cadet of the house of Brooke and Warwick, who won Jockey Club Plates in 1758, 1762, 1763, and 1765, with Mirza (by the Godolphin Arabian, and bred by Lord Godolphin, but sold to Mr. Panton, then to Mr. Swymmer for 100 guineas, then to Mr. Greville for 450 guineas, then to Sir J. Lowther for 1,500 guineas), with Prospero, and (1763 and 1765) with Dorrimond (or Dorimond), sold to Mr. Greville by the 'Culloden' Duke of Cumberland. This seems to have been undoubtedly the Fulke Greville who (as he was a sportsman) very much astonished our friend Horace Walpole by writing 'Maxims and Characters,' and whose wife wrote the once well-known 'Ode to Indifference,' or 'Prayer for Indifference.' This Mr. Greville was evidently a notable member of the Jockey Club; and of his house and lineage was another very notable member of the Jockey Club in more recent times, the Mr. C. C. Greville, Clerk of the Council, confederate on the Turf for a time of the great Lord G. Bentinck.

Mr. HOLMES (or HOLME, according to disputed orthography) is found among the signatories of the Jockey Club in 1758, and is apparently identical with a great Northern breeder of that name, John Holmes (or Holme), Esq., of Carlisle, who bred the famous Matchem, besides Brown Slipby, Bay Slipby, Brown Starling, Bay Starling, &c., and whose horses were sold in 1764 at York. To have bred Matchem is fame enough for a member of the Jockey Club; if, indeed, the Mr. Holmes who bred the horse was the same person as the signatory of the Jockey Club document of 1758.

Mr. HUTCHINSON is he who ran a brown filly by Oroonoko for the Jockey Club Plate won by Mr. Naylor's Sally in 1759; but nothing further can be ascertained about him than that he was certainly not the Mr. John Hutchinson (ex-stable-boy and then 'Esquire') of Shipton, near York, and that he was certainly not so great a Turfite as the latter.

Mr. JENNISON (or JENISON), one of the Jockey Club signatories in 1758, was Ralph Jennison, Esq., of Walworth, Durham, the last of that name among the proprietors of (High) Walworth, and he seems to have been connected with Messrs. (*Jenison* and Robert) Shafto, who are described as of Whitworth, Durham. He had been Master of the Staghounds (Buckhounds) to King George the Second, and M.P. for the Isle of Wight. At his death, in 1758, his widow is said to have sold Walworth to Alderman Stephenson of Newcastle, for 16,000*l.*, and he to John Harrison, Esq., for a sum not mentioned. Mr. Jennison owned Collier, by Locust; Regulus, by Regulus; Ruffler, by Orion; Now or Never, by Cartouch; Why Not (late Mr.

Leonard Hartley's, a great breeder), by Cartouch; Bashful, by Cartouch; Tawney (not the famous horse that ran in Lord March's 'carriage match'), Grantham, Warhawke, &c.; and he ran his filly Black Eyes, by Blaze, for a Jockey Club Plate in 1756. In fact, he ran both in the North and the South, at Durham, at Ascot, at Newmarket, at Swaffham.

Mr. MARCH, who ran the grey colt Drummer (son of Driveler or Driver) for a Jockey Club Plate in 1771, can be almost certainly identified as John March, Esq., of Horsley Park, Huntingdonshire, whose daughter married in 1785 the Hon. Richard Howard (Secretary to Queen Charlotte), brother of the Earl of Effingham. Mr. March was also a subscriber to the Jockey Club Challenge Cup in 1768, and signed a Jockey Club 'agreement' in 1771; but he does not seem to have left a very deep mark upon the Turf or the pedigrees, though he was temporary owner of Holyhock (son of Cypron, dam of King Herod), bred by the 'Culloden' Duke of Cumberland.

Mr. MEYNELL, who was a signatory of Jockey Club 'Resolutions' of 1758 and 1767, and among the subscribers to the Jockey Club Challenge Cup in 1768, was Hugo Meynell, Esq., the never-to-be-forgotten 'Father of Foxhunting.' He was the second son of Littleton Poyntz Meynell, Esq. (who married Miss Judith Alleyne, of Barbados), of Bradley, Derbyshire. Mr. Hugo Meynell was High Sheriff of the county of Derby in 1758, and was M.P. for Lichfield. He was married twice, in 1754 and 1758, his second wife being a daughter of Thomas Boothby Scrimshire, Esq., of Tooley Park, Leicester, and a sister of 'Prince' Boothby, whose acquaintance we have already made. Mr. Meynell, who was a friend of Horace Walpole's (as we know from his 'Letters') and of Sidney Smith's, was the very famous Master of the Quorn Hounds, which, together with Quorndon Hall, were sold to Lord Sefton in 1800. Mr. Meynell, who died in 1808, at the age of seventy-three, or, as others say, eighty-one, was, of course, better known as a hunting than as a racing and breeding member of the Jockey Club, and is found running dogs, instead of horses, sometimes at Newmarket.

Mr. NAYLOR, who won a Jockey Club Plate in 1759 with his famous mare Sally, by Blank, and was a signatory of Jockey Club 'Resolutions' in 1758 and 1770, appears very little upon the scene. The name seems to point to Mr. Francis Naylor, of Hurstmonceux, Sussex, whose property is understood to have passed to a Mr. Hare (son of a Bishop of Chichester), who consequently assumed the name of Naylor. Whether the family had aught in common with that of the Mr. R. C. Naylor, so celebrated upon the Turf in our own day, there is nothing in the records to show.

Mr. (also Captain and Admiral) NORRIS, one of the signatories of the Jockey Club document of 1758, seems to have been Henry Norris, Vice-Admiral, who died June 13, 1764, at his house in Grosvenor Square, and was probably identical with the 'Harry Norris' mentioned in a letter of 'Gilly' Williams to Selwyn, and with the Admiral Norris whom Walpole represents to have been anxious to give evidence in favour of the unfortunate Admiral Byng. The appearance of an admiral so early among the members of the Club foreshadows the coming of *the* Admiral who, under the name of Rous, was for so many years the leading spirit of the Club and the Dictator of the Turf. Admiral Norris, however, has left but little impression as a member of the Jockey Club.

Mr. OFFLEY, one of the signatories of the Jockey Club document in 1758, was almost certainly the gentleman mentioned in Walpole's 'Letters,' and by 'Gilly' Williams (in Jesse's 'Selwyn'), among the 'fashionables,' including Lord Ashburnham (a member of the Jockey Club) and 'Tommy' Pelham, who were on a visit at Stow in 1764 or thereabouts. He owned the brown filly (by Oroonoko) that became a noted brood-mare, dam of Stoic (Lord Rockingham's); but he was not among the most memorable owners and breeders. That there was a 'horsey' strain in his family, however, is to be inferred from the chronicles, which mention 'horse-matches' between a Mr. Ofley and a Mr. Izinson (of Northampton) at Newmarket as early as 1681.

Mr. OGILVY, a subscriber to the Jockey Club Cup in 1768, a signatory of the Jockey Club documents in 1770 and 1771, and runner for a Jockey Club Plate with Denmark in 1772, is called in the records Charles Ogilvy, Esq., and his 'harlequin' colours seem to point to a connection with the family of the Earls of Airlie. He was a great Turfite, and the hero of the match run on May 22, 1772, when he ran his horse Pincher against Messrs. Foley and Fox (who were confederates) represented by Trentham and Pyrrhus, the confederates betting 2,500 guineas to 2,000 guineas that Pincher would be last. Pincher, on the contrary, was first, though the betting at the start was 6 to 4 that Pincher was last. However, the match was run over again the next year at the Newmarket Craven Meeting (April 2) on the same terms (8 stone 7 lb. each, B.C.), the confederates betting 500 guineas, even this time, that Pincher was last; the betting at the start was 5 to 2 that Pincher was last, and he was last. Was it ' the riding that did it '?

The name of * OTTLEY covers two gentlemen, probably father and son, both conspicuous on the Turf, designated respectively as William Ottley, Esq., and William Ottley, jun., Esq., ' of Cambridge.' They belonged to the West Indian patrons of the Turf, as they 'hailed' from the Island of St. Christopher; and one of them ran Portius (by Cato) for a Jockey Club Plate in 1770, so that he was certainly a member of the Jockey Club. Whether they were both members is not so easily determined. He who ran Portius for the Jockey Club Plate owned the Cade mare (dam by

Hip) that bred (for Mr. Ottley) Corsican, Portius, Cassandro (a colt), Hengrave, and Grand Seignior; but the name of Ottley has not remained in evidence to any great extent.

Mr. PANTON, a subscriber to the Jockey Club Cup in 1768, and to nearly all the early 'orders' of the Jockey Club, was Thomas Panton, Esq., of Newmarket, the 'polite Tommy' Panton, whose father had been 'keeper of the King's running horses at Newmarket,' and whose sister Mary married the third Duke of Ancaster and was Mistress of the Robes. Both the Pantons were great upon the Turf. The elder, whom Horace Walpole calls 'a disreputable horse-jockey named Panton,' died in 1750 at the age of eighty-two, and the younger died in 1809 at the great age of eighty-seven or eighty-eight. It was the younger, the member of the Jockey Club who won the Derby with Noble, by Highflyer, in 1786, and was the owner, if not the importer or breeder, of the Panton Arabian, sire of Virago, dam of Hollandaise, winner of the first properly called St. Leger, in 1778.

Mr. (Colonel and General) PARKER, one of the signatories of a Jockey Club document in 1767, and of the subscribers to the Jockey Club Cup in 1768, is made out to have been the Hon. George Lane Parker, second son of the second Earl of Macclesfield. If so, he was born in 1724, married the widow of Sir Cottrell Dormer in 1782, and died September 1791. He was an officer in the Guards, and was at one time

M.P. for Tregony. He is not to be confounded with another Mr. Parker (afterwards Lord Boringdon), who was also a member of the Jockey Club, and was more distinguished upon the Turf. To him we shall come hereafter.

Mr. PIGOTT, who is upon the list of subscribers to the Jockey Club Cup, and is a signatory of the Jockey Club documents in 1769 and 1771, was Robert Pigott, junr., Esq., of Chetwynd Park, Salop, and of Chesterton Hall, Hunts, the gentleman who has already been mentioned as 'backing' his father's life at Newmarket against young Mr. Codrington's father's; whence arose a curious decision of Lord Mansfield's. The case is probably well-known, but will bear repetition. It so happened that Mr. Robert Pigott, senr., was already dead at the very time when the aforesaid bet was made, but the news of the death had not reached Newmarket, nor was it so much as suggested that either of the bettors knew of the death, or had any suspicion of it. When, however, Mr. Robert Pigott, junr., heard of his father's death, and found by calculation that it must have taken place before the bet was made, so that he had no chance of winning, he refused to pay. Meanwhile Mr. Codrington had transferred his bet to Lord March, afterwards 'Old Q.,' a very awkward customer to deal with, who appealed to the law, which did not then ignore wagers, and won his case; Lord Mansfield, before whom it came, deciding that 'the impossibility of a contingency is no bar to its becoming the subject of a wager when the impossibility is unknown to both parties.' This queer decision is of no consequence now that 'all contracts by way of wagering are void' in law; but obviously the accepted rule that 'you cannot win when you cannot lose' is the only safe and fair one. The 'impossibility of the contingency' may generally be proved without difficulty; but, especially in these days of rapid communication, it is not so easy to make sure that the impossibility was unknown at a given time to some interested person or persons. Mr. R. Pigott, member of the Jockey Club, is said to have been so alarmed by the aspect of affairs in America (1768–71) that he sold his estates (or as much of them as he could) for much less than they were worth, and retired to Geneva. Certainly there was a sale of his horses, conducted by Mr. Pond, the auctioneer, at Newmarket in 1772; and he died at Thoulouse in July, 1794, having married abroad and had an only son, who died before him. According to a writer in the 'Sporting Magazine' (about 1821 or 1822), he was the eldest of three brothers (as he undoubtedly was), and the three were called respectively, 'Shark' Pigott (from a famous horse), 'Louse' Pigott (for a reason to be given hereafter), and 'Black' Pigott (presumably out of respect for 'the cloth,' for he was a parson); but more will be said upon this subject when we come to the younger brother, Charles (*alias* 'Louse') Pigott.

Mr. PRATT, whose membership of the Jockey Club is established from several other sources besides the group of subscribers to the Jockey Club Challenge Cup in 1768, was the celebrated John Pratt, Esq., of Askrigg, Wensleydale, Yorkshire, probably the first case, and undoubtedly one of the very few cases, of a plebeian admitted to the Jockey Club; that is to say, with the plebeian stamp so very fresh. For—tell it not in Gath, publish it not in the streets of Ascalon —his father is said to have risen to be a hackney-coach driver (from the condition of ostler), and then a hackney-coach proprietor, and ultimately a small landed proprietor near Askrigg. The future member of the Jockey Club, however, was sent to the University of Cambridge, where, no doubt, he was affected by the neighbourhood of Newmarket, and where he studied after the fashion described in some once well-known verses:

> At Trin. Coll. Camb., which means in proper spelling
>   Trinity College, Cambridge, there resided
> One Henry Dashington, a youth excelling
>   In all the learning commonly provided,
> That is to say that he could drive a tandem,
>   etc., etc.

Mr. Pratt, who died at Newmarket May 8, 1785, was so respected that somebody wrote an epitaph or elegy, rather longer than the High Street, to commemorate his vicissitudes and virtues. He never had more than 700*l.* a year, it is stated, from the estate left to him by his father, but for some forty years (the duration of his career upon the Turf) he kept up a handsome house, large stabling, vast paddocks, twenty domestic servants, a pack of hounds, huntsman, whippers-in, numerous excellent hunters, and an extensive stud of racehorses (whereof the most successful were bred from the famous Squirt mare, bred by the Duke of Bolton, and purchased from Mr. Hammond, in Cumberland, about 1754); but then he married a Miss Hammond, of Naburn, near York, and she brought him a handsome fortune, which, of course, helped to keep him afloat, insomuch that, at his death, his friends were delighted, his enemies were dumbfounded, and the indifferent were surprised to find that, when his stud and other properties were sold, he had died not only solvent (as to which there had been a general and a considerable doubt), but with ' a very respectable surplus' over his liabilities. The worthy gentleman's death is supposed to have been hastened in so curious a manner that the story deserves to be told. Intelligence reached him that a horse which he had sold to a certain person for a certain sum had been resold to the Prince of Wales (George IV., who always paid, or at any rate promised to pay, far too much) for a great deal more. The shock, it is said, was fatal. Of course this is the Mr. Pratt who is gazetted as having won the St. Leger in 1782 with Imperatrix (bred by the Rev. Mr. Goodricke and very likely his property, run in Mr. Pratt's name only), and he owned (at any rate at the time of his death) The Ruler, winner of the St. Leger of 1780 in the name of Mr. William Bethell, of Rise, Holdernesse, a real old Yorkshire gentleman, who was confederated with Mr. Pratt, and may very well have been himself a member of the Jockey Club, though there is no proof that he was (and the membership of Mr. Pratt would be 'enough for two'). Of this Mr. Bethell it was remarked, at his death in July 1799, that he had 'never discharged a servant, never raised a rent, and never turned out an old tenant.' It is a pity that his name cannot be claimed for the Jockey Club.

Mr. READ, one of the signatories of the Jockey Club documents in 1758, is presumed to have been Wilberforce Read, Esq., of Grimthorpe, near Market Weighton, Yorkshire, who is described as a gentleman of good family but small means, but 'moving in the first circles.' His chief title to commemoration is that he introduced to the Turf the celebrated jockey, John Singleton, sen.

Mr. SCOTT, one of the Jockey Club signatories of 1758, was almost certainly the gentleman whom Horace Walpole mentions as a Captain Scott, who, in 1755, won a vast sum of money at hazard from the unfortunate Sir John Bland, of Kippax Park, Skipton, Yorks, and who apparently developed into the 'celebrated General Scott,' whose daughters became Duchess of Portland, Viscountess Downe, and Vis-

countess Canning, almost throwing into the shade
the 'lucky Burrells' of the Gwdwyr family. He
seems to have been identical with the General Scott,
M.P., who was so staunch a supporter of Warren
Hastings (himself, it is said, though not proved, a
member of the Jockey Club). It is undoubtedly he
whom 'Old Q.' (when Earl of March) mentions in his
correspondence with Selwyn, and it seems to have
been he who, when Mr. Panton betted that the
General's horse would be last in a race for which the
horses were just going to the post, took the bet
promptly, rode off after the horses, was just in time to
overtake them, and ordered his jockey to 'pull.' This
was done; and, as will readily be believed, is said to
have led to a 'dispute.' But it was smart.

*Mr. SELWYN, whose name is attached to Jockey
Club 'Resolutions' in 1767, and whose membership
is also attested by a letter to him from Lord Holland
of about the same date, remarking upon Selwyn's
refusal 'to sign at the Jockey Club,' is George Selwyn,
Esq., the celebrated wit, and his name bears the
asterisk, as he was one of the 'West Indian' members
(having property and holding a sinecure office in
Barbados, besides various little lucrative appointments
under Government, such as were then conferred upon
favourites by what would be now denounced as 'jobs').
It is not to be discovered that he ever ran a racehorse
in his own name, though he may very well have had
a share in one or more belonging to his intimate

friend Lord March ('Old Q.,' with whom he was supposed to share the responsibility for the birth, so far as paternity was concerned, of Maria Fagniani, Marchioness of Hertford), or that he delighted much in Newmarket; for we learn from Jesse's 'Selwyn' that he was 'chaffed' by a correspondent about being a blind guide for some Frenchmen who paid a visit to Newmarket and had Selwyn for their *cicerone*. Still, he was evidently an active member of the Club, as his signature to the 'Resolutions' shows; and he probably betted on horse-racing, for we find from his correspondence that he was 'dunned' both by Mr. Jenison Shafto and by Lord Derby, great horse-racers, for money due to them, though it may have been lost at play and not on the Turf. Selwyn's wonderful popularity and strange hankering after scenes of death are both illustrated by the story told of Lord Holland, who, being very near his end, and hearing that Selwyn had called upon him and had not been admitted, is reported to have said: 'Should Mr. Selwyn come again, show him up. If I am alive, I should like to see him; and, if I am dead, *he* will like to see *me*.' Selwyn was a welcome visitor at Goodwood House, and there it was his rare luck (in 1783) to look upon the (well preserved) face of the notorious Madame de la Querouaille (Duchess of Portsmouth), then between eighty and ninety years of age, and not much more dilapidated or a whit more ashamed than Ninon de l'Enclos at about the same age. In the very next year, if the authorities err not, Selwyn would have been too late, for the Duchess (of Portsmouth in England and d'Aubigny in France) is said to have died in 1734. Selwyn, who was M.P. for Ludgershall at one time, and during many years for Gloucester, and whose lovely country-seat called Matson, full of historic and romantic memories, is known far and wide by name to lovers of picturesque antiquity, himself died in 1791, and, though he had been a *viveur*, is said to have been one of those members of the Jockey Club who have 'made a good end.'

The name of SHAFTO covers two great Turfites and members of the Jockey Club, Messrs. Jenison and Robert, both sometimes styled 'Captain,' supposed to have been brothers. Jenison is the greater, Robert the lesser.

JENISON SHAFTO, Esq., of Whitworth, Durham, and of West Wratting, near Newmarket, was a subscriber to the Jockey Club Challenge Cup in 1768. It was he who is said to have cleared 16,000*l*. in bets by riding 50 miles at Newmarket in 1759 in 1 hour, 49 minutes, 17 seconds, using ten horses for the task, having been allowed two hours and as many horses as he pleased. It was he who in 1761 backed a Mr. Woodcock (using as many horses as he pleased, not exceeding 29), for a wager of 1,000 guineas a side (laid with the famous Mr. Hugo Meynell) to ride 2,900 miles in 29 successive days, that is, 100 miles a day on one and the same horse. Mr. Woodcock accomplished the feat at Newmarket, but by the skin of his teeth; for on one of the days the horse he was riding broke down after going 60 miles, and Mr. Woodcock had to begin all over again on a fresh horse, so that he rode 160 miles on that day. Mr. Jenison Shafto, who was an ornament of the Legislature (M.P. for different places at different times) as well as of the Turf and of the Jockey Club, appears to have died about 1770; at any rate his Stud was sold by auction at Newmarket by Mr. Pond, Oct. 5, 1771.

Mr. ROBERT SHAFTO, whose membership of the Jockey Club is established by Tandem, beaten by Pot8os for a Jockey Club Plate in 1780 (in which year Mr. Shafto, who had, no doubt, been a member of the Club for some years previously, seems to have died on June 11), is also described as of Whitworth, Durham, and of West Wratting, Cambs. He was also a mighty 'gentleman-jockey,' but did not attain, apparently, to the height of Mr. Jenison; and he appears also to have been M.P. as well as horse-breeder, horse-owner and horse-racer, and to have belonged to what was known as the great 'Northumberland Confederacy,' consisting of Messrs. Swinburne and Shafto (brothers), all members of the Jockey Club.

Mr. SCRYMSHER (*v.* BOOTHBY) is the same person as 'Prince Boothby.'

Mr. SHIRLEY, whose signature is appended to Jockey Club 'Resolutions' of 1767 and 1771, was the Hon. Thomas Shirley, belonging to the family of the

Earls Ferrers (one of whom, not a member of the Jockey Club, came to be hanged). Mr. Shirley, or Captain Shirley (as he is sometimes called), was a great 'gentleman-jockey,' and won at Newmarket a match in 1764 (on his horse Romeo) against Mr. Blake (on his horse Babram) over the B.C., in April, and at the same meeting another match (again on his own horse Romeo) against Mr. Payne (on his own horse Heart-of-Oak), *five* times over the R.C. (more than 15 miles). As, however, he evidently had brothers or near relations (of whom the Hon. George Shirley ran Papist for a Jockey Club Plate in 1775, and must therefore have been a member of the Club) running horses at the same time, it is a little difficult sometimes to discriminate between them. But he was certainly a notable patron of the Turf and member of the Jockey Club.

Mr. SKRYMSHER, *v.* SKRYMSHIRE or SCRYMSHER, and BOOTHBY, for the orthography of this name is very various.

Mr. W. SMITH (a notoriously difficult patronymic to deal with) is he who subscribed to the Jockey Club 'Resolutions' of 1771, and was undoubtedly a General Smith (he, no doubt, who was known as 'India-General Smith,' and is frequently met with in 'Hansard's Debates,' as he was a prominent M.P.). He is reported to have secured 'loot' to the handsome amount of 150,000*l.* during his service in India. According to 'Louse' Pigott (himself, as will appear hereafter, a member of the Jockey Club at one time), 'the old General' was one of the very plebeian members of the Jockey Club, having in early life (according to that same somewhat doubtful authority) 'carried cheeses on his head' to his father's customers. The 'old General' kept his 'Arabian,' and ran the laborious Rosaletta and many good horses and mares. According to Pigott, the son of the 'old General,' called the 'young General,' was also a member of the Jockey Club—at least he is included in the personages of Pigott's scurrilous 'Jockey Club'; but there is no tangible proof of his membership, which, however, is by no means improbable.

Mr. SMITH-BARRY is made out to have been the Hon. John Smith-Barry (whose son, Mr. James Hugh Smith-Barry, born 1748, bore a name which tells still more plainly the story of his father's alliance with an heiress), youngest son of the fourth or fifth Earl of Barrymore, and a relative (whether uncle or other) of the three brothers, 'Cripplegate,' 'Newgate,' and 'Hellgate,' already mentioned. Mr. Smith-Barry, as has been said, married one of the two co-heiresses of the millionaire Mr. Hugh Smith, and is described as of Foaty Island, county Clare, and of Marbury Hall, Belmont, Cheshire. He seems to have been born about 1725, and to have died about 1784; and to have been a breeder, owner, and runner of race-horses on a large scale and with no little success—witness All Fours (by Regulus), Amaranthus (by Old

England), Forester (by Dionysius), Ragamuffin (by Northumberland), &c., &c.; and he is credited with two 'Arabians' at least—a grey and a chestnut. He ran Amaranthus unsuccessfully for the Jockey Club Plate won by the Hon. Mr. Foley with Trentham in 1772, and was a very notable member of the Jockey Club.

Mr. STAPLETON, a subscriber to the Jockey Club Challenge Cup in 1768, was Thomas Stapleton, Esq., of Carlton, near Snaith, Yorkshire, one of the Northern lights of the Turf and of the Jockey Club. He has already been mentioned in connection with Sir Thomas Gascoigne, whose confederate he was upon the Turf, and with whose family he was allied by marriage. It was in his name (not Sir T. Gascoigne's) that Tommy (by Wildair) won the St. Leger of 1779; and it was in his name that Parlington (so named after Sir T. Gascoigne's place in Yorkshire) ran for the Jockey Club Plate won by Lord Sherborne's (Mr. Dutton's) Spectre in 1784. Mr. Stapleton was an ancestor of the Lords Beaumont of our day, if he was not the very gentleman who established his right to the title after a period of abeyance.

Mr. STRODE, whose membership, no doubt, commenced at an earlier date than 1775, when it is established by his running Bon Vivant for a Jockey Club Plate, is described in the records as Edward Strode, Esq., ' of Berkshire,' and sometimes as ' Captain' Strode (with customary orthographical variations, such as Stroud). He was a great owner and runner, and seems to have laid himself out to become the temporary possessor of every noted horse of his day; and among them the celebrated Priestess (bred by the Rev. Mr. Hewgill, of Hornby Grange, Northallerton, Yorkshire), by Matchem, and the great Paymaster (ex-Jesmond), sire of Paragon. There is some reason to think that he belonged to the Strodes, of whom one married a sister of the then Lord Salisbury, and was M.P. for Reading; and he not improbably could claim relationship with the Strode who was one of the famous 'five members.' He was for awhile a brilliant meteor upon the Turf, but he disappears as abruptly and as unnoticed from the records as if, in the expressive American phrase, he had 'gone under'; an ending very likely to have been brought about by his apparently reckless expenditure.

Mr. SWINBURNE, in whose name Alipes (dam of Lord Grosvenor's Grasshopper and Imogen) won a Jockey Club Plate in 1761, was William Swinburne, Esq., of Long Witton, Northumberland, belonging to a very ancient and distinguished family, and conspicuous as one of the very great Northern lights of the Turf, the head of the famous 'Northumberland Confederacy,' which did great execution on the race-courses both North and South, and owned the famous Wildair (son of Cade), imported temporarily by Colonel Delancey into America (where he became the sire of many celebrated horses and mares), but re-purchased by Mr. Leedes, of North Milford, Yorkshire. Mr. Swinburne bred Sprightly (sire of Pyrrhus), whose fate resembled that of Mr. I'Anson's celebrated Queen Mary, and was not unlike that of the once despised Marske (till he begot Eclipse) and of Squirt (sire of Marske and Syphon, after narrowly escaping being shot as worthless); for Sprightly, at seventeen years of age (in 1771, the very year in which Pyrrhus first appeared at Newmarket and began his victorious career), was sold for ten guineas to a miller (who used him as a *cadging* horse), was repurchased by Mr. Swinburne (after the appearance of Pyrrhus) for twelve guineas, and a fortnight afterwards had 500 guineas offered for him, which Mr. Swinburne refused. Pyrrhus, however, like Mark Anthony, Conductor, Pantaloon, and, in more modern times, Melbourne and Touchstone, was a 'first foal' (against which there is still some unreasonable prejudice), and may have been more indebted to his dam (a Snip mare) than to his sire for the excellence he displayed. In any case, there was much reason in the remark of the philosopher who propounded that 'Natur's a rum un.'

* Mr. SWYMMER, who won a Jockey Club Plate with Standby (son of Shepherd's Crab) in 1758, and thus proved his membership of the Jockey Club, was Anthony Langley Swymmer, Esq., M.P. for Southampton, and one of the 'West Indians' apparently, for he died in Jamaica in 1760. He was fairly great on the Turf, and he married into a racing family, having espoused a daughter of Sir J. Astley and sister to the Countess of Tankerville. The very year after Mr. Swymmer's death his widow married Sir F. Vincent, and that is all that can be discovered about this member of the Jockey Club.

Mr. VAREY, signatory of the Jockey Club 'Resolution' in 1769, is made out to have been William Varey, Esq., familiarly called 'Billy Varey' in Selwyn's correspondence, where he is mentioned in conjunction with 'Bet Thompson and Charley Price' as likely to be (as he was) a pall-bearer at the funeral of Lord Bath (Pulteney). He is himself one of Selwyn's correspondents, and he seems to have been of Ixworth Abbey, near Bury, Suffolk, all in the way, as it were, to Newmarket and the Jockey Club. It was probably he who in 1769 was appointed 'Superintendent of all His Majesty's gardens belonging to all and any his Royal palaces in England.' Mr. Varey, however, does not seem to have left his mark upon the history of the Turf or of the Jockey Club.

Mr. VERNON, whose membership of the Club is plain from a hundred pieces of evidence, among which it will suffice to mention that he won one of the two Jockey Club Plates of 1753 (the year of the Club's first appearance at Newmarket), was Richard Vernon, sometimes styled (erroneously, apparently) the Hon. Richard Vernon, and sometimes Captain Vernon (correctly, as he began life in the Guards), whom Horace Walpole frequently mentions, sometimes under the style and title of Mr. 'Jockey' Vernon. He lived at Newmarket, and was the 'oracle of Newmarket'; and it was he whose tenants certain members of the Jockey Club became when he built the rooms which the Club rented in 1771. He bred, owned, and ran almost innumerable horses; he possessed, if he did not import, the useful Vernon Arabian (sire of the dam of Emigrant, winner of the July Stakes, 1796); he won the Jockey Club Challenge Cup, the first year of asking, in 1768, with Marquis (son of the Godolphin Arabian); and he won the Oaks with Annette (by Eclipse) in 1787. Nor did Mr. Vernon confine himself to the improvement of the thoroughbred at Newmarket; he was a notable breeder of peaches, and acquired quite a great reputation for his treatment of them.

It was with Mr. Vernon, at Newmarket, that Holcroft, the dramatist, served his apprenticeship as a stable-boy (by way of preparation for dramatic literature), and, whilst in that service, the future playwright is represented to have seen that determined struggle (over the B.C. for 500 guineas a side, in 1759 apparently) between Mr. Jenison Shafto's Elephant and Mr. Vernon's Forester, on which occasion, according to Holcroft, Forester, finding himself beaten, 'made one sudden spring, and caught Elephant by the under jaw, which he gripped so violently as to hold him back.' No match between Elephant and Forester later than 1759 can be found in the records (such as are at hand to consult), and Holcroft says that it took place 'about a year and a half' after he took service with 'Captain' Vernon at Newmarket, whereas Mr. Christie Whyte (whose misprints, however, are as the sand upon the sea-shore for multitude) says that Holcroft did not enter the service until after 1760. However, no doubt Holcroft did see a case of 'savaging,' between those very two horses, perhaps; but the 'holding back,' as Forester certainly lost (and not apparently 'on a foul'), is rather a strain on credulity, and one cannot help thinking that Holcroft, when he wrote his 'Memoirs' (edited by W. Hazlitt), put in a few 'dramatic touches' under the influence of a long course of play-writing. Perhaps it is not to be taken more literally than the story about Mr. Vernon himself and the 'automatic extinguisher,' which he is said to have had erected by way of sounding-board to the pulpit of his parish church at Newmarket, and which was warranted to come down over the parson's head if he preached for more than a certain tolerable number of minutes.

Mr. Vernon belonged politically to what was known as 'the Bloomsbury gang,' which accounts for his sitting in Parliament (on the nomination of the Duke of Bedford) as M.P. for Tavistock and for Bedford, as well as for Okehampton, and for his obtaining the office of Clerk of the Board of Green Cloth, as well as for the bestowal of his name upon Vernon Place,

Bloomsbury Square. Mr. Vernon married the Countess-Dowager of Upper Ossory in 1759, and died in 1800, at the great age of 85. One of his daughters married Lord Warwick, and another Mr. Robert Percy Smith. Mrs. R. P. Smith was the mother of the Rt. Hon. Mr. Vernon Smith, of munificent memory. About 'Mr. Vernon, the jockey,' Horace Walpole tells a curious story to illustrate 'the honour of the young men of the age.' Mr. Vernon, in 1752, was proposed for 'Old' White's Club, and was blackballed, though of the twelve members present eight had promised him their votes, and after the ballot ten 'assured him *on their honour* that they had put in *white* balls.' It must be concluded that the remaining two were his own proposer and seconder: so that the result was certainly curious.

Mr. WARDE (or WARD, for so sometimes, but apparently contrary to orthography, it is spelt) must have been the gentleman who ran Habit for a Jockey Club Plate in 1760; Fairplay for a Jockey Club Plate in 1767; and Cleaver (by Warde's, or Ward's, Arabian) for a Jockey Club Plate in 1772; and he again must have been John Warde, Esq., of Squerries (where Warde's, or Ward's, Arabian stood in 1767), Kent. He was the father of 'glorious John' Warde (who was probably and inferentially, but not quite demonstrably, himself a member of the Jockey Club, and ran the significantly named Adieu-to-the-Turf at Canterbury in 1778, meaning, apparently, that he would thenceforward devote his money, his talents, and what he was pleased to call his mind to the more congenial pursuits of hunting and mail-coach driving), the famous Nimrod and Jehu, who drove a mail-coach for so many years to so much admiration. The family, though settled in Kent, was of 'horsey' Yorkshire by origin, and the elder of this noble pair, having been twice married (the second time to an heiress), died in 1775, leaving one son (and, if there be no mistake, a great many daughters), known in sporting circles as 'glorious John.' The younger of the noble pair, the said 'glorious John,' was born in 1753, and died in 1838. He was High Sheriff of Kent, M. F. H., and is commemorated by admiring chroniclers as an unfailing attendant, almost to the day of his death, at Messrs. Tattersall's 'Monday dinners,' at which he would distinguish himself by his manner of tossing off the contents (port wine) of a silver fox-head, holding nearly a pint and precluding 'heel-taps,' at the end of a banquet (whereat much other liquor had been 'punished'), and then rising 'steady as a rock' and refusing, in the small hours of the morning, to leave 'until he had gone up to the drawing-room to bid Mrs. Tattersall good-night' (much to the dismay and dread, no doubt, of the worthy lady, who would, probably, have dispensed gladly with the alarming ceremony and questionable compliment). The Warde Arabian is not quite unknown in the pedigrees; and, according to Bruce's American Stud Book, the elder of the Messrs. Ward's Antæus (by Spectator) went to America and stood there (at Jacksonborough, South Carolina) in 1771, but has not become famous as a progenitor (even if he was thoroughbred, which is by no means certain).

Mr. WARREN, who won a Jockey Club Plate in 1761 with Sportsman (by Cade), is to be identified with John Borlase Warren, Esq., of Stapleford, Notts, whose second Christian name is traceable to Sir John Borlase, of Cornwall. Mr. Warren was plainly related (whether as father, uncle, cousin, or what not) to the celebrated Admiral John Borlase Warren (died 1822), who came in for the Stapleford property, and whose name and profession (whether there be any lineal descent or not) are combined in the person of the present gallant Captain J. B. Warren, of H.M.S. *Rodney*. The Mr. Warren of the Jockey Club was one of the great guns of the Turf; he bred not only Sportsman (sire of the celebrated Sportsmistress, dam of the great Pot8os), but Careless (by Regulus), Fearnought (sent to America in 1764, by Regulus), and a colt by Cade (sent to America in 1762 and there called Cade), all from the same mare, Silvertail (by Mr. Heneage's Whitenose), also bred by him. From the 'horsey' point of view, at any rate, he was a credit to the Turf, to the Jockey Club, and to his horse-breeding county of Nottingham.

Mr. WASTELL, whose membership of the Jockey Club at an early period of its existence is explicitly

L

declared by Pigott and inferentially attested in many ways, and who was also (as many other members of the Jockey Club were) a member of 'Brookes's,' was John Wastell, Esq., of Risby, near Bury St. Edmunds (but originally of Eaglescliff, Yarm, Yorkshire), where he died in 1811 at the age of seventy-five. He was a perfect 'Talleyrand of the Turf' (as appears from what is said about him in the hackneyed 'Receipt to make a Jockey,' wherein he and his 'advice' are mentioned among the 'ingredients'); and, as for horse-breeding (with which he combined a great deal of horse-racing), it will suffice to say that he bred the famous Conductor (though he ran in Mr. Pratt's name), Ainderby (sold to Lord Bolingbroke and then to Lord Clermont), and Alfred (sold to Lord Bolingbroke), all by the famous Matchem from a Snap mare (bred by the Duke of Kingston in 1762 and sold at an early age to Mr. Wastell). He won the Oaks in 1802 with Scotia (by Delpini, a wonderful horse that never shed his coat during the last three years of his life, presenting so curious an appearance as to have suggested—it is supposed—to the enterprising showman a hint for evolving and exhibiting the ingeniously-contrived phenomenon of the 'woolly horse'). Mr. Wastell was, according to credible accounts, one of the happy few who have 'made a good thing' (as one of 'the talent,' not of 'the ring') by the Turf and its concomitants (including betting). He was 'horsily' connected, too, for a Miss Wastell married the gallant

General Philip Honywood, proprietor of Honywood's White Arabian (*alias* Sir Charles Turner's White Turk, *alias* Sir W. Strickland's Turk), sire of the famous 'Two True Blues.' Mr. Wastell, then, from the 'horsey' point of view, was a worshipful member of the Jockey Club, though, according to scurrilous Mr. Pigott, he was too much attached to 'ale and tobacco,' to vulgar associates, and 'a fat greasy housekeeper,' and 'never once betrayed a symptom of charity or benevolence.' It would clearly have been lost time to try on Mr. Wastell the hoax lately perpetrated, with qualified success, upon two present eminent Turfites, Lords Dudley and Rosslyn, of whom the former is a lately elected member of the Jockey Club, and the latter is the son of a late member.

Mr. WENTWORTH, subscriber to the Jockey Club Challenge Cup in 1768 and winner of a Jockey Club Plate in 1785 with Rockingham (ex-Camden), was the renowned Peregrine Wentworth, Esq., who died at Towlstone (or Tolstone) Hall, Yorkshire, August 30, 1809, aged eighty-eight, and was the founder of the fortunes of Mr. John Hutchinson (the ex-stableboy) in the training business, and of the celebrated Mr. Leonard Jewison, in the jockeying business. Mr. Wentworth, whose membership of the Jockey Club is, so to say, perpetuated by the Fitzwilliams at the present time, was famous not only for his racehorses, but also for his hunters; not only for his successes on the Turf (as confederate for a time with Sir Lawrance Dundas, progenitor of the spotty' Earls of Zetland), but for his performances with hounds; not only for the thoroughbreds he possessed, but for the valuable paintings (representing sporting subjects of various kinds, and including a portrait of the notorious Mr. Tregonwell Frampton and a view of the Earl of March's, that is, 'Old Q.'s,' famous 'carriage-match') he had collected. His feat in 1759, when at the peril of his own life (so well worth living with his many advantages) he saved Miss Howe from imminent drowning, after a run with the hounds, (in the melancholy fashion of Sir C. Slingsby of the York and Ainsty in later days), when his liberal offers had failed to tempt anybody with less to lose, would have earned him the medal of a certain excellent society at the present time. His horse Thornville (bred by Colonel Thornton, by Herod out of Cleopatra, by Spectator) is *said* to have run *four miles* at York August Meeting, 1782, in $7\frac{1}{2}$ minutes; but Mr. Orton (in his 'Annals') merely says that the race (for the Great Subscription) was 'supposed to have been run in less time than any race since the year 1766, when Bay Malton beat Jerkin,' &c., and then it was run in 7 minutes $43\frac{1}{2}$ seconds. But 'clocking' is altogether unsatisfactory; for by that means you may seem to prove that Merry Hampton and Ayrshire were better over the Derby course than The Flying Dutchman, West Australian, and Ormonde.

Mr. WILBRAHAM, who ran Shakspeare for a Jockey

Club Plate in 1753 (the first year of the Club's career), is called in the 'Calendar' Mr. Roger Wilbraham, so that the gentleman was presumably he who was of Nantwich, Cheshire, M.P. (son, to all appearance, or nephew, of Roger Wilbraham, Esq., High Sheriff of Cheshire in 1714), and seems to have been the founder of the branch of the Wilbrahams of Delamere. The name also appears in the 'Calendar' with the prefix or affix (indifferently) of Bootle; whence one would conclude that there were two relations racing at the same time, for it seems to have been a Richard (not Roger) Wilbraham who became Wilbraham-Bootle or Bootle-Wilbraham (according to the will of Sir Thomas Bootle, whose heiress he married apparently), and was the father of the first Lord Skelmersdale. Anyhow, Mr. Roger Wilbraham is not among the most prominent members of the Jockey Club and promoters of 'the cause.'

Such were the most conspicuous among the royalties, noblemen, and gentlemen who composed the Jockey Club from its entrance upon public life up to the year 1773. They were, almost to a man, of royal or noble or hereditarily gentle birth; and they were, almost to a man, either hereditary or elective legislators, for nearly all the commoners, or at any rate a large proportion of them, were Members of Parliament. To them, as we have seen, not only nearly all the imported 'Sons of the Desert' (which were about that time, however, beginning to lose the mysterious influence undoubtedly exercised by them for many years upon the English breed of horses), but all the good horses in the country belonged, or by them and by their families before them had been bred; and it was only through the sales which took place upon the death or the retirement of such owners and breeders that the 'cracks' fell into the hands of persons whose social rank precluded them from becoming members of the Club—as Regulus, for instance, into the hands of Mr. Martindale (a saddler, of St. James's Street); Eclipse into the hands first of Mr. Wildman (a meat salesman, of Newgate Market), and then of Mr. (Captain, Major, and Colonel) O'Kelly (a disreputable adventurer); and Highflyer into the hands of Mr. Tattersall (an auctioneer, though of excellent repute). It is true that the Shem, Ham, and Japhet of all our present race of thoroughbreds, that is, the Byerley Turk (the charger ridden by a Captain Byerley in the wars of King William the Third), the Darley Arabian (which was purchased by an English merchant in Smyrna, and presented, or sold, or bequeathed to his brother, Mr. Darley, of Aldby Park, Yorkshire), and the Godolphin Arabian or Barb (imported from France by Mr. Coke, of Leicester, and given by him to Lord Godolphin, of Gogmagog, Cambridgeshire), did not belong to members of the Club; but it is enough to say that the least ancient of the three died in 1753, the very year in which the Club made its first appearance at Newmarket with its two

Jockey Club Plates. And a similar remark applies to Curwen's Bay Barb, and other early 'Sons of the Desert,' whose influence, having been transmitted *par les femmes*, is less conspicuously in evidence, and whose owners and importers might very well have been members of the Jockey Club but for temporal obstacles. We have seen, too, that the Club was not a mere 'Southern' institution, but that it was composed of members from the North and the South, from Ireland and from the West Indies (or having some connection with the West Indies), as if one of the objects kept in view at the foundation of the Club had been to weld together various interests, to promote intercourse, to foster mutual improvement, substituting for the spirit of almost hostility which had formerly prevailed between the horse-racers and horse-breeders of the North and of the South a feeling of reasonable and profitable emulation. Altogether it would seem that the Club, at the time at which it was started, had the elements of an almost ideal representative body, so far as the best interests of the Turf were concerned.

CHAPTER VI

FIRST PERIOD (*concluded*)

We have seen that, away from Newmarket, the Club (or a quorum thereof) would meet in the earliest days at the Star and Garter, Pall Mall, or at the Clarendon, Bond Street, or at the Thatched House, St. James's Street, or at one another's houses, whether in town or country, as in 1768 at the Duke of Grafton's at Euston; but they, of course, wanted headquarters at Newmarket, which was not so accessible as it is now, and where members of the Jockey Club would stay for the whole duration of a meeting, and where, not having houses of their own (as many, if not most, of them have now), they would naturally look out for some place of their own, to save them from the necessity of being intruded upon by all and sundry who, if only they had the necessary money at command, would be as free as the members of the Jockey Club themselves of the public hostelries, assembly rooms, &c. Now at Newmarket the Club, at its incipience, did not possess a single inch of ground (in its aggregate capacity, whatever may have been the

case with some individual members, such as Mr.
'Jockey' Vernon) from which to 'warn off' anybody
who incurred its displeasure. Accordingly, in or about
the year 1752, it seems that the members of the Club
seceded (save for purposes of dining) from the Red
Lion (the hostelry at which it appears to have been
customary for the 'quality' to assemble, as well as
probably for the most affluent and most masterful,
but by no means the least offensive, of the 'blacklegs'), and acquired for themselves, on a lease for fifty
years, from a certain Mr. Erratt (a name which occurs
pretty frequently in the records of that time as the
patronymic of a jockey, a groom, or other person pro-
fessionally engaged in horse-racing and horse-keeping)
a plot of ground whereon they caused a tenement to
be built for their accommodation. This tenement,
or a certain portion of it, was called the Coffee-room;
and, before half of the said fifty years had expired,
the ground lease was transferred to Mr. 'Jockey'
Vernon, whose tenants, as has been observed already,
such members of the Club as chose to become shareholders or subscribers, or whatever they were called,
became. This tenement, at any rate, was adopted as
the headquarters of the Club. There they transacted
what business there was to do; and there they spent
their evenings, which, as 'Bozzy' would lead us to
understand from his 'Cub at Newmarket,' were not
passed in that singing of anthems to which Sir John
Falstaff attributed his hoarseness. Nor, after the

brief biographical notices which have been given of the earliest members, will it seem likely that they commenced each day's proceedings with family prayer, and then turned their attention entirely to legislating for the Turf and reforming it, after the fashion most gratuitously ascribed to them by certain writers about the Turf and its abuses. Take the evidence of Lady Sarah Bunbury upon the point, who thus writes to Selwyn in 1767: 'A Mr. Brereton (a sad vulgar) betted at a table where Mr. Meynell, the Duke of Northumberland, and Lord Ossory were playing cards *in the morning* at the Coffee-house; he lost, and accused Mr. Meynell and Mr. Vernon (who had just come in) of having cheated the Duke of Northumberland, and [accused] Lord Ossory, &c., of being cheats in general.' An additional side-light may be thrown upon the ordinary occupations of the members by referring to the antics (already mentioned) of the 'Cripplegate' Earl of Barrymore, and to what is said to have taken place at the Coffee-room some few years later, when the noted Col. George Hanger (who will be encountered hereafter), a member of the Jockey Club and a 'bruiser' of renown, was worsted in a 'turn-up,' as the pugilists say, by a more scientific but less aristocratic brother-member and brother-bruiser, Mr. T. Bullock. Not that there is any intention here of insinuating that the members of the Jockey Club had not a perfect right to play cards, even in the morning, and to bet and to box, if they pleased, whether in the morning or in the evening; but the little sketch of such proceedings has been proffered for the benefit of those who insist upon preaching as if the main intention of the Club at its foundation had been professedly a severe, business-like reform of the Turf, its racing and its morals. The absurdity of the idea will appear at once from the reflection that the Club, having at first no property from which to 'warn off' anybody, and no command over the 'Calendars,' so as to keep out of them the programmes and advertisements of disobedient race committees or individuals, had absolutely no means of asserting its power against recalcitrants. True, about nine-tenths or more of the horses which ran at Newmarket belonged to members of the Club, who would be subject to laws made by it or to 'agreements' made one with another; but as regards the remaining tenth and the whole racing world outside Newmarket, the Club had only very indirect means of exercising influence, by hoping that its example would be followed by the peers of its members, by threatening persons of low degree with disqualification for employment by members of the Club, and by appealing to the general sense of the racing community.

Let us now see how the new Club began to work its way towards its ultimate position of paramount authority, from 1753 to 1773.

Be it premised that the only laws and regulations to which horse-racing was subject at the advent of the

Jockey Club were partly statutory and partly traditional; the former contained in an abstract of certain Acts of Parliament, and the latter in a collection of 'Rules concerning Racing in General,' published in Pond's 'Kalendar' for 1751. Both the abstract and the collection will be found—by whoever cares to read them—in the Appendix.

The Club having founded, as we have already seen, two Jockey Club Plates to be run for by horses belonging to its own members only, appears first of all (in 1756) in the rare character of the physician who heals himself. For one of these Plates was originally run in heats, but it was found that the hereditary and elective legislators who competed for it had so many violent disputes over 'the posting of the horses, &c.,' that the Club agreed to substitute for the three heats a single heat, called by the Americans a 'dash,' a very salutary example, recommended by the Club to the Master of the Horse (in 1851) for Queen's Plates, but not adopted for them until ten years later (in 1861), and not even now expressly enforced in the rules of racing. The only possible excuse for races in heats is such a scarcity of horses that a sufficiency of sport could not otherwise be insured. The case of dead heats might be made exceptional. To the same year, 1756, belongs a decision of the Jockey Club (in respect of placing the horses in the Jockey Club Plate won by the Duke of Ancaster's Spectator) which became a generally but not universally received precedent, quoted in 1786 by a commentator, who writes of 'so respectable an authority as the Jockey Club' (alluding to a dispute as to the places of Privateer and Duchess in a race at Malton in 1782). From which we may conclude that between 1753 and 1773 the Jockey Club was only gradually attaining the degree of 'high respectability' as an arbiter in the North, and was not likely to be harbouring the design, as yet, of becoming the Lycurgus of the whole English Turf.

In 1758 the Club felt strong enough to publish two resolutions; one allowing two pounds over weight, and the other disqualifying (for riding at Newmarket) any rider who should fail to declare, or to have declared for him, 'that the rider is above the weight allowed of by the aforesaid resolution'; but it is not clear how the resolutions were to be enforced if the rider were employed by somebody who did not belong to the Club, and defied its authority. In 1759 the Club instituted the 'Weights and Scales Plate' of 100 guineas, 'out of the fund arising from the weights and scales,' over which and the fees thereof the Jockey Club had apparently succeeded in establishing its control; and, as it was to be 'free for any horse,' it seems to have been intended by the Club *pro bono publico*. In 1762, under the auspices of the Club, there was instituted a Second October Meeting, so that the hitherto October Meeting became known as the First October; and in the same year eighteen members signed a 'Resolution and Agreement' to sport certain 'colours' of their own, which was a great boon to race-goers, for though 'colours' had been worn long before, they were adopted apparently at haphazard, and without discrimination or permanence. In 1767 two resolutions were passed, one (signed by eighteen members) relating to bets, the other (signed by twenty-one) relating to the admission of members to the Coffee-room. In 1768 the Jockey Club Challenge Cup was founded (for horses the property of members of the Jockey Club only), the subscribers being twenty-seven, according to Messrs. Weatherby's 'Calendar,' until 1861, but altered, without explanation, in 1862, to twenty-five, the former being, almost without a doubt, the proper number, as will be shown hereafter. In 1769 there was a 'Resolution,' signed by twelve members, touching entries to be made to the keeper of the match-book. In 1770 there were numerous 'Resolutions,' to the effect that 'the members of the Club shall meet annually at dinner on the day preceding the King's birthday'; that the number of stewards shall be three (there having been but one steward, apparently, before); that certain disabilities shall be incurred for 'watching trials,' or causing them to be watched (though, of course, there was as yet no awful threat of 'warning off,' almost as tremendous as 'naming' a member of Parliament); that bets made 'from signal or indication, after the race has been determined at the post,' shall be regarded as 'fraudulent, *illegal*, and totally void'; that the age of the horses which run at Newmarket shall be ascertained and vouched for by an expert 'at the ending post, immediately after running' (if it be the first time, and unless the requisite examination has taken place before); that certain 'colours' shall be adopted by certain owners (neither the colours nor the owners being the same as those already specified for the year 1762, which shows that the practice had 'caught on' satisfactorily); and that want of punctuality on the part of 'grooms' (when 'trainers' did not figure so prominently as now in racing matters) shall entail a fine of 'five guineas each time,' to be paid to the Club. The most important resolution (so far as the public are concerned) is that concerning the certificate of age, for in that resolution express mention is made of two-year-olds, and express sanction given (by the words used) to the novelty of two-year-old racing, the responsibility for which has been saddled for so long upon Sir Charles Bunbury (perhaps because he was the single steward at the time when the innovation commenced, though, as we have seen, he does not seem to have been himself among the earliest runners of two-year-olds), who was certainly elected one of the stewards in this year (1770), when the number was fixed at three, and when two-year-old racing was officially sanctioned, but with Lord Bolingbroke and Mr. Jenison Shafto to share the responsibility with him.

In 1771 there were passed and published five

'Resolutions' (with the signatures of twenty-one members) and one 'Agreement' (with seventeen signatures), whereof the most important provided that 'all disputes relative to racing at Newmarket' should 'for the future be determined by the three stewards and two referees to be chosen by the parties concerned'; that 'dead heats' should 'be run off after the last match on the same day'; and that 'in match or sweepstake, without specified weights, the horses' should 'carry 8 stone 7 lb.,' but with specified weights, 'the highest weight' should be 'fixed at 8 stone 7 lb.,' a plain proof that the Club was drifting away from the old 12 stone and 10 stone imposts towards the light weights which in subsequent years became ridiculous and led to no end of controversy. In 1772 the Club does not appear to have published any resolution or agreement of public importance. Meanwhile, under the auspices of the Club, sport at Newmarket had been promoted by the establishment (in 1765) of the July Meeting, of the Houghton Meeting (1770), and of the Craven Meeting (1771, when two-year-olds were first officially admitted to compete with older horses, in the eponymous Craven Stakes), making altogether the seven Meetings to which the racing world thenceforward became accustomed, though they were sometimes reduced to six (when the Second Spring was abandoned for many years), sometimes (as in 1890, by the introduction of a Second July) increased to eight. We have now reached the dawn of the 'Weatherby era,' when the Jockey Club became almost complete masters of the situation by means of the publication which has been known all over the racing world in its book form for about 120 years as 'Weatherby's Racing Calendar,' whereof the first sole proprietor was Mr. James Weatherby, keeper of the match-book at Newmarket and the Jockey Club's devoted henchman. The event is so important as almost to deserve a fresh chapter for the history and consideration of it.

As hand washes hand, so the Weatherbys, by means of their 'Calendar,' have assisted the Jockey Club, and the Jockey Club, by their patronage, have assisted Messrs. Weatherby. The history of that 'Calendar' is as follows:

As long ago as 1670, according to the evidence that can be obtained, there was a 'Calendar of Horse-racing' set up at Newmarket 'by request,' the author being a certain Mr. John Nelson, and the price being half a crown. But little, if any, more information is forthcoming in respect either of the work or of its author. After, though probably not immediately after him (else we should undoubtedly know more about him and his work), came a Mr. John Cheney, whose pedigree and performances have not been handed down quite so carefully as they might have been had he boasted to be the son of a quadrupedal sire distinguished upon the Turf, and who, to trust to memory, is somewhere described, a little vaguely, as

M

'of Arundel, Sussex.' At any rate, he published in 1727, after prodigious travelling, labour, and inquiry (prosecuted chiefly, if memory may be relied upon, according to his own account, among the clergy, the natural repositories of the required information, as we may presume from the fact that they were strictly charged by statute of Henry the Eighth to interest themselves in horse-breeding, and from the cases of the Rev. Mr. Tarran, who was noted for his 'Black Barb'; the Rev. Mr. Hewgill, who bred the famous Priestess; the Rev. Mr. Goodricke, who bred a multitude of grand racehorses, won several St. Legers, and is credibly reported to have had a hand in the introduction of two-year-old racing; the Rev. 'Passon' Harvey, who used to ride Young Vandyke to service, they say, at Westminster Abbey, and hang on to his tail in Tattersall's yard; the Rev. 'Passon' Nanney-Wynn, owner of the celebrated Signorina (by Champion); and in more recent times the Rev. Mr. 'Launde' King, fellow of Corpus Christi College, Oxford, and breeder, owner, and runner of the famous mare Apology), the first volume of a work which may be considered to have been continued annually, though of course with variations of form, arrangement, size and name, down to the present day, when it has become the incomparable 'Weatherby'—with so much variation of size, indeed, that at last, in 1846, or about that year, it grew so stout as to burst asunder into two parts, like as two peas, and in those two parts, themselves increasing year by year to bursting-point, has ever since been presented to a public undeterred by their ridiculous expensiveness.

Upon the death of Mr. Cheney (who was mortal) in 1750 or 1751, his shoes were promptly stepped into by a certain Reginald Heber (not to be confounded with the perhaps equally celebrated Bishop, whose pretty turn for hymn-writing is well known and still appreciated). He, as we gather from his instructive advertisements, combined the sale of 'mild York River tobacco,' of stationery, of sporting and other (somewhat mysteriously indicated, as if to suggest a possibility of impropriety) pictures, with the business of compiling and selling his 'Historical List of Horse-matches, &c.,' in professed succession to Mr. Cheney, first at Fulwood's Rents, Holborn, and then elsewhere in the neighbourhood of Chancery Lane and Long Acre.

But, 'nil sine magno vita labore dedit mortalibus'; and Mr. Heber's succession to Mr. Cheney was not secured without a struggle. There was a determined opposition made with a 'Sporting Kalendar' by Mr. John Pond (with whom and his equestrian daughter we have already made acquaintance). He, however, was worsted evidently in the contest, and it is to be feared that he fell upon evil days, for in the 'Obituary' of 1786 it is recorded that his wife 'died in Covent Garden Workhouse.' Mr. Heber, the victorious, continued his publication by annual volumes from 1751 to 1769 (the latter year not inclusive), and then (for he too was mortal) slept with as many fathers as he may be supposed to have had. Again a struggle took place for the succession, between a Mr. B. Walker (who published a volume for 1769) and Messrs. William Tuting and Thomas Fawconer (who jointly also published a volume called 'The Sporting Calendar' for 1769). Poor Mr. Walker went to the wall against this combination; no matter of surprise, inasmuch as Mr. William Tuting described himself as 'Keeper of the Match-book at Newmarket,' and Mr. Thomas Fawconer described himself as 'Secretary to the Jockey Club.' Messrs. Tuting and Fawconer therefore triumphed together, and together carried on the publication for a year or two; but in 1773 Mr. Tuting was dead, and Mr. Fawconer (who, after the first year of the joint publication ceased to describe himself as 'Secretary to the Jockey Club,' having apparently either assumed a title to which he had no right or been deprived of it for some reason) published a volume for that year on his own account, with a preface in which he makes serious charges against his late partner and 'Mr. James Weatherby,' for conspiring to defraud him and for forcing him into a Chancery suit. This suit seems to have killed poor Mr. Fawconer: at any rate, he was in his grave before another volume was due, and Mr. James Weatherby (who had published an opposition volume in 1773) reigned supreme and sole in 1774, having succeeded

Mr. Tuting as 'Keeper of the Match-book' and, to all appearance, Mr. Fawconer (if he ever held the post) as 'Secretary to the Jockey Club.' Of course it is impossible here to enter into the dispute between Mr. Fawconer and Mr. J. Weatherby. Suffice it to say that the latter retorted on the former with accusations of pilfering and so on, and remained in 1774 complete master of the situation. Thus commenced that monopoly which the Weatherbys have enjoyed ever since, unendangered and almost unassailed, and that close connection between them and the Jockey Club, which has been equally advantageous to both parties, has helped to make the Jockey Club the paramount authority that it is, and the firm of the Weatherbys a nondescript commercial house of no mean standing and financial importance. No doubt the issue of the 'Stud Book' (1791 and 1808), published by the family of Weatherby (one of whose members is understood to have been the original compiler), helped to strengthen the hands both of the Weatherbys and indirectly of the Jockey Club, whose representatives they were and are, and whose place of business in town is looked upon as identical with that of the Weatherbys. This was not always in Old Burlington Street, but at first in Hamilton Street, Park Lane, then at Bury Street, St. James's, then at Oxenden Street, Haymarket, whence (about 1843) it was removed to the present locality. To show the Protean character of the Weatherby's official personality it will be enough to state that at a certain trial, when the question of 'warning off' was discussed, the Mr. Weatherby called for the Jockey Club was described as ' the solicitor, treasurer, and agent for the Club, keeper of the match-book, and publisher of the " Calendar." ' Perhaps 'stakeholder' might also have been added; in any case the 'stakeholdership' at Newmarket and elsewhere became hereditary in the family.

We have now reached the point at which the Jockey Club had their own ' organ ' (the ' Calendar ') played by their own Weatherby, which marks conveniently the beginning of the second period in the existence of the Club. But before we deal with that it will be convenient to point out that, about the time at which the ' Weatherby era ' began, it seems to have occurred to the members of the Club that it would be a good thing to have a few more permanent officials of their own, such as judge, starter, &c. Up to that date the judging and starting had been performed in the most casual manner, as we read of jockeys 'calling one another back,' of the 'judges not having arrived,' and of some baker or linendraper or man-in-the-street (if only they would swear that they had no bet on the race) being raised to the judicial bench for the occasion. We do (in 1754) read of ' Mr. Deard, the judge,' at Newmarket, as if he were a regular official, whether appointed by the new Jockey Club or by the stewards of Newmarket races, but it is just as likely that he was the keeper of 'Deard's Coffee-house' at Newmarket, enlisted for the occasion. Anyhow, the first recorded regular judge at Newmarket (though he may have been really the second, successor of Mr. Deard) was Mr. John Hilton (appointed about 1772, died 1806), whose office was in time extended to Epsom, Brocket Hall, Bibury, and probably to other meetings; and he was succeeded by the dynasty of John Clark (grandfather, father, and son), lasting down to the recent accession of Mr. Robinson. About the same time other regular officials were appointed, whose names have been handed down, as, for instance, 'John Hammond, weigher of jockeys' (otherwise, 'Clerk of the Scales'), and 'Samuel Betts, starter of horses,' &c. How such offices have grown in dignity and emolument may be inferred from the fact that nowadays a live lord or other aristocrat does not disdain to discharge the arduous duties (which is one thing) and draw the salary (which is another) of a professional starter. It only remains for a Prince of the Blood to advertise himself as a public trainer, and horse-racing will have attained its apogee (though not much custom may come to the Prince of the Blood from owners who know what they are about).

THE SECOND PERIOD

1773—1835

CHAPTER VII

THE PRINCE OF WALES AND THE DUKES

IN 1835, so far as can be discovered, there was published for the first time (whether for the purpose of striking awe into 'touts' and other desperadoes with no fear of the Jockey Club before their eyes, or for mere information's sake, and out of a considerate regard for racing folks' natural and legitimate desire to know by whose authority and by what manner of men they would be 'warned off' in case of possible delinquency) that 'List of Members of the Jockey Club' which has ever since been annual, and has ever since remained one of the most interesting and useful portions, if not an indispensable portion, of the 'Racing Calendar' in its book form. So that from 1835 to the present day there is accessible to anybody who chooses to take a little trouble a complete list of the members for any particular year; and from 1773 to 1835 will be a convenient range to take for our Second Period.

Now, from 1773 to 1835 we find, on similar evidence to that previously employed, that the most notable, prominent, and active among those magnates who composed the Jockey Club, either certainly or with a probability amounting almost to certainty, were the following:

Royalties.—The Prince of Wales (afterwards George the Fourth), the Duke of York, the Duke of Clarence (afterwards William the Fourth, titular 'Patron' of the Jockey Club), the Duke of Cumberland (died 1790, who has already been dealt with), [the Duke of Gloucester, already dealt with in the 'First Period,' *q.v.*], and the French Duc d'Orléans (or de Chartres, otherwise 'Philippe Égalité').

Dukes.—Bedford (the fifth), Bolton (the last), Cleveland (the first), *Dorset (the third), Grafton (the fourth), Hamilton (the eighth), *Leeds (two), *Montrose, *Norfolk, *Portland (two), Richmond (two or three), Rutland (the fifth).

Lords.—*Auckland, *Belgrave (second Earl Grosvenor), *E. Bentinck, G. H. Cavendish, *Chesterfield (two), *Coventry, Darlington (*v.* Duke of Cleveland), Derby, Egremont, Exeter, Foley, *Grenville, *Guildford, *Harrington, *Hawkesbury, Jersey, *Kenyon, *Lansdowne, *Leicester, Lowther, Sackville, Sherborne, [Stawell], Stradbroke (two), Suffield, Tavistock, Titchfield (*v.* Duke of Portland), *Thurlow, *John Townshend, Verulam.

Sirs.—*W. Aston, *C. Bampfylde, J. Byng, C. Davers, F. Evelyn, H. F. Fetherston, J. Lade, *F.

Molyneux, F. Poole, F. Standish, H. T. Vane, H. Williamson, M. Wood.

Messrs. (with or without military or naval 'handles,' &c.).—Batson, Bertie, *Buller, Bullock, Cookson, Cussans, *Dalrymple, Dawson, Delmé (Delmé-Radcliffe), Douglas, *Dundas, Dutton, *Erskine (afterwards the famous Lord Erskine), *Fitzpatrick, Gascoyne, Gower, Grosvenor, Hale, Hallett, Hanger, *Hare, *Hastings (Warren), Howorth, *Jekyll, Jennings, Kingsman, Lake, Lamb, Maynard, Mellish, Neville, *Northey, *Onslow, O'Kelly, Parker (Lord Boringdon), Pigott (C. or 'Louse'), *P . . . t (? Admiral Pigot), *Pitt, *Robinson, Rous, Rush, *St. John, Shakspear, *Sheridan, *Tarleton, Taylor, Thornhill, *Topham, Udney, Vansittart, Vernon (H.), Villiers, Walker, Watson, Wilson, Wortley, Wyndham.

The names branded with an asterisk are those of persons who are mentioned by Pigott in his book, and are not expressly stated by him not to have been members of the Jockey Club, and some of whom, therefore, though their membership cannot be absolutely proved in the manner adopted in this work, may very well have been members; for it is difficult to see why Pigott should only now and then, and not always, mention the exceptions. And the exceptions which he does mention are noticeably few.

Notice may conveniently be taken here of certain Frenchmen who, like 'Philippe Égalité,' were (whether officially or unofficially) resident for a longer or shorter time in England, were affected by the 'Anglomania' then prevalent among the French aristocracy, cultivated horse-racing *à l'Anglaise*, visited Newmarket, causing Mr. Hugo Meynell to complain of the nuisance, and to wish that 'we were comfortably at war again,' and undoubtedly received attention from the Jockey Club, probably to the extent of being made temporary members of it, as we have seen that 'Jemmy' Boswell professes to have been made on the introduction of Lord Eglinton. These Frenchmen, or the chief of them, were the Marquis de Conflans (whose name was given to the Conflans Stakes at Brighton, or rather Brighthelmstone, and who purchased and imported into France the famous race-horse and sire King Pepin, whether on his own account or that of the Comte d'Artois, purchaser of Barbary and Comus); the Marquis de Fitz-James (descendant of our James the Second, and a great favourite at Newmarket); the Comte de Guerchy (the well-known ambassador); the Comte de Lauraguais (who was one of the famous little Gimcrack's many owners, and three or four of whose sisters successively obtained the questionable distinction of being mistress to Louis the Fifteenth); the Duc de Lauzun (who ran successfully with Taster and Patrician against Lord Clermont with Creeper at Newmarket in 1773, and raced at Lewes and elsewhere in 1774); and last, but by no means least, the Comte de Mirabeau (who visited England about 1782-83, saw horse-races at Epsom or elsewhere, and, as 'Mr. Grossley,' described them in print after a fashion worthy of his great imaginative powers, and wonderful for an Englishman to contemplate).

Some of the members dealt with in treating of the 'First Period,' such as the Duke of Cumberland, of course lived well into the 'Second Period,' but it was not necessary to repeat their names. Nor need we say more than a very few words about the asterisked members, whose membership rests almost entirely upon the fact that they appear in 'Louse' Pigott's gallery. These are the third Duke of Dorset (who succeeded to the title in 1769 and died in 1799, was Lord Steward of the Household, after having been ambassador to France, and stood high in Royal favour); the Duke of Leeds (father of the Duke who won the St. Leger with Octavian, and was very likely, but cannot be proved to have been, a member of the Jockey Club, the father having been rather a political than a racing character, and, according to Pigott, better fitted to be a director of concerts than a minister, a statesman, or a politician); the Duke of Montrose (who figures, as Marquis of Graham, in 'The Rolliad'); the Duke of Norfolk (who, in the language of Pigott, 'quitted the religion of his ancestors for his country'—in other words, became a Protestant—and who, as Lord Surrey, ran Judge Jefferies, Captain Tart, General Bandbox, and Sir Thomas Jellybag, and may therefore, very probably, have been a member of the Jockey Club); the Duke of Portland (the third, who died in 1809, was Lord-Lieutenant of Ireland for a short time, and Prime Minister in 1807, and was brother of the racing Lord E. Bentinck, and father of the racing fourth Duke of Portland); Lord Auckland (who was the Rt. Hon. W. Eden, third son of Sir Robert Eden, third Baronet, of Castle Eden, Durham, a family most distinguished in the annals of racing, so that he may very well indeed have been an actual member of the Jockey Club, though he has left no personal impression upon the Turf); Lord Belgrave (who is not best known by that name as a racing member of the Jockey Club, but will appear hereafter in that character under the style and title, first, of the second Earl of Grosvenor, and then of the first Marquess of Westminster); Lord E. Bentinck (a great racer and gentleman-rider, who married the daughter of Richard Cumberland, the author, and was brother to the third Duke of Portland, and almost without doubt a member of the Jockey Club); Lord Chesterfield (the Lord to whom the 'Letters' were addressed and who was very likely indeed a member, if only because his predecessor had put in his will a provision that 'if his successor should keep racehorses or hounds, or resort to Newmarket Races, or lose 500*l.* in one day by gambling, he should forfeit 5,000*l.* to the Dean and Chapter of Westminster,' a body chosen by the testator on the amusing plea that he had transacted business with them and had found them so 'hard' that they would be sure to exact the penalty to the uttermost farthing); Lord Coventry (who was George William, sixth Earl, husband of Maria Gunning, one of the two historically beautiful sisters); Lord Grenville (who was Prime Minister in 1806); Lord Guildford (second Earl, better known as the humorous Minister, Lord North, who had the misfortune to go blind in his latter days, but was so irrepressibly cheerful and witty under his affliction as to remark that he and his inveterate enemy, Col. Barré, who, singularly enough, had met with the same misfortune, would be 'very glad to see one another'); Lord Harrington (who served with distinction in the American War, and was an uncle of the 'Cripplegate' and 'Newgate' Earls of Barrymore, for the sixth Earl of Barrymore married Amelia Stanhope, daughter of the Earl of Harrington, father, apparently, of the Earl here in question); Lord Hawkesbury (Charles Jenkinson, afterwards Earl of Liverpool, Home Secretary under Pitt); Lord Kenyon (Lord Chief Justice); Lord Lansdowne (the Marquess of Lansdowne, better known as Lord Shelburne, patron of learning, science, and sport); Lord Leicester, (not a Coke, but George Townshend, Master of the Mint, who was created Earl of the County of Leicester, May 18, 1784, succeeded his father as Marquess Townshend in 1807, and died 1811); Lord Thurlow (the 'Jupiter Tonans' Lord Chancellor, of swearing notoriety); Lord John Townshend (brother of Lord

Leicester) a witty writer, a man of fashion, and a duellist, having fought with Mr. Fawkener, Clerk of the Privy Council, whose domestic peace he had disturbed, quite like a member of the Jockey Club, in 1786; Sir Willoughby Aston (very intimate with the Prince of Wales, and a runner of 'yearlings' in 1790 and 1791); Sir C. Bampfylde, who was murdered under very painful circumstances in 1823, for having —very many years before—seduced, it was supposed, the wife of the murderer and suicide (for the murderer immediately shot himself), and whose son was created Lord Poltimore in 1831; Sir Francis Molyneux (who, according to Pigott, first drove mankind to invent the word 'bore' to describe him, and to perpetuate it as applicable to his kind); Mr. Dalrymple (whether of the House of Stair or not, a General, intimate with the Prince of Wales, and known, according to Pigott, as 'Agamemnon the Great'); Mr. Buller (the celebrated Mr. Justice); Mr. Dundas (Henry, who became Viscount Melville); Mr. Erskine (the Hon. Thomas, of the Buchan family, the celebrated advocate, who became Lord Chancellor, having served in early life both in the army and—like another celebrated Lord Chancellor, Sir Frederick Thesiger, Lord Chelmsford—in the Navy); Mr. Fitzpatrick (Colonel and General, the accomplished brother of the second and last Earl of Upper Ossory); Mr. Hare (the famous 'Hare of many friends,' who was for many years M.P. for Knaresborough, the intimate of C. J. Fox and Lord Carlisle,

of great reputation as an orator and a wit, but of
small accomplishment in the former capacity) ; Mr.
Jekyll (the celebrated wit and brilliant barrister) ;
Mr. Hastings (Warren Hastings, the ever-memorable
'oppressor of Begums'); Mr. Northey (whose membership may be considered almost certain, though it
is difficult to prove to demonstration, for the family
of Compton Bassett, Wilts, and of Epsom, Surrey, is
most prominent on the Turf from early times, and
one of them was owner of brood mares poisoned by
Daniel Dawson at Newmarket, 1809-11); Mr. Onslow
(afterwards second Earl of Onslow, whose prowess as
a 'whip' is attested in some doggerel, running,
'What can Tommy Onslow do? He can drive a
chaise and two. And can Tommy do no more? He
can drive a chaise and four'); Mr. P ... t (almost
certainly Admiral Pigot, a great gambler of the day,
whose daughter, or one of whose daughters, is most
scurrilously assailed by Pigott, and who was a brother
of the unfortunate Lord Pigot, already dealt with in the
'First Period'); Mr. Pitt (the famous Prime Minister,
whose family were decidedly 'horsey') ; Mr. Robinson
(John Robinson, Esq., of Wyke House, Middlesex,
Secretary to the Treasury, father-in-law to Lord
Abergavenny, and a holder of pensions to an extent
which gave rise to questions in Parliament); Mr. St.
John (the Hon. John, a younger brother of the 'Bully'
Lord Bolingbroke, and a writer of opera and tragedy,
as well as a man of fashion, one of the regular

'macaronis,' as so many members of the Jockey Club were); Mr. Sheridan (the witty author of 'The School for Scandal,' but not 'of much account at horse-racing,' as an American would say); Mr. Tarleton (General Sir Banastre Tarleton, Bart., G.C.B., Governor of Berwick, and for twenty-two years M.P. for Liverpool, who ran Wilbraham at Newmarket in 1789-92); and Mr. Topham (Captain, Major, and Colonel, editor and proprietor of *The World*, a periodical whereof the title, and perhaps partly the style and spirit, is still preserved amongst us, an officer in the Horse Guards, it is said, originally, and a man of means and fashion, connected probably with Dr. Johnson's fashionable friend, Mr. Topham Beauclerc).

In not one of these cases does 'Louse' Pigott warn his readers, as he does in others, that the person mentioned was not really a member of the Jockey Club, but was joined with them as being 'tarred with the same brush,' and there is very good reason to think that the great majority of them did belong to the Club, though their credentials are not forthcoming. That Judges should be members of the Club, at that date, is not at all surprising; we have had and have such cases of Saul among the prophets in our own day—witness Mr. Baron Martin and Mr. Justice Hawkins, to seek no further.

We may now get on to the personages whose membership is capable of actual proof.

Let us begin with the three royal brothers, of

whom the least promising (being no sportsman, or, at any rate, no devotee of horse-racing), namely, the Duke of Clarence, turned out in the end to be the Jockey Club's best friend.

The PRINCE of WALES, whose membership of the Club, dating probably from the moment that he arrived at years of indiscretion, is first publicly attested in the records of 1786, when, being just twenty-four years of age, he ran second with Anvil (purchased by him in October 1784 from Mr. Parker, who was afterwards Lord Boringdon) to Mr. Wyndham with Drone, for a Jockey Club Plate, had three periods of display upon the Turf. The first, from 1784 to 1786, was brought to a premature and ignominious close (for a time) by pecuniary embarrassments, from which Parliament released him (again for a time) by paying his debts and increasing his income; the second, commencing from his reappearance with a clean slate and a larger revenue, was terminated in 1791-92 by what is known as 'the Escape affair,' when the Prince, who very honourably and pluckily stuck by his jockey, Sam Chifney the elder, accused (as the Prince believed, very unjustly) of riding Escape 'booty,' as it was called, was virtually 'warned off' Newmarket Heath by the Jockey Club, represented by the three stewards, Sir Charles Bunbury, Mr. Ralph Dutton, and Mr. Panton (the 'polite' Tommy Panton): for Sir Charles, the mouth-piece, intimated to His Royal Highness that, if he continued to employ Chifney, no gentleman would run against him; and the third, begun in 1800, was concluded in 1830 by the intervention of grim Death himself. It is well known how His Royal Highness, before he withdrew—mightily and not perhaps unjustly incensed—in 1791 from Newmarket, if not entirely from the Turf, had indulged in high jinks at 'head-quarters'; how he would 'post' thither in queer fashion, himself riding the near leader and the illustrious Mr. C. J. Fox (the statesman and orator) riding the near wheeler of the four horses that drew the chaise, with the two 'jolly post-boys' enjoying the unwonted luxury of 'going inside,' and reflecting, no doubt, that it is 'a mad world, my masters'; how he once 'shoved Orléans into the pond' in front of the palace at Newmarket, to the unspeakable indignation of old 'Égalité,' who had been intently observing the gold-fish in the tank, and whom it took twenty-four hours of envoy-sending, apologising, and diplomatic parleying to pacify; how, with the best and kindest and most polite intentions in the world, when the Bibury Club Meeting was held at Burford, he would call on his old tutor at Christ Church, Oxford, in full 'Bibury Club costume,' to the consternation of the worthy divine who ruled 'the House'; and how, at a very early age, in the Second Spring Meeting of 1784, when he was barely twenty-two, he had an opportunity of studying the difference between professional and unprofessional riding, when, weight and distance the same in both cases, his horse Hermit

(Mr. Panton up) was beaten by Sir H. Fetherston's Surprise (owner up), but, when jockeys were substituted for gentlemen, Surprise was beaten by Hermit on the same day and within an hour or so. It was in later days that he headed the gay scenes at Brighton (or Brighthelmstone) in his 'German waggon' (as a barouche was then called), drawn by six horses, and with Dr. Johnson's 'fast' young friend, Sir John Lade, for coachman; and it was in still later days that he introduced the gorgeous processions and the second meeting (instead of one only) at Ascot, when he seemed to have racehorse on the brain, buying here, there, and everywhere, whenever a horse took his fancy, and of course paying through the nose—at any rate on paper, though the colour of his money may not always have been so visible as his signature —for what he had afterwards to sell for a mere song, and when he had a tale to tell of reckless expenditure and very disproportionate success, though (chiefly in the name of Mr. D. Radcliffe) he won a considerable number of races, including the Goodwood Cup with Fleur-de-lis in 1829, the year before his death. He won the Derby once, in 1788, with Sir Thomas (by Pontac), and he won a Jockey Club Plate (w.o.) in 1788 with Gunpowder (bought of the notorious Mr. Denis O'Kelly, owner of Eclipse). The Prince is sometimes said to have won the Newmarket Challenge Whip with Anvil; but Anvil won the Whip in 1788, when he belonged to Mr. Parker (Lord Boringdon), and had not yet been sold to His Royal Highness, who, by the way, when George the Fourth, seems to have instituted the annual dinner to the members of the Jockey Club, continued by William the Fourth, and resumed by the present Prince of Wales. George the Fourth also presented to the Irish Turf Club in 1821 the Royal Whip run for at the Curragh.

The DUKE of YORK, next brother to the Prince of Wales, who was born in 1763 and died in 1827, three years before his elder brother, does not seem to have run for a Jockey Club Plate, but the evidence of 'Louse' Pigott that he was a member of the Club is supported by so much of tradition and circumstance as to leave no room for doubt. It is supposed to have been in the Coffee-room at Newmarket that His Royal Highness most delighted to show with what inimitable grace he could propose the famous toast, 'I drink to Cardinal Puff,' accompanied by gestures and contortions beyond the attainment of less gifted beings. He is understood to have been even greater when proposing this toast than when commanding our army, of which he (assisted by his fair associate, Mrs. Clarke) was so long Commander-in-Chief. He was perhaps the only Bishop who ever belonged to the Jockey Club; for he, at the tender age of six months, was declared (Prince) Bishop of Osnaburgh, with the accumulated revenues of which unlaborious office, it is said, was purchased for him the estate of Allerton, in the West Riding of Yorkshire, which, as well as his well-known property of Oatlands, near Weybridge, he is said to have lost by gambling, not on the Turf but at play, whether at Cheveley with the Duke of Rutland or elsewhere with other nobles and gentles. Indeed, he was an inveterate gambler; and, though he won a fair amount of money by his successes on the Turf, it was but a drop in the ocean compared with the stupendous debts which he left behind him, and which, we are told, the Government of the day ceded Cape Breton to his creditors to discharge. He is said to have been a good judge of a horse, and he won the Derby twice, in 1816 with Prince Leopold, and in 1822 with Moses; and the Ascot Cup twice, in 1815 with Aladdin, and in 1821 with Banker (w.o.). Neither he, however, nor his elder brother, can be regarded as model-members of the Jockey Club or model-patrons of the Turf.

The DUKE of CLARENCE, the Prince's next brother, afterwards known familiarly as the 'Sailor King,' was notoriously indifferent to horse-racing, though he seems to have run about twice in his life before his brother's death; after which, as King and 'Patron' of the Jockey Club, he ran his brother's colt by Mustachio for the Derby of 1831, and was first, second, and third with his brother's Fleur-de-lis, Zingance, and The Colonel, for the Goodwood Cup of 1830 (August —George the Fourth, having died in June of the same year), upon which occasion he gave the sailor-like order to 'start the whole fleet.' He agreeably surprised the Turfmen, for he not only improved the Royal Stud and increased the number of Royal Plates, but at one of the annual dinners which he gave to the members of the Jockey Club, on May 16, 1832, he presented the Jockey Club with one of Eclipse's hoofs, set in gold, as a prize (called ' The Eclipse Foot ') to be run for annually (plus ' 200 sovs. added by His Majesty and a sweepstakes of 100 sovs. each [afterwards 50 sovs.] for horses the property of members of the Jockey Club ') at Ascot. It was first run for in 1832, and won by Lord Chesterfield's famous horse Priam, and was last challenged for, apparently, in 1835, by Mr. Batson (owner of the great Plenipotentiary), after which it seems to have commanded neither race nor even challenge, and to have become ultimately a snuff-box at the Jockey Club Rooms, Newmarket. (The more is the pity, one feels inclined to say). Not that it was at all extraordinary for a sailor to patronise the Turf; it is extraordinary rather that he should have had so little personal liking for it—witness Admirals Norris, Rous, Harcourt, and the names, at any rate, of Boscawen, Howe, Hawke, &c. Why, one of the earliest ' horsey ' anecdotes of this century has for its hero ' a naval officer ' who ' undertook, for a wager, to ride a blind horse round Sheerness racecourse, without guiding the reins with his hands,' which the wily ' salt ' accomplished by cutting the reins and fastening them to the stirrups so as to ' steer ' with his feet. It was in Mr. D. Radcliffe's name that George the Fourth's horses, run by William the Fourth, were entered; a practice not in accordance with the present Rule, that ' a horse cannot be entered in the real or assumed name of any person as his owner unless that person's interest or property in the horse is at least equal to that of any other one person, and has been so registered.' Even under the present Rules Mr. Radcliffe might of course have been deputed to enter the horses, but, if he were merely the King's deputy, and not himself the original subscriber, the entries would be voided by the King's death. Mention having been made of ' The Eclipse Foot,' it may be interesting to remark here that a Mr. William Worley, of Weybridge, claims to have had in his possession for about thirty years (on July 7, 1891) a pin with a horse's head made from one of Eclipse's hoofs, and the property originally of a William Worley who had been in the service of the ' Culloden ' Duke of Cumberland and afterwards manager of the Duke of York's stud at Oatlands, and who had actually cut off the hoofs of Eclipse (died 1789, when the Duke of York would be very much interested in such matters). Another relic of Eclipse is the ' wrist-band' made out of hair from his tail and attached to the famous ' whip.' There is no reason to doubt that Mr. Worley's claim is well founded, and that he possesses a very desirable souvenir. The skeleton of Eclipse also is preserved in the museum of the Royal College of Veterinary Surgeons, 10 Red Lion Square, Holborn, London.

The DUC D'ORLÉANS (formerly Duc de Chartres, under which title also he ran racehorses in England) was, of course, the notorious 'Égalité,' guillotined in 1793, who had voted for his illustrious relative's (Louis XVI.) death, when even the notorious 'Tom' Paine (one of two Englishmen elected to the National Assembly) voted against it, and whose membership of the Jockey Club is not only well attested in various publications, but certified by the fact that he was running his horse Conqueror for a Jockey Club Plate at Newmarket (where the site of his stables is pointed out even to this day) in 1790, on the very eve, as it were, of Madame de Pompadour's famous 'Deluge,' which was so soon to swallow him up. He does not seem to have been very popular; but he ran freely, both English horses and horses 'bred in France' (some of them two-year-olds), such as Rouge, Vert, and Petit-gris. In his nomination ran Cantator for the Derby of 1784 and Orleans for the Derby of 1786; but he has left little more than an ill savour behind him as regards both the Turf and the Jockey Club and history.

The DUKE of BEDFORD was Francis, the fifth Duke (born 1765, died 1802), who won half a dozen Jockey Club Plates (one in 1789, one in 1790, two in 1791, and two in 1792), whose 'horsey' qualifications are commemorated in the 'Receipt to make a Jockey,' and who was as distinguished upon the Turf as it was prophesied that he would be (and as he very probably would have been had he not died at the early age of thirty-seven) in the field of politics and statesmanship. He succeeded his grandfather in 1771, his father having been killed, when Marquess of Tavistock, by a fall from his horse. Duke Francis is said to have owed his early death to an accident which occurred at cricket when he was a boy at Westminster, and which caused some mischief necessitating, after many years, a very painful and heroically borne but fatal operation. He was a great gentleman-rider, and in November 1792 at Newmarket he won a match ('owners up') with his horse Dragon against Dr. Johnson's young friend, Sir John Lade, with his horse Clifden (5 years, *fifteen* stone each, B.C.), a match which nowadays, with such a weight and over such a distance (4 miles, or a little more), would be voted both preposterous and cruel, though in 1879 Sir J. D. Astley and Mr. Caledon Alexander (both, like the Duke of Bedford and Sir J. Lade, members of the Jockey Club) rode a similar match (also at Newmarket), carrying at least *sixteen* stone each, the distance, however, being only about a mile and a half (Suffolk Stakes Course); and in the same year Sir J. D. Astley (carrying *sixteen* stone *and ten pounds*) broke down his horse, poor Drumhead, in another similar match, distance *two miles*. The Duke of Bedford, young as he was at his death, had won the Derby three times (in 1789, 1791, and 1797, with Sky-scraper, with Eager, and with a colt by Fidget out of Sister to Pharamond), and the Oaks three times (in 1790, 1791, and 1793, with Hippolyta, Portia, and Cælia). Whether the Duke bred Sky-scraper is a question which has troubled Israel, but cannot be answered with certainty. All that is certain is that Sir John Shelley (who died in 1783) bred and for some years owned Everlasting (dam of Sky-scraper); but she passed from his stud to Lord Egremont's first, and then to the Duke of Bedford's, and between those two owners lies the breedership of Sky-scraper. Altogether, the fifth Duke of Bedford was one of the most worshipful among those members of the Jockey Club who have promoted the 'cause.' He was confederate with Mr. Ralph Dutton, which will account for the fact that Sky-scraper was entered for the Derby in Mr. Dutton's name.

The DUKE of BOLTON was the last Duke (whose natural daughter married Mr. T. Orde, that is, Mr. T. Orde-Powlett, created Lord Bolton in 1797), and he ran Brother to Johnny for a Jockey Club Plate in 1781 (having probably been a member of the Club for some years previously). The Duke ran a filly by Syphon for the very first Oaks (in 1779), and Bay Bolton (by Matchem) for the very first Derby (in 1780), and he 'strained back' to the Duke who was the owner (though Sir M. Peirson was the breeder) of the very famous Bay Bolton (*alias* Brown Lusty, by

Grey Hautboy), that died at Bolton Hall, Yorkshire, 1736, aged thirty-one, which Duke was the father of the Duke who shot himself in 1765, not from any cause connected with the Turf, but, it was said, from dudgeon at not receiving a certain honourable office on which he had set his heart.

The DUKE of CLEVELAND (who died in 1842, aged seventy-five) of course lived into the times at which the annual official list of 'Members of the Jockey Club' began to be published, and duly figures therein, but he (first Duke of the new creation in 1833, who was successively Lord Barnard, Earl of Darlington, Marquess of Cleveland, and Duke of Cleveland and Baron Raby) was a member of the Club as early certainly as 1797, for in that year he, as Lord Darlington, won a Jockey Club Plate with St. George. He was for fifty years a shining light of the Turf (though he was even greater perhaps in 'scarlet' than in 'silk,' with the hounds of Raby than with the racehorses at Doncaster, where, as Marquess of Cleveland, he won the St. Leger with Chorister in 1831). He, of course, was the Lord Darlington who won the Two Thousand with Cwrw in 1812, under circumstances which, as related by the late Admiral Rous, create a curious impression, and which will receive due notice hereafter. He is said to have paid any price that anybody chose to ask for a horse that he was set upon (in the figurative sense of the word); he was temporary owner of almost countless good horses (including

Barefoot and Memnon, sold by him to Mr. Watt, unfortunately, just before they won the St. Leger); and he is credited with the excellent remark that he 'bought the best horses he could get for money, and had too much respect for them to run them in handicaps.' He won the Ascot Cup in 1818, 1823 (Mr. Dilly's Netherfield being disqualified), and 1827, with Belville, Marcellus, and Memnon (repurchased from Mr. Watt). He was a Vane, connected in some far-off way with his earliest predecessors (whether Fitzroys or Vanes), and therefore had racing bred in the bone and bound to come out in the flesh; and his immediate predecessor in the Dukedom (not in some of his other titles), the Duke of Cleveland and Southampton (a Vane-Fitzroy), may very well have been a member of the Jockey Club, though there is no proof of it, his great racing-ground having been the North, where he was very prominent (especially in Give-and-Take Plates) with Charon, Dainty Davy (winner of the Richmond Gold Cup five years in succession, from 1759 to 1763), Meaburn, Raby, &c. The Duke of Cleveland, created in 1833, married a daughter and co-heir of the last Duke of Bolton (Powlett), whence the name of Powlett adopted by the third Duke.

The DUKE of GRAFTON is a title which covers two persons, the third Duke (who lived into this period, but has already been dealt with), and the fourth Duke, who (born 1760, died 1844) did not 'cross and jostle' his father on the Turf, but, on the death of the third Duke (in 1811), at once stepped into the vacant shoes (though he is not gazetted as a runner for a Jockey Club Plate till 1836, when his horse Ulick, with 6 to 4 *on* him, was beaten by no less a distance than 100 yards by Lord Exeter's Luck's All), and, availing himself of his father's stud, including the celebrated mares Prunella and Penelope, surpassed the paternal success, great as that had been. The fourth Duke won the Derby once (in 1815, with Whisker), the Oaks six times (in 1813, 1815, 1822, 1823, 1828, and 1831, with Music, Minuet, Pastille, Zinc, Turquoise, and Oxygen), the Two Thousand five times (in 1820, 1821, 1822, 1826, and 1827, with Pindarrie, Reginald, Pastille, Dervise, and Turcoman), and he almost 'farmed' the One Thousand from 1819 to 1827, since Lord Jersey's Cobweb (in 1824) alone broke the continuity of his successes, with Catgut, Rowena, Zeal, Whizgig, Zinc, Tontine, Problem, and Arab.

The DUKE of HAMILTON is the eighth, who succeeded to the title on the death of his brother (at an early age) in 1769, and died *s.p.* in 1799. He ran Hercules for a Jockey Club Plate in 1778, and fulfilled all the traditions of the Club, having been divorced, 'at the suit of her Grace,' in 1777-78, on account of his relations with a Mrs. Esterre, and having run for Derby, Oaks, and St. Leger, but he was completely overshadowed on the Turf by his uncle and successor, Lord Archibald Hamilton, the 'cock of the North.'

O

The DUKE of LEEDS is a title covering both the Duke abused by 'Louse' Pigott (and already dealt with) and his son and successor (born 1775, died 1838), who is in the list of members of the Jockey Club for 1835, and had no doubt been a member for some years, as he won the St. Leger with Octavian as early as 1810. A curious story is told of Octavian (by Stripling), to the effect that the Duke purchased the animal 'when a foal with its dam, from one of his own tenants, having taken a fancy to it *while following its dam in the plough.*' This looks as if the Duke must have had a pretty good eye for a horse; and the prevalence of a 'horsey' strain in his blood may be inferred from the fact that a Lord Carmarthen ran Spot at York in 1722.

The DUKE of PORTLAND, again, is a title covering both the third Duke (already treated of) and the fourth, who succeeded in 1809 and died in 1854, and who, as Marquess of Titchfield, ran Viret for a Jockey Club Plate in 1796. It was he who won the Derby in 1819 with Tiresias, who was instrumental (in 1827) in establishing the right of the Jockey Club to 'warn off' people from Newmarket Heath, who advanced funds to the Jockey Club in 1831, and who, above all, was the father of the celebrated Lord George Bentinck.

The DUKE of RICHMOND is a title covering two (and perhaps three) personages, the third Duke (who has already been dealt with, though he lived to 1806, well within this ' Second Period ') ; perhaps his nephew and successor (known as the Colonel Lennox who fought a duel with the Duke of York, whose wife gave —or did not give, according to the latest version of the affair—the famous ball at Brussels on the eve of the Battle of Waterloo, and who died in 1819 from hydrophobia, caused by the bite of a dog, or, as some say, of a tame fox), though his membership of the Jockey Club lacks indisputable proof; and certainly the fifth Duke, who is on the list for 1835, who won the Oaks with Gulnare in 1827 and with Refraction in 1845, the Goodwood Cup with Linkboy in 1827 and with Miss Craven in 1828, and the One Thousand with Pic-nic in 1845, and died in 1860. It is to this fifth Duke that Lord George Bentinck was 'managing man,' to such purpose that the Goodwood Meeting won the now stereotyped epithet of ' glorious,' though, no doubt, alliteration had something to do with it, as in the case of ' The Fighting Fitzgeralds,' &c., &c., down to ' Bloody Balfour.'

The DUKE of RUTLAND is John Henry, the fifth, who died in 1837, having won a Jockey Club Plate (w.o.) in 1830 with Cadland and (also w.o.) in 1831 with Oppidan. He won the One Thousand in 1816 with Rhoda, the Oaks in 1811 and 1814 with Sorcery and Medora, and the Two Thousand and Derby in 1828 with Cadland, Cadland and The Colonel having first run a dead heat for the Derby, the first on record for that race.

CHAPTER VIII

THE LORDS

LORD BELGRAVE (second Earl Grosvenor), whose father, the first Earl, the great racer and bettor, lived well into the 'Second Period' (as he died in 1802), won a Jockey Club Plate with Labrador in 1817, as Lord Grosvenor, but he will be deferred till the 'Third Period' (since it was then that, as the first Marquess of Westminster, he became most prominent on the Turf).

LORD G. H. CAVENDISH (who was third and last for a Jockey Club Plate with Furbisher to Lord Verulam with Vitellina and the Hon. C. Wyndham with a chestnut colt by Phantom in 1825) was a younger brother of the fifth Duke of Devonshire, and is said to have come in for the greater part of his uncle Frederick's immense fortune. He 'went a-head' in his primrose days, but he appears to have had everybody's good word. He was born in 1754, and soon developed a taste for gambling, but bore himself so coolly and discreetly that he was considered proof against danger, and he was so beyond suspicion of anything questionable that even the scurrilous Pigott observes, 'We do not believe the mines of Peru could seduce this nobleman to commit a dishonourable act.' He maintained for many years upon the Turf the prestige of the family which owned (but did not breed) the famous 'Devonshire' or 'Flying' Childers. He won the Two Thousand with Nectar in 1816, the One Thousand with Young Mouse in 1829, and the Ascot Cup with Bizarre in 1824 and 1825. He bred and owned Competitor (foaled 1786), the 'last of the Eclipses' that was named and ran (Horizon, foaled 1772, having been the first), and started him unsuccessfully for the Derby of 1789. Competitor died in 1816; Lord G. H. Cavendish about a quarter of a century later, at a very great age.

LORD CHESTERFIELD is a title covering two personages, one of them already dealt with (and abused by 'Louse' Pigott); the other, the sixth Earl (son of Pigott's, who was the fifth), who was born in 1805, succeeded in 1815, received forfeit in 1831 with the famous Priam for the Jockey Club Challenge Cup, won the Eclipse Foot (for members of the Jockey Club only) in 1834, and was a heavy bettor as well as a great racer. A long minority had secured to him a vast income when he came of age in 1826, and he at once proceeded to expend a considerable part of it upon a stud of racehorses. He had some notable successes. He won the Ascot Cup with Zinganee in 1829, and with Glaucus in 1834; the Goodwood Cup in 1831 and 1832 with Priam, and in 1836 and 1837 with Hornsea and Carew; the Oaks in 1838 and 1849 with Industry and Lady Evelyn; the St. Leger in 1838 with Don John; and he issued two unaccepted challenges for the Whip, with Zinganee in 1831 and with Glaucus in 1834. He was at one time confederate with the famous Mr. C. C. Greville, Clerk of the Council, and was for awhile Master of the Buckhounds, at his retirement from which office, in 1834, there was given to him at the Clarendon a complimentary dinner, of which somebody has thought it worth while to preserve the following account:

Menu OF DINNER GIVEN IN MAY, 1834, TO LORD CHESTERFIELD, ON HIS QUITTING THE OFFICE OF MASTER OF THE BUCKHOUNDS, AT THE CLARENDON.

The party consisted of thirty.

PREMIER SERVICE.

Potages.—Printanier à la reine, *turtle (two tureens).*

Poissons.—Turbot (*lobster and Dutch sauces*), saumon à la Tartare, rougets à la Cardinal, friture de morue, *whitebait.*

Relevés.—Filet de bœuf à la Napolitaine, dindon à la chipolate, timbale de macaroni, *haunch of venison.*

Entrées. — Croquettes de volaille, petits pâtés aux huîtres, côtelettes d'agneau purée de champignons, côtelettes d'agneau aux points d'asperge, fricandeau de veau à 'oseille, ris de veau piqué aux tomates, côtelettes de pigeon à la Dusselle, chartreuse de légumes aux faisans, filets de canneton à la Biggarrade, boudins à la Richelieu, sauté de volaille aux truffes, pâté de mouton monté.

Côté.—Bœuf rôti, jambon, salade.

SECOND SERVICE.

Rôts.—Chapons, quails, turkey poults, *green goose.*

Entremets.—Asperges, haricots à la Française, mayonnaise d'homard, gelée Macedoine, aspics d'œufs de pluvier, Charlotte Russe, gelée au Marasquin, crême marbre (*sic*), corbeille de pâtisserie, vol-au-vent de rhubarb, tourte d'abricots, corbeille de Meringues, dressed crab, salade au (*sic*) gélantine (*sic*), champignons aux fines herbes.

Relevés.—Soufflée à la vanille, Nesselrode pudding, Adelaide sandwiches, fondues, pièces montées, &c.

DESSERT.

'The price,' we are told, 'was six guineas a head,' and though that probably included ' something to drink ' (if only a little beer), the dinner seems to have been very dear at the price, even for the Clarendon and for the time of year.

LORD DERBY (born 1752, died 1834) is the twelfth Earl, grandson of the eleventh, and son of the nobleman who persisted (as we have seen) in calling himself Lord Strange, and who introduced a Smith (worth her weight in gold) among the aristocratic Stanleys. The twelfth Earl won both the Jockey Club Plates of 1783, with Oliver Cromwell and Guildford, as well as the Oaks (which he was instrumental in establishing, and which was named after his estate The Oaks, purchased from his relative General Burgoyne, on Banstead Downs) in 1779, the very first year it was run for, with Bridget, and in 1794 with Hermione, and the Derby (which also he was instrumental in establishing, and which received its name from him) in 1787 with the immortal Sir Peter Teazle, commonly called Sir Peter *tout bref*, and not only owned but bred by him. This of itself would be enough to place the twelfth Earl of Derby on the topmost pinnacle of fame as a member of the Jockey Club and a supporter of the Turf. He was twice married; first to Lady Elizabeth Hamilton (from whom he was divorced in the orthodox style of the early members of the Jockey Club, whether because she not unnaturally objected to cock-fighting in the drawing-room, a practice to which the noble Earl was addicted, or for a more potent reason, more cognisable by law), sister and heiress of her brothers, the seventh and eighth Dukes of Hamilton; and secondly, to the celebrated actress, Miss Ellen Farren, whose 'Lady Teazle,' no doubt, suggested to the noble Earl a portion of some of the names or a whole name given to some of his horses, and who, having more than Lady Elizabeth Hamilton can have had to gain by such a matrimonial alliance, was more ready perhaps to smile upon cock-fighting even in the drawing-room. This lord had a pleasant, easy, reckless, selfish way with him, according to Horace Walpole, who tells us that the Earl 'nearly killed his cook with late suppers,' and, when the heart-broken *chef* remonstrated (at the same time admitting that the 'place' was in other respects quite unexceptionable), bade the poor man be content and put down 'wear and tear of life' at a fixed sum. We have already encountered him in the character of a 'dun,' when he applied to George Selwyn, the wit, for payment of a debt of honour. Which of this noble Earl's characteristics it was that made him so very popular—whether it was the horse-racing or the hunting, to which he was equally devoted, or the cock-fighting in the drawing-room, or the late suppers and the cavalier treatment of the long-suffering cook, or the elevation of an actress to be the wearer of a coronet—is not easy to determine; but his popularity was tremendous, and, ' Ah, he was English, sir, from top to toe!' was said of him by an admirer, with tears in his eyes, who was probably himself a cock-fighter.

LORD EGREMONT is he who ran Claret for a Jockey Club Plate in 1787, and of whom Horace Walpole, we find, wrote (1774) : 'Lord Thomond is dead . . . could not bring himself to make a will . . . and the whole real estate falls to his nephew, L. E.' He was to have married Walpole's niece, Lady Maria Waldegrave, but thought better (or rather very much worse) of it (for which he is roundly abused by the moralist of Strawberry Hill), and 'opted' to live unmarried with a Miss Iliffe (who bore the name of Mrs. Wyndham). He is said to have ' begun life with 45,000*l.* a year, and ended with 81,000*l.* a year.' He naturally took to Newmarket and horse-racing and horse-breeding (witness Thomond House there, and the Earl of Thomond's stud in the time of Charles the

Second), as became a relative of the Thomonds; and when he slept with his fathers (November 11, 1837, in his eighty-sixth year), he had bred Gohanna (the Ney of racehorses, the gamest of the game, though Waxy was one too many for him), and had won the Derby five times (1782, 1804, 1805, 1807, 1826, with Assassin, Hannibal, Cardinal Beaufort, Election, and Lapdog), and the Oaks—oddly enough—exactly the same number of times (1788, 1789, 1795, 1800, and 1820, with Nightshade, Tag, Platina, Ephemera, and Caroline), as well as the Goodwood Cup (in 1825 and 1826, with Cricketer and Stumps), a specially appropriate trophy for him, as Goodwood races were the successors, as it were, of the races which had been held by Lord Egremont at Petworth, where, it may be remarked in passing, a most mysterious murrain (in 1825) raged not only among the blood-stock but among the cart-mares and even the asses, causing great mortality and never traced to any ascertainable source. It is related of this Lord Egremont that he was by natural constitution so disinclined for a legitimate alliance with the other sex as to declare his honest conviction that, if he were to marry, he should inevitably hang himself, and yet of so benevolent a disposition that he for many years spent 20,000*l.* annually in relieving distress and contributing to charitable institutions.

Lord Exeter, who by family name 'strains back' to the very early days of horse-racing (for we find the

Hon. William Cecil racing in company with Her Majesty Queen Anne for Her Majesty's own Gold Cup, at York in 1713), is the second Marquess (born 1795, succeeded 1804, died 1867), who appears in the official list of 1835 (having, almost certainly, been a member some years before), and was a great upholder of the Turf, of an excellent type. He won the Two Thousand in 1825, 1829, 1830, and 1852, with Enamel, Patron, Augustus, and Stockwell (having just been in time to purchase this great horse as a yearling from Mr. Theobald, the hosier, his breeder, who was near his end); the One Thousand in 1832, with the 'flying' Galata; the Oaks in 1821, 1829, and 1832, with Augusta, Green Mantle, and Galata; the St. Leger in 1852, with Stockwell; and the Whip in 1854, with Stockwell. Add to all this a number of matches, and the Ascot Cup, with Galata in 1833. How unfortunate he was not to win the Derby with Stockwell (amiss, as he so often was) needs no demonstration. This is the Lord Exeter whose name is associated with a well-known but ill-understood method of selling race-horses, which are then said to be sold 'under Lord Exeter's conditions' (as he was the originator of the process). Those conditions, as they are imperfectly 'understanded of the people,' it may be well to append:

The horses are sold without their engagements, but the purchaser has the right of running for any of them by paying half the stake, and in the event of the horse winning, or being entitled to second or third money, one-third shall be paid to the vendor, but the vendor reserves to himself the right of striking the horse out of any race in time to save a minor forfeit or discount, unless the purchaser shall give notice that he wishes to run for any particular race, when he will become liable for half the stake or forfeit. Horses purchased under Lord Exeter's conditions cannot be resold under the same conditions without the written consent of the original vendor.

These conditions are now officially recognised by the Jockey Club and inserted in the Rules of Racing. Briefly, they exempt the purchaser from all vexatious liabilities.

LORD FOLEY (though his father, the confederate of the Hon. and Right Hon. C. J. Fox, overlaps into this period, since he died in 1793) is, of course, William Thomas, third Baron of the second creation, who ran Duenna for the Jockey Club Plate won by Lord Grosvenor with Labrador in 1817; and that is as much as need be said about him.

LORD JERSEY, who won a Jockey Club Plate with Cannon-ball in 1818, is the fifth Earl (succeeded 1809, died 1859), who was twice Master of the Horse. He was perhaps the most conspicuous member of the Jockey Club and patron of the Turf in his time. It was he who was for a time confederated with the great Turfite Sir J. Shelley (sixth Baronet, of Phantom and Cedric celebrity), and he kept an excellent stud at Middleton Stony (whence the name of two famous horses), Oxon, and, so far as his family name of Villiers goes, he carries us back in memory to the Duke of

Buckingham's Helmsley Turk, bred by the Lord-Protector Cromwell's stud-groom, one Mr. Place. His famous horses included the two Middletons (chestnut by Phantom, and bay by Sultan), Mameluke, and Glenartney. The chestnut Middleton (like Amato in 1838) was a case of 'Veni, vidi, vici,' for he came out for the first and only time in 1825, won the Derby, and disappeared from public life. Glenartney was his own brother, and, according to public statement at the time, could not have lost the Derby of 1827, for which Lord Jersey started his other 'crack,' Mameluke also, and won with this other, whereat there was a great outcry. There had been no 'declaration'; but, on the contrary, it was publicly stated that Lord Jersey's jockeys had positive orders to run independently. Still, as Lord Jersey and his friends were supposed to have derived advantage from the result, there was, of course, much unpleasantness and sarcastic congratulation, especially when Lord Jersey refused 5,000 guineas for Glenartney after the race and sold Mameluke for 4,000 guineas at Ascot. On the other hand, Mameluke is known to have been a most ungenerous, uncertain brute, but a 'tickler' when in the mood; and, moreover, a jockey (and that jockey the notorious Harry Edwards) may think sometimes that he may disobey orders if that will win his employer's bets (and his own).

Lord Jersey won the Derby in 1825, 1827, and 1836, with Middleton, Mameluke, and Bay Middleton;

the Oaks in 1824, with Cobweb; the Two Thousand in 1831 and 1834-37, with Riddlesworth, Glencoe, Ibrahim, Bay Middleton, and Achmet; the One Thousand in 1824 and 1830, with Cobweb and Charlotte West; the Ascot Cup in 1835, with Glencoe; and the Goodwood Cup in 1834, with Glencoe. The fifth Earl died on October 3, 1859, and singularly enough, his son and successor, the sixth Earl, on the 24th of the same month in the same year.

LORD LOWTHER, who ran Tot for a Jockey Club Plate in 1808, and is famous in Turf annals for winning the Derby of 1831, with the outsider Spaniel (at 50 to 1), beating Lord Jersey's strong favourite Riddlesworth (at 6 to 4 *on*), must be he who became (in 1844) the second Earl of Lonsdale, President of the Council in 1852, and died in 1872. How much the Turf has been and is indebted to the Lowthers has been shown in the case of Sir J. Lowther, member of the Jockey Club in the 'First Period.' Lord Lowther's descendant, the fourth Earl, who won the Two Thousand with Pilgrimage, does not appear to have been invited to become a member of the Jockey Club, to the advantage of the Club and to the credit of its discernment.

LORD SACKVILLE, who ran second with Sober Robin to Lord Darlington with St. George for a Jockey Club Plate in 1797, was the second Viscount Sackville and fifth and last Duke of Dorset (having succeeded in 1815 his young cousin, who met with a fatal accident out hunting, when only just of age). It may be well to write a few words of explanation on the subject. The first Duke of Dorset, then, created 1720, and Lord-Lieutenant of Ireland (1730–37 and 1750–55), had several sons, of whom the third was George Sackville (better but not more favourably known as that strange compound of gallantry and apparent cowardice, Lord George Germaine, the name and title which he had been permitted to assume), who (died April 1785) was created Viscount Sackville; and his son, the second Viscount and fifth and last Duke of Dorset, died unmarried on July 29, 1843, when all the honours became extinct. He was temporary owner or nominator of many good horses, including Kitt Carr, Silver, Magic, Spread-Eagle (Sir F. Standish's, winner of the Derby in 1795), Commodore, Expectation (won a Jockey Club Plate in 1800), and Dick Andrews (w.o. for a Jockey Club Plate in 1803). In 1814 he ran Hocus-pocus (Lord Suffield's) under his title of Lord Sackville, and in 1815 of Duke of Dorset, under which title he appears in the Jockey Club list of 1835. It is of the poor fourth young Duke (whether a member of the Jockey Club or not there is no saying, as he only came of age in November 1814 and met with his fatal accident in Ireland in February 1815) that the story is told about 'the gross irreligion of sportsmen.' It appears that he was placed by Lord Powerscourt and other friends on one of those hard and slippery couches (of which many of us must have had experience) to be found in country inns, and feeling himself gliding apparently to the ground exclaimed, 'I'm off!' which Mrs. Grundy, as it was just before he died, attributed to profanity.

LORD SHERBORNE (born 1744, died 1820), by name a Dutton (James, son of the great Turfite James Lenox Dutton, who was running Ajax, by Second, and many other good horses all over the country about the time or even before that the Jockey Club was foaled), won a Jockey Club Plate with Spectre in 1784, in which year, having been M.P. for Gloucester for many years, he was created Lord Sherborne, from the family estate of Sherborne, Gloucestershire. How great the Duttons were upon the Turf may be inferred from the fact that a certain course at Newmarket was named Dutton's Course after one of them; though it has not held its own, as 'Rowley's Mile' and 'Bunbury's Mile,' and so on, but has passed away from remembrance, like the 'Duke's Course' and the 'Clermont Course,' and the rest of them. The name of the family was originally Naper, which Lord Sherborne's next brother, William (Ralph being the third), resumed on succeeding to the Naper portion of the family property at his father's death (about 1775). Hence the records of racing may be found a little puzzling sometimes; the same horse appearing under the name both of Dutton and Naper occasionally.

[LORD STAWELL], having found his way on to the list without credentials that can be verified beyond a doubt, is retained (in a bracket) on grounds of high probability, even if it cannot be said of him, as Voltaire said of the Prophet Habakkuk, 'il était capable de tout.' He was apparently Henry Stawell, son of the Rt. Hon. Bilson Legge (who had married the lady created Baroness Stawell in 1760), and he seems to have succeeded to his mother's title in 1780, and to have died in 1820, leaving no male issue, so that the title became extinct, and, being unfamiliar accordingly, is often written erroneously Stowell. His only daughter had married in 1803 a son of Lord Sherborne, himself a mighty racer. Lord Stawell was a very noticeable Turfite, and won the Derby with Blucher in 1814. He had a curious horse in Goldenleg (so-called because it was a bay with one chestnut leg), which died on its way to the Cape, about 1817, after having belonged to Lord G. H. Cavendish; and one of the few twins (besides Mr. Rogers's Nicolo) that were ever worth a rap in Elizabeth, by Waxy (ran unplaced for the Oaks of 1803).

LORD STRADBROKE is a title which covers two personages, father and son, the first and the second Earls.

The first Earl (born 1750, died 1827), who ran second for a Jockey Club Plate in 1822 with Incantator to Lord Egremont with Centaur, and who is better known on the Turf, as well as in 'Hansard,' under the style and title of Sir John Rous, and afterwards Lord Rous, winner of the Two Thousand with

P

Tigris in 1815, and owner of Jerboa (by Gohanna), and most of her progeny, though not without claims to rank among the benefactors of the Turf and ornaments of the Jockey Club, cannot of course compare in those respects with his two famous sons, the second Earl of Stradbroke and the memorable Captain (and Admiral) Rous. As for the racing strain in the family, witness a Major Rous who runs against the notorious Mr. Tregonwell Frampton at Newmarket in 1721. There is reason to believe that they do err who attribute to this family the origin of the expression 'Bravo, Rous!' (tracing it to the Admiral's feat with his ship *Pique*); one Rous, who kept the Eagle Tavern in the City Road, and performed to the great delight of the vulgar at his theatre there, is said to have been the true first great cause of the popular cry, now almost obsolete, and of the interpretation placed upon the letters 'O.P.Q.R.,' namely, 'O particularly queer Rous.'

The second EARL of STRADBROKE, John Edward Cornwallis Rous (born 1794, died 1886, at the great age of 91–92), was a member of the Jockey Club long before he appears on the list of 1835 in company with his brother, Captain the Hon. H. Rous; in fact, they are both expressly stated in print and on good authority to have been elected members of the Club in 1821, during their father's lifetime. The second Earl was probably greater as a patron of coursing than of horse-racing, though he won the Two Thousand with Idas in 1845, and was for a time confederate with the Duke of Richmond; and he paled before his brother, the Admiral, with whom he had originally been associated. Not that the 'Great Twin Brethren' were all their lives altogether at one on all questions connected with the Turf. They were, no doubt, both equally anxious for the improvement of its morality, as well as of its business and the accessories thereof, but they differed often, not to say generally, and voted on opposite sides. The Admiral, for instance, was very angry with people who said that the English racehorse had degenerated; the Earl agreed with them. The Admiral and the Earl, moreover, voted on opposite sides on Sir J. Hawley's proposal in 1869 to limit the racing of two-year-olds, the Earl being for the limitation and the Admiral against. When two such honest experts differ on such questions it seems almost hopeless to arrive at the true conclusion.

LORD SUFFIELD is a title which covers two single gentlemen; the first is he who married the co-heiress of the Earl of Buckingham, and was well known on the Turf as Mr. Harbord before he aired his lordship at Ipswich in 1810, which was eleven years before he ran Vandyke Junior for a Jockey Club Plate in 1821, in which year he died; and the other (? son of the former) is he who was 'obliged to decline the Turf' in 1839, but had already deserved honourable mention for joining those members of the Jockey

Club who protested in 1837 against the sale of the Royal Stud at Hampton Court.

LORD TAVISTOCK is the Marquess of Tavistock who ran his mare Leeway for a Jockey Club Plate in 1828, and he will be better dealt with in the 'Third Period' as Duke of Bedford (the seventh, nephew of the fifth, the great racing Duke), to which title he succeeded on the death of his father in 1839.

LORD VERULAM (first Earl) won a Jockey Club Plate with Vitellina (by Comus) in 1825, and seems to have aired his new-fledged title (created 1815) first of all in 1819 at Ascot, running his roan filly Vaharina for the Wokingham Stakes. This Lord Verulam (a Grimston) has nothing, of course, but his title and his property at Gorhambury Park, near St. Albans, Herts, in common with the celebrated Lord Bacon (who, as if he had not worked sufficiently in his own line, has been credited in our own day with the achievements of the voluminous William Shakespeare); but he deserves to be commemorated as a public benefactor for instituting races at Gorhambury, which at one time bade fair to rival Goodwood (bar the Trundle Hill and the scenery generally). Gorhambury came to the family through their ancestor Sir Harbottle (or Airbottle) Grimston ('barrow-knighted' in the reign of James the First), descended, it is said, from a de Grimston who 'came over with the Conqueror'; but the estate is, of course, called after Robert de Gorham, with whose four-legged namesake Lord

Verulam ran second to Attila for the Derby of 1842 at 100 to 1 against his winning, having won two or three times with him at Gorhambury previously. It was the 'Gothic' father of this first Earl who is said to have destroyed Lord Bacon's old place and built a new one.

But perhaps the Grimston whose memory is most cherished by sportsmen of all descriptions is Robert, fourth son of the first Earl of Verulam; that all-round sportsman who was well-known on the Turf, better in the hunting-field, and best as President of the M.C.C. and who died in 1884, aged sixty-seven.

CHAPTER IX

THE COMMONERS

Sir J. Byng, who won a Jockey Club Plate with Morisco in 1824, was of course the gallant General and Field-Marshal Sir John Byng, created Baron Strafford in 1839 and Earl of Strafford in 1847, father of the late Earl (George Stevens Byng), who was also a member of the Jockey Club. Sir John was a very great racing man, unfortunately of the betting persuasion, whereby hangs a tale of a long friendship which should have had a nobler origin; for it is said that his long friendship with the late General Peel —another regrettable example of the betting persuasion—began when the latter, being a subaltern, dined at the mess of a regiment of which the former was colonel. During dinner the colonel expressed a desire to take 50 to 1 about a certain horse for the St. Leger, and was electrified by hearing the stranger-subaltern, whose presence he had not noticed, take him up with the ready response of 'I will lay you fifty hundreds to one, sir.' Whether the future Field-Marshal accepted the offer, and was drawn towards the subaltern by the powerful attraction of 5,000*l.*, is not stated; but it is more likely that he lost his own 'century.'

Sir CHARLES DAVERS, Bart., ran Attack for a Jockey Club Plate in 1777. He was apparently son of Sir Robert Davers, M.P., a mighty Nimrod, whose name is found among the subscribers to Heber's 'Calendar' about 1760. Sir Charles, who was likewise a mighty Nimrod, M.F.H., M.P. for Edmundsbury (*alias* Bury St. Edmunds), was of Rougham, Suffolk, and, like so many of the early members of the Jockey Club, appears to have belonged to a family of West Indian connections. Sir Charles would be remarkable if only as one of the few members of the Jockey Club against whom 'Louse' Pigott can find nothing to say; but he is also remarkable as a great benefactor of the Turf. For, at the death of the famous Mr. Jenison Shafto, and the consequent sale at Newmarket, October 24, 1771, he purchased the broodmare Miss Ramsden (by Cade), and from her bred Quicksand, Wormwood, Whipcord, and above all the celebrated Woodpecker, a great racehorse, and one of the very greatest sires of the 'Stud Book.' In his capacity of M.F.H. also Sir Charles was remarkable, for it is recorded that his pack of hounds on one occasion found a leash of foxes, whereupon it split up into three packs, each of which had a splendid run and killed. Sir Charles, again, was remarkable in being the last of his race (so far as the baronetcy was concerned), for he, like the famous Turfite Sir

T. Gascoigne (as we have seen), lost his only son (who was a captain in the navy, and caught yellow fever on service), in 1804; so that the title became extinct.

Sir FREDERICK EVELYN, who ran second to Lord Sackville for a Jockey Club Plate in 1800, was one of the oldest members of the Jockey Club when Pigott sneered at his 'pitiful desire of excelling and distinguishing himself at a country race,' and at his having 'acquired a particular and curious method of making a horse sink while measuring for a *give-and-take plate*.' However this may have been, it is certain that Sir Frederick was the owner of some good horses (including Signal and Atom, both by the Damascus Arabian, as early as 1769, and Prize, by Snap, and Gallant, by Dorimant, later); and that he ran Wotton (by Vauxhall Snap) for the very first Derby (1780), and bred Egham, Maria (sister to Wotton), and Mira (by Woodpecker), &c. So that he contributed to the good cause. The family seems to have been connected by marriage with the Boscawens (in fact, Sir Frederick's father, Sir John, married a daughter of Viscount Falmouth), whence the familiar name of Evelyn Boscawen, Viscount Falmouth, late pillar of the Turf, if the expression be admissible.

Sir H. FETHERSTON, Bart., though his membership of the Jockey Club may not be proved quite to demonstration by actual facts, may be confidently accepted on Pigott's evidence, backed by hereditary connection (v. Sir M. Fetherstonhaugh in the 'First Period') and by other signs and tokens (v. Prince of Wales, with whom Sir H. Fetherston was intimate, and for whom he rode), and is he who ran third with Smart, afterwards Claret (by Bourdeaux), for the Derby in 1786, and second for the Oaks with Countess (by Count, Mr. 'Chillaby' Jennings's) in 1782.

Sir JOHN LADE, Bart., whose membership of the Jockey Club is proved by his running Adonis for a Jockey Club Plate in 1780, when he was but twenty-three years of age, is not to be confounded, of course, with his quasi-kinsman, 'Counsellor' Lade (so-called because he was bred to the law, which he neglected for the Turf, whereon he ran half-starved horses), who died in 1799. Sir John is he to whom Dr. Johnson, the lexicographer, addressed the lines 'On a Young Heir's coming of Age,' containing the sarcastic quatrain:

> Wealth, my lad, was made to wander;
> Let it wander, as it will;
> Call the *jockey*, call the pander,
> Bid them come and take their fill.

How the lexicographer came to be acquainted with such a young 'rip' is very easily made out, for young Lade's mother was sister to Henry Thrale, the Lades and the Thrales were fellow-brewers at one time in Southwark, and young Lade was 'uncle Thrale's' ward. Not that Sir John was a true Lade; for his father was an Inskip, a cousin apparently of a Sir

John Lade, Bart., a brewer (who died in 1747, when the baronetcy became extinct), and inherited the brewer's property, assumed his name, and was himself created a Baronet in 1758, died apparently the very next year, and was succeeded in title and property by Dr. Johnson's young friend. Sir John, the member of the Jockey Club, made a questionable marriage with a certain Mrs. Smith ('off the streets,' according to Pigott), died without issue (at Egham) in 1838, at the age of eighty-one, and the title again became extinct. Sir John had evidently ceased to be a member of the Jockey Club before his death, for his name is not in the official list for 1835. He was remarkable for many things: for his intimacy with the 'First Gentleman' Prince of Wales (whose famous hunter Nottingham had been his, though he did not breed the horse, and whose 'gentleman-coachman' he was); for his skill as a 'whip' (to which, no doubt, he owed his preferment as coachman to the heir to the Throne, and which is said to have been so great that he made a bet to drive the wheels of his 'coach' over a sixpence placed upon the road, and 'realised the stakes'); for his riding, whether of horse or mule (and he rode matches on both at Newmarket, once, as we have seen, on Clifden, in 1792, when he was beaten by the young Duke of Bedford on Dragon); for being the first person to appear in public in *trousers* (according to the scroll of Fame); and for winning a wager under the following amusing circumstances. He,

being a little man and a light weight, made a bet
(not of large amount, else perhaps decency would
have gone to the wall) that he would carry on his
back Lord Cholmondeley, being a big man and a
heavy weight, twice round the Steyne at Brighton,
in 1795. The story of the wager got about, and a
number of ladies assembled to see such sport. Lord
Cholmondeley with great confidence essayed to mount,
but Sir John slipped away, saying, 'Strip!' Lord
Cholmondeley turned pale, repeating, 'Strip! What
the devil do you mean?' Said Sir John, 'I betted
that I would carry *you*, not you and your clothes;
your clothes are more than 2 lb. over weight. So
make haste and strip; you are keeping the ladies
waiting.' This pointed observation was too much for
the noble lord, who was unequal to the occasion and
was compelled to acknowledge that he had lost the
wager. If it had been possible, Dr. Johnson's opinion
as to his young friend's liability to carry clothes upon
the occasion would have been worth hearing; but Sir
John had evidently cut his eye-teeth.

Sir FERDINANDO POOLE (who won Jockey Club
Plates in 1794, 1795, and 1796, with Waxy, Kerenhappuch, and Pelter, and the Derby with the illustrious Waxy, the 'ace of trumps' of the whole pack
of sires, from his time to the time of Touchstone)
came of a very ancient family in Cheshire, with seats
at Poole, Wirrall, Cheshire, and The Friary, Lewes,
Sussex, succeeded Sir Henry in the baronetcy in

1767, and was himself succeeded by the Rev. Sir Henry in 1804, with whom the title was extinguished. He was not only the owner but also the breeder of Waxy; and Waxy was one too many for Gohanna, and was the sire of 'Waxy' Pope, Whalebone, Whisker, Music, Minuet, &c.; so that Sir F. Poole did his duty as a 'Father of the Turf' to an extremely lively tune.

Sir F. STANDISH, of Duxbury, Lancashire, winner of the Derby in 1795, 1796, 1799, with Spread Eagle, Didelot, and Archduke, and of the Oaks in 1786 and 1796 with the Perdita filly (known as The Yellow Filly, by Tandem) and with Parisot (so-called after a famous she-dancer of the day, *cf.* Baccelli, Violante, &c.), was 'Frank' Standish, whose Christian name is not a diminutive of Francis, but the surname of his cousins (the Franks of Campsall, Yorks), to whom his property (as he died intestate, suddenly, of apoplexy, whilst his servant was preparing breakfast, in Lower Grosvenor Street, 1812) descended. He ran second for a Jockey Club Plate in 1786 with Lepicq, when the Duke of Grafton won with Oberon.

Sir HARRY TEMPEST VANE, otherwise Sir HARRY VANE TEMPEST, Bart., whose famous Cockfighter was beaten by Mr. F. Dawson's Quiz for a Jockey Club Plate in 1802, bears a name redolent of horse-racing from the earliest times to the present day, when it is represented on the list of the Jockey Club by Marquesses of Londonderry. Sir H. T. Vane, or Sir H. V. Tempest, was he who purchased (in 1796) Ham-

bletonian, and ran the great match with him against
Mr. Cookson's Diamond in 1799 at Newmarket; after
which Sir Harry is said to have ridden Hambletonian
in the Park, where it would create a sensation nowadays to see an Ormonde ridden by a Duke of Westminster, or a Donovan by a Duke of Portland, or any
winner of Derby or St. Leger by any member of the
Jockey Club.

Sir HEDWORTH WILLIAMSON, Bart., who was beaten
with Walton by the Duke of Grafton with Parasol for
a Jockey Club Plate in 1805, was another of the great
Northern lights of the Turf and of the Jockey Club.
He won the Derby twice—in 1803 with Ditto (by Sir
Peter) and in 1808 with Pan (by St. George). Ditto
(ridden by W. Clift) was said to have been the only
horse up to his day who had won the Derby 'in a
trot' (though, of course, it may have been done since);
and the fact was commemorated by the curious name
of Trotinda (foaled in 1822, a daughter of Zoraïda and
Ditto), which would be incomprehensible to anybody
unacquainted with the reason. Sir Hedworth's
Christian name is continued to this day among the
members of the Jockey Club in the person of Mr.
Hedworth Trelawney Barclay (descended maternally,
it is understood, from Sir Hedworth Williamson),
owner of the great handicap-horse Bendigo, so popular
with the public. The baronetcy dates from 1642, but
the only one of the Baronets to distinguish himself
greatly upon the Turf appears to have been he who

owned (and apparently bred) the own brothers Ditto and Walton (a great sire, of St. Patrick, winner of the St. Leger, and of Partisan, &c.) and their half-brother Pan; but that is enough for a single member of the Jockey Club.

Sir MARK WOOD, who received forfeit for the Jockey Club Challenge Cup both with Lucetta (by Reveller) in 1830 and with Camarine (by Juniper) in 1832, was he whose early death in 1837 was so deeply regretted by the friends of the Turf. He had been racing since 1829 only, after selling his 'estate and borough of Gatton, in Surrey, to Lord Monson for 180,000*l.*'—of which sum (such was the value of a 'borough' in the 'good old times') it is calculated that Lord Monson lost about 100,000*l.* by the passing of the Reform Bill —and removed to Hare Park, Newmarket. Sir Mark 'illustrated' both himself and the Turf by the performances of his two famous mares, already mentioned (of which Camarine was bred by the eccentric Lord Berners, and Lucetta by Mr. Stanlake Batson —neither by Sir Mark himself), a pair surpassing, perhaps, the excellence in performance of the celebrated Beeswing and Alice Hawthorne, though neither of the former produced a Newminster or a Thormanby, or even a Nunnykirk or an Oulston. Sir Mark won the Ascot Cup in 1830–31–32; the Oaks in 1833; the One Thousand in 1831; and yet his whole stud (at the sale which took place after his death), consisting of six brood-mares, seven horses in training, three two-year-olds, five yearlings, and four foals, fetched a little less than 9,000 guineas, though Camarine and Lucetta were among them. Horseflesh was comparatively cheap in those days; or there were no Colonels North and Barons Hirsch and Messrs. Blundell Maple to pour out money like water.

Of the Messieurs who can be proved to have been members of the Jockey Club, Mr. Stanlake Batson ran his bay mare Luss for a Jockey Club Plate in 1822; Mr. (or Captain) Bertie is he who ran Hugh Capet (or Caput) for a Jockey Club Plate in 1780; Mr. Bullock ran Messenger for a Jockey Club Plate in 1784; Mr. Cookson won a Jockey Club Plate in 1798, with Ambrosio; Mr. Cussans is he who ran second with Wouvermans to Lord Jersey with Cannon-Ball in 1819; Mr. Dawson is he who won a Jockey Club Plate with Coriander in 1793, and with Quiz in 1802; Mr. Delmé (afterwards D. Radclyffe) is he who ran Petruchio for the Jockey Club Plate won by the Duke of Grafton with Parasol in 1805, and was the 'double' (on the Turf) of George the Fourth and William the Fourth; Mr. Douglas is he who won a Jockey Club Plate in 1778 with Bourdeaux, and another in 1779 with Sting (both by Herod); Mr. Dutton is he who is known to have been one of the Stewards of the Jockey Club at the time of the Prince of Wales's trouble about Escape in 1791-92; Mr. Gascoyne is he who ran Thetford for a Jockey Club Plate in 1776, and is identified with Joseph Gascoyne, Esq., a 'keeper of

the Royal Stables,' but is often wrongly confused with
Mr. Gascoigne (whose original name was Oliver),
winner of the St. Leger in 1811 and 1824; Mr.
(General, or even Field-Marshal) Gower is he who
ran second with Pelisse to Mr. Lake with Nymphina
for a Jockey Club Plate in 1808; Mr. (General and
also Field-Marshal) Grosvenor is he who won a
Jockey Club Plate with Defiance in 1813; Mr. Hale,
of King's Walden, Herts, High Sheriff, uncle of Lord
Verulam, having married a Miss Grimston in 1777,
is he who ran for Jockey Club Plates with Dromedary
in 1787, and previously with Camel in 1785, and died
at a great age in 1829; Mr. Hallett is he who ran
third for a Jockey Club Plate with Stickler in 1797,
was second with Stickler for the Derby of 1796, and
second for the Oaks in 1800 with Wowski (bred, however, by Sir Ferdinando Poole), the illustrious dam of
the great Smolensko, winner of both Two Thousand
and Derby in 1813; Mr. (Colonel) Hanger is he who
ran Columbine for a Jockey Club Plate in 1776, and
was the Hon. George, youngest of three brothers
successively Earls of Coleraine; Mr. Howorth is he
who ran Vole and Plantagenet for Jockey Club Plates
in 1800 and 1806, and was confederate for a time
with the ' Phantom ' Sir John Shelley, and is believed
to be identical with the gentleman who (having the
celebrated Colonel Mellish for his second) stripped to
the ' buff' to fight a duel with the Earl of Barrymore,
lest any particle of clothes should get into any wound

that might be inflicted; Mr. Jennings is the unfortunate Mr. Henry Constantine (*alias* 'Chillaby') Jennings, who ran Count for a Jockey Club Plate in 1777, and of whom more will be said presently; Mr. Kingsman is he who ran Olive, winner of the Two Thousand for Mr. Wyndham in 1814, for a Jockey Club Plate in 1815; Mr. Lake is he in whose name Nymphina won a Jockey Club Plate in 1805, who was, apparently, Mr. Warwick Lake, Master of the Horse to the Duke of York, and third and youngest son (and third and last Viscount Lake) of the celebrated General Lake (Lord Lake, of Delhi and Laswaree), and who died in 1848, having ceased, apparently, to be a member of the Jockey Club, as his name does not appear on the list of 1835; Mr. Lamb is he who, according to Admiral Rous (very likely indeed to know), was a Steward of the Jockey Club in 1797 (*v.* 'Horse-Racing,' p. 68), and who must have been the Hon. J. Peniston Lamb (son of Lord Melbourne), M.P. for Herts from 1802 to 1805 (in which year he died), of Brocket Hall, where races were held under the auspices of the Lords Melbourne and their family; Mr. Maynard is he who ran his chestnut colt Smith for a Jockey Club Plate in 1786; Mr. Mellish is, of course, the famous Colonel Mellish, of whom and his ruin everybody has heard, and who won a Jockey Club Plate with Staveley in 1806; Mr. Neville (afterwards Lord Braybrooke in 1825, and editor of 'Pepys's Journal') is the Hon. Richard, who won a Jockey

Club Plate with his filly Ridicule in 1814, and won the tremendous match in 1816 with Sir Joshua (died in December of the same year) against Mr. Houldsworth with Filho da Puta; Mr. O'Kelly, nephew and heir of the adventurer O'Kelly, owner of Eclipse, is he who ran Cardock for a Jockey Club Plate in 1793; Mr. Parker, afterwards Lord Boringdon, is John Parker, Esq., of Boringdon and Saltram, Devon, who ran Anvil for a Jockey Club Plate in 1784, and won the Derby with Saltram (bred by him), by Eclipse, in 1783; Mr. C. Pigott (or 'Louse' Pigott) is he who ran Piccadilly, &c., in 1774, &c., for Jockey Club Plates, and of whom more will be said hereafter; Mr. (Captain and Admiral) Rous is the Hon. H. Rous, who, as everybody knows, was for many years a father to the Jockey Club and a dictator to the Turf; Mr. Rush is George Rush, Esq., who is made out to have been born 1782, died 1848, to have been of aldermanic antecedents, *par les femmes*, J.P., D.L., High Sheriff of Northamptonshire, and to have run a chestnut colt by Rubens for a Jockey Club Plate in 1823; Mr. Shakspear is Arthur Shakspear, Esq., who ran Nuncio for a Jockey Club Plate in 1810; Mr. Taylor is he who ran second with St. George (Mr. Herrick's) for a Jockey Club Plate won by Buzzard in 1794; Mr. Thornhill is the famous Master of Riddlesworth, who ran Anticipation for a Jockey Club Plate in 1817; Mr. (or Colonel) Udney is he who ran Barmecide for a Jockey Club Plate in 1822, won the Derby with Emilius in 1823, and the One Thousand and the Oaks in 1818 with Corinne, and was John Robert Fullarton Udney (born at Leghorn in 1772, died 1861), of Udney Castle and Dudwick, Aberdeen; Mr. Vansittart is he who won a Jockey Club Plate with Burleigh in 1811; Mr. (H.) Vernon is he who ran Ratoni for a Jockey Club Plate in 1774; Mr. Villiers (apparently identical with the Right Hon. J. C., who succeeded his unmarried brother as third Earl of Clarendon, and died in 1838) is he who won a Jockey Club Plate with Don Cossack in 1815; Mr. Walker is he who was fourth with Antipas for a Jockey Club Plate in 1776; Mr. Watson (the Hon. George Watson, a relative of Lord Rockingham and Mr. Peregrine Wentworth, and therefore bound to have racehorse on the brain) is he who ran St. George (Lord Darlington's) for a Jockey Club Plate in 1798; Mr. Wilson is he who was so well known and so popular as Mr. 'Kit' (Christopher) Wilson, the 'Father of the Turf' in his old age, and who won a Jockey Club Plate in 1794 with Buzzard; Mr. Wortley (the Right Hon. Stuart Wortley, who became Lord Wharncliffe in 1826 and died in 1845) is he who is known to have been a Steward of the Jockey Club in 1827, when the case of Mr. Hawkins, who had been 'warned off,' established the right of the Jockey Club to exercise their 'warning power'; and Mr. Wyndham (the Hon. C. Wyndham, brother to the Earl of Egremont, and at one time Secretary at War) is he who won a Jockey Club Plate with the celebrated Drone in 1785, and again in 1786, but is of course overshadowed among the members of the Jockey Club by his 'big brother' who 'belonged to' Gohanna.

Having thus established their membership of the Jockey Club in the case of all these gentlemen, we may proceed to say a little more about some of them.

Let us single out Messrs. Charles Pigott and Constantine Jennings, because both, though in different ways, were 'shocking examples' of the Jockey Club; because both belonged rather, perhaps, to the 'First Period' than to the 'Second Period,' though proofs of their membership are found in the latter; and because they were evidently acquaintances as well as fellows in misfortune.

Mr. Charles Pigott is the poor gentleman whose decease was announced in a public paper after the following fashion in 1794: 'On the 27th of May, Charles Pigott, Esq., commonly called "Louse" Pigott. . . . Interred in the family vault, Chetwynd, Shropshire.' Old Mr. Robert Pigott (whose life, as we have seen, was made the subject of a disputed bet, which was decided in a court of law by no less an authority than the great Lord Mansfield), of Chetwynd Park, Salop, and Chesterton Hall, Hunts, left three sons (and four daughters), the Robert Pigott already dealt with in the 'First Period,' the Charles Pigott with whom we are engaged at present, and William Pigott (the Reverend, who held the living of Chetwynd); and, according to a writer in the 'Sporting Magazine,' as has already been mentioned, they were known respectively as 'Shark' Pigott, 'Louse' Pigott, and 'Black' Pigott. But there is some reason to doubt the accuracy of the writer quoted; for the great racehorse Shark, distinctly stated by Pick to have been bred and to have been run by Mr. *Charles* Pigott (and we have seen that Mr. *Robert* Pigott's stud was sold in 1772), did not run till 1774, and Lord Carlisle, writing to George Selwyn in 1772, says: 'Nothing will surprise me about Lord H.; not if he were to come upon the Turf and be a confederate with *Black* Pigott.' Unless, then, we are to understand that the Rev. William Pigott was, like his brother, on the Turf (not by any means an impossibility, but his name never appears in the records), and that the epithet 'Black' is in honour of 'the cloth,' it is more natural to suppose that 'Shark' Pigott, 'Louse' Pigott, and 'Black' Pigott (the epithet applying figuratively either to character or looks), are but one and the same person. Anyhow, there is no doubt that Mr. Charles Pigott and 'Louse' Pigott are one and the same person. Nor is it quite certain that 'Louse' was a nickname conferred upon him for some reason derogatory to him; on the contrary, there is authority for saying that it stuck to him in consequence of a creditable proficiency in the French language, which enabled him, when a boy at Eton, to turn 'pou' into the equivalent English. And it is quite clear from the works which he published, called 'The Jockey Club' and a 'Political Dictionary,' that he was a man of considerable education and even scholarship, that he was for awhile the social equal of such men as the Hon. and Rt. Hon. C. J. Fox, and that, scurrilous as his works were (so scurrilous that the printer was imprisoned in 1793), he knew what he was talking about and was quite right in the main about the noblemen and gentlemen whom he libelled. He was a great gentleman-jockey (as well as an owner of numerous good racehorses), having ridden and won races against Sir John Lade, Mr. Walker, and other 'crack' riders among the members of the Jockey Club. That he lost his fortune on the Turf (though he won upwards of 16,000 guineas with Shark alone, the great horse that was imported into Virginia and died there) is lamentably true; that he had to withdraw from the Jockey Club appears to be certain; that he was scouted and 'cut' by its members cannot be doubted; that he went swiftly down the easy road to Avernus is as plain as large print; and he was ultimately charged with uttering seditious language, fell into debt apparently, was confined in the Sumpter Prison in 1793, and was only released from his troubles by death in the following year. He seems to have married a sister of Sir Charles Cope, of Brewerne, Oxon, and certainly to have belonged to the same class as those persons whom he scurrilously attacked, and better than whom he probably was not. That he possessed a certain sardonic humour may be gathered from his 'Political Dictionary,' wherein he defines 'half seas over' as 'the most respectable state of sobriety among princes and ministers,' and 'Nethermost Hell' as 'the country-seats of Loughborough, Dundas, Pitt, and the whole crew of rascals round the throne,' and tells us that 'Grace, when in conversation applied to a Duke, means nothing: thus "His Grace the Duke of Leeds" has absolutely no signification,' or that 'honour in high-life means the debauching your neighbour's wife or daughter, killing your man, and being a member of the Jockey Club and Brookes's gaming-house.' That his 'colours' in racing should have been 'yellow shot with red' was appropriate enough in the case of a gentleman gifted with so lurid a humour; but the history of the age assures us that his remarks may be taken without any very large admixture of salt.

Mr. Jennings (of whom 'Louse' Pigott naturally speaks with sympathetic respect) was Henry Constantine Jennings, of Shiplake, Oxon, a gentleman of good estate and illustrious descent, having 'Royal blood in his veins' (from George, Duke of Clarence, *par les femmes*, through the beheaded Countess of Salisbury, it is said). He was born in 1731, and died ('within the Rules of the King's Bench') in 1819, so that his life, whatever may be said of his fortune, cannot have been very much abridged by his career upon the Turf, to which he does not seem to have taken until he was at least forty years of age. He is generally supposed to have been ruined by his late-developed 'horseyness,' and he has been regarded as one of the 'victims' of 'Old Q.'; but we have seen already that he himself bore witness to the perfect honour, though undoubted superiority as a 'jockey,' of his friend 'Queensberry.' Mr. Jennings was known as 'Dog' Jennings, a name which he did not at all like; as 'Alcibiades' Jennings, a name which was very agreeable to him; and as 'Chillaby' Jennings, a name which, recalling the failure of his pet 'Arab,' called Chillaby, cannot have been so much to his taste. He was a celebrated 'virtuoso,' and two of his names he owed to an achievement of his in that capacity, when he purchased a tailless dog (in marble or stone of some kind), which was considered by high authorities to be a veritable genuine effigy of the historical 'Dog of Alcibiades,' and which, because it was so considered, fetched as much as a thousand guineas, in 1778, at one of the many sales forced upon poor Mr. Jennings, not less, perhaps, from his recklessness as a 'virtuoso' than from his inexperience as a horse-racer and 'jockey.' His third nickname he owed to his unfortunate belief in a reputed 'Arabian' purchased by him and called Chillaby (perhaps after King William the Third's white Barb, Chillaby), but commonly known as 'The mad Arabian.' For this animal Mr. Jennings took some eighty acres of ground in

Essex, introduced to him certain brood-mares, and matched their future produce for large sums of money against the produce to be brought to the post by such astute breeders and judges as ' Old Q.,' the first Earl Grosvenor, and perhaps even ' Louse ' Pigott himself. To his own lack of knowledge and judgment (as he himself seems to have suspected and to have confessed at last), rather than to the villainy which ' Louse' Pigott has hinted at, Mr. Jennings seems to have owed his ruin (so far as the Turf was concerned); for the produce of Chillaby (the sire that he stuck to through thick and thin), when they came to be sold under the hammer, are said to have realised about a guinea and a half apiece. That they were not all quite worthless, however, is proved by the case of Mr. T. Douglas's Emetic (by Chillaby), winner of several races in 1780-82, including the 1,200 guineas Subscription at Newmarket. Mr. Jennings, nevertheless, had some considerable successes with animals of whose existence Chillaby was perfectly innocent. Chillaby's madness was such, it is said, that he would rush at ' scarecrows ' in a field and tear them limb from limb, under the impression that they were live men. He came at last into the hands of a Mr. Hughes, who kept a circus in St. George's Fields, and who, having tamed the horse to some noticeable extent, exhibited him to a gaping public. It was during this period that an incident occurred illustrative of the dread in which ' The mad Arabian ' was held. In the absence of

Hughes from his place in St. George's Fields, a friend, to whom he was in the habit of lending horses to ride, called to beg for a mount, and, the master being away, took the first that came, a horse which went very well to Croydon and back, only just once walking, tail first, into a public-house on the road, but displaying no other eccentricity. On arriving at the circus, however, the rider encountered Mr. Hughes, who had returned home, and who greeted him with a horror-stricken face and a cry of 'My God! you've been out on Chillaby!' which is said to have so affected the friend that he had to be put to bed and supplied with 'strong waters' before he could be brought round. Yet even Chillaby, like so many 'savages,' had his gentle friend, in the shape of a 'lamb which would butt flies off the horse's shoulder,' and which the horse would not attempt to injure. It is curious that neither in the old nor in the new edition of the first (or any other) volume of the 'Stud Book' is this Chillaby discriminated from King William the Third's, though progeny of his (not including Emetic, so that he may have been half-bred, notwithstanding the statement of his parentage, Chillaby and a Herod mare, ? h. b., in the 'Calendar') is registered (for instance, Viscount, *alias* Young Chillaby) in the 'Stud Book,' which ought not to be if Chillaby were regarded as no genuine Arabian.

Mr. Batson deserves further mention as the gentleman who last challenged for the Eclipse Foot, and, his challenge being unaccepted, had the trophy handed over to him (to be transferred eventually to the Jockey Club), and whose horse Plenipotentiary created so great and painful a sensation by winning the Derby in a canter and being 'nowhere' for the St. Leger, though the easy explanation (if any were needed in the case of so honourable a gentleman) has since been given, that the horse met with an accident (of which even his owner knew nothing till long afterwards) on his way to Doncaster. Mr. 'Tom' Bullock is, of course, the plebeian member who (according to Pigott) outfisticuffed the redoubtable Colonel Hanger at the Jockey Club Rooms at Newmarket, and from whom the Americans obtained Messenger (foaled 1780, by Mambrino), their famous 'Father of Trotters.' Mr. Cookson (who had a share in a bank at Newcastle, and was at one time an officer of the Guards) was Mr. James Cookson, a great 'Northern light,' winner of the Derby with Sir Harry in 1798 and of the St. Leger with Ambrosio in 1796, and is notable as one of the few members of the Jockey Club who have been publicly stated ' by strict attention to business on the Turf to have won a large fortune.' Mr. (Thomas) Douglas, of Grantham, Lincolnshire, won the Oaks with Tetotum in 1780, and appears to have died (at a comparatively early age) on December 22, 1787, and to have been a brother of the Rev. Mr. Douglas who was chaplain to the Prince of Wales (George the Fourth), and who was an author of some repute, of 'Naenia Britannica,' &c. Mr. (Ralph) Dutton is remarkable as one of the few members of the Jockey Club whom 'Louse' Pigott deals gently with, and the gentle treatment is quite in accordance with the quotation, 'Honor virtutis præmia,' which was addressed to him on the occasion of his marriage in 1806 to Miss 'Honor' Gubbins. He was a younger brother of the first Lord Sherborne, and was confederate for a time with his other brother William (who reassumed the name of Naper), and also at one time (as has been mentioned) with the young Duke of Bedford (twenty-one years of age in 1786), whose Skyscraper he nominated for the Derby of 1789. Mr. (that is, General or Field-Marshal Leveson) Gower, whose name recalls the celebrated Gower stallion (which belonged to his family), distinguished himself upon the Turf by winning the Oaks with Maid of Orleans in 1809 and with Landscape in 1816, as well as the Ascot Cup in 1809 with Anderida. Mr. (General and Field-Marshal) Grosvenor is notable for winning the Oaks with Briseis in 1807 and in 1825 with Wings (purchased in 1837 by M. A. Lupin, the now venerable *doyen* of the French Jockey Club and the French Turf), but still more interesting as the breeder of Copenhagen, the horse that was ridden by the Duke of Wellington at the Battle of Waterloo, and, at the end of the day, was so fresh as nearly to kick the Duke's brains out and turn the victory into mourning. By the way, Copenhagen, though he is in the 'Stud Book' (where the flaw in his pedigree is pointed out), though he ran and won several races (some at two years of age), and though his statue (which was not taken from him at all) opposite Apsley House has been pointed out to 'a young man from the country' by an equally ignorant *cicerone*, cockney-born, as that of a horse that 'won the Derby,' was not thoroughbred (though it is often asserted that he was), but was the son of Lady Catherine (herself ridden by General Grosvenor 'in the wars'), daughter of the Rutland Arabian and of 'a hunting-mare not thoroughbred.' As for Mr. (Colonel) George Hanger, he was a very strange character, not only an owner, breeder, runner, and rider of racehorses, a bruiser, and a bully (with a club, which he playfully christened 'The Infant'), a 'hanger'-on of the Prince of Wales (so long as His Royal Highness affected Newmarket), and in his advanced years an Earl of Coleraine, but also a literary gentleman, who is believed to have been the author of 'Military Observations on the Attack and Defence of London,' and is understood to have written and published in two volumes his own 'Memoirs,' with a frontispiece representing himself *sus. per coll.*, in sardonic allusion, it is supposed, rather to the family name than to the fate which he contemplated for himself. Mr. Maynard (who no doubt belonged to the family whereof a certain Lord Maynard is said to have married the notorious Nancy Parsons, *alias*

Mrs. Horton) synchronises and is apparently identical with the Mr. Maynard who won the cruel match at York Spring Meeting, 1788, against the celebrated Mr. Baker, of Elemore Hall, with his bay mare against a grey horse, one mile, *thirty stone* each (owners up, apparently), when it was '2 to 1 *on* the horse,' and the 'bay' mare proved the better. Mr. O'Kelly is very remarkable as the nephew whom the adventurer Denis O'Kelly (owner of the famous Eclipse) made his heir, with the express stipulation (*cf.* the case of the fifth Earl of Chesterfield and his godson the sixth, to whom the 'Letters' were written) that he should forfeit vast sums if he took to the Turf, and who, nevertheless, managed to evade the forfeits, owned, bred, ran, and rode race-horses, and was—what his uncle could never manage to become—a member of the Jockey Club. Whether old O'Kelly 'got religion' at the end of his life is not stated; but his nearest approach to it during his active career appears to have been that he kept a wonderful parrot which whistled the 104th Psalm, the only religious service old O'Kelly is known to have countenanced. As for Mr. Mellish (the celebrated Colonel), whose name should have preceded that of Mr. O'Kelly, junior (who, by the way, unlike his uncle, won none of the 'classic' races), he 'illustrated' the Jockey Club not only as a good soldier (being commended in despatches by the Duke of Wellington himself), but as a racer, for he won the St. Leger with

Sancho and Staveley in 1804 and 1805, and, in fact, was so good a judge of horses and horse-racing that, it was said (as was said of the unfortunate young Marquess of Hastings, another member of the Jockey Club in after times), he might have retrieved his heavy losses on the Turf and kept his property intact if only he could have 'kept his elbow still' and avoided the 'bones.' He was a gallant gentleman, but scarcely a 'model' member of the Jockey Club. Mr. Parker (afterwards Lord Boringdon, founder of the Earls of Morley) was a very notable member of the Jockey Club, not only for his intimacy with the Prince of Wales (whom he supplied—not *gratis*—with Anvil and other horses), but also as winner of the Derby with Saltram (by Eclipse) in 1783, and of the 'Whip' with Anvil in 1784, and as owner of the famous brood-mare Virago (dam of Saltram), and of a 'Parker' or 'Boringdon' Arabian. Saltram, by the way, was imported into the United States in 1800 by Mr. Lightfoot, of Virginia. Mr. Parker was M.P. for many years before he became Lord Boringdon and versed in Parliamentary matters; but it was his successor, the second Lord Boringdon, who advocated a Compulsory Vaccination Act in 1813–14, and was so far in advance of his age. The name of Shakspear is, of course, very tempting, but our Mr. Shakspear, the member of the Jockey Club, was Arthur, not William, and though he bought Lord Egremont's Cardinal Beaufort, winner of the Derby in 1805, did not himself win any 'classic' race or leave upon the history of the Jockey Club and of the Turf anything like the impression which his namesake William has left upon the history of literature. Mr. Thornhill is a very noteworthy member of the Jockey Club. He was the famous Master of Riddlesworth (the name of his estate in Norfolk, from which the once very fashionable Riddlesworth Stakes at Newmarket received its designation, and also the horse Riddlesworth, that was so strong a favourite for the Derby in 1831, but was beaten by the rank outsider Spaniel), who won the Derby with Sam on May 28, 1818, which was the anniversary of Sam's birth, and with Sailor (died at exercise in the autumn of the year) in 1820, and 'sandwiched in,' as it was said, an Oaks with Shoveler (own sister to Sailor) on May 28, 1819, all three winners bred by him and by the same sire, called Scud (by Beningbrough), so that when Sailor won the Derby in a hurricane it was considered to be mighty appropriate. Mr. Thornhill also won the Ascot Cup with Anticipation in 1816, and the One Thousand with Extempore in 1843, ran a dead-heat with Euclid (beaten by Charles the Twelfth in a decider) for the St. Leger in 1839, and was himself beaten in a match by Death in 1844, when he was found to have bequeathed, it is said, to his favourite jockey, Sam Chifney, junior, the hero of the 'rush' (after whom the horse Sam was named), his Newmarket house and stables 'for life,' though the jockey left them altogether in 1851 for Hove, near Brighton, where he died, aged sixty-eight, in 1854. Mr. Thornhill's yellow phaeton was one of the sights of Newmarket towards the end of his life, but at the date of Sam, Shoveler, and Sailor, when he was about forty years old, he rode on horseback regularly on the Heath, though he weighed the Daniel-Lambert-like weight of more than 23 stone, having been fortunate enough to fall in with a Mr. Dobito, a sporting farmer in Suffolk, who, bearing an avoirdupois similarity to Mr. Thornhill, had given his mind to the breeding and training of roadsters up to that weight. Mr. H. Vansittart (belonging to the family of Shottesbrook and Foot's Cray) is notable as having married in 1812 Teresa, widow of the famous young Northern racer Sir Charles Turner (once owner of Beningbrough, Hambletonian, and Oberon), whereby he became Mr. Vansittart of Kirkleatham, York, J.P., D.L., and High Sheriff, and as having 'split' Mr. Ridsdale's St. Giles (an easy winner) and Trustee (third) with Perion for the Derby of 1832. He died in 1848, and is therefore, naturally, on the official list of members of the Jockey Club in 1835. Mr. (Henry) Vernon, of Hilton Park, near Wolverhampton, has claims to special mention, as regards the Turf, because he was nephew of the memorable Mr. 'Jockey' Vernon, the oracle of Newmarket, and, as regards matters in general, because he was the gentleman who made a voyage to the Crimea (or travelled in the

Crimea) in company with the notorious Margravine of Anspach (ex-Lady Craven), and is understood to have published an account of his travels, as also did Her Highness (for whom Horace Walpole was 'printer in ordinary' at Strawberry Hill). Mr. Walker is entitled to further notice because he is supposed to be identical with the Thomas Walker, Esq., of Mickleham, Surrey, who in August 1773 rode a cruel match for 400 guineas from London to York on his hackney (said to have died within six miles of Tadcaster) against a Captain Mulcaster on his mare (which drank twelve bottles of wine on the road, finished the task, and was quite well after two days' rest), when the first ninety miles were ridden in six hours, and when, after the match was over, some severe strictures were made in the papers of the day on the cruelty and uselessness of such performances (unless, of course, you are a Dick Turpin riding your Black Bess for life, liberty, and a place in fiction); and because he was probably a son or nephew of the 'old Tom Walker' at whom Horace Walpole sneers in his 'Letters' (1748) as 'a surveyor of roads, a kind of toad-eater to Sir Robert Walpole and Lord Godolphin, a great frequenter of Newmarket' (not unnaturally, as there is mention made in the 'State Papers' of a 'Thomas Walker, housekeeper of Her Majesty's house at Newmarket'), 'and a notorious usurer' (as other 'horsey' gentlemen have been, like the late Mr. Padwick, who, according to Admiral Rous, played 'spider' to the 'fly' played by the last Marquess of Hastings). Mr. (the Hon. George) Watson, a relation of Lord Rockingham, Lord Fitzwilliam, and Mr. Peregrine Wentworth, was notable on the Turf and as a member of the Jockey Club for winning the One Thousand and the Oaks in 1817 with Neva (by Cervantes). Mr. (Christopher) Wilson (who is said to have been a son of Christopher Wilson, Bishop of Bristol) was one of the most notable and popular members of the Jockey Club in his own day or in any other, and he is the more entitled to special attention because there were, besides himself, at least three other Wilsons on the Turf at the same time with him (namely, Mr. Richard Wilson of the Bildeston Stud Farm, Suffolk, who had been bailiff to the Duke of Northumberland, had a legacy of 40,000l. left him by Lord Chedworth, had little or no success upon the Turf, and died in 1835, aged seventy-four; Major and Colonel Robert Wilson, better known as the eccentric Lord Berners, who won the Derby with Phosphorus 'on three legs' in 1837, and died the next year at the age of seventy-six; and Mr. William Wilson, the original owner of Duchess of Lieven, afterwards simply Duchess, winner of the St. Leger in 1816 for Sir Bellingham Graham; but none of these three—not even Lord Berners—seems to have been a member of the Jockey Club). Mr. Christopher Wilson belonged both to the North (where he dispensed a good old English hospitality at Oxton Hall, near Tadcaster, or Ledstone Hall, or elsewhere) and to the South (where he died at 'Christie's' in St. James's Street, aged seventy-eight, on the Derby Day—singularly enough—May 25, 1842); and on the Turf it was his distinction to be the first person to win both Derby and St. Leger with the same horse (Champion, by Pot8os), and to be the winner both of the first Two Thousand (with Wizard, by Sorcerer) in 1809, and of the first One Thousand (with Charlotte, by Orville) in 1814. Enough distinction for any member of the Jockey Club, and not dissimilar to Sir Charles Bunbury's with Diomed, Eleanor, and Smolensko. To Mr. (the Hon. Charles) Wyndham's credit must be placed the Two Thousand, won in 1814 by Olive (a bay colt by Sir Oliver, and bred by Lord Egremont), and the Ascot Cup won in 1826 by Château-Margaux (bred also by Lord Egremont, by Whalebone).

Having now disposed of what may be called the personal question, we will proceed in a fresh chapter to get a bird's-eye view of what the Club in its corporate capacity had done for the Turf in general and for itself in particular during the 'Second Period,' from 1773 to 1835.

CHAPTER X

A BIRD'S-EYE VIEW

BY 1773, as we have seen, the Jockey Club had their own organ (the 'Calendar') played by their own organist (Mr. James Weatherby), of whom, being under their authority as the holder of several offices in their gift, they were in a position to demand any tune they pleased. He would in all probability take his cue from the Stewards, and insert or exclude whatever they thought it best for their purposes that the 'Calendar' should admit or omit. But before they could make it the vehicle for the promulgation of their views and the instrument for the enforcement of their will over the whole area of the Turf in Great Britain, they had to strengthen the weak proprietary rights which belonged to them at Newmarket.

This, whether they had any clear idea of what they were about, and were carrying out a preconceived and well-laid plan, or merely acted haphazard and lived from hand to mouth, as it were, taking advantage of unforeseen chances, they did in the following manner.

It has been mentioned that in 1771 Mr. Richard Vernon, the oracle of Newmarket and of the Jockey Club, had purchased (for a term of sixty years) the lease of the ground on which the Coffee Room was built and of that on which the New Rooms were erected subsequently, and that in the same year the Stewards and as many members of the Club as chose to subscribe became Mr. Vernon's tenants, under an agreement to pay him an annual rent; he for his part having entered into a compact to build rooms for the Club. In 1831, of course, Mr. Vernon's lease expired, and the freehold of the lots comprising the Coffee Room, the New Rooms, and adjuncts thereof, was purchased (with money advanced, it is said, by the 'Tiresias' Duke of Portland, father of Lord G. Bentinck) of the Erratts (a well-known Newmarket family of stablemen, grooms, jockeys, trainers, and the like), and the estate was conveyed (in trust) to Lord Lowther, the Duke of Richmond, and the Earl of Verulam, who were presumably the Stewards for the time being.

Meanwhile the Inclosure Acts of George II., whereby, it has been calculated, 'ten thousand square miles of untilled land were added under their operation to the area of cultivation,' enabled the Club to acquire certain portions of Newmarket Heath. The Acts which particularly concerned the Club were the Swaffham Bulbeck Act of 1798, 'for allotting, draining, &c., waste lands, &c., in the Parish of Swaffham

Bulbeck (wherein are certain Heath Grounds, which form a part of Newmarket Race Ground, commonly called the Beacon Course and Round Course),' and the Swaffham Prior Inclosure Act, wherein mention is made of John Peter Allix, Esq. (of Swaffham House, Cambridgeshire, and a descendant of the celebrated Dr. Peter Allix, a French ecclesiastical refugee in this country), who is described as being ' seised of divers lands in Swaffham Prior'; and on both occasions when the Acts were passed, as well as when the Exning Inclosure Act of 1807 was passed, the Club (whose members included, as we have seen, many influential hereditary and elective legislators) no doubt was instrumental in taking care that conditions were inserted which provided that certain portions of the lands 'and a space of fifty yards at least in breadth on either side of the course be preserved for ever for racing.' The Club, then, between 1805 and 1808, bought of the aforesaid Mr. J. P. Allix, or his immediate successor, certain of the aforesaid lands of which he was ' seised '; other adjacent lands in 1808 of a Mr. Salisbury Dunn and a Mr. C. Pemberton; and by 1819, partly by buying up Crown property and partly by exchanging bits of land with the representatives of Pembroke College, Cambridge, became practically masters of Newmarket Heath, as proprietors of nearly all the Beacon Course (of which the other courses are but subdivisions or embranchments), upwards of four miles in extent. Further purchases, whether of lease or freehold, the Club has made since: of the exercise-grounds known as the Bury Hill, the Warren Hill, the Limekilns, where there is now a straight gallop of two miles, and the winter-ground, with what is considered to be the finest 'tan gallop' in the world, dwarfing to insignificance that which was laid down in the North by the famous Mr. John Bowes, of Streatlam, and his trainer, John Scott, of Whitewall; and lastly, in 1882, when the Exning estate, lying close to 'The Flat' from end to end, was for sale, the Club was constrained to purchase it lest speculative builders should erect upon it houses which, overlooking the Heath, might be used as 'stands' at race-time and as 'tout-nests' on other days. The outlay, says Lord Suffolk and Berkshire, was so great as to necessitate a mortgage on the whole property; but there were hopes that great gain rather than some loss might result after all, if that part of the estate from which neither race nor trial can be seen, and which borders upon the growing town of Newmarket and the village of Exning, should be utilised for building purposes and the rest for 'gallops.' The foreshadowed sale took place on June 30, 1891, when not all the lots found purchasers at a price beyond the reserve; but most of them were sold, the principal purchasers being Lord Durham, Captain E. W. Baird, and Mr. Hewes, at bids which may or may not have come up to expectation. Perhaps not, as sixteen lots, including Exning House and Park, went to Captain Baird for 32,000*l.*

It may here conveniently be observed that neither Messrs. Bowes nor John Scott (the former as owner and the latter as trainer) with their tan gallop of more than a mile at Langton Wold, nor the Jockey Club with theirs, still finer, at Newmarket, can lay claim to that useful invention which was due, it is stated on excellent authority, to Mr. John Whyte, the originator of the short-lived Hippodrome (in 1837), Bayswater, whom everybody tried to dissuade from the use of tan, on the ground that it would 'entirely destroy the grass.' He, however, tried it first of all over a small portion of his Hippodrome, and found that it not only 'formed an elastic carpet' which saved the horses' legs from jarring, but actually 'promoted the growth of the grass.' So much for English prejudice, which is nearly always dead against any new thing; whereas Americans try a novelty first and object to it (if it fails) afterwards.

Let us now proceed to inquire how the Jockey Club, first with nothing but its organ (played by Mr. James Weatherby) and its social prestige to sustain its authority, and then with proprietary claims over the principal portions of Newmarket Heath to give it rights which would be enforced by law, entered upon that course of progressive domination which has culminated in undisputed autocracy; what were the chief rules and regulations which it passed for observance at Newmarket only (as was expressly stated from time to time in a sort of deprecatory spirit), and what were the main innovations which it encouraged.

As regards innovations, to begin with, the Club is found to have sanctioned the racing of yearlings as early as 1786, in which year (though, as it happened, no yearling ran in the race) there was announced a 'Subscription Plate of 50 Guineas; yearlings a feather, &c.,' at Newmarket Craven Meeting; and by 1792 yearling races were in full swing under the auspices of the Jockey Club at Newmarket. Indeed, in 1788 there was a regular 'Yearling Course (being the first third of R.M.),' and thereon Mr. 'Jockey' Vernon ran (but at an off-meeting in March) his bay colt Ventilator, one year old, against two-year-olds belonging to two other members of the Jockey Club (Mr. Panton and Lord Clermont). From that time the mischievous practice (as it is generally acknowledged to be) continued at Newmarket and was adopted all over the country until 1859, when Lord Stamford (a member of the Jockey Club) and Mr. W. Day (eminent among jockeys and trainers) ran first and second for the Anglesey Stakes 'for yearlings' at Shrewsbury, after which the Jockey Club, repenting of its sanction, stepped in and prohibited the running of yearlings for *public* stakes, though it was not until 1876 that 'yearlings shall not run for any race' was inserted among the Rules of Racing.

The next innovation was an attempt (in 1792-93)

to put a stop to the detestable practice of 'crossing and jostling,' by resolving, 'That when any match is made in which crossing and jostling are not mentioned, they shall be understood to be barred'—a rule which, commendable as it is, shows that the practice had been customary before; and it was very dear to the heart of Mr. Denis O'Kelly (owner of Eclipse), who, having negotiated for a match with a noble lord, and having been unable to come to terms, observed, with tears in his eyes: 'Be Jasus, me dear, had it been cross and jostle, I'd a brought a spalpeen from Newmarket that should dhrive his lordship's horse into the bushes and keep him there for a fortnight.'

The next innovation, whether introduced into the 'Calendar' by the Jockey Club at the suggestion of Mr. James Weatherby or by Mr. James Weatherby on the suggestion of the Stewards or some influential member of the Jockey Club, was a master-stroke of policy, eminently calculated to spread the authority and prestige of the Club all over the country, wherever a copy of the 'Calendar' was accessible; this was the publication of 'Adjudged Cases,' with a notification that 'with a view to promote the uniformity of decisions, as well as to prevent the trouble of application to the Stewards of the Jockey Club, on points already decided, we intend, with the consent of the Stewards, to publish occasionally such adjudged cases as may be useful as precedents.' We have seen that from the first the Jockey Club had included the stars of the Northern as well as of the Southern Turf, and such a step as that just mentioned could scarcely fail to find favour both in the North and in the South, and augment the influence of the Club in both regions.

But the most important innovation is that of 1833, which effected, so far as the breeding of race-horses is concerned, a complete revolution. For on April 25 in that year it was decreed by the Club that ' from and after the end of the year 1833 horses shall be considered *at Newmarket* as taking their ages from January 1 instead of May 1. With respect to other places, they will be considered as taking their ages from May 1 until the Stewards of those races shall order otherwise.' It is noteworthy that this Resolution, though expressly said to apply to Newmarket only, is prefixed not to the ' Rules and Orders of the Jockey Club,' but to the ' Rules concerning Horse-racing in General,' as if it were a *ballon d'essai* in the direction of universal legislation; that by the year 1851 the exception relating to ' other places ' had been omitted, and that in the new list of Rules in 1857 that which had been a complete innovation in 1833 was incorporated, probably after consultation with the Stewards of the various meetings outside Newmarket, or on account of the general acceptance of the novelty, and made the very first ordinance without a word about Newmarket or any exceptive clause. That innovation, no doubt, was a salutary one in many respects, especially because it put a stop to the confusion caused by a sudden change of age in the very middle of the racing season; but as regards the physiological question, it is worthy of notice that so experienced a breeder and trainer as Mr. John Porter of Kingsclere has lately advocated a certain amount of retrogression towards the old practice, and that in the year 1869 Lord George Manners (a member of the Jockey Club) proposed to have the rule so far altered that two-year-olds should be considered to take their age from May 1. There is no doubt that January 1 is a very inconvenient date for breeders in Australia (where horses take their age from August 1) who wish to compete for our great weight-for-age races, but whether May 1 would suit them any better is very questionable indeed. What is said about May as the natural month for foaling may be all very true; but it has been urged on the other hand, not without point, that the modern thoroughbred intended for racing is a wholly, or almost wholly, artificial product, and less adapted for natural than for artificial processes and unseasonabilities.

With the Rules of Horse-racing in General the Jockey Club apparently did not trouble themselves at all until, in 1797, all on a sudden, Mr. Weatherby printed in his 'Calendar' the Rules 'taken (with some few alterations) from "Pond's Racing Calendar" for the year 1751' (a literal copy of which will be found in the Appendix). We gather from what Admiral

Rous says in his 'Horse-Racing' (edition of 1866, pp. 67–68), that this was done at the suggestion of Sir Charles Bunbury, who, according to the Admiral, to sanction a decision given by a Committee of the Jockey Club in his (Sir Charles's) favour, but 'protested against by the Stewards of the Club,' 'introduced' a certain Rule. But the fact is that the Rule, as given by Admiral Rous, runs thus: 'If a horse wins the first heat, and all others draw, they are not distanced, if he starts no more; but, if he starts again by himself, the drawn horses are distanced.' Now, without entering into the bearing of this Rule upon Sir C. Bunbury's case or into the case itself, it is sufficient to remark that the reader will find the Rule, just as it is quoted by Admiral Rous, in 'Pond' (in the Appendix), and that all that Sir Charles and the Committee seem to have done, on the Admiral's own showing, is to have stuck by the old and accepted Rule. The Admiral goes on to say that 'in 1803, being ashamed of their proceedings, the Jockey Club expunged this *order* [as if it had been something of their own], and virtually condemned the decision which the general meeting of the Jockey Club had confirmed.' Certainly the Admiral, if anybody, should have known what he was talking about, and should have been able to consult the archives of the Club, and certainly the said Rule is expunged after 1803, but, oddly enough, there is nothing to be found in Weatherby's book 'Calendar' about a '**Commit**tee of the Jockey Club' (though 'a

Committee' is said there to have decided in favour of Sir Charles Bunbury, which need not have been a Committee of the Jockey Club, for the case seems to have been decided on the spot at a provincial race-meeting), nor, either in Weatherby or in other records which have been consulted, is there a word about any protest, and we have seen that the Rule stands in 'Pond.' Nor is anything said about the matter in the 'Adjudged Cases'; so that, if Admiral Rous is correct (which he certainly ought to be), there is in 'Weatherby' a very culpable omission of what undoubtedly ought to have been made known to the public; such an omission of information, interesting and of importance to the public, as has given rise in these latter days to a complaint that the proceedings of the Club are not made so fully known as they should be.

However, the main point established is that the Jockey Club first took cognisance (in the 'Calendar') of General Rules of Racing in 1797, and first made its own version of them in 1803 by expunging one which had stood since the days of 'Pond' (1751). After this the Club published their own version of those Rules pretty regularly, changing here a little and there a little, from 1803 to 1833; and then, in 1857, having found themselves securely seated in the saddle, they appointed a Committee which framed what Sam Weller would have called a 'reg'lar new fit out o' Rules,' that came into operation in 1858, another in 1876, and yet another—the present elaborate and voluminous 'fit out'—in 1890. Their own 'Rules and Orders' for home use—that is, applicable to Newmarket only—have been published in a collected body, almost annually, since the dynasty of Weatherby began to rule over the 'Calendar,' with an occasional 'new fit out' beginning from 1828, and repeated in 1858, 1876, and 1890. The most important alteration, as regards the public, in these latter was when in 1842 it was announced that ' the Jockey Club and the Stewards thereof will henceforth take no cognisance of any dispute or claims in respect to bets.' This, of course, saved them a great deal of trouble and unpleasantness, which was transferred to the Committees of Tattersall's and of the Subscription Rooms at Newmarket (the Committees, however, consisting largely of members of the Jockey Club); but it does not at all mean, as it is often represented to mean, that the Club 'ignores betting': it only means that the Club waits for an official report from the Committee of Tattersall's or of the Subscription Rooms at Newmarket before proceeding against defaulters for bets, thus shirking the painful duty of taking the initiative against such members of the Club or of the Rooms as (like Lord Foley in the very old times and the Marquess of Hastings more recently) may be notoriously in default, but, for some reason or other, may not be reported by the aforesaid Committees. Up to 1842, however, it is not too much to say that questions having something to do with betting were those which chiefly occupied the Club's attention.

We may now consider some of the immediate consequences of the proprietorship which the Jockey Club had acquired by 1819 in certain portions of the Heath. In July of that very year it was 'Resolved that . . . one guinea annually shall be paid in respect of every racehorse that shall be trained and exercised or shall run any private trial, &c., &c.'; and ever since that date, to listen to the jeremiads of trainers and owners (who, of course, have to pay the piper ultimately), what with a fine for this and a fee for that, the Jockey Club has come to be regarded as the horse-leech's two daughters, whose constant cry was 'Give! Give!'

In 1821 comes the first instance recorded in the book 'Calendar' of a 'warning off,' when a poor devil of a 'tout,' whose name was William Taylor, *alias* Snipe (his nickname, no doubt), was 'warned by notice from Mr. Weatherby to keep off the Heath grounds occupied by tenants of the Jockey Club,' for the heinous offence of 'watching a trial with a telescope,' and for 'refusing to say who his employers were.' Apparently Mr. Snipe did not show fight— that is, did not withstand the Jockey Club, and render an appeal to the law necessary; but in 1827, when a decision of the Stewards of the Jockey Club in the case of a disputed bet (a sort of business which, as

s

we have seen, the Club very judiciously, if a little selfishly, declined for the future in 1842) had given offence to a Mr. Hawkins (one of the parties to the dispute), and caused him (as so often happens) to find balm for his wounded feelings in heaping violent abuse upon Lord Wharncliffe (Mr. Stuart-Wortley), and to get 'warned off the course' for his pains, the 'warned off' person was recalcitrant, causing the action Duke of Portland *v.* Hawkins, for trespass, to be brought (at Cambridge Assizes), upon which occasion (as the law reports of the time will show anybody who cares to refer to them), the right of the Jockey Club to 'warn off' was amply confirmed. This heart-burning question was tried again, about 1862, in connection with what is known as the 'Tarragona case,' when Mr. Irwin Willes, the well known 'Argus' of the *Morning Post*, refused to acquiesce in the 'warning off' decreed against him, but was worsted when an appeal was once more made to the law; and it was touched upon in 1869, when the action Bray *v.* Jennings, for assault, was tried, and when Mr. Bray, a 'tout,' being less chivalrous apparently than Mr. Snipe (of whom mention has been made), not only did not refuse to say 'who his employers were,' but gloried in stating that he was employed by the Right Hon. the Earl of Stamford and Warrington, a most conspicuous member of that Jockey Club to which a 'tout' is as the dead fly that makes the apothecary's ointment to stink.

We may now get on to the Jockey Club's 'Third Period,' from 1835 to the present day, having first remarked that a measure of the respect paid by that date to the opinion of the Club may be obtained from the significant fact that the appearance in the records from 1819 to this day of Antonio as the winner of the St. Leger in 1819, is due to a decision of the Stewards of the Jockey Club, to whom the question had by agreement been referred as to whether the Stewards of Doncaster Races had been right in allowing a second race to be run (on the ground that certain horses had not been ready to start in the first), and who promptly overruled the Stewards of Doncaster, and gave the race to Antonio, a non-starter for the second race. The power and influence of the Club were still farther extended and consolidated in 1844, when, in consequence no doubt of the 'Running Rein' case, it was arranged that the Stewards of the Jockey Club for the time being should be *ex officio* Stewards of Epsom; in 1857, when the like provision was applied to Ascot; and some time between 1878 and 1881, when Goodwood also was included in their (joint) Stewardship.

THE THIRD PERIOD

1835—1891

CHAPTER XI

DEPARTED MEMBERS

FROM 1835 (included) to the present day the Jockey Club has comprised the following members, substantive and honorary, the same name or title sometimes representing two or three different bearers of it, generally in regular succession, as of son to father, or brother to brother, and so on, and the same Royal or Imperial personage occasionally being represented by two different titles.

Imperial and Royal Personages.—King William the Fourth (Patron), the Prince of Orange, the King of Holland, the Prince of Wales, Prince Christian, the King of the Belgians, the Duke of Edinburgh, the Duke of Connaught, the Duke of Cambridge, Prince Vladimir of Russia, the Czarewitch (the Emperor of All the Russias), the King of the Netherlands (Holland), the Grand Duke Vladimir of Russia, the Crown Prince of Germany, the Duke of Clarence and Avondale.

Official Honorary Members.—The President, Vice-President, and three Stewards of the French Jockey

Club; the President of the American Jockey Club, New York; the Chairman of Committee of the Victoria Racing Club, Melbourne, Australia; the Chairman of Committee of the Australian Jockey Club (A.J.C.), New South Wales.

Princes.—Batthyany, D. Soltykoff.

Counts.—Batthyany (Prince), de Berteux, Tasselo Festetics, F. de Lagrange.

Barons.—De Teissier, Meyer de Rothschild.

Dukes.—Beaufort, Bedford, Cleveland, Dorset, Grafton, Hamilton, Leeds, Montrose, Newcastle, Portland, Richmond, Rutland, St. Albans, Westminster.

Marquesses.—Ailesbury, Anglesey, Conyngham, Drogheda, Exeter, Graham (Duke of Montrose), Hastings, Hartington, Hertford, Londonderry, Normanby, Tavistock (Duke of Bedford), Waterford, Westminster.

Earls.—Albemarle, Annesley, Aylesford, Bessborough, Bradford, Bruce (Marquess of Ailesbury), Cadogan, Caledon, Carlisle, Cawdor, Charlemont, Chesterfield, Clarendon, Cork, Coventry, Derby, Durham, Eglinton, Egremont, Ellesmere, Erroll, Feversham, Fitzwilliam, Glasgow, Granville, Hardwicke, Howe, Howth, Ilchester, Jersey, Lichfield, Lincoln (Duke of Newcastle), Lonsdale, March (Duke of Richmond), Milltown, Mulgrave (Marquess of Normanby), Orford, Portsmouth, Rosebery, Rosslyn, Spencer, Stamford and Warrington, Stradbroke, Strafford, Strathmore, Suffolk and Berkshire, Uxbridge (Marquess of Anglesey), Verulam, Westmorland, Wilton, Zetland.

Lords.—Alington, G. Bentinck, Burleigh (Marquess of Exeter), Calthorpe, Castlereagh (Marquess of Londonderry), Randolph Churchill, Clifden, Colville of Culross, Courtenay, Dorchester, Downe, Dupplin, Enfield (Earl of Strafford), Falmouth, John FitzRoy, Folkestone, Hastings, Kelburne (Earl of Glasgow), Lascelles, H. G. Lennox, Londesborough, Lowther (Earl of Lonsdale), Maidstone (Earl of Winchilsea), C. Manners, G. Manners, (de) Mauley, Milton (Earl Fitzwilliam), Mostyn, Newport (Earl of Bradford), Palmerston, Penrhyn, W. Powlett, Rendlesham, Ribblesdale, Royston (Earl of Hardwicke), St. Vincent, Saye and Sele, John Scott, Southampton, Stanley (Earl of Derby), Strafford (Viscount Enfield, Earl of Strafford), Suffield, Villiers (Earl of Jersey), Vivian, Wharncliffe (Mr. Stuart-Wortley).

Sirs.—D. Baird, R. W. Bulkeley, G. Chetwynd, H. Des Vœux, J. M. Errington, J. Gerard, R. Graham, S. Graham, H. Hawkins (Mr. Justice), J. Hawley, G. Heathcote, F. Johnstone, C. Legard, W. A. Lethbridge, S. Martin (Mr. Baron), Hercules Robinson, C. Rushout, J. Shelley, J. V. Shelley, T. S. M. Stanley, W. M. Stanley, R. Wallace, M. Wood, W. W. Wynn.

Messrs. (whether Hon. or with military or naval 'handles').—Alexander (Caledon), Allix, Anson (the Hon. Col. and Gen.), Astley (Col. and Sir J. D.),

D. Baird, H. D. Barclay, F. Barne, S. Batson, S. R. Batson, H. Biggs, J. Bowes, Bulkeley (Capt.), G. Byng (Hon.), Carington (Hon. Rupert), Carleton (Col. Dudley Wilmot, Lord Dorchester), T. E. Case (Case-Walker), Chaplin (Rt. Hon. H.), R. H. Combe, T. H. Cookes, T. Cosby, Craven (Hon. Berkeley), J. A. Craven, W. G. Craven, Crawfurd (W. S. Stirling), J. S. Crawley, J. Douglas, T. T. Drake, R. C. Elwes, R. Etwall, Fitzwilliam (Hon. G. W., C. W., and H. W.), Forester (Hon. Col. H.), T. Gardnor, Gerard (Hon. W., Lord Gerard), A. Goddard, C. C. Greville (Clerk of the Council), Grosvenor (General and Field-Marshal), W. Hallett, T. Houldsworth, J. H. Houldsworth, J. Hunter, W. H. Irby, R. Jardine (Sir Robert), Lane (Capt. Douglas), W. J. Legh (of Lyme), Lloyd (Cynric), Lowther (Col., third Earl of Lonsdale), Lowther (Rt. Hon. J.), Lupin (Monsieur Auguste, *doyen* of the French Jockey Club), J. Mills, W. M. E. Milner (Sir W.), E. M. Ll. Mostyn (Hon.), R. H. Nevill, G. E. Paget, Payne (J. and G.), Pearson (Col. and Gen.), Peel (Col. and Gen. the Rt. Hon. Jonathan), Petre (Hon. E.), W. R. Phillimore, W. A. Roberts, C. D. Rose, Rothschild (Leopold de), Rous (Hon. Capt. and Admiral), G. Rush, H. Savile, W. Scott-Stonehewer, H. Seymour (Capt.), J. V. Shelley (Sir), J. Spalding, Spencer (Hon. Capt.), Smith (T. Assheton), S. Stanley, M. Stanley, W. M. Stanley, W. Sloane Stanley, J. Stanley, J. M. Stanley, Sturt (Gerard, first Lord Alington), R. Sutton

(Sir R.), Synge (Col.), Tharp (Montagu), T. Thornhill, C. Towneley (Col.), J. R. Udney (Col.), Vansittart (H.), Villiers (Hon. A. and Hon. F.), Vyner (H. F. Clare), H. S. Waddington, R. Watt, Major Wickham, W. Wigram, Williams (Col. and Gen. Owen), C. Wilson, Wood (Gen. Mark), G. Wyndham (Col.), Yates (General).

Of these personages many 'overlap' from the previous period and have already been accounted for, and many, being members of the Club at present, may be deferred for awhile. Of the rest, some may be passed by altogether; upon others, a little space will be bestowed, either because they are historical figures, or because they achieved some special distinction upon the Turf, or because they were 'shocking examples,' or for some similar or dissimilar reason.

Of the Royal and Imperial personages, the foreigners are, for the most part if not entirely, 'honorary,' and cannot be expected to have done much for the English Turf. Still, the Kings of Holland (Netherlands) and Princes of Orange—though there may remain but an indistinct remembrance of the Orange Plate—are commemorated by the Nassau Stakes at Goodwood, and a King of Holland, as we have seen, came to the front at the beginning of the present reign (when a young queen could not very well, even had she been inclined, become the avowed patroness of such an institution as the Jockey Club, and was married to a consort whose inclinations certainly did not lie that way), and gave the Jockey Club that

Royal countenance which is one reason of the immense prestige enjoyed by the Club. And the substitution of 'Emperor's Plate' for 'Ascot Gold Cup,' from 1845 to 1853 (both inclusive), before the days of Sir Hamilton Seymour, the Emperor Nicholas, the talk about 'the Sick Man,' and the siege of Sevastopol, bears witness (as also the Cesarewitch and the Grand Duke Michael Stakes testify) to Russian co-operation and encouragement in the cause of British horse-racing. Of the personages with the foreign titles of Prince, Count, and Baron, Prince Batthyany—who died suddenly at Newmarket, just after the race for the Two Thousand in 1883—was, like Prince Soltykoff, who is still among us, to all intents and purposes an English sportsman, having been on the English Turf from 1829, and a member of the Jockey Club since about 1859, and won the Derby with the famous racehorse and sire Galopin (sire of St. Simon, bred by the Prince, though Galopin was not), in 1875. Count de Berteux, of the Cheffreville Stud, Normandy, is one of the very best customers English breeders of blood-stock have ever had. Count Tasselo Festetics is understood to be brother-in-law to the Duke of Hamilton, excellent credentials for a member (honorary) of the Jockey Club. Count F. de Lagrange was as well known in this country as in his own (and perhaps better) as a breeder, owner, and runner of horses—especially of Fille de l'Air and Gladiateur. Baron de Teissier was English in all but his name and title (one of a French family naturalised in this country, of whom James Teissier—grandfather, apparently, of the member of the Jockey Club whose father, Lewis de Teissier, died in 1812, or thereabouts, worth half a million of money —was 'de''d, or ennobled, by Louis XVIII. for kindness to the French refugees in London); lived at Woodcote Manor (whence the Woodcote Stakes), near Epsom; was perpetual Steward, in combination with the popular Sir Gilbert Heathcote, of Epsom Races; nominated a filly for the Durdans Stakes at Epsom, October 9, 1833, which seems to have been as near as he ever got to actual horse-racing; and was elected a member of the Jockey Club about 1839. Baron (Meyer de) Rothschild (born 1818, died 1874, whose family was ennobled by the Emperor of Austria in 1815, and received from him the title of Baron in 1822), was, of course, he of Mentmore, whose only daughter, Hannah, was the late lamented Countess of Rosebery, and who bred and owned Favonius (winner of the Derby in 1871), Hannah (winner of the One Thousand, the Oaks, and St. Leger in 1871), and Corisande (winner of the Cesarewitch in 1871), so that the year 1871 was called 'the Baron's year.' He also won the One Thousand in 1853 and 1864 with Mentmore Lass and Tomato (both bred by him), and the Goodwood Cup in 1869 with Restitution (bred by him), by King Tom, and in 1872 with Favonius. It was not he, of course—as he died in 1874—but Baron Lionel (of Gunnersbury), who raced as Mr. Acton and was not a member of the Jockey Club, that won the Derby with Sir Bevys in 1879. Though untitled, Monsieur A. Lupin, who has been a member of the French Jockey Club almost from the day that it commenced existence in 1833, may be conveniently brought in here. He imported Wings (winner of the Oaks in 1825) into France in 1837, and from that time for many years continued to import expensive English mares (including Songstress, winner of the Oaks in 1852, imported in 1859); and it was his distinction to win the first notable French success on an English race-course, when he won the Goodwood Cup with Jouvence (bred in France, but of English sire and dam, Sting and Currency) in 1853, on which occasion the French Jockey Club was illuminated, and the Seine was very nearly set on fire. M. A. Lupin has been very successful in his own country, but not in proportion to his efforts, and he was thought to be especially unfortunate in 1885, when he sacrificed the all but certainty of winning the French Derby with Xaintrailles to the honourable desire of winning the English Derby, for which he was but a bad fourth. But he won 'half an Oaks' with Enguerrande (a deadheat with the French-bred Camélia) in 1876.

Among those whose names are found in the batch of members of the Jockey Club from 1835 to the present day, some, as has been said, belong to the general history of the country. Prominent among them are the following:

The fourteenth EARL of DERBY, the 'Rupert of debate,' the Prime Minister, statesman, orator, scholar (translator of the 'Iliad'), and sportsman (born 1799, died 1869), who could not win 'his own' Derby (even with Toxophilite in 1858) but did succeed (as Lord Stanley) in winning the Oaks with Iris in 1851 (the year he succeeded to the Earldom), and the Two Thousand with Fazzoletto in 1856, as well as the One Thousand in 1848 (as Lord Stanley) with Canezou, and in 1860 with Sagitta, three years after he had written his famous letter to the Stewards of the Jockey Club (in 1857), calling upon the Club to do their duty towards their neighbour, if he was a cheating scoundrel.

LORD GRANVILLE (the second Earl, born 1815, died 1891), is he who was so prominent as a statesman and minister. He is said to have had a share in racehorses very often, but never ran a racehorse in his own name; though, as a Leveson-Gower, great-grandson of the Earl of Gower, who was a member of the Jockey Club in 1753, and bred the famous Gower stallion, he belonged to a family celebrated as breeders and runners of great racehorses, and as patrons of the Turf in the earliest days of the Jockey Club.

LORD GEORGE BENTINCK (third son of the fourth or 'Tiresias' Duke of Portland) and his brilliant career both on the Turf and in the senate, with its melancholy termination 'by the visitation of God—to wit, a spasm of the heart' (as the jury found), in one of his father's fields at Welbeck, will never be forgotten. He won the Two Thousand in 1838 with Grey Momus; the Two Thousand, One Thousand, and Oaks in 1840 with Crucifix; the One Thousand in 1837 with Chapeau d'Espagne, and in 1842 with Firebrand; the Ascot Cup with Grey Momus in 1838, and the Goodwood Cup with Miss Elis in 1845; and he just missed the 'blue ribbon' (for which he had hungered and thirsted so long) by the sale (in 1846) of Surplice, winner of the Derby in 1848 (the very year in which Lord George died, September 21, aged only forty-six).

The famous LORD PALMERSTON, again, will always be held in remembrance. He was one of the stars of the Jockey Club, though his success upon the Turf was infinitesimal, notwithstanding his hopes of the Derby in 1860 with Mainstone (by King Tom), and his winning of the Cesarewitch with the variously pronounced Iliona in 1841, and his diligent patronage of John Day, the trainer.

Sir SAMUEL MARTIN is almost historical, too, for he was a famous judge; and, if his membership of the Jockey Club was only honorary, he was devoted to the Turf, and is said to have been nominated, with Mr. Rudston Read, one of the executors in the will of Mr. John Scott, the celebrated trainer at Whitewall.

Sir RICHARD WALLACE, the philanthropic, reputed son of the eccentric Lord Henry Seymour (of racing renown in France, and a son of a Marquess of Hertford) is another honorary member, whose generous qualities

and open hand should secure him long remembrance;
he was not a racing man, but still he was always
ready to place his villa called Bagatelle, near Longchamps, at the service of English gentlemen who ran
candidates for the Grand Prix de Paris.

Colonel, afterwards General, ANSON (the Hon.),
may certainly be considered historical, if only as a
descendant of the famous 'circumnavigator' Commodore (and afterwards Lord) Anson, the figure-head of
whose ship (the Centurion, in which he went round
the world) was set up at Goodwood House on a
pedestal with an inscription in doggerel. But General
Anson himself was Commander-in-Chief in India,
where he died in 1857, and whence his body was
removed to England and buried in Kensal Green
Cemetery in 1860. The gallant General was a great
racer; he won the Derby in 1842 with Attila, and the
Oaks in 1844 with The Princess (ridden by his favourite
jockey, the celebrated Frank Butler).

Colonel and General the Right Hon. JONATHAN
PEEL is another of the historical members, for he was
a Cabinet Minister and Secretary for War, and a
member of Parliament for forty-two years, from 1826
to 1868. He gave evidence in the trial (1827) which
established the right of the Jockey Club to 'warn off'
offenders from Newmarket Heath. He won the Two
Thousand with Archibald in 1832, and the sensational
Derby of 1844 (when his friend, Lord George Bentinck,
exploded a villainous plot) with Orlando; and by his

T

death (at eighty years of age) on February 13, 1879, at his beautiful place Marble Hill (once the seat of Mrs. Howard, George II.'s Countess of Suffolk), Twickenham, the great horse Peter (so called from the General's friend, the eccentric Lord Glasgow, whose nick-name it was), by Hermit, was disqualified for (winning) the Derby of that year.

Admiral Rous, again, may be classed among the historical group; for his feat in bringing home the sinking *Pique* is a historical feat of seamanship, though perhaps his 'mates' (at a time when there was no such term or rank as 'sub-lieutenant'), including the late Rear-Admiral Robert Dawes Aldrich, deserved as much credit as Admiral Rous himself.

Among the dead and gone 'shocking examples' of the Jockey Club comprised in this batch of members were those that follow.

There was the DUKE of NEWCASTLE (the sixth), who at one time owned the good horse Julius (that managed to beat Hermit in a match) and whose very hippic name disappears from the list of members in 1869 (after a short and stormy career, both as Earl of Lincoln and as Duke of Newcastle), the year after he had won the Goodwood Cup with Speculum. He is understood to have used the race-horse principally as an instrument of gambling, and to have made terrible havoc of things in general.

The (fourth and last) MARQUESS of HASTINGS is, of course, he who was the hero of a very romantic matrimonial incident, who won the One Thousand with Repulse in 1866, the Grand Prix de Paris with that mysterious horse The Earl in 1868, the Ascot Cup with Lecturer in 1867, the Goodwood Cup with The Duke in 1866, who paid 6,000 guineas or more for the impostor Kangaroo, in the hope of winning the Two Thousand and Derby won by Gladiateur, who was the owner of the sensational Lady Elizabeth, who was 'fly' to Mr. Padwick's 'spider,' and who, having commenced racing when he was barely twenty years of age in 1862 with a 'plater' called Consternation, before the end of 1868, at twenty-six years of age, had finished his career and his life—'all out.' It is only fair to add, though, that the ruin of his fortunes has been attributed, not without reason and credibility, rather to\the 'bones,' the cards, and generally extravagant expenditure, than to his losses, enormous as they were—more than 100,000*l.* on Hermit's Derby— on the Turf.

The next 'warning' is the (seventh) EARL of AYLESFORD (one of the 'black funereal Finches'), who was born in 1849, and, having been for some years a member of the Jockey Club after the kind to which the 'Cripplegate' and 'Newgate' Earls of Barymore belonged, but not having gained so much distinction as the former of that noble pair of brothers on the Turf, was constrained to leave his country (perhaps for that country's good) for Texas, where he died (not, it is understood, in the odour of sanctity) on his 'ranche' in 1885. He was not unknown on the Turf as Lord Guernsey, but it was as Lord Aylesford that he covered himself and the Jockey Club with as much glory as can be derived from covering other people with flour 'shied' in bags from a drag on the way to London after the Derby. That is 'the sort of man he was.'

As for LORD COURTENAY (afterwards twelfth Earl of Devon, who died on January 15, 1891), he was so badly hit that he had to retire from the Jockey Club, after a certain number of years' membership, some time between 1869 and 1872. Nor had he anything to show for his financial ruin (which was supposed to be caused by betting on the Turf principally); for, though he may have had a share in many race-horses, and though his colours (violet, green sleeves, and white cap) were duly registered, memory fails to recall a single notable success won by him.

The next is (the third) LORD RIBBLESDALE (whose family name of Lister recalls memories of the 'Lister Turk,' and is eloquent of hereditary horse-raciness), of Gisburn Park, West Riding, Yorkshire, whose melancholy death (by his own hand, it is said) at Geneva in 1876, gave rise to sinister rumours, whether founded or unfounded, of misfortune connected with the Turf, as is always the case when the person who is the subject of the rumours has to do with horses and horse-racing.

Of (the third) VISCOUNT ST. VINCENT, winner of the

St. Leger with the famous Lord Clifden in 1863, it is understood that he burnt his fingers very badly during his connection with the Turf, which is highly credible, as he certainly had dealings with the notorious Mr. Padwick (the 'Spider'), from whom he is said to have purchased at a cost of something like ten thousand pounds a half-share only in the unfortunate race-horse Klarikoff (burnt in his van in 1861, on his way from Epsom after the Derby to Whitewall) one of the favourites for the Two Thousand and the Derby in 1861, when it was common to bet 'the three D.'s against the three K.'s' (Diophantus, Dundee, and Dictator against Klarikoff, Kettledrum, and Kildonan).

VISCOUNT DUPPLIN (eldest son of the eleventh Earl of Kinnoul), who had the misfortune to have his marriage dissolved (which, however, as we have seen, was quite in accordance with the early fashion of the Jockey Club), and who died at Monte Carlo in 1886, if not a 'shocking example' exactly, belonged rather to that category than to the model members or the highly distinguished members, though he won the Two Thousand (not with Kaleidoscope, as had been expected, though nobody seems to have known why) and the St. Leger in 1876 with the beautiful horse Petrarch, that, as a two-year-old, had 'spread-eagled' his field for the Middle Park Plate. That a Lord Dupplin should be a horse-racer by heredity is plain when we see that as early as 1717 a Lord Dupplin ran Smiling Betty at Hambleton and (as Lord Kinnoul) ran her again at the same place in 1722.

LORD VIVIAN (Charles Crespigny, second Baron), who, with Lord Hardwicke, was very pronounced in his anti-Gallican sentiments at the time (1876–77, when he was quite a new member of the Jockey Club) of Lord Falmouth's 'Reciprocity' agitation, is another of those to whom common report, rightly or wrongly, attributes badly burnt fingers from playing with the Turf.

Mr. (the Hon.) BERKELEY CRAVEN (winner of the Oaks with Bronze in 1806, and once at least a Steward of the Jockey Club) is one of the most deplorable cases among the 'shocking examples,' for this poor gentleman, in consequence of a fear that he might not be able to meet his losses incurred by betting against Bay Middleton for the Derby of 1836, shot himself on the night of the Derby Day. And what made the affair more melancholy was that (it is stated) he would have recouped himself over the Oaks, had he waited till the next day (for the Derby was then run on Thursday, the Oaks on Friday). Nor was such not altogether condemnable sensitiveness always confined to the noblemen and gentlemen of the Jockey Club; for in Smolensko's year (1813) a 'bettor round' (or 'bookmaker,' as we should now say), a Mr. Robert Brograve, shot himself rather than face creditors to whom he owed 8,000*l.* (which he had laid against Smolensko) with but 4,000*l.* (which he had at his bank).

This sensitiveness is the more noticeable, because, had the debt or debts been due to the widow, or the orphan, or the hardworking father of a family for 'work and labour done' and for 'value received,' both the member of the Jockey Club and the 'bettor round' would probably have considered an offer of ten shillings in the pound extremely handsome.

Mr. GEORGE PAYNE (who was nephew to Mr. John Payne, the winner of the Derby with Azor in 1817) must reluctantly be added to the 'shocking examples,' inasmuch as he lost two or three fortunes by racing, cards, dicing, and other objectionable practices, though he was a most amiable, agreeable, witty, and clever man, reminding one forcibly, in failings and talents, of the illustrious C. J. Fox. He died September 2, 1878, having achieved very little distinction in the public life for which his talents (as his friends said) were eminently adapted (had he not concealed them in a figurative napkin), or on the Turf (beyond winning the One Thousand with Clementina in 1847).

The (twelfth) EARL of WESTMORLAND, who has passed away just as this work was being finished, must, it is to be feared, take his place among the 'shocking examples,' because, though in many respects a most worshipful member of the Jockey Club and patron of the Turf, he was a very heavy bettor sometimes, and had to retire, badly hurt, from his favourite pursuit (to which he was more addicted than to hunting, shooting, fishing, and cricket, all congenial sports to him) about 1868, and returned to the Turf only in the character of adviser and coadjutor to Lord Hartington. Lord Westmorland (who had served his country both in India, and in the Crimea as aide-de-camp to Lord Raglan) never owned any very noted horse, though with Rama he managed to beat the famous Lord Lyon for the Doncaster Cup in 1866; and he was once owner of Marigold, the dam of Doncaster (sire of Bend Or, sire of Ormonde). His great disaster was in 1863, when the discovery that the scales had been tampered with prevented the race for the Cambridgeshire (together with bets to the tune of many thousands of pounds) from being given to his horse Merry Hart, second to Catch-'em-Alive, which latter would have been disqualified but for the timely discovery referred to.

Mr. (the Hon.) EDWARD PETRE was also among the 'shocking examples,' for though he won four St. Legers, once with Theodore (at odds of '100*l*. to a walking-stick' against him) in 1822, and three years running (1827, 1828, and 1829) with Matilda, The Colonel, and Rowton, yet his end is said to have been 'sold up.' He belonged to a family which is especially interesting, because one of its members was he who, by stealing a lock of hair from the beautiful Arabella Fermor, gave Pope the subject for the finest mock-heroic poem in existence.

CHAPTER XII

DEPARTED MEMBERS (*continued*)

IT remains to single out from the defunct members of the club from 1835 to 1891 those who have been notable for distinction gained upon the Turf.

The (seventh) DUKE of BEDFORD, who succeeded to the title in 1839, and had previously raced as Marquess of Tavistock, and who died in 1861, won the One Thousand in 1855 with Habena (bred by him), by Birdcatcher, and bred the famous Asteroid (by Stockwell), chosen by Admiral Rous (the Duke's 'managing man,' to whom the Duke bequeathed the choice of a horse from his stud) and sold by him for 1,500 guineas (it is stated) to Sir J. Hawley, who won with him (but without a race) both the Jockey Club Challenge Cup and the Whip in 1862.

The (second) MARQUESS of AILESBURY is he who was summoned to the House of Lords as Baron Bruce in 1839, and died in 1878, when he was succeeded by his brother (died 1880), who was succeeded by his grandson (with hereditary racing tendencies strengthened maternally, as his mother was a Craven), who had the strange experience of being 'warned off' (as if he had been Mr. 'Snipe,' the 'tout') by that very club of which his relative, the second Marquess (a Master of the Horse), had been a conspicuous ornament. The second Marquess (who in 1868 succeeded his relative the Earl of Cardigan, the 'Crimean hero') won the St. Leger with St. Albans in 1860, and the Goodwood Cup with Aventurière in 1875, all but won the Derby and the St. Leger in 1866 with Savernake (own brother to St. Albans), and, according to superstitious persons, would have won them if the colt had been named when he ran for the Derby. He came out strongly and handsomely in true English fashion against Lord Falmouth and the anti-French party in the controversy (1876–77) about 'Reciprocity.'

The (third) MARQUESS of CONYNGHAM (who died in 1876) was naturally better known on the Irish turf than on the English; but he won the Cambridgeshire in 1855 with Sultan, by Crescent, under circumstances (to wit, odds of 40 to 1 against him) which might well earn for his trainer, Mr. William Day (of the well-known house of Day of Danesbury, a jockey, a trainer, an owner, a breeder at the extensive Alvediston stud, and ultimately a literary author), his great character as a trainer of handicap horses especially.

The (first) MARQUESS of WESTMINSTER (died 1845), who has already been nibbled at as Lord Belgrave and (second) Earl Grosvenor, is he who bred Touchstone (and was near to having him destroyed, because he was a *first foal*!) and won the St. Leger in 1834 with him, in 1840 (when the 'leading case' of a 'declaration to win' occurred, as Maroon was 'pulled double,' when he could have won by a hundred yards, it is said, to allow Lord Westminster's other horse to win) with Launcelot, Touchstone's own brother, and in 1841 with Satírist. As to the case of Maroon and Launcelot, it should be noted that Launcelot had run second to Little Wonder (a reputed instance of a horse 'very older' than he should have been, according to scandal) for the Derby (which the Queen and Prince Albert witnessed, and after which the royal consorts presented Little Wonder's rider, Macdonald, with a complimentary whip), that the public therefore would have backed him, and that the marquess, for that reason, it is supposed, declared to win with him. The family of the marquess is admirably represented at the present day both on the turf and in the Jockey Club by the Duke of Westminster.

The (fourth) EARL of ALBEMARLE (who died in 1849 and was succeeded by his son, who died *s.p.* in 1857, and was succeeded by his brother, the late venerable earl, an author, who died February 21, 1891) is he who was Master of the Buckhounds, and seems to have raced chiefly because of his official position. He won the One Thousand with Barcarolle in 1838, the Two Thousand with Ralph in 1841, and (as became a Master of the Buckhounds) the Ascot Cup with Ralph in 1843, and in 1844 and 1845 (when it was called the Emperor's Plate) with the Emperor (imported into France, where he became joint sire of the famous Monarque, and died in 1851), by Defence. His unfortunate horse Ralph (a son of the celebrated Dr. Syntax) is said to have been poisoned just before the race for the Ascot Cup, and (though he won) to have died soon afterwards, whereby a valuable 'cross' was lost.

The (fourth) EARL of ANNESLEY (died 1874) won the Goodwood Cup in 1860 with Sweetsauce.

The (thirteenth) EARL of EGLINTON, it is scarcely necessary to say, was the famous Lord of the Tournament of Eglinton, one of the most popular members of the Jockey Club ever known. He won the Derby of 1849 with the celebrated horse The Flying Dutchman (nearly beaten, however, by the half-bred Hotspur, and ultimately imported into France); the St. Leger of 1842, 1847, and 1849 with Blue Bonnet, Van Tromp, and The Flying Dutchman; the Ascot Cup in 1849 and 1850 with Van Tromp and The Flying Dutchman; the Goodwood Cup in 1848 with Van Tromp; and, above all, the memorable match in 1851 with The Flying Dutchman (5 yrs., 8 st. 8½ lb., ridden by Marlow), against Lord Zetland's Voltigeur (4 yrs., 8 st., ridden by Flatman, *alias* Nat), for 1,000 guineas, at York Spring Meeting, distance two miles.

The (fifth) EARL of GLASGOW (who began his career upon the Turf as Viscount Kelburne) was the eccentric

nobleman, known among his intimate associates as
'Peter,' who won the Two Thousand with General
Peel (runner of a dead-heat for the Ascot Cup with
Ely in 1865, but beaten in the decider), and was
known principally for his heavy betting (having
offered to lay Lord George Bentinck 90,000*l.* to
30,000*l.*, when the latter nobleman expressed a desire
to back his horse Gaper for the Derby of 1843 'to
money'), for his objection to name his horses until
they had deserved a name (which seldom happened),
for his extreme irritability, his strong language, his
curious dress, his 'sleeping draughts' (nothwithstanding which he had lived to the good age of
seventy-seven, when he died in 1869), for his amusing
habit of anathematising his jockeys for not 'making
play' with his horses according to his orders (when
he started animals that could not beat a jackass),
and for his noble and ingenuous inability, it is said,
even to the last day of his life, to understand the
trickery practised in running races in heats so as
to win. He was also a mighty Jehu, and drove a
famous match (which, of course, he lost through illluck) with Lord Kennedy, on a night as dark as
pitch.

The (third) EARL of HOWTH (died 1874), a great
judge of all matters pertaining to horseflesh, was
better known, no doubt, on the Irish than the English
Turf, but his name of St. Lawrence was given to a
stout horse well-known on English racecourses, and

sire of the famous Saucebox, winner of the St. Leger in 1855.

The (first) EARL of LICHFIELD (created 1831, and previously Thomas William, Viscount Anson, son of the grand-nephew of the 'circumnavigator') is he who died in 1854, and who, under the auspices of Lord G. Bentinck, won the St. Leger of 1836 with Elis (originally Mr. C. C. Greville's), and the Two Thousand of 1839 with The Corsair (when it was 7 to 2 *on* Lord Jersey's Cæsar, and there were only three runners).

The (third) EARL of LONSDALE (nephew of the second Earl, who, as Viscount Lowther, won the sensational Derby of 1831 with Spaniel) is he who was better known upon the Turf and in the Jockey Club as Colonel Hugh Lowther (born 1818, succeeded 1872, died 1876, so that he did not wear out his coronet), and who covered his new earldom with glory by winning the Cesarewitch of 1873 with King Lud (bred by Lord Zetland).

The EARL of ORFORD (the third of the new creation in 1806, the old having expired with the celebrated Horace Walpole), who died in 1858 at the age of seventy-eight, won the Two Thousand with Clearwell in 1833, and the One Thousand with a filly (afterwards called Lady Orford), by Slane out of Exotic, in 1850, and so 'kept the pot a-boiling,' which had been set on by the 'mad' Lord Orford, one of the early members of the Jockey Club.

The (fourth) EARL of ROSSLYN, who died only the other day (September 6, 1890, at fifty-seven years of age), a descendant of the celebrated or notorious Lord Loughborough (Lord Keeper and Lord Chancellor during a part of Pitt's long administration, 1783–1801), was noted rather as a breeder than as a racer, having bred, among other good horses, the queer-tempered but highly meritorious Tristan (one of whose feats was to lift with his teeth out of a chaise and shake like a dog a reverend gentleman who was merely 'looking on' at Newmarket), but having injudiciously sold him at an early age to the famous M. Lefèvre, of Chamant, near Chantilly, for whom he was an Eldorado (though now repurchased at a long price for his native land). The Earl was a 'clayver' man with a turn, and a very pretty turn, for verse-writing, whether in Latin or English, and might have done for the English Turf as much as was done for it by an Oxford Professor of Poetry (Sir Francis Hastings Doyle), if not quite so much as was done for Grecian sport by one Pindar, whom a Rev. Professor of Greek at Cambridge used to describe patronisingly (in his sermons) as 'this benighted heathen.'

The EARL (seventh) of STAMFORD and (third) of WARRINGTON was the very persistent patron of the Turf, whose two marriages did not altogether meet with the approval of society, and whose employment of 'touts' (which was revealed in the action of Bray v. Jennings, for assault and battery, the plaintiff having been a 'tout' and the defendant a trainer, in 1869) was an outrage upon the tenderest feelings of the Jockey Club to which he belonged. The Earl won the Two Thousand with Diophantus in 1861, the One Thousand with Lady Augusta in 1863, the Oaks with Geheimniss in 1882, and the Ascot Cup with Rupee in 1860, and was especially notable for having purchased (when he saw that the French were coming to the front) the French horses Armagnac, Brick, and Le Maréchal in 1862 in a lump for 6,000*l*., and for having been the first Englishman to run for the French Derby (as he did with Armagnac in 1863, thus showing his countrymen how to dispense with 'Reciprocity'). That the Earl was a great shot and a great cricketer, and, in fact, a great 'all round' sportsman, is to his credit as a member of the Jockey Club.

The (second) EARL of STRAFFORD was apparently the eldest son of the first Earl (Field Marshal Sir J. Byng, *q.v.* in the 'Second Period'), and was George Stevens Byng, a Lord of the Treasury, &c., who died in 1886, and, as Viscount Enfield, won the Two Thousand with Hernandez (bred by the Hon. Col. Anson, and imported into France in 1853) in 1851.

The (twelfth) EARL of STRATHMORE and KINGHORNE (whose ancestor the tenth Earl was the father of the celebrated Mr. John Bowes, of Streatlam, and who not improbably was himself a member of the Jockey Club, when he won the St. Leger with

Remembrancer in 1803) was a great racing man, owner of Saccharometer (unbeaten as a two-year old, and equal in the betting with Macaroni for the Derby of 1863), and challenged for both the Jockey Club Cup and the Whip with Mouravieff in 1861, but was quite overshadowed by his relative Mr. Bowes (also a member of the Jockey Club) upon the Turf. He died in 1865.

The (third) EARL of WILTON, winner of the St. Leger with Wenlock in 1872, succeeded to the title and estates of his maternal grandfather (the first Earl of Wilton) in 1814, and died (only the other day comparatively) March 7, 1882, at the age of eighty-two. He had three great horses, and only three great ones, in his life : Gladiator (second to Bay Middleton for the Derby of 1836, and perhaps the very best sire the French ever purchased from us, giving 2,500*l.* for him in 1846), the aforesaid Wenlock, and Seesaw (a sensational winner of the Cambridgeshire, and the sire of Bruce, winner of the Grand Prix de Paris in 1882). But it was as a rider, whether on the flat or across country, that Lord Wilton was so admirable; it is said that no gentleman or even professional jockey could 'touch him.' He deserved well of the public by the establishment of races at Heaton Park; but the public showed such multitudinous appreciation that he was obliged to try (ineffectually) exclusive measures, and was probably glad when the meeting was moved to Liverpool (in 1839). He was a most accomplished man : a Turfite, a yachtsman, a surgeon, an organist, a saint, and a sinner, being partly a 'dissipated man of fashion' and partly a sort of domestic chaplain, who undertook to read the family prayers to his assembled household, including servants and visitors.

The (second) EARL of ZETLAND, who died in 1873, was he who won the Two Thousand in 1857 with Vedette (sire of Galopin), unable to run for the Derby or St. Leger (whether entered or not), else the famous Blink Bonny and the less famous Impérieuse might have won less distinction. The Earl had already, in 1850, won the Derby and St. Leger, and beaten The Flying Dutchman for the Doncaster Cup with Voltigeur; and he won the Ascot Cup in 1855 with Fandango (which horse won the Jockey Club Cup by 'half a distance' from Homily in 1856), and in 1857 with Skirmisher. The Earls of Zetland, of course, 'strain back' to Sir Lawrance Dundas, one of the earliest members of the Jockey Club, and, as we have seen, one of the founders of the Jockey Club Challenge Cup in 1768.

The (third) VISCOUNT CLIFDEN is memorable for ever through having 'Jacobed' Lord G. Bentinck, as it were, by winning the Derby and St. Leger (the 'blue ribbon' and its pendant) of 1848 with Surplice, sold by Lord George to the Hon. Mr. Mostyn, and by him to Lord Clifden, who thus did at the first time of asking what Lord George could not do during his whole racing career.

The (sixth) VISCOUNT FALMOUTH, who married Baroness le Despencer, a peeress in her own right, is a household word. He won 'everything,' to speak loosely; he never betted—after he took to racing and breeding at any rate; and by stakes and the sale of his stock is calculated to have made quite 200,000*l.* His successful horses were legion, and he was winner of the Derby in 1870 with Kingcraft, and in 1877 with Silvio; of the Oaks in 1863, 1875, 1878, and 1879, with Queen Bertha, Spinaway, Jannette, and Wheel of Fortune; of the Two Thousand in 1874, 1879, and 1883, with Atlantic, Charibert, and Galliard; of the One Thousand in 1862, 1873, 1875, and 1879, with Hurricane, Cecilia, Spinaway, and Wheel of Fortune; and of the St. Leger in 1877, 1878, and 1882, with Silvio, Jannette, and Dutch Oven. The story of his one bet, after he became a racing man in his own name and ceased to be 'Mr. Valentine,' is variously told, but it related to Queen Bertha, winner of the Oaks in 1863; it varies in amount, according to the story-teller, from half-a-sovereign to sixpence, and it was paid, according to the story-teller's fancy, to Mrs. Scott or to John Scott (Lord Falmouth's then trainer) in the form of a handsome brooch or scarf-pin, with the particular coin as a portion of the ornament.

LORD LONDESBOROUGH (first Baron) won the Oaks with Summerside in 1859 (the year before his death), and had already won the Ascot Cup with West Australian (sire of Summerside) in 1854, and was remarkable for having in his stud at the time of his death both West Australian and Stockwell, the former sold at the subsequent sale (at Londesborough Lodge, near Scarborough) to the French Count de Morny, and the latter to Mr. R. C. Naylor.

LORD MAIDSTONE (afterwards eleventh Earl of Winchilsea and Nottingham, born 1815, succeeded 1858) is entitled to notice rather as a rider than as a runner of horses, as a scholar (who took part in the learned discussion as to the pronunciation of Iliona, the name of Lord Palmerston's mare that won the Cesarewitch of 1841), and as one of the poet-members of the Jockey Club.

LORD MOSTYN is made out to have been the second Baron, apparently the same person as the Hon. E. M. Ll. Mostyn (born 1795, succeeded 1854, died 1884, grandfather of the third Baron), who won the Oaks and St. Leger with the famous Queen of Trumps (whose peculiarity it is said to have been that she 'went lame on all four legs, one after the other, before she could settle into her stride') in 1835.

LORD W. POWLETT (whose name recalls the family of the racing Dukes of Bolton and bewrays relationship to the racing Duke of Cleveland) is he who owned the gallant Tim Whiffler, beaten in the famous dead-heat with Buckstone for the Ascot Cup of 1863, and challenged with him (expatriated to Melbourne, Australia, in 1871) both for the Jockey Club Challenge Cup in 1862 and the Whip in 1863.

Lord Saye and Sele (twelfth Baron, died 1847) is remarkable among members of the Jockey Club rather as the bearer of a family name (Fiennes) which, in the form of Fines or Fynes, is found as early as the reign of Henry VII. (Thomas Fynes, who died 1534) among patrons of horse-racing, than for notable performances upon the Turf.

Lord John Scott (of the Cawston Stud) was the very popular nobleman who bred (from Touchstone's daughter Phryne) the brothers Elthiron, Windhound, and the once celebrated Hobbie Noble (the horse that came to the whistle like a dog, that was to have won the Derby of 1852, that Queen Victoria admired so much at Ascot, and that is said to have cost Mr. James Merry 6,500 guineas, but that sum apparently included other horses), who was the 'universal' sportsman (including a little 'bruising'), and who once for a bet rode his old charger Helen (by Octavian or Octavius out of Lady of the Lake) up the steps of the Bank of Dublin and down again, having duly cashed a cheque.

Lord Suffield is a title which apparently covers three members of the Jockey Club—namely, the second Baron (William Assheton), who died in 1821 (in which year he ran for a Jockey Club Plate with a colt or filly by Vandyke, Jun.); his brother Edward, the third Baron (who is on the published list for 1836), and the fourth Baron, who was the son of the third, and who died *s.p.* in 1853, when he was succeeded by his half-brother Charles (the present Baron, who is a member of the Jockey Club to be noticed hereafter, among the living members). The Suffields are not recorded among the most successful runners of race-horses; and the fourth Baron had to 'decline the Turf,' but deserves the most honourable mention as one of those twenty-three or twenty-four prominent members of the Club who protested (but in vain) against the dispersal of the Royal Stud at Hampton Court at the very beginning of the present reign, though it has since been re-established with so much success—witness the price given for Memoir, and the 5,500 guineas for her sister, La Flèche. The fourth Lord Suffield, however, ran second with Caravan for the Derby of 1837, won by Lord Berners with the 'cripple' Phosphorus.

Sir DAVID BAIRD (of Newbyth) is made out to have been the nephew of the celebrated Sir David Baird (the stormer of Seringapatam, created a baronet in 1802, died *s.p.* in 1822), and to have been a noted 'gentleman-jockey' (like Lord Wilton, Sir F. Johnstone, Messrs. Delmé-Radclyffe, Brand, and others of the same date) rather than a distinguished owner and runner of race-horses.

Sir JOHN GERARD cannot be discovered among the winners of any 'classic' race, but was undoubtedly of the family of which was also a Sir W. Gerard (a member probably of the Jockey Club, though proof is not forthcoming) who won the Oaks of 1810 with

Oriana, who was a considerable breeder, and whose family is represented at the present day among the members of the Jockey Club by Lord Gerard, and has been connected with the Turf from time immemorial.

Sir S. GRAHAM was Sir Sandford (died 1852), not so well-remembered a Turfite as his kinsman Sir R. Bellingham Graham, who was one of the great 'Northern lights' (winner of the St. Leger with Duchess in 1816), and was very likely himself a member of the Jockey Club (though no actual proof of his membership is forthcoming, and, like Mr. Hugo Meynell, he is perhaps better remembered as a great hunter). Sir Sandford is understood to have been of Kirkstall, Yorks, and Sir Bellingham of Norton Conyers, Yorks. They are not to be confounded with the Grahams (of the Yardley Stud) who have won so many great races with Regalia, Formosa, Gamos, &c.; but are represented to this day among the members of the Club, it is understood, by the Sir Reginald Graham of the present list.

Sir JOSEPH HAWLEY, of Leybourne Grange, Kent, is another of our 'household words' so far as the Turf is concerned. He was known as 'the lucky Baronet' (though, indeed, he had his ill luck as well as good), and won the Derby no fewer than four times, in 1851, 1858, 1859, and 1868, with Teddington (belonging really, it is said, to his confederate, Mr. J. M. Stanley, and bred by Mr. Tomlinson), with

Beadsman (bred by himself), with Musjid (purchased, it is said, by advice of the present Lord Alington, then Mr. Gerard Sturt, and bred by Mr. R. G. Lumley), and with Blue Gown (bred by himself), in the year when Lady Elizabeth was favourite, and when he 'declared to win' with Rosicrucian or Green Sleeve in preference to Blue Gown. He won the Two Thousand with Fitz-Roland in 1858; the Oaks in 1847 with Miami; the One Thousand with Aphrodite in 1851; the St. Leger with Pero Gomez (the horse that 'ought to have won the Derby') in 1869; the Ascot Cup with Teddington, Asteroid, and Blue Gown in 1853, 1862, and 1868; the Goodwood Cup with Siderolite in 1870; and he shocked his brethren of the Jockey Club by the introduction of revolutionary measures (1869–1870) concerning two-year-old racing and the admission of un-aristocratic persons as members of the Jockey Club. He betted on a gigantic scale, thereby setting an evil example; but he was a man of learning, science, and literary ability of no common order, and he collected at Leybourne a magnificent library.

Sir GILBERT HEATHCOTE, Bart., the extraordinarily popular 'perpetual Steward of Epsom races' (jointly with Baron de Teissier), predecessor of the present Lord Rosebery at 'The Durdans,' belonged to a family known from very early times upon the Turf, and was remarkable for winning the Derby of 1838 with the outsider Amato (buried in his grounds), that never started for a public race before or after (just like Chestnut Middleton, the winner of the Derby in 1825).

Sir J. SHELLEY, Bart., and his son, Mr. J. V. (afterwards Sir J. V.), may be taken together. The former was the sixth Baronet (born most likely in 1771, died in 1852), who commenced racing at a very early age (before he was five-and-twenty), and was confederate first with Mr. Howorth and then with the (fifth) Earl of Jersey, but does not appear upon the list of the Jockey Club until after 1835. He won the Derby in 1811 with Phantom (sire of Chestnut Middleton and Cedric, both winners of the Derby), and in 1824 with Cedric (when the field were all 'wheelers' and no 'leaders,' it was said), and the Two Thousand with Antar in 1819; and altogether was a great racing celebrity of a racing stock (as we have seen). His son, Mr. (afterwards Sir) J. V. Shelley, better known in connection with politics, Westminster, and the London Bank than with winners of the Derby, was elected a member of the Jockey Club about the same time, apparently, as his father, but retired from it in 1862, and died in 1867.

Sir W. W. WYNN was, of course, the excellent Baronet who died only a few years ago, was familiarly styled 'Sir Watkin,' and sometimes 'the other Prince of Wales,' and was better known for his hounds than for his racehorses, though he was a member of the Jockey Club for about half a century.

Mr. (CALEDON) ALEXANDER, who died in 1884, was very prominent on the Turf, though not as a winner of 'classic' races, and his heavy-weight match in 1879 with Sir J. D. Astley has already been mentioned (Briglia, 5 yrs. 16 st., *v.* Drumhead, 6 yrs. 16 st. 6 lb., Suffolk Stakes Course, Newmarket—that is, a mile and a half, owners up). He also ran the sporting match in 1866 with his Robin Hood, by Wild Dayrell, against Baron Rothschild's Robin Hood, by North Lincoln, 3 yrs. 8 st. 10 lb. each, Ditch mile, Newmarket, for '200 sovs. and the name—*i.e.* which should be entitled to be called Robin Hood,' and won 'the stakes.'

Mr. ALLIX demands special notice as one of the family (if not the very identical gentleman) from whom the Jockey Club made the memorable purchase which first gave the Club proprietary rights over a portion of Newmarket Heath and laid the foundation of 'warning off.'

Mr. F. BARNE (of Sotterley, Norfolk) is noticeable as having been connected maternally (through the Mr. Miles Barne, High Sheriff of Suffolk in 1790) with the family of General Philip Honywood (one of the great lights of the Turf with his Honywood Arabian and two True Blues), and for having apparently disputed with the late Lord Granville the position of *doyen* of the Club (for he was a member before 1848, and was still on the list in 1885) without having attained any distinction on the racecourse, though he (unlike Lord

Granville) ran a good many horses in his own name.

Mr. HENRY BIGGS, though now no longer remembered, was very well and favourably known in his day, and was of Stockton, Wiltshire.

Mr. JOHN BOWES, of Streatlam, Durham, who died only a few years ago, was one of the most interesting characters of the Jockey Club. He was all but eleventh Earl of Strathmore, but missed the earldom through his father's dilatoriness in the matter of marriage; and he himself was twice married, but each time to a foreigner; first (in 1872) to Josephine Benôite, Countess de Montalbo or Montalba, who died in 1874; and secondly (in 1877) to Alphonsine Marie, Countess de Courten. Thus it was that he lived abroad a great deal, insomuch that George Fordham (who rode for him very often in latter times, though not, of course, in the palmy days, not being old enough) is said not to have known him by sight. It was in his earlier days that Mr. Bowes (who won the Derby in 1835, 1843, 1852, and 1853, with Mündig, Cotherstone, Daniel O'Rourke, and West Australian; the Two Thousand in 1842, 1843, and 1853, with Meteor, Cotherstone, and West Australian; and the St. Leger in 1853 with West Australian) laid down, in conjunction with John Scott the trainer, the famous 'tan gallop' at Langton Wold.

Mr. T. E. CASE-WALKER is the gentleman who was Mr. Case when he was elected a member of the Jockey

Club, and who died about 1882; and is not to be confounded with Mr. T. E. Walker, winner of the One Thousand with Elizabeth in 1880.

Mr. T. COSBY, belonging probably to the family of Strabally Hall, Queen's County, Ireland, which is connected by marriage with the racing family of the Duncombes (Lord Feversham), is he who won the Eclipse Foot (for members of the Jockey Club only) in 1833 with Galopade at Ascot, and the Oaks with Pussy in 1834. He was a well-known 'gentleman jockey,' especially at Heaton Park.

Mr. W. STIRLING-CRAWFURD, winner of the Two Thousand in 1868 and 1873 with Moslem (dead-heat with Formosa; Moslem walked over and divided) and Gang Forward; of the One Thousand in 1859, 1881, and 1882, with Mayonnaise, Thebais, and St. Marguerite; of the Derby in 1878 with Sefton; of the Oaks in 1881 with Thebais; and of the St. Leger in 1875 with Craigmillar, was he of Sefton Lodge, Newmarket; a sort of 'Duke of Montrose' from the domestic rather than the heraldic point of view. He is understood to have been very pronounced in favour of the betting persuasion.

Mr. THOMAS TYRWHITT DRAKE, of Shardeloes, Amersham, Bucks, who was born in 1818 and died in July 1888, though he did not start his racing colours of crimson and black cap much before 1870, though he ran no great horses (for Professor, Sunshade, and Quits did not belong to that category), and though he and his father before him were better known (as so many members of the Jockey Club have been) as M. F. H., agriculturists, cattle-breeders, and patrons of cricket, yet deserves special mention here as a recipient of property, and probably of descent, from the Stradlings of St. Donat's, Glamorganshire, to one of which family the famous Stradling (*alias* Lister) Turk is considered by some persons to have owed one of his distinguishing, or rather confusing, designations.

Mr. A. GODDARD, who is taken to have been Mr. Ambrose Goddard, of The Lawn, Swindon, Wilts, distinguished himself by winning the Ascot Cup in 1819 with Anticipation (Mr. 'Riddlesworth' Thornhill's).

Mr. T. HOULDSWORTH, winner of the One Thousand with Destiny in 1836, and the hero of the match between Filho da Puta and Sir Joshua (North *v.* South) in 1816, bore a name which has been connected with the Turf from very early times, and, as we shall see presently, is still prominent in the list of horse-racers and members of the Jockey Club. He belonged, of course, to the great manufacturing interest, to the 'men of business,' with one or two of whom the Jockey Club, much to its advantage, has had its aristocratic exclusiveness leavened from the very first. Great patron of racing as he was, however, Mr. Houldsworth, it is said, was by no means the man to let his hobby run away with him to the neglect of other matters, and very often did not know what horses he had in his stables when a question arose about a sweepstakes for which he was challenged to enter. He is represented in the Jockey Club of the present day by the very popular Mr. J. H. Houldsworth, whose election dates from 1874.

Mr. HUNTER is the gentleman whose unique fortune it was to win the Derby with a *grey* horse, Gustavus, in 1821. The horse was bred at what had been the Prince Regent's stud-farm, near Six Mile Bottom, on the road to Newmarket, and afterwards Colonel Leigh's; and the horse's dam was Lady Grey, very significant of the colour which she conferred from herself upon five of her progeny in succession. Mr. Hunter was strongly of the betting persuasion, and is said to have won largely upon Gustavus in the Derby, but his successes upon the Turf were not conspicuous otherwise.

Mr. HENRY SAVILE (who died about 1880–1881) was the famous racer of Rufford Abbey, Notts, and of Ryshworth, Ripponden, Yorks, breeder, owner, racer, and bettor, winner of the Derby in 1872 and of the Ascot Cup in 1873 with the famous Cremorne, by Parmesan (sire of Favonius). He admitted into his stud ('unbeknown' very likely, and with the best intentions) certain American-bred mares (including Cincinnati, by Star Davis, and Desdemona, by Glencoe), which investigation showed not to be thoroughbred, though the two named have found their way into the Stud Book (not without due warning, however ; *vide* vols. ix. and x.).

Mr. SCOTT-STONEHEWER, a conspicuous member of the Club in his day, won the Two Thousand in 1817 with Manfred, and the Oaks with Variation in 1830.

Mr. J. M. STANLEY is the gentleman who was confederate (when Teddington won the Derby) with the overshadowing Sir Joseph Hawley.

Mr. (Sir RICHARD) SUTTON is the heavy bettor who died in 1875, having won in 1866 the Derby, Two Thousand, and St. Leger with the famous Lord Lyon, leased, it was understood, from General Pearson (breeder both of Lord Lyon and of his celebrated sister Achievement). A gentleman who 'owns all Piccadilly,' as was said of him, can afford to bet heavily; but the example is not the less to be deprecated.

Mr. (Colonel in the Lancashire Militia) TOWNELEY is he who won the Oaks of 1860 with Butterfly (in Mr. Eastwood's name), and the Derby of 1861 with Kettledrum; Charles Towneley (of the family known in connection with 'the Towneley marbles'), born 1802, married into the hippic family of Molyneux (Earls of Sefton, of whom the first was a member of the early Jockey Club, and whose titular name was given to a winner of the Derby), and died about 1873 (in which year Kettledrum found a home in Hungary). Col. Towneley's first important success was in the Royal Hunt Cup at Ascot in 1858, with the celebrated half-bred Hesperithusa, though she ran in the name of Mr. Eastwood.

Mr. H. F. CLARE VYNER (died 1882) is he who won the Two Thousand of 1875 with Camballo, and was brother to the present racing celebrity, Mr. R. C. Vyner, who purchased the property of Fairfield, Yorkshire, which one belonged to the 'Leviathan' bookmaker, John Jackson, known as 'Jock o' Fairfield.' Mr. R. C. Vyner, who has won the Grand Prix de Paris (with the celebrated Minting in 1886), the One Thousand (with Minthe in 1889), the St. Leger (with The Lambkin in 1884), and other notable races, is understood to have declined membership of the Jockey Club on the tit-for-tat principle, which leads people to refuse when it is offered that which was not given when it was sought.

Mr. (RICHARD) WATT, winner of the One Thousand with Cara in 1839, of the St. Leger in 1813, 1823, 1825, and 1833, with Altisidora, Barefoot, Memnon, and Rockingham, and virtually winner of it in 1817, when his great horse Blacklock was foolishly 'pulled back to his horses' by way of 'swagger,' and 'snapped' by Ebor at the finish, was he of Bishop Burton, Yorks, one of the great 'Northern lights,' of Tramp and Blacklock memory, and not to be confounded—as he very often is—with Mr. Watts (of Ireland), an owner of much later date, winner, in 1845, of the St. Leger with The Baron (sire of Stockwell), and breeder both of him and of his dam, Echidna, by Economist.

General MARK WOOD cannot be passed over without special commemoration, both because he was a nephew of the famous Sir Mark Wood, of the Hare Park, Newmarket, whose achievements on the Turf have already been recorded, and because, like his friend Lord Falmouth, he was no bettor, or, if he betted at all, made merely nominal bets of no importance. He served his country in the 60th Rifles (in Jamaica) and in the Coldstream Guards (Crimea). He has left no impression upon the Turf, on which he raced as 'Mr. Lambourne'; but, as regards 'the curse of horse-racing,' which is betting, he has left an example 'pour encourager les autres.'

CHAPTER XIII

PRESENT MEMBERS

Of the present members of the Jockey Club, the most noteworthy as not belonging to the betting persuasion are Lord Cadogan, the Duke of Portland, and the Duke of Westminster; and there are others who, like Mr. James Lowther and General Pearson, are understood to bet very little, if at all, and certainly not by 'throwing large commissions into the market,' as the saying is, that is, by doing systematic and large business with 'the Ring.' Of the rest, the majority (including Lord Durham, the modern reformer of the Turf) are believed to consider horse-racing and betting to be inseparable. The most noteworthy members, as present or past participators in high offices and public affairs, reminding one of the days when it was said (truly, however ironically) that 'the country was governed from Newmarket,' are (to say nothing of the Royalties, some of whom serve their country in various prominent capacities) the Duke of Beaufort (twice Master of the Horse), the Earl of Bradford (a Master of the Horse), Earl Cadogan (in the Cabinet), the Rt.

Hon. H. Chaplin (in the Cabinet), Lord Randolph Churchill (an ex-Chancellor of the Exchequer, and ex-Leader of the House of Commons), Lord Colville of Culross (a Master of the Buckhounds), the Earl of Cork and Orrery (twice Master of the Buckhounds, and a Master of the Horse), the Earl of Coventry (a Captain of the Gentlemen-at-Arms and Master of Buckhounds 1886), the Earl of Durham (the 'Reformer'), the Marquess of Exeter (a Treasurer of the Queen's Household, and a Captain of the Gentlemen-at-Arms), the Earl of Hardwicke (a Comptroller of the Queen's Household, and a Master of the Buckhounds), the Marquess of Hartington (an ex-Secretary of State), Sir Henry Hawkins (a distinguished Judge), Earl Howe (ex-Military Secretary to the Commander-in-Chief in India), the Earl of Ilchester (a Captain of the Gentlemen-at-Arms), Sir Robert Jardine (head of the great China firm of Jardine, Mathieson and Co., and M.P. for Dumfriesshire), the Marquess of Londonderry (a Lord-Lieutenant of Ireland), the Rt. Hon. James Lowther (a Chief Secretary for Ireland), Mr. G. Ernest Paget (a notable Chairman of public Railways), General Pearson (a distinguished officer), the Duke of Portland (a Master of the Horse), Sir Hercules Robinson (a distinguished Governor of several Colonies), the Duke of Richmond and Gordon (Secretary for Scotland, etc., etc.), the Earl of Rosebery (ex-Foreign Secretary), the Duke of St. Albans (ex-Captain of the Yeomen of the Guard), Lord Suffield (Superintendent of Stables to the Prince of Wales), the Duke of Westminster (a P.C. and a Master of the Horse), General Owen Williams (a distinguished officer), and the Earl of Zetland (Lord-Lieutenant of Ireland). No doubt some of the posts held by these noblemen and gentlemen are 'no great shakes'; but in these days, when every appointment is so closely scrutinised, to hold the least of them is more indicative of worth than it would have been in days gone by, and the holders of them, taken all together, form as competent a Board of Control for the Turf as heart could desire.

Of the present members the most successful upon the Turf have been (to go by the 'classic' races only) Lord Alington (confederate with Sir F. Johnstone) with Common; the Duke of Beaufort with Vauban, Petronel, Siberia, Scottish Queen, Rêve d'Or; Sir Robert Jardine (represented by Mr. J. Johnstone) with Pretender, Bothwell; the Duke of Westminster with Shotover, Ormonde, Farewell, Bend Or; Mr. Douglas Baird with Enterprise, Enthusiast, Briar-Root; the Duke of Portland with Ayrshire, Semolina, Donovan, and Memoir; General (Colonel) Pearson with Achievement; Lord Hartington with Belphœbe; the Duke of Hamilton with Miss Jummy, Ossian; Mr. Chaplin with Hermit; Sir F. Johnstone (sometimes confederate with Lord Alington) with St. Blaise, Brigantine; Lord Hastings with Melton; Lord Cadogan with Lonely; Lord Calthorpe with Seabreeze; Lord R. Churchill with L'Abbesse de Jouarre; Lord Rodney with Kilwarlin.

Of the present members, hereditary tendency towards Newmarket, the Turf, and the Jockey Club is most pronounced in Lord Alington (both through the Alingtons, to whom the manor of Newmarket came by marriage from the Argentines, and through the Humphry Sturt who was connected with the Turf at the birth of the Jockey Club); in Sir J. D. Astley (whose name is of great antiquity on the Turf, and in the records of it); in Mr. Hedworth T. Barclay (descended maternally from the winner of the Derby 'in a trot' in 1803)'; in the Duke of Beaufort (whose ancestor, Edward Somerset, Earl of Worcester, was Master of the Horse to James I., of Newmarket renown); in the Earl of Bradford (descended maternally from the racing family of Sir David Moncreiffe); in Lord Cadogan (whose name is recorded in ' Pond ' before the Jockey Club was known); in Lord Calthorpe (who 'strains back' maternally to the Dukes of Beaufort, Noachian patrons of the Turf); in Lord Cawdor (connected maternally with the Thynnes, a noted racing family as early as 1669); in Mr. H. Chaplin (one of whose ancestry it probably was who ran as long ago, at least, as 1719 Smiling Nanny for a Gold Cup at Newmarket; and one of whose ancestry it obviously was who ran his grey colt, Blankney, at Grantham and Stamford, Lincolnshire, in 1765); in Lord R. Churchill (who strains back to a Duke of Marlborough, a member, as we have seen, of the Jockey Club in its earliest days); in Lord Colville of Culross, very likely (as a

Colvill, or Colvil, or Colvile, is caught running Smiling Molly at Newmarket, as early as 1733, with Lord Gower and the rest of the 'quality'); in the Earl of Cork (connected by marriage with the great racing family of the Marquesses of Halifax, whose name is conspicuous in the early Calendars); in Messrs. Craven (a name redolent of the noble lord from whom came the designation of the Craven Stakes, in 1771); in Mr. Harvey Combe (a relation, no doubt, of the Mr. Harvey Combe who, in 1838, had a controversy about his horse Cobham, a favourite for the Derby, with his trainer, John Scott); in Mr. Ambrose Crawley (if he be maternally descended from Mr. Christopher Musgrave, of Kempton Park—which has become a very centre of horse-racing—and he be connected with the Ambrose Crawley, alderman of London, whose daughter married the Earl of Ashburnham, one of the early members of the Jockey Club, and who himself seems to have done a little racing in 1753); in Lord Dorchester (whose predecessor, or one of whose predecessors, in the title bred the famous horse Buccaneer—once the property of Lord Portsmouth, but sold to happy Austria-Hungary in 1865—and whose possible ancestor, Sir John Carleton, did the first bit of recorded 'warning-off' from Newmarket Heath in 1636); in Viscount Downe (belonging to a very old horse-racing family of Danby Lodge, Yorkshire, of whom one ran a match at Newmarket as early as 1748, against the Lord March, better known as 'Old Q.'); in the Marquess of Drogheda (whose ancestor would run horses at Newmarket in the days before the fact that Queen Anne was dead was so generally known as it now is, with names, varying from the gentle Tom Tit to the tremendous Hell Fire, which would scarcely pass muster nowadays); in the Earl of Durham (who, as a Lambton, connected with the Curwens, of Curwen Bay Barb celebrity, bears a name which carries us back to horse-racing at York some time before Queen Anne died); in the Earl of Eglinton (one of whose predecessors introduced 'Bozzy' to the Jockey Club in 1765, and another 'belonged to' the Flying Dutchman); in the Earl of Ellesmere (who is positively saturated with Jockey Club, so to speak, inasmuch as he is connected in family with the Duke of Bridgewater, who, as we have seen, was an original member of the Club; he married a daughter of the second Marquess of Normanby, a member of the Club, and the first Earl of Ellesmere married a daughter of Mr. C. C. Greville, a member of the Club, who himself had married a daughter of the Duke of Portland, a member of the Club); in the Marquess of Exeter (who, by his name of Cecil, takes us back in the history of the Turf as far at least as 1713 and 1714, when the Hon. W. Cecil's Creeper ran, in company with Queen Anne's Mustard and Star, at York); in the Earl of Feversham (whose family name of Duncombe has been shown to have appeared in the records of horse-racing before the foundation of the Jockey Club); in the Fitzwilliams (whose racing fame is connected with that of their kinsman, the 'Bay Malton' Marquess of Rockingham); in Colonel the Hon. H. Forester (whose family appears to have matrimonial ' crosses ' with the racing families of Manners, and Maltzahn, and Lamb [Lords Melbourne, of Brocket Hall]) ; in Lord Gerard (whose family is supposed to have gone horse-racing some time B.C., and certainly, as long ago as 1623, a Lord Gerard is credited with a notable race-horse called Captain); in Sir Reginald Graham (through the famous Sir Bellingham Graham, to go back no farther); in the Duke of Hamilton (whose predecessors, the tenth and eleventh dukes, appear to have eschewed the Turf and the Jockey Club) through the great northern horse-racer, Lord Archibald, ninth duke, and back to the first duke, who was Master of the Horse to Charles I. ; in the Marquess of Hartington (who recalls memories of Flying Childers, the property of a Duke of Devonshire) ; in Lord Hastings (whose ancestor, Sir Jacob Astley, appears once in the extraordinary character—for an Astley—of a prohibitor of a horse-race at Catterick in 1639, for the name is connected rather with the promotion of such sport from the earliest times) ; in Mr. J. H. Houldsworth (with memories of Filho da Puta in 1816) ; in Earl Howe (whose title, and whose name of Curzon both recall the earliest days of the Club); in the Earl of Ilchester (whose compound name of Fox-Strangeways tells in its first part a tale of the Rt. Hon.

C. J. Fox, member of the Jockey Club, and runner of many race-horses); in Sir F. Johnstone (a name of early and notable distinction upon the Turf, of a family whose members rode as well as ran their race-horses); in Captain Douglas Lane (closely connected with Newmarket by descent, it is understood, from the Colonel John Lane, who was the intimate friend of Charles II.); in Lord Lascelles (related, no doubt, to the Rev. Mr. Lascelles, of Gilling, near Richmond, Yorkshire, who is mentioned as a temporary owner of the fabulous Tartar mare, dam of Mr. O'Kelly's famous Queen Mab); in Mr. W. J. Legh (inasmuch as in 1751, just at the birth of the Jockey Club, there was to be run for at Newton 'a Gold Cup, value 50*l.*, given by Mr. Legh, of Lyme,' which was won by Mr. Barker's Sweet William); in Sir W. A. Lethbridge (since the first Baronet, Sir Hesketh, of that surname appears to have married an Astley, and the third, predecessor of the present Sir Wroth Acland, to have married the only daughter of the once too well-known 'Jack' Mytton, of Halston, who verily watered the Turf with his fortune); in the Marquess of Londonderry (whose name of Vane carries us back to the annals of racing in 1612, to penetrate no farther into antiquity, and whose compound name of Vane-Tempest is eloquent of Sir Harry V. T. and the great Hambletonian); in the Right Hon. James Lowther (whose name is an epitome of excellent hippic records, as regards both horse-racing and horse-breeding); in the Earl of March (who telescopes into the Duke of Richmond, taking us back to the first Duke, Master of the Horse, about 1681-82, and to Old Rowley and Newmarket in olden time, and conjuring up all the glories of Goodwood); in the Duke of Montrose (as the Grahams or Græmes are almost antediluvian patrons of horse-racing, and one of them ran Champion against Queen Anne's 'nutmeg-grey' Mustard at York in 1713); in Mr. G. E. Paget (if by any chance his family 'belonged to' the Paget Turk, which, however, is very uncertain); in General Pearson (if haply, which is again uncertain, he 'strain back' to the Mr. Anthony Pearson, so frequently met with in 'Pick' as a mighty breeder of good racehorses); in Lord Penrhyn (who is a grandson of the Hon. John Douglas, a name prominent upon the Turf, and who married, as it were, into the Jockey Club, for the first Lady Penrhyn was a daughter of Sir C. Rushout, a member of the Jockey Club); in the Duke of Portland (whose family produced Lord George Bentinck, which suffices); in the (now deceased) Earl of Portsmouth (for a Wallop, a Viscount Lymington, runs his horse Toy at Windsor as early as 1744, before there was a Jockey Club); in Lord Rendlesham, one of whose family it was, no doubt, who, as Mr. C. Thelusson, was racing at Doncaster in 1810 (early enough—when the foreign origin of the 'accumulator' who caused the 'Thelusson Act' is considered), to say nothing of intermarriage with

the family of the racing Earls of Eglinton; in the
Duke of Richmond (as a descendant of 'Old Rowley');
in Lord Rosebery (of a family 'full of running
blood,' *par les femmes*); in Mr. Leopold de Rothschild
(through Baron Lionel, *alias* Mr. Acton, the owner of
Sir Bevys, and also through the more famous Baron
Meyer, of Mentmore); in the Duke of St. Albans
(through 'Old Rowley' again); in the Earl of Suffolk
and Berkshire (a Howard, descended from Bernard
Howard, it is understood, who was a sort of Admiral
Rous in the days of 'Old Rowley'); in Mr. Montagu
Tharp (who, though an honorary member only, and
not known upon the Turf, has his estate of Chippenham Park, Cambs., handy for Newmarket, and is
great-grandson of the Mr. John Tharp who raced
as long ago as 1799 at Newmarket with the eponymous horse Chippenham, and other horses); in the
Duke of Westminster (from the Sir Richard Grosvenor,
who was the first Earl, a member of the Jockey Club
at the beginning, and adopter of the popular 'yellow
and black cap'); in the Earl of Westmorland (whose
title is that of a Master of the Horse in 1796, to go
back no farther, and one of whose ancestors married
the daughter of a Bristol merchant bearing the
racing name of Swymmer, perhaps the Antony Langley Swymmer whom we have encountered among
the early members of the Jockey Club, or a relation
of his, and who himself married into the racing
family of Howe); in General Owen Williams (if, by

any chance, he be connected by lineage with the Sir
J. Williams of the famous 'Turk,' otherwise 'Honywood's Arabian'); and in the Earl of Zetland
(through the Sir Lawrance Dundas who, according
to the more credible version, was one of the subscribers to the Jockey Club Challenge Cup in 1768).
Since these lines were written the Earl of Westmorland (the twelfth) has died (July 31, 1891), and he
has been added to the 'departed' members of the
Jockey Club. The Earl of Portsmouth has also died
(October 4, 1891).

CHAPTER XIV

A BRIEF REVIEW

DURING this Third Period, towards the end of which a 'reg'lar new fit out o' rules' (to come into effect from January 1, 1890) was published, the Club had to deal with a great many important matters, whereof the most interesting, so far as the public is concerned, were the following:

In 1835 sanction was given to the publication (for the first time, so far as can be discovered), in the book Calendar, of a list (continued annually ever since) containing the names of the noblemen and gentlemen belonging to the Jockey Club at the time of issue. What the reason was is a mere matter of conjecture; perhaps to overawe the common herd, perhaps to let it be publicly known by how obviously trustworthy and competent a body the authority over the affairs of the Turf had been partly gained through conferment or acquiescence, and partly usurped through self-assertion, so that feelings of animosity might be allayed, and a sense of confidence and security established in the breast of everybody who might take an interest in the Turf. Cynicism would incline towards the former explanation, Christian charity towards the latter.

In 1838 the Club declared its 'extreme disapprobation of horses being started for races without the intention on the part of the owners of trying to win' (of which more will be said presently), and enacted a rule (for Newmarket) that 'any member of a Racing Club riding in with the leading horses, shall be fined 25 sovs., and anybody else 5 sovs.' This objectionable practice had been very common with the illustrious and Rt. Hon. C. J. Fox, and with that stern reformer of abuses Lord G. Bentinck himself (insomuch that the Judge Clark of that day, having had his placing of the horses called in question, remarked that he 'ought properly to have placed a tall gentleman in a white macintosh first,' Lord George being a tall gentleman who wore a white macintosh), and called aloud for stringent repression. It has already been noticed that the Club in 1842 declined to have anything further to do with disputes about bets; so we may get on to 1844, when the 'Running Rein' scandal in connection with the Derby of that year, as well as the 'Leander case' and the 'Ratan case' in connection with the same Derby, and the 'Bloodstone case' in connection with the New Stakes at Ascot in the same year, gave the Jockey Club no end of trouble. There is no intention here of re-telling the threadbare stories of rascality. They are merely alluded to for the purpose of pointing out that they testify to a terrible weakness of the knees on the part of the Jockey Club, which, having in this year 1844, and in the next year 1845 (on account of what was called the 'Old England conspiracy,' for the 'nobbling' and even cruelly 'maiming' a horse called Old England, which was expected to win the Derby), 'warned off' certain miscreants for about as heinous offences as anybody could conceive, by the year 1847 had relented and restored to the scoundrels, or to the most dangerous of them, the privileges which had been removed either righteously (as appears from the Jockey Club's own account) or unrighteously. If unrighteously (which is not to be thought for a moment) a handsome apology should, of course, have accompanied the public notice of the restoration of privileges, or at any rate a dignified explanation. It is that Gallio-like method of treating great offences, combined with a more Draconic mode of procedure against small offenders, which has caused a doubt sometimes whether the Jockey Club is morally sound at the core.

In 1845 the Jockey Club passed that Rule which was enough to make 'Old Q.' and the earliest members of the Club turn in their graves : 'that no races for gentlemen riders be allowed at Newmarket during the regular meetings, without the sanction of the Stewards, and that, in the event of such sanction being obtained, these races be the first or last of the day.' Henceforth the name 'Jockey Club' became a misnomer, though there can be little doubt about the soundness of the Rule. Between 1840 and 1845, too, the Club (chiefly through the Duke of Richmond, and of Lord Palmerston, who was consequently elected a member of the Club) procured the repeal of an obnoxious Act of Parliament (13th year of George II.) as to running two horses in a race (for a Plate) and obtained the passage of the Gaming Acts Discontinuance Bill, whereby *qui tam* actions were prevented, and scoundrels who raked up an obsolete statute for purposes of black-mail were checkmated.

In 1852 the Jockey Club publicly, by decreeing the weights to be carried, gave its sanction to a race in which *two-year-olds* were to run *three miles* at Newmarket; but, it should be remembered, in the Houghton week, when they would be 'rising three' very rapidly, though, even so, it was a 'heavy order' well discharged in 1870 or thereabouts. But in 1852, the Jockey Club countenanced the racing of yearlings, as we have seen. That, in 1855, the Club should have discontinued the Second Spring Meeting is the more noticeable because, in 1890, when the Meeting had been renewed (1870–71), a Second July was added (some days, however, being at the same time docked from other meetings). That in 1856 a Rule was passed 'that if either party in a case which is heard before the Stewards of the Jockey Club, desires to have a short-hand writer engaged to take down the evidence, the Stewards may, if they think proper, engage a

shorthand-writer at the expense of the person making
the request,' does not seem to have been generally
known at the time of the Chetwynd-Durham affair a
year or two ago, after which a proposition was made
as to the employment of a shorthand-writer at all
meetings of the Club, else perhaps it would have been
pointed out that (with the exception of defrayment of the
expense) not much advance was made, by the concession then obtained, upon the position secured in 1856.

In 1857 came the letter, already mentioned, in
which Lord Derby vigorously called on the Club to
do their duty, and which deserves to be read in connection with Mr. Baron Alderson's observations at the
conclusion of the 'Running Rein' case, when he said:
'Before we part, I must be allowed to say that this
case has produced great regret and disgust in my
mind. It has disclosed a wretched fraud, and has
shown noblemen and gentlemen associating and
betting with men of low rank, and infinitely beneath
them in society.' There we have it: but for the
betting the close association would not be tolerated,
that betting which the majority of the Jockey
Club have encouraged from the first. Perhaps Lord
Derby (whose letter related especially to a Mr.
Adkins, a convicted swindler) had in his mind's eye,
when he wrote, the race for the Hunt Cup of 1856,
when he himself raced in company with the said
Mr. Adkins, or that pretty picture in the Cesarewitch
of the same year, when Mr. Adkins raced in company

with Lord Anglesey, Lord W. Powlett, Sir R. W. Bulkeley, and Captain Douglas Lane, all members or soon to be members of the Jockey Club, and when the race was won by Vengeance (which must have recalled memories of the Rugeley poisoner, William Palmer), with Pole Star (which was eloquent of Palmer's victim, Mr. J. P. Cooke) second, and December (belonging to the W. Day who had been 'warned off' in consequence of the 'Old England' affair) third. If poverty makes strange bed-fellows, so does betting make strange associates. If it were not for the betting, Messrs. Adkins and Co. would not find it worth their while to run horses, and the 'noblemen and gentlemen' would not find it worth while to tolerate such gentry if they did.

In 1858, under the auspices of the Club, there came into operation a 'reg'lar new fit-out o' Rules,' of which that which has given rise to most controversy, and which (though not precisely in the same words) remains in force to the present day, decrees that: 'All nominations are void by the death of the subscriber;' a rule enforced in scarcely any, if any, other country. It evidently grew out of the old rule in 'Pond,' that: 'Matches and bets are void on the decease of either party before the match or bet is determined.' But there is no need to point out how different is the case when matches have almost become obsolete, and sweepstakes, etc., for which horses are entered two or three years before determination, are the order of the day. [As to bets, of course nothing will be said here.] But it is by no means certain that the rule is not a good one, or as good a one as is possible under the circumstances. It may be a case of England against the world; but England (as Free-traders will allow) may be right all the same.

What says the French rule? It used to run, and probably still runs thus: 'L'engagement d'un cheval est annulé, si la personne sous le nom de laquelle il a été engagé meurt avant l'époque fixée pour le paiement de l'entrée ou du forfait. Dans les courses où il est stipulé que l'entrée sera représentée par un billet, l'époque du paiement sera considérée comme fixée au jour de la souscription de ce billet;' with the following important modification:

'Le montant du forfait, ou de l'entrée lorsqu'il n'y a pas de forfait, doit être versé au moment de l'engagement.

'Dans les courses pour lesquelles les engagements se font un an ou plus d'un an à l'avance, le montant de l'entrée ou du forfait peut être représenté par un billet à ordre.

'Lorsque les conditions de la course admettent plusieurs forfaits, c'est le forfait le plus élevé qui doit être déposé ou souscrit.

'Tout engagement qui n'est pas accompagné du montant de l'entrée ou du forfait exigé peut être refusé.'

This, of course, is tantamount to a rule that

'nominations are *not* void by the death of a subscriber' (which is the Australian rule in so many words); and one seems to remember that Archiduc thus became incapable of running for the English Derby by the death of Count Lagrange, but could and did run for the French, and was second to Little Duck.

The German rule (Union Klub's) used to run, and probably does still run: 'Die zu den Rennen gemachten Anmeldungen bleiben gültig, selbst wenn der Unterzeichner oder Nenner stirbt' (nominations *not* void by death of subscriber).

The Austro-Hungarian: 'Abgegebene Unterschriften oder Nennungen erlöschen, wenn der Unterzeichner oder Nenner stirbt, ausser wenn ein angemeldetes Pferd vor dem eingetretenen Todesfall seines Nenners mit Engagements verkauft und die gehörige Anzeige hievon erstattet wurde' (nominations *are* void by the death of a subscriber, unless the nominated horse shall have been sold with engagements before the death, and due notice of the sale shall have been given; which is the English rule with a very important modification).

Still there is a great deal to be said in favour of the English rule as it now stands; it is so simple, so trenchant, so downright, so preventive of mistakes, disputes, litigation and dishonesty, unless in the event (which is likely to be very rare) of the almost simultaneous occurrence of the subscriber's death and the decision of a race to which he may have subscribed.

There is a sort of dog-in-the-manger plea which is sometimes urged in favour of the rule as it stands; but that deserves little attention. It is, that a deceased subscriber would probably have subscribed for a great many horses, of which only one perhaps would be good, and that the purchaser of that 'crack' would be quit of all the liabilities incurred by the original subscribers for the bad ones, and the various stakes, if the purchaser did not win them, would be so much the less valuable to another, and, if he did, so much the more to himself. But, even if the plea were not too mean to be considered, it should be borne in mind that for the Derby, for the Grand Prix, and for many, if not most, of the great stakes there is now a minor forfeit, which the subscriber would most likely have paid for the bad ones before his decease, so that there would be little of the anticipated loss. Another point which should be looked at, and which tells in favour of the rule as it stands, is this: that those who object to the rule consider the cases only of good horses (in which there is no doubt a depreciation of property sometimes) and of horses with great reputation, or of owners (like the late Mr. White, the Australian representative) possessing such horses to be left to their 'executors, administrators, and assigns,' but the good horses, and even the reputed good horses, are to the bad as one to a hundred (or more), and both the good and the reputed good horses very often belie their promise (as the notorious Lady

Elizabeth testifies), so that the present rule, which certainly does rather good than harm to the inheritors of bad horses, may also very often save the inheritor or purchaser of good or reputed good horses from disappointment or ruinous disaster.

The year 1859 is also noteworthy in the history of the Club as the year in which Admiral Rous (by continuous re-election till his death in 1875) commenced his career of a sort of Perpetual President (as Sir C. Bunbury is said to have been in his day), during which, it is asserted, he raised the revenues at the command of the authorities at Newmarket from a bare 3,000*l.* a year to 18,000*l.*

In 1860 the Jockey Club was threatened with the intervention of a meddlesome Legislature in the form of a Bill concerning race-horses and horse-racing, but the danger was averted by means of a petition presented on behalf of the Club by Lord Derby; in 1861 the remaining one of the originally two 'exclusive' Jockey Club Plates (of 1753) was thrown open (with an augmentation of value) to the public; in 1862 Admiral Rous, for the Jockey Club, debated with the Vicomte Daru, for the French Jockey Club, the question of running the race for the newly instituted Grand Prix on some other day than Sunday, but was beaten by the Sabbath-breaking Frenchmen (so that some of the most eminent members of our Jockey Club, such as the late Lord Falmouth and the present Duke of Westminster, have abstained from running

for that valuable prize), and in the same year the
Club again established (against 'Argus') its right to
'warn off'; in 1863 the Jockey Club opened to 'the
horses of members of the Rooms at Newmarket, as
well as to members of the Jockey Club,' the old exclusive Jockey Club Challenge Cup, which has been a
failure almost from the first; in 1864 the Club, which
had ceased to bask in the smiles of Royalty (with the
exception of Dutch representatives thereof), revived,
with the Prince of Wales to give it fresh vitality and
lustre; in 1865 the Club had to thank Mr. Blenkiron
(of Eltham Stud Farm) for the institution of the Middle
Park Plate (with 1,000*l*. 'added'), touching which in
1869 (when the Club took it over with the substitution
of 500*l*. for 1,000*l*.) there was a somewhat ungracious
proposal (defeated by a majority of the Club, it is
pleasant to relate) made that 'as the money is added
by the Jockey Club, it shall be called the Jockey Club
Plate'; in 1866 the Jockey Club paid the French the
well-deserved compliment of making M. de Lagrange,
M. Lupin, and the President, Vice-President, and three
Stewards of the French Jockey Club, honorary
members of the English; in 1867 it was resolved
that the Master of the Buckhounds for the time
being should be *ex officio* a member of the Jockey
Club; in 1869 the Club determined to enlarge the
Betting Enclosure for the convenience of persons
engaged in that of which the Club is supposed to
'take no cognisance,' as the excellent Mr. Tattersall

in former times, though himself inimical to betting, built, for the accommodation of his patrons who were addicted to what he deprecated, a 'house of call' more commodious than his parlour, which had previously served their purpose as well as it could; in 1869 and 1870 the Jockey Club successfully wrestled with Sir J. Hawley in his attempts to revolutionise horse-racing and the constitution of the Club, after the fashion advocated (though not to the same extent, apparently) in these latter days by the reforming Earl of Durham; and in 1872 Admiral Rous, on proposing (with Lord Falmouth, represented by Lord Calthorpe, as seconder) that 'no person starting one, two, or more horses, shall give orders to his jockey to pull up a horse that has a chance of winning, on any plea of declaration, or under any circumstances,' was promptly defeated by 22 votes to 4.

This is the more extraordinary because, as we have seen, the Club had in 1838 expressed its extreme disapprobation of starting horses without the intention of winning with them; and plain folk will have a difficulty in understanding how that can mean anything else than 'without the intention of winning with that which turns out to be the best of them in the race for which they are run,' for that is surely the end and aim of racing, and any other way of racing, as Admiral Rous clearly saw and as clearly stated, may be turned to sinister purposes. It is only fair to say that members of the Jockey Club, who were quite as honourable as Admiral Rous, voted against his proposition. And here again comes in the ever-recurring question of betting; but for which it is not easy to see why an owner should prefer to win with one of his horses rather than another, though certainly it would appear that in the One Thousand of 1890 the Duke of Portland was moved by sentimental regard for the Semolina he had bred in preference to the Memoir he had purchased, unless, indeed, he may have understood that Semolina had been backed by the public, and may have allowed himself to be influenced by that understanding. Mr. William Day, in his 'Racehorse in Training' (edition 1880, pp. 169-172) waxes quite enthusiastic in favour of the 'declaration to win,' considers it 'a disgraceful exhibition' when a jockey wins 'in defiance of orders' (to 'pull,' when a 'declaration' has been made), and opines that 'the offending jockey should in every case be heavily fined and suspended' (because he will probably have played havoc with the owner's *betting*, not with the owner's legitimate winning of stakes). How the minds of the most chivalrously honourable runners of race-horses may become tainted and perverted by this doctrine of the 'declaration' may be best illustrated by an account of what happened in 1850, when the proverbially chivalrous Lord Stanley (afterwards the Prime Minister Lord Derby) and his friend (and perhaps confederate for the time being) Mr. C. C. Greville, the celebrated Clerk of the Council, were concerned in a transaction of what seems to ordinary persons a very peculiar kind, akin to the 'declaration to win.' Lord Stanley, who was a bettor and sometimes a pretty heavy one, ran his mare Canezou for the Goodwood Cup, and it was well known that Canezou would have the better chance if she had 'something to make the running for her,' as the phrase is. Mr. C. C. Greville, therefore, kindly started his horse Cariboo to give her that assistance. The account goes on to say: 'Cariboo *was declared* to start merely to make the running for Canezou; but *he went so well that it was all Charlton [his jockey] could do to pull him up* in front of the Stand, in order that Butler might win with the mare.' Now, Mr. William Davis, the 'Leviathan' bookmaker, had betted heavily against Canezou, it is said, and it is no wonder, therefore, that he indulged in strong language, as he is reported to have done, at this exhibition of what the most chivalrous aristocrats consider honourable, or that some newspaper-writers of the day made unfavourable comments upon the proceedings. Of course both Mr. Davis and those writers were laughed at for their ignorance by more discriminating judges of what is right and proper, fair and unfair, honourable and dishonourable; but it is worthy of remark that, though a 'declaration' was made and a perfect understanding existed (it was asserted), yet on this occasion Canezou and Cariboo did not even belong to the same owner, but to different owners (unless, as was observed above, Lord Stanley and Mr. Greville were confederates at the time, which is not stated in the account to have been the case). Anyhow, to take a broad view of such questions, it is not very wonderful if persons, in whom the moral perception is not naturally very acute, or has not been sharpened by culture and practice, cannot see why, if you may have one of two or more horses pulled for the sake of winning not a race, be it observed, but the money you have betted on a race, you may not have a single horse pulled for the same commercially legitimate object, or why you may not juggle with three horses (to the deception and pecuniary spoiling of the Egyptians) as with three cards. However that may be, the Jockey Club has at last (in the Rules of 1890) officially sanctioned (Part XIX. Rule 141) the 'declaration to win' (in spite of the disapprobation expressed in 1838), but has made it compulsory, whereas it was formerly quite voluntary.

This is as opportune a place as any for telling another little anecdote (related by Admiral Rous) illustrative of the example set by a noble member of the Jockey Club for the edification of the Ring and of horse-owners. The noble owner (who was Lord Darlington, afterwards Duke of Cleveland) of Cwrw, winner of the Two Thousand in 1812, says the Admiral (who was certainly a little given to 'fouling his own nest') in his 'Horse-racing, had another horse, a colt by Remembrancer, in the Two Thousand.

This latter, before the race (which, it must be remembered, was not at that time a P.P. race, otherwise a 'Pay or Play' race, otherwise a race in which bets laid against a horse which did not start were not won), was 'ridden past the Ring with Chifney on his back and a stable-boy on Cwrw,' which was, of course, as much as a 'declaration to win' with the Remembrancer colt. But 'at the starting-post, Chifney changed his mount, Cwrw became the first favourite and won an immense stake,' and 'the Remembrancer colt did not start, by which the Ring lost a great portion of their field-money.' Yet this Lord Darlington was so far the very soul of honour, that when he became Marquess of Cleveland he, mounting upon the table at the Subscription Rooms, Doncaster, in the 'Ludlow' year (1832), denounced 'horse-cheats' with a fervour worthy of Peter the Hermit, and declared that thenceforth 'no *gentleman* could have anything to do with the Turf, at Doncaster at any rate.' His conduct in the case of Cwrw was, to say the least of it, 'shady,' but has been defended on the ground that the Ring had very often 'had' him. It should be recollected, however, that 'noblesse oblige'; and that, if you condescend to be an example of 'diamond cutting diamond,' you become a 'diamond.' To this may be added the instance recorded of the great reformer but gigantic bettor, Lord George Bentinck himself, when he threatened to have Elis scratched for the St. Leger of 1836, unless the required 'odds' were forthcoming, and so gave the sanction of his high authority to the abominable practice of 'putting on the screw.'

In 1875 the Jockey Club, marching with the times, actually erected a Grand Stand; and, as for many years a charge had been made for carriages of all kinds, Newmarket became, to all intents and purposes, almost as much a 'gate-money' race-cours as Kempton, Sandown, etc., which, joined to the fact that so many members of the Jockey Club have houses at Newmarket, makes the Heath a more private race-course (of which the members of the Jockey Club are the proprietors) than many another which is so-called but belongs to a company of shareholders. It may be a matter of regret, from certain points of view, to see the old delightful freedom and costlessness and openness to everybody departing from that which was peculiarly a popular spectacle, but the 'gate' gives an excellent means of excluding the professional 'bettor,' whenever it seems proper to adopt that course.

We may now pass on to 1876, when there was another 'reg'lar new fit out o' rules,' which will be found in 'Weatherby'; and it may be noted in passing, that the President of the American Jockey Club was by this time admitted among the honorary members of the English. In this year the Club had to deal with a representation made to them by certain 'owners and trainers of horses,' who desired to put an end to the 'Training Reports,' which had been introduced into some of the 'sporting newspapers'; and on the suggestion of Admiral Rous, it was agreed that 'the Committee lately appointed to consider the new rules should advise on the best mode of dealing with the subject.' What conclusion the Committee came to, matters little; for we all know that the 'nuisance' (if that be the proper name for it), so far from being abolished or abated, has become greater than ever, and that the information afforded (though perhaps of no practical use to any living creature) is daily paraded in detail and devoured with avidity by thousands, who derive as much comfort, if as little profit from it, as the old lady derived from 'that blessed word Mesopotamia.' In this year 1876, moreover, the Club had its attention drawn to the question of 'reciprocity' between the English Turf and the French, a reciprocity demanded, it was said, by the success of French horses on our race-courses in 1876, to the tune of some 26,000*l*. So that Lords Falmouth (of all men in the world), Vivian, and Hardwicke gave notice of measures to be brought before the Jockey Club in 1877 in restriction of French liberty to win our stakes. It was to be 'reciprocity' or 'warning off.' Ultimately, as we know, the measures were all shelved, and the question was not revived until Plaisanterie won both Cesarewitch and Cambridgeshire in 1885 (as Foxhall, the American, had done in 1881, without raising any desire among English owners to take vengeance for their losses by a descent upon Jerome Park). Then, at length, the Club was roused to action, and passed a resolution which rather contributed than not to make the French mare Ténébreuse win the Cesarewitch of 1888, and turned the laugh against the proposer. The Jockey Club had, so to speak, to eat its own words.

Of course reciprocity is to be desired, if only for the look of the thing; but for a perfectly equitable reciprocity there should be something like equal conditions on both sides. The arena on which the championship of the world is decided must be open to all comers; but it does not follow that every smaller arena, whence competitors come thither to achieve a few successes at long intervals, is bound to 'reciprocate' at the risk of having all its prizes won by strangers. At any rate, the Jockey Club would do well to think twice before they pass measures which, debarring the French from our courses, would keep their subscriptions from swelling our stakes, their owners from training in England, and employing hundreds of 'hands,' and their purchasers from buying in our market (either because they would no longer have to contend against our breed of horses, and would be content with their own; or because they would take our action as a proof that their horses were as good as ours, else we should not be afraid of them). Lord Stamford and Warrington, as we have seen, showed how to obtain the right of running on French racecourses; and since then the present Duke of Hamilton has taught the Jockey Club a similar lesson.

As a red rag to a bull, so is Mr. Anderson's Metropolitan Racecourse Bill of 1879 to a member of the Jockey Club, who will deride it as a 'posthumous act,' inasmuch as the club, 'with a view to the abolition' of such public nuisances as Kingsbury, Bromley, and *hoc genus omne*, had already before 1879, and, indeed, in the new rules of 1876-77, made such a sum of 'added money' *per diem* obligatory that the aforesaid meetings had 'been smothered out of existence' before the said Bill 'came into operation.' But these nuisances had been in existence for years and years (amidst outcry and lamentation) before the Jockey Club adopted the very roundabout course of which it boasts; and that course had certainly not 'smothered out of existence' Bromley by 1881, or Kingsbury by 1879; and it is problematical whether the entire smothering would have been effected by this time, had it not been for the fear inspired by an Act of Parliament. The Jockey Club might long before have put down the nuisances by the strong measure of denouncing the conduct of those meetings, and resolving that horses which had run there should be disqualified from running anywhere under Jockey Club rules. It is this dilatoriness, this hesitation to strike home, this habit of pleading 'Please, sir, we were just a-going to begin,' or 'we had as good as done it,

when some exterior pressure is brought to bear, that
has always characterised the Club, and brought under
a sort of jealous suspicion the authority which it has
so excellent a right to claim and exercise.

From 1879 to 1884 the Club was chiefly employed
in devising means for the suppression of the evils
which arise from the existence of jockeys who not
only bet, and bet to an extravagant extent, but are
owners or in part owners (as well as trainers) of race-
horses; but though elaborate measures (including
the licensing of jockeys, and the securing of the fees
due to them, as far as possible, so that they should
no longer have their old excuse for betting) were
passed and still remain in force, it is extremely
doubtful whether the impracticable object has been
so much as approached within measurable distance.
Impracticable, so long as jockeys are human, with
eyes to see the example set them by their employers,
with ears to hear the suggestions of the tempter
(whether brother-jockey, trainer, bookmaker, or
another), and with wits to understand how to shift
their own personality beyond all reasonable chance of
identification.

In 1885 the successes of Plaisanterie in the
Cesarewitch and Cambridgeshire led to the passing
of a rule which, known to the French as 'la proposition Craven' (Mr. W. G. Craven's), was intended, it
is supposed, to make things hard for French candidates in the future; but which, according to the

z

opinion of French authorities, had the contrary effect, and led indirectly to the success of Ténébreuse in 1888. The rule was afterwards withdrawn.

We now come to the gravest matter with which the Club has had to deal since it first came into existence—for the 'Running Rein' business was not settled by the Club but by a court of law, and, moreover, did not involve the credit of one of its own members—the 'Chetwynd-Durham Case,' which was left to the arbitration of the stewards of the Jockey Club, and was, in fact, an indictment framed by one member of the Club against another. There is no intention here of going into the details of the matter. It will suffice to call to mind that in a speech delivered at the Gimcrack Club, York, Lord Durham, in the most outspoken manner, brought certain charges which Sir G. Chetwynd considered to be levelled against himself, and said so. Lord Durham admitted that the cap had been put upon the right head. Whereupon Sir George, in the good old-fashioned way, wished to fight. Lord Durham naturally declined; not only, it may be presumed, because duelling is obsolete, as well as illegal, but because to have accepted the challenge would have proved nothing more than that two gentlemen were ready to stand fire or cold steel, as everybody would have taken it for granted that they were, and as 'Tommy Atkins' is whenever he is called upon. There was, therefore, nothing for it but the law; from which, with the necessary formal technicalities, the case was transferred to the Stewards of the Jockey Club for arbitrament. A dreadfully long inquiry ensued. Lord Durham proved a great many things (especially that between a member of the Club, a trainer, and a jockey of large pecuniary means, great ability, and questionable character, there were extraordinary relations, such as certainly would not have met with the approbation of the Lord Derby who wrote the letter to the Club of June 30, 1857), but, as most people thought, did not prove the particular allegations he had made. In the end Lord Durham incurred a great deal of expense, and won a great deal of credit. The Stewards delivered a sort of half and half award in spirit, though they awarded but one farthing instead of the 20,000*l.* claimed; and Sir George Chetwynd retired from the Club, announcing his retirement in a letter which Mr. James Lowther read to the Club, and commented upon in terms which made one wonder what the pother had been about, and why Sir George, instead of resigning, should not have been elected a Steward once more. To many an outsider it seemed to be eminently a case which the Stewards ought to have taken up (and, indeed, it appeared that they were 'just a-going to begin,' as usual, when the plaguy law interfered again and pricked them into premature action) long before, and settled within the four corners of the Jockey Club's own room; for, according to Lord Durham, the disgraceful matters which drove him to speak had been 'notorious' for a long time past, and ought not to have escaped the notice of the Stewards. Mr. Lowther very properly declines to be a 'detective,' but the common complaint has been for years and years (before and after Lord Derby's letter of 1857) that the Club and its Stewards will not see what is going on under their very eyes. To many an outsider, again, it was evident that the accursed betting was at the bottom of the whole wretched affair; and to many an outsider it occurred that the place of a gentleman, or a nobleman, or a semi-nobleman, who confesses to owing a considerable portion of his annual income to systematic, scientific betting, is not in the Jockey Club but in the Ring, whether with or without a stool and an umbrella, and a clerk and a slate and a white hat, whereof the brim is turned up with blue or red. At any rate, Sir G. Chetwynd's virtual condemnation seems to have had no effect beyond depriving the Club of his services and the benefit of his experience—perhaps only for a while.

CONCLUSION

CHAPTER XV

CONCLUSION

NOBODY can deny that the roll of the Jockey Club, from its commencement to the present day, generation after generation, has been a splendid one. The Club, as we have seen, has consisted from the very first, to all intents and purposes, of King, Lords and Commons (though the King, at its initiation, was represented by a Royal Duke only), as if it were modelled on the lines of the British Constitution. Its members have been—almost to a man, one might say—hereditary and elective legislators, versed in public affairs, and familiar with Parliamentary proceedings, and, in very many cases, holders of the highest offices in the realm; not a few have been the wits and social leaders of the day; a great number have won literary distinction; and most of them have claimed descent from families which were conspicuous, long before the Club was so much as dreamt of, not only in society, but in horse-breeding and horse-racing, and all that relates to the Turf, in bygone days and dark ages before that term had any special significance, and to which most of the famous sires of the 'Stud Book' (with the exception of the three primal 'Sons of the Desert,' for reasons mentioned already) can be traced. So far no better or more legitimate Governors of the Turf could possibly be desired; and it has been shown that they themselves, from 1753 to the present day, have kept continually in the front rank as owners, breeders, and runners, which makes them still more unexceptional as the components of the governing body.

On the other hand, it cannot be denied that they have been sinners from the first in the matter of that betting which is, and always has been, the curse of horse-racing. It is true that they have only followed the traditions of their fathers, who had no idea of horse-racing unconnected with betting; but there was then no organised Ring, and the members of the Jockey Club betted—for the most part—one against another, a comparatively unobjectionable mode of wagering.

Certainly there were 'blacklegs,' such as Messrs. Quick and Castle (who, about 1771-73, were 'warned off' certain race-courses, but not 'by order of the Jockey Club'), Dennis O'Kelly, Dick England, and others, to whom noblemen and gentlemen (including the 'Culloden' Duke of Cumberland) would condescend to lose their money (indeed, Mr. O'Kelly is said to have held 'post obits' to the amount of 20,000*l*. from a notorious Lord Belfast), but they did not as yet form a distinctly recognised body, with enclosures set apart for them at race-meetings all over the country, with a sort of 'Exchange' at Hyde Park Corner or Knightsbridge, with Clubs called after the reigning sovereign, and that sovereign's consort, with clerks and all the paraphernalia of a legitimate business, with a committee composed of nobles and gentles (mostly members of the Jockey Club), with town councillors and churchwardens (it is said) among their most conspicuous brethren, with the public press to aid and abet them, and with their mystic appellation of 'the Ring.' Besides, it was not until the Jockey Club had been in existence for some years that O'Kelly and England and their compeers were in full force. So that, when the Jockey Club first appeared upon the scene, their members may be truly said to have conducted their betting much in the same way in which it was conducted when, as the records relate of the famous match between Old Merlin and Mr. Tregonwell Frampton's unnamed horse, 'the South-country gentlemen observed to those of the North, that "they would bet them gold whilst gold they had, and then they might sell their land."' It is true that this reckless betting resulted in the ruin of 'several gentlemen,' and that Parliament had to take the matter up; but there was an absence of the sordid appearance which is characteristic of the modern system, when august personages whose 'ancestors came over with the Conqueror' try (generally, it must be acknowledged, in vain) to swell their revenues by winning the money which 'the Ring' has collected from more or less questionable sources.

That Ring, which it was the bounden duty of the Jockey Club, if they took upon themselves to be the Fathers and Governors of the Turf, to discourage at its first formation, and break up, as far as possible, when once it was formed, they have encouraged, accommodated, and even now accept as a great convenience and a blessing. Yet what, in the opinion of the Club, is the greatest evil on the face of the earth? A 'tout.' And what bred the 'tout'? Trials—the severe ones—for which a trial-horse is sometimes borrowed. And what necessitates such trials, which break down perhaps more great horses (like Velocipede and many another) than the races themselves? Betting; the desire to anticipate the result of a race, and, with the knowledge supposed to be thus acquired (supposed, be it said advisedly, for the trial may be, and—almost as often as not—is, illusive) to 'get the money on.' And whence comes the money which a member of the Jockey Club wins, if he should win? From the Ring. And whence does the money which the Ring pays come? Partly, no doubt, from members of the Jockey Club and gentlemen of their class, but partly—shall we say mostly?—from what Lord Suffolk and Berkshire correctly calls 'the perennial stream of the savings, the stealings, or the superfluities of the backing million.' A nice thing that a member of the Jockey Club, of the Governing Body, a Royal Prince, or a Duke, or a Marquess, or an Earl, or a Baron, or a mere Baronet or other Commoner of the higher and wealthier class, should win, if he do win, the money of his own tradesman or valet. But the winner would probably say '*num olet?*' Such is the state of mind engendered by betting.

To what, again, do we owe the practice of giving to jockeys preposterous sums (of 1,000 and even 'the whole stakes') for winning the Derby or other great (or even small) races? To betting, obviously.; for only the owner who wins large bets could afford to give away thousands of pounds to his jockey for winning. The practice has been severely condemned over and over again by such members of the Jockey Club as the late Lord Derby, the late Lord Glasgow (though himself a heavy bettor), the late General Peel, the late Admiral Rous, and other members like them; and yet the Club (to which many of these injudicious donors belong) do nothing, as a body, to stop the practice, as they very well could (so far as their own members are concerned), by a 'rule and order' or an 'agreement' of the kind already frequently exhibited. The conclusion, therefore, is that the Club on the whole approve of the practice.

To betting, again, we owe the unedifying spectacle (such as shocked Mr. Baron Alderson, when he had the facts of the 'Running Rein' affair before him) of 'noblemen and gentlemen associating and betting' with 'blackguards,' and, what is more, of members of the Jockey Club acting as agents (perhaps commission agents) for their own jockeys by 'putting on the money' for them, and of a member of the Jockey Club publicly squabbling with Mr. 'Plunger' Walton. To betting may be traced nearly all the 'nobbling' that has ever taken place, nearly all the trouble and misery that have resulted from horse-racing, nearly all the questionable proceedings recorded in the annals of the Turf, nearly all the calumnious reports to which the most honourable owners, trainers, and jockeys have been subjected, and nearly all the lawsuits which have arisen out of horse-racing. Nor is it going too far to say that betting is the great first cause of the ridiculously exorbitant charges, the downright robberies, to which everybody who follows the sport of horse-racing, to however small an extent, is invariably exposed, whether travelling by road or rail, or water or air, whether eating or drinking, or resting or sleeping, at the hotel or the hired house, or the 'apartments let furnished,' whether requiring a stable for his horses or a horse or horses from a stable. As Admiral Rous very truly said ('Horse-Racing,' p. 7): 'The owner of a racehorse in the United Kingdom is like Cain—the hand of every man who profits by the trade is against him.' The argument appears to be this: 'Lightly come, lightly gone; everybody who follows the sport of horse-racing makes or loses money by betting; the winner, having got his money so easily, is careless what he pays, and is ready to pay through the nose, and to the loser the exorbitant charges are but as another drop in the ocean.' No doubt overcharge is the rule everywhere where any kind of sport is a-foot, or any holiday-making is toward, so that the very tram-cars are said to charge double fares on Sundays and 'holy' days or holidays, and the tolls at Putney Bridge and Hampton Court used to be doubled in old times for whoever took an outing on Sunday; but for him who goes a-horse-racing or a-horse-race-seeing, prices are multiplied from tenfold to an hundredfold.

On the other hand, unfortunately, there is no gainsaying the fact that betting is the manure to which the present enormous crop of horse-racing and race-horse-breeding in this and other countries is to a very considerable extent due; and that, without betting, we should never have seen the establishment of those prodigious prizes (though, of course, they are obtained by clever alchemy from subscriptions and profits), and those high prices which make it possible for a few (and still comparatively only a few) owners, runners, and breeders of the thoroughbred, such as the late Lord Falmouth and the present Duke of Portland (with whom Mr. H. Chaplin may be joined, although he belongs conspicuously to the betting persuasion), to make racing and breeding pay handsomely without any sort of gambling. The late Lord

George Bentinck, no doubt, used to maintain that nobody but a Crœsus could afford to race without betting; but that noble lord, though he did a great deal to improve the Turf, and more than any among his brethren of the Jockey Club to augment the comfort and pleasure of the public at race-meetings, did some very queer things, uttered some very unsound doctrine, and in many respects was a very unsafe guide, philosopher, and friend. He was very hard on the man who lost 4,000*l.* to him, and asked for time to settle; so that there is the less hesitation in being hard on him (dead though he be) and saying, by a paraphrase of his own stern remark, that 'no man has a right to keep racehorses if he cannot pay for them out of his own pocket.' No doubt one of the reasons why horse-racing was called 'the sport of kings' was that those potentates (being then able to tax their subjects *ad libitum* almost) were at the head of the very few who could stand the expense of horse-racing, as a rule, though of course a few 'small men' might occasionally light upon a horse or mare that would be as good as a gold-mine (witness O'Kelly with Eclipse, and the I'Ansons with Queen Mary). Horse-breeding is, of course, a business, and a legitimate profit may be expected justly from it; but horse-racing is not only a test, but above all a sport, and why a man should expect to make money out of it any more than out of any other sport or fancy, out of yachting, or hunting, or shooting, or gardening, passes comprehension. A man, therefore, who takes to horse-racing should first calculate how much he can afford to spend annually on his 'pertickler wanity,' that is, how much he can afford to lose, and make his arrangements accordingly, taking for his motto 'quod Fors . . . cumque dabit, lucro Appone,' and considering whatever he wins a sheer godsend. This may seem to be a hard saying, but it is the only principle on which horse-racing can be conducted with as little as possible of that rascality which, with the curious irony that characterises life, seems to be inseparable from whatever appertains to the handsomest, noblest, most useful, most honest (with rare exceptions) of four-footed (or two-footed) animals. That a man should have in training, as Lord George Bentinck had, so many horses so heavily 'engaged' that their mere forfeits and travelling expenses would amount to twenty thousand and more pounds a year, and be unable to pay their cost unless he got the money out of other people's pockets, is simply monstrous. And this such a man could hardly hope to do, year by year, but for his middlemen, represented by the Ring.

Acquiescence in the existence of the Ring, even on the part of the Legislature, appears to have become the order of the day, as if the institution were a necessity; and as for the Newmarket Legislature, represented by the Jockey Club, they not only tolerate the Ring, instead of 'warning off' the monster, but they provide it there and allow it to be provided elsewhere with accommodation. The Ring, moreover, is likened very frequently to the Stock Exchange, and the members of the former to the members of the latter. But there is really no sort of analogy. It is obvious that an institution like the Stock Exchange, or the Bourse, or the Rialto, or whatever name be given to it, is absolutely necessary for the transaction of legitimate business between country and country and countries and individuals, and the regrettable 'jobbing' and speculation that become appurtenances of it can no more be prevented than the dirt that adheres to indispensable machinery; but the legitimate business of no country requires either betting or a Ring. A model Jockey Club would refuse to sanction any race-meeting where accommodation was provided for a Ring, and would 'warn off' all persons known to belong to the Ring; and a model Government would support such a Jockey Club with the strong arm of the law, would make short work of 'Tattersall's,' and the 'Subscription Rooms' at Newmarket, and such clubs as are known to exist for betting purposes by the 'quotations' issuing from them. The newspapers, even the most respectable of them, those that daily lecture us upon the state of public morality, 'encourage gambling' (as Admiral Rous truly said years ago), and uphold the Ring, by publishing 'quotations' and by having long articles written almost entirely from the betting point of view, and by giving 'tips' (to which if a man trusts he shall inevitably be 'broke'); whereas, if they would lend their assistance (which, of course, they will not do, from commercial considerations) by ignoring 'odds' and 'tips' altogether, the suppression of the monster would not be beyond hope entirely. For it is said, though it may not be generally known, that there was in olden times an idea of abolishing cricket on account of the gambling to which it gave rise; yet, though there is no doubt some betting on cricket-matches still, there is now no systematic and 'quoted' gambling connected with that game. Nobody wants to prevent anybody from forming an opinion and backing that opinion in the good old English fashion by a wager in reason; what one would like to suppress is the 'Society for the Propagation of Gambling on Horse-Racing' (without the trouble of forming an opinion, or caring for anything but the nimble ninepence).

It has been conceded that without the Ring there would be less horse-racing, less valuable prizes, less handsome prices for thoroughbred horseflesh, and there would perhaps be no drawing-room meetings (like Sandown and Kempton); but that might not be a matter for regret, inasmuch as there is a general complaint of over-racing, and (as it would leave horse-racing pretty much to those persons, hundreds of thousands in England who delight in the 'strength of an horse') it would render 'nobblings' and other obstacles in the way of ascertaining which is really the best horse of a season less likely, and might result in the production of a better class of horses than has ever yet been seen, even in the country that produced Flying Childers, Eclipse, Blacklock, Touchstone, Bay Middleton, Newminster, Stockwell, Galopin, Barcaldine, St. Simon, and Ormonde.

We have seen that, as regards the fitness of the Club to be the Moses of the Turf, its composition in many—nay, in most—respects leaves nothing to be desired. True, it has never done much for the public (though some of its members, individually, are not open to that reproach) until in 1875 it accomplished the construction of a Grand Stand, and cynics do say that even then the public might have waited another century or so, had not a more than usually acute member perceived how great a pecuniary advantage the Club might derive from the innovation. However that may be, it is proverbially ungracious to look a gift horse in the mouth.

Some thirty years ago, and even less, it was the fashion to sneer at the small amount of 'added money' which the Club from the very first had doled out for the encouragement of racing, even at Newmarket (to say nothing of the other race-meetings which were under its fostering care, but received from it no pecuniary nutriment whatever); but we have seen that it had heavy expenses of its own, whilst it was engaged in establishing its proprietorship of lands and tenements, or rather tenements first and lands afterwards, on and near the Heath, not to mention the salaries of the many officials whom it had to employ. Besides, at a very early period of its career it was as good as a grandmother to the provincial meetings, offering gratuitous advice and arbitration in the hour of dispute and difficulty. Nor could it reasonably be expected that the Club should supply subventions to associations which it assisted gratis with its authority and from which it derived no sort of emolument. As to the Club's acceptance from time to time of donations from private individuals (for instance, Lord Stamford, Mr. Blenkiron, and—quite recently—Mr. Rose), or from the town of Newmarket, or the Great Eastern Railway, it is all very well to urge that it is beneath the dignity of such a body to accept contributions towards a show of which the members of the Club are to all intents and purposes the proprietors, that the mere offer of a donation is a reflection upon the Club, as if it were needy or niggardly or inattentive to a certain class of races; but there is another side to the question, and that is the ungraciousness of refusing to let enthusiasts participate in the promotion of the good cause. At any rate, the Club is certainly less open nowadays than it was wont to be to the charge of illiberality. It is to be feared, however, that credit cannot be given to the Club for having originated the idea of an institution with which it is now intimately connected and which has flourished under its auspices, the excellent Bentinck

Benevolent and Provident Fund. That fund is understood to have commenced with the sum of money subscribed for a testimonial to Lord G. Bentinck on account of his services in the detection of the 'Running Rein' fraud, but to have been projected some years before by that same Mr. Whyte, of the Hippodrome, Bayswater, who first invented or is said to have been the first to invent the invaluable 'tan gallop.'

Lord Suffolk and Berkshire (Badminton Library, 'Racing,' p. 55) says : 'To ordinary minds, however, it seems that the only beneficial method by which Parliament could exercise a control over racing would be that of bestowing some form of incorporation on the Jockey Club, and having thus asserted its supremacy, the Legislature might well leave the general management and direction of Turf matters in the hands of that body, which for a hundred and thirty years has held an undisputed authority, which now rules over many thousands of the inhabitants of the kingdom, and whose laws and regulations, obeyed and respected here, receive the sincere flattery of imitation from other countries.' Here is a statement which, as we have seen, is perfectly true on the whole, but requires some modification ; for the authority of the Club, by its own published acknowledgment, did not extend necessarily (as appears from the case of the alteration, in 1833, from May to January of age-taking) beyond Newmarket till within the last thirty-two years, when (in 1858) the Club first assumed the right to dictate the whole Rules of Racing, though it had previously taken the liberty of making an alteration or addition (chiefly by way of explanation) from time to time; and as lately as 1854, when exception was made at some country race-meeting or race-meetings (advertised to be held 'under the same rules and regulations as Newmarket') of one particular rule, the Club simply 'recommend to the Stewards of all races not to allow this exception in future,' without announcing any penalty for disobedience. 'Other countries,' moreover, have undoubtedly paid the Jockey Club the compliment of imitating its rules in most respects (as they could not well help doing, unless they studied to be original and eccentric) ; but, as we have seen, some of them have a rule diametrically opposed to that of the Club concerning nominations and the death of the subscriber. Add to this that the Club itself apparently adopted the rules published by Mr. Pond, stuck to them for about fifty years or more, and made no notable alteration in them before 1803, when they omitted one article; so that the mere argument of adoption and imitation does not carry much weight.

Be it fully granted, however, that the Club is the best conceivable ruling body for the Turf. Still, it does not follow that the best thing that Parliament could do, either for the Club or for the public and the

Turf, would be to grant it a charter of incorporation and supremacy. An incorporated body of that kind, entrusted by the Government with legislative authority in matters appertaining to owners, trainers, breeders, and their numerous adherents and various interests, could not remain, it is obvious, a private, social Club, as it is now, when it certainly is not and does not profess to be representative of any but a single class. Besides, it is quite impossible that a Government, so keenly alive as ours is supposed to be to the evils arising from the existence of the Ring, the 'Society for the Propagation of Gambling' (and its dreadful consequences), could commit by express enactment the charge of the Turf and all its appurtenances to a Club which, from its infancy, has suffered from the curse of betting, and in these latter days has hailed the Ring as a blessed medium for indulging the more easily in what the law refuses to recognise as legitimate, and the Government regards as vicious. Such a Government, so acting, would stultify itself egregiously. Let the Jockey Club make a compact to assist the Government by not only declining to provide an enclosure for the Ring, but by 'warning off' the members of it from Newmarket Heath and from all other race-courses under Jockey Club rules, by abolishing the Subscription Rooms at Newmarket, and by passing a rule that no member of the Jockey Club shall bet with any member of the Ring, either personally or by commission, on pain of losing his membership by so doing; and then it will be time enough to expect that Parliament will give to the Jockey Club the plenary sanction it desires.

Of course the Jockey Club will not do anything of the kind, any more than the Government will give the public prosecutor orders to proceed against 'Tattersall's,' or the newspapers, the very best of them, will drop their 'quotations' and their 'gambling articles,' and cease to spread the 'Ringworm.' Yet the small bettor of the public-house, or the shop, or the lodging, or the pavement, is daily brought before the magistrate, and not unnaturally asks, 'Why don't you try it on with the big men?' Possibly the small men cause the most actual crime, but it looks mean to tackle them only, and, moreover, it is of little use, as they are the most numerous, and the conviction of them produces little effect and attracts little notice. Kill a bishop if you wish to prevent avoidable railway accidents; make an example of a 'Leviathan' if you mean to stop the plague of public betting.

Meanwhile, there are a few more points to be considered as regards the Jockey Club. We have seen that the members of that Club, and of the class in society to which they belong, either bred or owned in olden time all the horses and mares (with few exceptions in each case) from which the present splendid and unequalled English thoroughbred is descended, supplied nearly all the horse-racing that was of any account, and, in nearly every case, were the winners of the races whereof the names have become household words, and that it was only when the studs of such personages were disposed of, either in consequence of death, or retirement, or inability to win any more wagers with certain animals, that persons belonging to a very different class, persons with whom members of the Jockey Club had and could have no social connection, became possessed of a noted horse or mare, the sire or dam of progeny which earned great sums of money both in stakes and bets, and world-wide celebrity upon the Turf. Still, there were in the very early days one or two such persons: the Quicks and Castles, the Wildmans, the O'Kellys, the Englands, with more reputable contemporaries or successors, such as Mr. Tuting, Clerk of the Course at Newmarket; Mr. Martindale, the saddler of St. James's Street; Mr. John Hutchinson, the ex-stable boy of Shipton, near York; and Mr. Tattersall, the auctioneer who made a fortune by Highflyer. As time went on, the number of such persons, both reputable and disreputable, grew and multiplied, until at last jockeys, and trainers, and bookmakers, as well as men 'in business,' of high character perhaps and of enormous wealth, and members of Parliament to boot, but not of sufficient culture or standing in society to be admitted among the aristocratic members of the Jockey Club, and, even had they been eligible in those respects, too numerous for a Club which had always been of somewhat circumscribed dimensions—for a club—were conspicuous among the breeders as well as owners and runners of the best horses in England, and the names of Chifney, Ridsdale, Sadler, Gully (ex-butcher, ex-prize-fighter, ex-publican, but M.P.), Pedley, I'Anson, Snewing, J. Day, W. Scott, W. Day, J. Dawson, Forth, J. Scott, Crockford (of 'fishy' antecedents), B. Green, and a host more, some of them men of the very highest character, but nevertheless bookmakers, trainers, and jockeys, or persons 'in business' (whether in the line of hosiery, or ' Nicholson's gin,' or iron, or carpets and furniture), as Messrs. Theobald (breeder of Stockwell), Graham (who 'belonged to' Regalia), Blenkiron (of Middle Park), Merry (the 'Glasgie body'), Cartwright (owner of the 'beautiful Ely'), and *tutti quanti*, were constantly in the mouths of men as winners of the 'classic' races, or breeders of the horses that won them. Meanwhile the era of Stud Companies had set in, and they too sent forth horses conquering and to conquer. Observing all this, certain reformers arose with propositions, and among them, Sir Joseph Hawley (himself a prominent member of the Jockey Club) raised the question, as we have seen, whether the time had not come for 'extending the basis' of that Club which ruled the Turf and nearly everything that appertained thereto, and rendering it more representative; and the same question has been lately raised again by Lord Durham (another prominent member of the Jockey Club). It is a curious fact that a complaint similar to that which is implied in the proposal to 'extend the basis' of our Jockey Club has lately been made by a French writer (Monsieur A. de Saint Albin) concerning the 'exclusiveness' of the French Jockey Club (which consists of about two thousand members, more or less). 'Il est très regrettable,' we read, 'que pour faire partie du Comité de la Société d'Encouragement, on doive nécessairement faire partie du Jockey Club,' and 'ce que je regretterai toujours, c'est que le Comité de la Société d'Encouragement reste fermé pour une foule d'hommes de valeur, que leur situation dans le monde de l'élevage désignerait tout naturellement pour avoir voix au chapitre.' What is curious in this is that the 'Société' was the original foundation out of which the now obstructive 'Club' or 'Cercle' grew; that it was possible at first to belong to the 'Société' without belonging to the 'Cercle,' but not to belong to the 'Cercle' without belonging to the 'Société'; that the subscriptions were kept separate; and that it was ruled that 'tout Membre de la Société peut, sur sa demande, être admis sans ballottage à faire partie du Cercle,' in February, 1836, by which time (only three years from the foundation of the 'Société') it seems obvious that nobody was likely to be elected to the 'Société' who would not be an eligible member of the 'Cercle.' And, in fact, it appears that by 1838 there were but eight members of the 'Société' who were not (however eligible they may have been) members of the 'Cercle,' namely, Baron de la Bastide, Marquis de Marmier, Comte Edouard de Montgregon, le Chevalier Nogent, Monsieur Couret Pléville, Marquis de Miramon, Comte Max de Béthune Sully, and Major Cadogan. Thus, in France, a huge fashionable Club has grown out of a horse-improving Society, and has usurped the dominion which, there is reason to believe, was originally intended for a very different body, consisting of all manner of men interested in horse-breeding and horse-racing. The reason, of course, is that, the founders having been men of rank, station, wealth, and fashion, and the idea of combining the business of a company with the sociality of a club having occurred to them, the social question prevailed over every other, and the main object, after the first year or two, was to keep out all that was uncongenial. How much more must that be the case with a club such as our Jockey Club, which seems to have been started for the express purpose of knitting together men of like class and pursuits, and keeping at arms' length men of different class, though of like pursuits? You may 'extend the basis' of such a Club; but, as Lord Durham proved when he was challenged to mention the names of eligible persons, and accepted the challenge, you will not make it much more representative as regards variety of class. Nor is there any reason in the world why a Club of gentlemen, who have acquired the supreme authority in all matters relating to the sport which they pursue, should throw open their doors to uncongenial followers or promoters of the same sport, and be put to the inconvenience of social incongruity. There is no just cause or impediment why a suggestion should not be borrowed from the original French arrangement, whereby the 'Société' and business were kept separate from the 'Cercle' and sociality; why there should not be in this country a 'Turf Society' to which anybody might belong, and which should deal generally with all business connected with the Turf, and distinct from it, as a social Club, the present Jockey Club, a certain number of whose members should be *ipso facto* members of the Committee of the Turf Society, and whose Stewards should have the power of *veto* in all cases of proposals originating with the Society. In this way the Club might preserve its undoubted right to be as private and even as exclusive as it pleases, and might keep intact its prestige and authority and usefulness (which would be seriously endangered if nothing more than a property qualification or a prominent connection with the Turf were considered to give Tom, Dick, or Harry a claim to membership).

We have seen that in many respects the Jockey Club has been, from time immemorial, the best conceivable governing body for the Turf; but we must not forget that under its auspices many abuses have been permitted, and even encouraged. It sanctioned for a long while those yearling races which it now forbids altogether, and which nearly everybody agrees to condemn. It cannot be altogether exonerated from the charge of allowing two-year-old racing (which in moderation is good, perhaps, rather than bad) to be carried to excess, and of contributing to the multiplication of short-distance races (which, no doubt, became more numerous as yearling courses and two-year-old courses grew more and more common, and of which it now seems at last to have repented). It sanctions the pernicious 'declaration to win' (which can be turned to villainous account) ; it has shut its eyes to all sorts of scandals, until one of its own members has felt called upon to protest; and it has used its power of 'warning off' too often against petty offenders, and too seldom against notorious scoundrels. It has done absolutely nothing to diminish the evil of gambling, but, indeed, has rather encouraged it collectively and individually (with a few bright exceptions). It has certainly declined to settle disputes between bettors, but that was obviously rather to escape trouble, and the necessity perhaps of having a disagreeable duty to perform towards some of its own members, than to express disapprobation of the practice, and to throw obstacles in the way of it. And until it takes for its motto 'Delenda est Corona' (to paraphrase Cato's famous saying), and ceases to give facilities to the Ring for plying its questionable trade, it is ridiculous to suppose that a Legislature whose chief difficulty, as regards horse-racing, is in dealing with the curse of betting, will so far stultify itself as to bestow upon the Jockey Club, whose members are (some, not to say most, of them) among the greatest offenders, the charter which is so self-complacently claimed for it by Lord Suffolk and Berkshire.

The Club, collectively, may not have been noticeable for a desire to promote the pleasure, comfort, and advantage of the public; but individually they have many of them at different times deserved well of the community, either by establishing race-meetings on their property, as, for instance, the Dukes of Richmond at Goodwood, the Earl of Egremont (previously) at Petworth, the Fetherstons at Uppark, the Lambs (Lords Melbourne) at Brocket Hall, the Brands at the Hoo, the Earls of Eglinton at Eglinton Park, the Earl of Wilton at Heaton Park, the Earls of Verulam at Gorhambury, &c., or, as for instance Lord G. Bentinck, by improving the spectacle and increasing the means of enjoying it.

APPENDIX

APPENDIX

Up to the time at which the Jockey Club was established, and for many years afterwards, the only Rules of Racing (to be found in the records) consisted of two distinct parts, of which one may be termed the Statute Law and the other the Common Law. The former, in the shape of 'An Abstract of an Act passed in the 13th year of his Majesty's [George II.'s] reign, relating to Horse-Racing,' and the latter, in the guise of a document copied *verbatim et literatim* (but numbered, as it is not in the original), are both inserted here, that the curious may see out of what material the Jockey Club eventually elaborated its present voluminous and minutely constructed code. There were also separate articles referring to the Royal Plates and issued under the authority of the Master of the Horse for the time being; but as the Plates, so far as England is concerned, are obsolete, there is no occasion to deal with those articles.

PART OF AN ACT PASSED IN THE 13TH YEAR OF GEORGE II.'s REIGN, RELATING TO HORSE-RACING.

Horses to be enter'd by the Owners. And no more than one at a Time.—That from and after the Twenty-fourth Day of *June*, one Thousand seven Hundred and Forty, no Person or Persons whatsoever shall enter, start, or run any Horse, Mare, or Gelding, for any Plate, Prize, Sum of Money, or other Thing, unless such Horse, Mare, or Gelding shall be truly and *bona fide* the Property of and belonging to such Person so entering, starting, or running, the same Horse, Mare, or Gelding, nor shall any one Person enter and start more than one Horse, Mare, or Gelding, for one and the same Plate, Prize, Sum of Money, or other Thing; and in Case any Person or Persons shall, after the said Twenty-fourth Day of *June*, one Thousand seven Hundred and Forty, enter, start, or run any Horse, Mare, or Gelding, not being the Property truly and *bona fide*, of such Person so entering, starting, or running the same for any Plate, Prize, Sum of Money, or other Thing, the said Horse, Mare, or Gelding, or the Value thereof, shall be forfeited, to be sued for and recovered, and disposed of in Manner as is herein after mentioned, and in Case any Person or Persons shall enter and start, more than one Horse, Mare, or Gelding, for one and the same Plate, Prize, Sum of Money, or other Thing, every such Horse, Mare, or Gelding, other than the first entered Horse, Mare, or Gelding, or the Value thereof, shall be forfeited, to be sued for and recovered, and disposed of in Manner as herein after is mentioned.

On Penalty of 200*l.*—Any Person that shall enter, start, or run a Horse, Mare, or Gelding, for less Value than fifty Pounds, forfeits the Sum of two hundred Pounds.

On Penalty of 100*l.*—Every Person that shall print, publish, advertise, or proclaim any Money or other Thing to be run for of less Value than fifty Pounds, forfeits the Sum of one hundred Pounds.

Races to be begun and ended in one Day.—Provided also, that every Race that shall be hereafter run for any Plate, Prize, or Sum of Money, be begun and ended in one Day.

APPENDIX 371

Matches may be run at Newmarket and Black-Hambleton for any sum under 50l.—Horses may run for any Sum on *Newmarket* Heath, in the County of *Cambridge* and *Suffolk*, and *Black-Hambleton*, in the County of *York*, without incurring any Penalty.

Entrance-Money to be paid to the Second-best Horse.—And be it further enacted by the Authority aforesaid, That from and after the Twenty-fourth day of *June*, one Thousand seven Hundred and Forty, all and every Sum and Sums of Money to be paid for entering of any Horse, Mare, or Gelding, to start or run for any Plate, Prize, Sum of Money, or other Thing, shall go and be paid to the second-best Horse, Mare, or Gelding, which shall start or run for such Plate, Prize, or Sum of Money, as aforesaid.

Gifts left for annual Races not to be alter'd.—Provided always, That nothing herein contained shall extend, or be construed to extend to prevent the starting or running any Horse, Mare, or Gelding, for any Plate, Prize, or other Thing or Things, now issuing out of, or paid for, or by the Rents, Issues, and Profits of any Lands, Tenements, or Hereditaments, or of or by the Interest of any Sum or Sums of Money now chargeable with the same, or appropriated for that Purpose.

RULES CONCERNING RACING IN GENERAL.

(From Pond's 'Kalendar' for 1751.)

Horses take their Age from *May Day*:
1760 Yards is a Mile.
240 Yards is a Distance.
Four Inches is a Hand.
Fourteen Pounds is a Stone.

1. Catch Weights is each Party to appoint any Person to ride without weighing.

2. Give and Take Plates are fourteen Hands to carry ( ) [the weight not specified, as it varied by agreement]; all above or under to allow the Proportion of seven Pounds for an inch.

3. A Whim Plate is Weight for Age and Weight for Inches.

4. A Post Match is to insert the Age of the Horses in the Articles, and to run any horse of that Age, without declaring what Horse, till you come to the Post to start.

5. A Handy-Cap Match is for *A.*, *B.*, and *C.* to put an equal sum into a Hat, *C.* which is the Handy-Capper, makes a match for *A.* and *B.* which when perused by them, they put their Hands into their Pockets and draw them out closed, then they open them together, and if both have Money in their Hands, the Match is confirmed; if neither have Money it is no Match: In both Cases the Hand-Capper draws all the Money out of the Hat; but if one has Money in his Hand, and the other none, then it is no Match; and he that has the Money in his Hand is intitled to the Deposit in the Hat.

6. If a Match is made without the Weight being mentioned, each Horse must carry ten Stone.

7. If no Power is allowed in the Articles to alter the Day of Running, and it should be run on another Day, the Bets before altering are all void.

8. Where a Power is allowed in the Article for altering the Time of Running, all Betters must conform to the changing the Day.

9. *Crossing and jostling allowed in Matches, if no Agreement to the contrary.* [Italicised for emphasis.]

10. When started, if a Rider attempts to go off, and his Horse by taken the rest [= by taking the rest = by becoming restive], or any Accident should prevent it, he

would be distanced though he did not pass the Post [*i.e.* the starting-post].

11. The Horse that has his Head at the ending Post first, wins the Heat.

12. Riders must ride their Horses to the weighing Post to weigh, and he that dismounts before or wants Weight, is distanced.

13. Horse Plates, or Shoes not allowed in the Weight.

14. If a Rider falls from his Horse, and the Horse is rode in by a Person, that is sufficient Weight, he will take place the same as if it had not happened, provided he goes back to the Place where the Rider fell. [Case in point at Melton Mowbray, August 29, 1728.]

15. Horses not intitled to start, without producing a proper Certificate of their Age, at the Time appointed in the Articles, except where aged Horses are included, and in that case a *junior* Horse may enter without a Certificate, provided he carries the same Weight as the aged.

16. All Betts are for the Best of the Plate, if nothing is said to the contrary.

17. A Horse that wins the first and second Heats, wins the Plate, but is obliged to start again if required by any one of the other Riders, and no Clause in the Articles against it, and must save his Distance to intitle him to the Plate.

18. For the best of the Plate, where there are three Heats run, the Horse is second best that wins one.

19. For the best of the Heats, the Horse is second, that beats the others twice out of three Times, though he doth not win a Heat.

20. A confirmed Bet cannot be off without mutual Consent.

21. Either of the Bettors may demand Stakes to be made, and on Refusal declare the Bett void.

22. If a Party is absent on the Day of Running, a publick Declaration of the Bett may be made on the Course, and require if any Person will make Stakes for the absent Party; if no Person consents to it, the Bett may be declared void.

23. Betts agreed to pay, or receive in Town, or at any other particular Place, cannot be declared off on the Course.

24. The Person that lays the Odds has a right to chuse his Horse, or the Field.

25. When a Person has chose his Horse, the Field is what starts against him, but there is no Field without one starts with him.

26. Betts made for Pounds are paid in Guineas.

27. If Odds are laid without mentioning the Horse before it is over, it must be determined as the Betts were at the time of making it.

28. Betts made in running, are not determined till the Plate is won, if that Heat is not mentioned at the Time of Betting.

29. Betts are void for the best of the Plate, on Horses that have run, not being qualified.

30. Betts are won and lost, for the best of the Heats, if Horses are not qualified.

31. Where a Plate is won by two Heats, the Preference of the Horses is determined by the Place they are in at the second Heat.

32. Horses running on the wrong Side of the Post, and not turning back, distanced.

33. Horses drawn before the Plate is won, are distanced.

34. Horses distanced, if their Riders cross and jostle, when the Articles do not permit it.

35. [If a Horse wins the first Heat, and all others draw, they are not distanced if he starts no more, but if he starts

again by himself, the drawn Horses are distanced.] [This Rule was expunged by the Jockey Club in 1803.]

36. A Bett made after the Heat is over, if the Horse betted on does not start, is no Bett.

37. When three Horses have each won a Heat, they only must start for a fourth, and the Preference between them will be determined by it, there being before no Difference between them.

38. No Distance in a fourth Heat.

39. Betts determined, though the Horse does not start, when the Words absolutely, Run or Pay, or Play or Pay, are made Use of in Betting.

Example, I bett *Robinson's* Bl. H. *Sampson* absolutely wins the King's Plate at *Newmarket* next Meeting, the Bett is lost though he does not start and win [won] tho' he goes over the Course [by] himself.

40. Betts made, a Horse wins any Number of Plates in a fixed Time, no Bett if he does not start for one, after he has started for one, provided there is a Field, the Bett is lost if he starts no more.

41. In Sweep-Stakes Match or Plate of one Heat, where two Horses come in so near that it cannot be decided, they two only must start again, and the Betts are determined on the others the same as if it was won.

42. In running of Heats, if it cannot be decided which is first, the Heat goes for nothing, and they must all start again, except it be in the last Heat, and then it must be between the two Horses that if either had won the Plate would have been over, but if between two that the Plate might not have been determined, then it is no Heat, and the others may all start again.

43. If betted, that two Horses wins their Matches, if the first is run, and the last not, the Betts are determined, and the Horse that pays Forfeit is the beaten Horse, but if

the first Match is not run, and the last is, then it is a void Bett.

44. If two Persons by Agreement or casting Lot, to chuse on two Matches, one is run and the other forfeits, that which is run is determined, and that which forfeits is void, they being two distinct Betts.

45. Horses that forfeit are the beaten Horses, where it is run or pay.

46. Betts made on Horses winning any Number of Plates that Year, remain in Force till the first Day of May.

47. Money given to have a Bett laid them, not returned, if not run.

48. To propose a Bett, and say done first to it, the Person that replies done to it, makes it a confirmed Bett.

49. The Party in a Match, that does not bring his Horse to the Post at the Time specified in the Articles, the other at the Expiration of it, may go over the Course without him, which intitles him to the Sum, or forfeit what the Match was made for.

50. Matches and Betts are void on the Decease of either Party, before determined.

Such, presented in the literal form in which it originally appeared, is Mr. Pond's List of Rules. It no doubt has concealed somewhere about it a faithful statement of the laws which were in his day accepted by the followers of horse-racing as a pursuit or pastime, but the interpretation of those laws is rendered somewhat difficult and uncertain by a grammatical construction which Mr. Pond himself would perhaps have accounted for by saying that he was 'no scholar,' but which, nevertheless, reminds one forcibly of the greatly admired Æschylus and Thucydides among the ancients, as well as of the celebrated Mrs. Gamp among more modern and more fictitious characters. The composition, indeed, can be highly recommended to school boards and school inspectors or examiners as a specimen of English wherewith to test the parsing capacities of their young victims as thoroughly as those of the less humble young scholars at the public schools are tested with choice examples of the Greek or Latin language, as 'she' was sometimes 'wrote' by poets and historians who ought to have known better.

INDEX

INDEX

The initials (J. C.) mean 'member of the Jockey Club'; Horse includes mare or gelding, colt or filly.

AAR

AARON (horse), 49
Abbesse de Jouarre l' (horse), 308
Abergavenny, Lord, 179
Abingdon, Earl of (J. C.), 12, 38–40
— Earls of, 25
Achievement (horse), 303, 308
Achmet (horse), 206
'Acton,' Mr. (Baron Lionel de Rothschild), 270, 315
Acts, Inclosure, &c., 246, 247, 369
Addison, Right Hon. Joseph ('Spectator'), 74
Adieu-to-the-Turf (horse), 143
'Adjudged Cases' (by the J. C.), 251
Adkins, Mr. (convicted swindler), 321, 322
Adonis (horse), 217
Æacus, the 'infernal' judge, 116
Age (of race-horses), different starting-points for the, 252, 253
Ailesbury, Marquess of (J. C.), 264, 281, 282
— — ('warned off'), 281, 282
Aimwell (horse), 50; (Mr. Conolly's), 112
Ainderby (horse), 146
Airlie, Earls of, 124
Ajax (horse). Sir J. Lowther's (by Carnatic), 88
Alabaculia (horse), 65
Aladdin (horse), 185
Albemarle, Earl of (J. C.), 264, 283
— Earls of, 283
Alcibiades, the dog of, v. Jennings, (Mr. 'Chillaby')

ANC

Aldby Park (Yorks), 150
Alderson, Mr. 'Baron' (on the 'Running Rein Case'), 321, 347
Aldrich, Admiral Robert D., 274
Alexander, Mr. Caledon (J. C.), 189, 265, 298
Alfred (horse), 146
Alice Hawthorne (horse), 222
Alington, Lord (J. C.), 265, 296, 308, 309
— the family of, 309
Alipes (horse), 138
All Fours (horse), 136
— Souls (Oxford), Library at, 110
Allerton (Mauleverer), (Yorks), Duke of York's estate of, 184
Alleyne, Miss Judith (of Barbados), 121
Allix, Mr. (J. C.), 247, 265, 298
— Messrs., 247
Alteration of age-taking, 252, 253
Altisidora (horse), 304
Alvediston Stud (Mr. W. Day's), 282
Amaranthus (horse), 136, 137
Amato (horse), 205, 296
Ambrosio (horse), 223, 235
Amelia, Princess (aunt of George the Fourth), 50
American Jockey Club, President of (J. C.), 333
Amersham (Bucks), 300
Ampthill (Beds), 61
Ancaster, Duke of (J. C.), 12, 23, 89, 113, 125, 156
— Duchesses of, 24
— Dukes of, 24–26

AND

Anderida (horse), 236
Anderson, Mr. or Capt. (Francis), (J. C.), 12, 99, 111
— Sir Edmund (of Kildwick), 99
— Mr., M.P. (his Racecourse Bill), 336
Angelica (horse), 89
Anglesey, Marquess of (J. C.), 264, 322
— Stakes (last public race for yearlings), 250
'Anglomania,' 174
Anne, Queen, 8, 19, 24, 203, 311
Annesley, Earl of (J. C.), 264, 284
Annette (horse), 141
Anson, Col. and Gen. (J. C.), 265, 273, 288
— Viscount (J. C.), 286
— Lord (Commodore), 273, 286
Anspach, Margrave of, 51
— Margravine of (Lady Craven), 51, 242
Antæus (horse), 145
Antar (horse), 297
Antelope (horse), 29
Anticipation (horse), 226, 240
Antipas (horse), 227
Antonio (horse), 259
Anvil (horse), 181, 183, 226, 239
Apella, the proverbial, credulous Jew, 59
Aphrodite (horse), 296
Apology (horse), 162
Appleby (Yorks), 87
Apsley House, 237
Arab, decline of the, 21, 22
— (name of a horse), 193
Arabians (breed of horses), *passim*; (failure of), 21, 22
Arachne (horse), 112
Archduke (horse), 220
Archibald (horse), 273
Archiduc (French horse), 324
Ardrossan (horse), 52
Argentine, family of, 309
'Argus' (a sporting writer's *nom de guerre*), 3, 258, 327

AZO

Aristotle (horse), 100
Armagnac (French horse), 288
Armytage, Sir John (J. C.), 12, 71, 72
— Sir George, 71
Artois, Comte d', 97, 174
Arundel (Sussex), 162
Ascham (horse), 89
Ascot (Berks), 8, 19 *et seq.*
— Cup, the, 268
— Races, the Father of, 19
Ashburnham, Earl (second) of (J. C.), 12, 40, 123, 310
Aske (Yorkshire), 81
Askrigg (Yorkshire,), 101, 128
Asparagus (horse), 55
Assassin (horse), 202
Asteroid (horse), 281, 296
Astley, Sir J., 140
— Sir Jacob, 312
— — J. D. (J. C.), 189, 266, 298, 309
Aston, Sir Willoughby (? J. C.), 172, 178
Astridge, Mr., 26
Athole, Duke of (Earl Strange), 68
Atlantic (horse), 291
Atlas (horse), 29
Atom (horse), 216
Attila (horse), 213, 273
Aubigny, Duchess d' (and of Portsmouth), 133
Auchinlech, the Laird of (J. Boswell), 105
Auckland, Lord (? J. C.), 172, 176
Augur (horse), 110
Augusta (horse), 203
Augustus (horse), 203
Australia (country), 253
Aventurière (horse), 282
Aylesford, Earl of (J. C.), 264, 275, 276
Ayrshire (horse), 148, 308
Ayrton, Mrs. (breeder of Bay Malton), 64, 65
Azor (horse), 279

INDEX

BAB

BABRAM (or Babraham), (horse), 20, 31
Baccelli (horse), (she-dancer), 107, 220
Bacchanal (horse), 53
Bacon, Lord (Verulam), 212, 213
Bagatelle (villa near Longchamps, Paris), 273
Baird, Sir David (of Seringapatam), 294
—— (J. C.), 265, 294
— Capt. E. W., 248
— Mr. Douglas (J. C.), 266, 308
Baker, Mr. (the celebrated, of Elemore Hall), 238
Ballyglasmin Park (Galway), 100
Bampfylde, Sir C. Warwick, murder of (? J. C.), 172, 178
— Lady, 107
Banker (horse), 112, (another) 185
Banstead Downs, 199
Barbados, 87, 110, 121, 131
Barbary (horse), 97, 107, 174
Barcaldine (horse), 48, 354
Barcarolle (horse), 283
Barclay, Mr. H. T. (J. C.), 221, 266, 309
Barefoot (horse), 192, 304
Barforth (Yorks), 113
Barmecide (horse), 226
Barnard, Lord (J. C.), (Duke of Cleveland), 191
Barnbow (Yorks), 83
Barne, Mr. F. (J. C.), 266, 298
— Mr. Miles, 298
Baron, The (horse), 304
'Baron's Year,' the, 269
Baronet, the 'lucky' (J. C.), v. Hawley
Barré, Colonel, 177
Barri (or Barry), Madame du, 44
Barry, Mr. J. (Smith), (J. C.), 13, 41, 68, 136
— Madame du, 44
Barrymore, Earls of (J. C.), 12, 41–44, 68, 79, 136, 154, 177, 224, 275

BEN

Bashful (horse), 121
Bastide, Baron de la, 363
Basto (horse), 29
Bath, Lord (Pulteney), 140
Batson, Mr. (senior), (J. C.), 173, 186, 222, 223, 234, 266
— (junior), (J. C.), 266
Batthyany, Count and Prince (J. C.), 264, 268
Bay Bolton (horse), 190
— Malton (horse), 64, 65, 148, 312
— Middleton (horse), 205, 206, 278, 289, 354
— Richmond (horse), (alias Sarpedon), 81
— Slipby (horse), 120
— Starling (horse), 120
Bayswater (hippodrome at), 249, 356
Beadsman (horse), 296
Beau, Le (horse), 29
—- Brummell, 30
— Clincher (horse), 53
Beauclerc } , Mr. Topham, 45, 180
Beauclerk }
— Lady Di, 44, 45
Beaufort, Duke of (J. C.), 264, 306, 308, 309
Beaumont, Lords, 137
Bedford, Dukes of (J. C.), 93, 142, 172, 188–190, 212, 218, 236, 264, 281
Beechwood (Herts), 91
Beeswing (horse), 222
Belfast, an Earl of, 344
Belgians, King of the, 263
Belgrave, Lord (second Earl of Grosvenor), (J. C.), 172, 176, 196, 282
Belle-de-Nuit (horse), 109
Bellina (horse), 55
Belmont (Cheshire), 136
Belphœbe (horse), 308
Belsay Castle (Northumberland), 89
Belville (horse), 192
Bend Or (horse), 280, 308

BEN

Bendigo (horse), 221
Beningbrough (horse), 75, 96, 241
Bentinck, Lord George (J. C.), 35, 119, 193, 195, 246, 265, 271-273, 285, 290, 314, 318, 332, 350, 351, 366
— — Edward (? J. C.), 172, 176
— Benevolent Fund, 355, 356
Berkshire, 40
Berners, Lords, 222, 243, 294
Berteux, Comte de (J. C.), 264, 268
Bertie, family of, 25
— Willoughby (fourth Earl of Abingdon), v. Abingdon
— Mr. or Capt. (J. C.), 173, 223
Berwick (place), The Governor of, 180
Bessborough, Countess of, 29, 30
— Earl of (J. C.), 264
Bethell, Mr. William (of Rise), 130
Béthune-Sully, Comte Max de, 363
Betting (the Jockey Club and), 256, 327, 337, 344-354
— (the newspapers and), 352
— Ring, v. Ring, The
Betts, Mr. Samuel ('starter of the horses'), 167
Bibury (Gloucestershire), 167
— Club, 10, 167, 182
Biggs, Mr. H. (J. C.), 266, 299
Bildeston (stud-farm), 243
Bishop Burton (Yorks), 304
Bizarre (horse), 197
Black and All Black (horse), (Othello), 63
— Bess (horse; Dick Turpin's), 85, 242
'Blacklegs' (ancestors of 'The Ring'), 344
— (horse), (*the Devonshire*), 115
Blacklock (horse), 304, 354
Bladen, Mr. or Colonel Thomas (? J. C.), 12, 99, 100

BOS

Bladen Stallion, the, 100
Blake, Messrs. (J. C.), 12, 78, 100, 103
— Sir Patrick (J. C.), 12, 100, 103
Bland, Sir John (the gambler), (suicide of), 14, 130
Blankney (place), 309
— (horse), 309
Blenkiron, Mr., 327, 355, 361
— (and the Middle Park Plate), 327
Blink Bonny (horse), 290
Bloodstone (horse), 318
'— Case,' the, 318
Bloody Buttocks (horse), 113
Blucher (horse), 209
Blue Bonnet (horse), 284
— Gown (horse), 296
Blundell, Mr. W. (father-in-law to the Duke of Ancaster), 23
Blythe, General, 71
Blunderer (horse), 53
Bohun, 114
Bolingbroke, Viscount ('Bully'), (J. C.), 12, 14, 44, 74, 146, 159, 179
— the celebrated, 44
Bolton Hall (Yorks), 191
— Bay (horse), 190
— Dukes of (whether J. C. or not), 129, 172, 190-192
— Lord (Mr. T. Orde-Powlett), 190
Bon Vivant (horse), 137
Bonny Black (famous mare) 36
Boothby, Mr. Scrymsher ('Prince'), (J. C.), 12, 103, 104, 122
— Mr. Robert, 105
— Scrimshire, Mr. Thomas, 122
Bootle Sir Thomas, 149
— Wilbraham, Messrs. (Earls of Lathom), 149
Boringdon, Lord (J. C.), 126, 181, 183, 226, 239
— (place), 226
Borlase, Sir John, 145
Boscawen, Admiral, 186

INDEX

BOS

Boscawen, Evelyn (Viscount Falmouth), 216
— Mr. George, 103
Boston (American horse), 80
Boswell, Mr. James (Dr. Johnson's biographer), (? J. C.), 12, 22, 23, 52, 91, 105, 106, 153, 174, 311
— 'The Cub at Newmarket,' by, 22, 91, 106, 153
Bothwell (horse), 308
Bounce (horse), 36
Bourdeaux (horse), 223
Bowes, Mr. John (J. C.), ('all but' Earl of Strathmore), 248, 249, 266, 288, 289, 299
'Bozzy' (James Boswell, Dr. Johnson's biographer), v. Boswell, Mr. James
Bradford, Earl of (J. C.), 264, 306 309
Bradley (Derbyshire), 121
Brand, Mr. Thomas (married Baroness Dacre), (J. C.), 12, 106–108, 294, 366
— Mr. (the 'Speaker'; Lord Hampden), 107
— Mrs. (Hon. Gertrude Roper, Baroness Dacre), 107
'Bravo Rous' (whence derived), 210
'Bray v. Jennings' (action for assault), 258, 287
Braybrooke, Lord (J. C.), 225
Brereton, Mr. (a 'sad vulgar'), (insolent at the J. C. rooms), 17, 154
Brewerne (Oxon), 230
Briar Root (horse), 308
Brick (French horse), 288
Bridget (horse), 199
Bridgewater, Francis third Duke of (J. C.), 12, 26, 57, 311
— — 'Father of Canals,' 26
— Scroop, first Duke, 26
— Treatises, 27
Brigantine (horse), 308
Brighton (Brighthelmstone), 36
Briglia (horse), 298

BUN

Brilliant (horse), 113
Briseis (horse), 236
Bristol, Bishop of, 243
Brocket Hall (Herts), 167, 312, 366
Brockton Hall (Salop), 225
Brograve, Mr. Robert ('bookmaker'), suicide of, 278
Bromley, suburban races at, 336
Bronze (horse), 40, 278
Brooke, Mr. Henry (and Lord Pigot), 62
Brookes's Club, 14
Brother to Johnny (horse), 190
Brown, Miss (Mrs. Fetherstonhaugh), 82
— Betty (horse), 67
— Lusty (alias Bay Bolton, by Grey Hautboy), 190, 191
— Slipby (horse), 120
— Starling (horse), 120
Browne, Mr. (ancestor of the Lords Feversham), 114
Bruce, Lord (J. C.), 264, 281
— (horse), 289
Brutus (horse), 95
Buccaneer (horse), 310
Buckhounds, Master of the, passim
— — ex-officio member of the J. C., 327
Buckhunter (horse), (the 'Carlisle' gelding), 47, 48
Buckingham, Dukes of, 114
— Earl of, 211
Buckstone (horse), 292
Bulkeley, Sir R. W. (J. C.), 265, 322
— Capt. (J. C.), 266
Buller, Mr. Justice (? J. C.), 173, 178
Bullock, Mr. Thomas (J. C.), 154, 173, 223, 235
'Bully' (Lord Bolingbroke), (J. C.), 14, 45, 58
Bumbrusher (horse), 112
Bunbury, Sir Thomas Charles (J. C.), 12, 45, 59, 72–78, 103, 113, 159, 181, 244, 254

C C

BUN

Bunbury, Mr. H. ('H.B.,' the caricaturist), (J. C.), 74
— Lady Sarah, 14, 72, 73, 112, 154
— Miss Annabella (Mrs. Blake), 103
Burdon, Mr., 76
Burgoyne, General, 199
Burleigh (horse), 227
— Lord (J. C.), 265
Burlington Street (Old), 165
Burlton, Mr. Philip (J. C.), 12, 108
Burrells, the 'lucky' (Lord Gwydyr, &c.), 131
Burton, Mr., 108
Bury Hill (Newmarket), 248
— St. Edmund's (Suffolk), 90, 140, 215
— Street (St. James's), 165
Bute, Earl of, 87
Butler, Frank (jockey), 273
Butterfly (horse), 303
Buzzard (horse), 40, 73, 227
Byerley, Captain (his 'Turk,') 150
Byng, Admiral, 123
— Field-Marshal Sir J. (Earl of Strafford), (J. C.), 172, 214, 288
— Hon. G. Stevens (Earl of Strafford), (J. C.), 214, 266, 288
Byron, Lord, 6
Bywell (Northumberland), 115

CADE (horse), (America), 145
Cadet (horse), 108
Cadland (horse), 195
Cadogan, Earl (J. C.), 264, 306, 308, 309
— Major (member of the Société d'Encouragement), 363
Cælia (horse), 190
Cæsar (a fox), 95; (horse), 286
Cæsario (horse), 35, 67
Caledon, Earl of (J. C.), 264
Calendars, Racing, 11, 161–166, 245, 253
Calthorpe, Lord (J. C.), 265, 308, 309, 328

CAR

Calvert, Mr. John (J. C.), 12, 109
Camarine (horse), 222, 223
Camballo (horse), 304
Cambridge (place), 124, 258
— the Duke of (J. C.), 263
Camden (horse), (*alias* Rockingham), 42
Camel (horse), 224
Camélia (horse, bred in France), 270
Camilla (horse), 89
Campbell, Mr. or Capt. Mungo, 52
Campsall (Yorks), 220
Canezou (horse), 271, 330, 331
Canning, Viscountess, 130
Cannon-ball (horse), 204, 223
Cantator (horse), 50, 188
Cape Breton (ceded to pay the Duke of York's debts), 185
Captain (horse), 312
— Tart (horse), 175
Cara (horse), 304
Caravan (horse), 294
Carabineer (horse), 81
Carbineer (horse), 81
Cardigan, Earls of, 282
Cardinal Beaufort (horse), 202, 239
— Puff (horse), 55, 65
'— —' (toast), 184
— York (horse), 39
Cardock (horse), 226
Careless (horse), 145
Carew (horse), 198
Cariboo (horse), 330, 336
Carington, the Hon. Rupert (ex-J. C.), 266
Carleton, Sir John, 3, 4, 310
— Col. Dudley Wilmot (Lord Dorchester), (J. C.), 266
Carlisle, (fifth) Earl of (J. C.), 12, 46, 178, 229, 264
— Gelding, the, 47, 48
Carlton Hall (Yorks), 137
Carmarthen, Lord, 194
Caroline (horse), 202
Carr House (Doncaster), 28
Carriage Match (Lord March's), 57

CAR

Carrick-glass (Ireland), 95
Cartouch (horse), 120, 121
Cartwright, Mr. W. S., 361
Case-Walker, Mr. T. E. (J. C.), 266, 299
Cassandro (colt), 125
Castle, Messrs Quick and ('black-legs'), 344, 360
— Eden (Durham), 176
Castletown (Ireland), 112
Castrel (horse), 40
Catch-'em-alive (horse), 280
— (and the Cambridgeshire), 280
Catgut (horse), 193
Cato (horse by Regulus), 113
Catterick (Yorks), prohibition of a horse-race at, 312
Cavendish (families of), 28
— Lord (Marquess of Hartington), (J. C.), 12, 28
— — G. H. (J.C.), 172, 196, 197, 209
Cawdor, Earl of (J. C.), 264, 309
Cawdry (or Cawdray), (Sussex), 19
Cawston Stud (Lord John Scott's), 293
Cecil, the Hon. William, 203, 311
Cedric (horse), 93, 204, 297
† Cell, Mr. (J. C.), 12, 109
Centaur (horse), 209
Centurion, Commodore Anson's ship, 273
Ceres (horse), 55, 115
Cervantes (horse), 243
'Cesarewitch,' the, 268, 269, 272, 286, 321
— a very pretty, 321, 322
Champion (horse), 244
Chancery Suit (concerning the Racing Calendar), 164
Chapeau d'Espagne (horse), 272
Chaplin, Right Hon. H. (Minister of Agriculture), (J. C.), 266, 307–309, 349
Charibert (horse), 291
Charlemont, Earl of (J. C.), 264
Charles the Second (King), 9, 19, 47, 313
— Twelfth (horse), 240

CHI

Charlotte (Queen of George the Third), 24, 121
— (horse), 244
— West (horse), 206
Charm (horse), 53, 192
Chartres, Duc de ('Égalité'), 172, 188
Château-Margaux (horse), 244
Chaworth, Mr. (killed by Lord Byron), 6
Chedworth, Lord (J. C.), 12, 48, 49, 116, 243
Cheffreville (Normandy), (Comte de Berteux's stud), 268
Chelmsford, Lord, 178
Cheney (or Cheny), Mr. John (and his Calendar), 161–163
Chesterfield, Earls of (? J. C.), 14, 71, 172, 176, 197, 238
— sixth Earl of (J. C.), 186, 197, 264
— dinner to the sixth Earl of (J. C.), 198
Chesterton Hall (Hunts), 126, 228
Chetwynd, Sir George (ex-J. C.), 265, 338–340
— Park (Salop), (the Pigotts'), 126, 228, 332
'— Durham Case,' the, 321, 338–340
Cheveley, The Hundred of, 36, 185
Chiffney (or Chifney), Messrs. (jockeys), 181, 240, 361
Childers, Mr. or Colonel, 28
— Flying, or Devonshire (horse), 28, 101, 197, 312, 354
Chillaby (horse), the 'mad' Arabian, 232, 234
— King William the Third's, 232–234
— Jennings, Mr. (J. C.), 217, 231–234
— (Young), (horse), (v. Viscount), 234
Chippenham (horse), 315
— Park (Cambs), 315

CHO

Cholmondeley, Lord (his bet with Sir John Lade), 219
Chorister (horse), 191
Christian, Prince (J. C.), 263
'Christie's' (St. James's Street), 244
Christopher, Island of St. (St. Kitt's), 124
Chrysippus ('the Father of the Porch'), 19
Chudleigh, the Hon. Miss (the 'infamous' Duchess of Kingston), 32
Chuff (horse), 56
Churchill, Lord Randolph (J. C.), 33, 265, 307–309
Cicero (the famous Roman orator), 74
Cincinnati (a h. b. American mare in Mr. H. Savile's stud and in the Stud Book), 302
Cincinnatus (the Roman dictator), 64
Circe (horse), 60
City Road (Rous, of the), 210
Clarence, George, Duke of, 231
— William, Duke of (William IV.), (J. C.), 172, 181, 185–187
— and Avondale, Duke of (J. C.), 263
Clarendon (hotel), 7, 152, 198, 199
— Earl of (J. C.), 227, 264
Claret (horse), (*alias* Smart), 217
Clark, Messrs. (official 'judges' to the J. C.), 167
Clarke, Mrs. (joint commander-in-chief of the British army with the Duke of York), 184
Clearwell (horse), 286
Cleaver (horse), 143
Clementina (horse), 279
Cleopatra (horse), 148
Clergymen-horse-racers, 162
Clermont, William Fortescue (first and last), Earl of (J. C.), 12, 30, 41, 49, 50, 53, 78, 79, 146, 174, 250
— Course (Newmarket), 50

COM

Cleveland, Dukes of, 191, 192
— Marquess and Duke of (J. C.), 172, 191, 192, 264, 331, 332
Clifden, Lord (Viscount), (J. C.), 12, 265, 290
— — (horse), 277
— (horse), 189, 218
Clift, Mr. W. (jockey), 221
Clio (horse), 53
Clopton, Mr. Boothby Scrymsher, 104
Closterseven (the Convention of), 71
Coates, Mr., 76
Cobham (horse), 310
Cobweb (horse), 193, 206
Cockfighter (horse), 220
Cockfighting (in the drawing-room), 200
Codrington, Mr. (J. C.), 12, 110, 111, 126
— Sir W., 110
— Colonel, 110
— Mr. Bethel, 111
Coke, Mr. (owner of Hobgoblin), 150
— Lord, vii
— Lady Mary, 23
Coleraine, Earls of (J. C.), 224, 237
Coleridge, S. T. (the poet), 29
Collier (horse), 120
Collinge, Mr., 92
Colonel, The (horse by Whisker), 185, 195, 280
Colours, first adoption of advertised by J. C., 157, 158
Columbine (horse), 224
Colville (of Culross), Lord (J. C.), 265, 307, 309, 310
Combe (or Coombe), Mr. Harvey (J. C.), 266, 310
Commodore (horse), 207
Common (horse), 308
Competitor (horse, the last of the 'Eclipses'), 197
Compton, Mr. (Henry), (J. C.), 12, 45, 111

Compton Bassett (Wilts), 179
Comus (horse), 60, 174
Conductor (horse), 50, 53, 139, 146
Conflans, the Marquis de, 107, 174
— Stakes, the, 174
Connaught, the Duke of (J. C.), 263
Conolly, Hon. and Rt. Hon. Thomas (J. C.), 12, 112
— Lady Louisa (sister of Lady Sarah Bunbury), 112
Conqueror (horse), 188
Consternation (horse), 275
Conyngham, Marquess of (J. C.), 264, 282
— (horse), 62
Cook (or Cooke), Mr. J. P. (poisoned by Palmer), 322
Cookes, Mr. T. H. (J. C.), 266
Cookson, Mr. J. (J. C.), 173, 221, 223, 235
Cope, Sir Charles (of Brewerne, Oxon), 230
Copenhagen (horse), the Duke of Wellington's, 236
Coquette (horse), 49, 92
Coriander (horse), 223
Corinne (horse), 227
Corisande (horse), 269
Cork and Orrery, Earl of (J. C.), 264, 307, 310
'Corner,' the (Hyde Park), 7
Corporal (horse), 52
Corsair, The (horse), 286
Corsican (horse), 125
Cosby, Mr. T. (J. C.), 266, 300
Cotherstone (horse), 299
Count (horse), 217, 225
Countess (horse), 217
Couret Pléville, M., 363
Course, the Duke's, 208
— the Clermont, 208
— Dutton's, 208
Courten, Comtesse de (Mrs. Bowes), 299
Courtenay, Lord (ex-J. C.), 111, 265, 276

Courtezan (horse), 112
Covent Garden workhouse, 163
Coventry, Earls of (J. C.), 172, 177, 264, 307
— the 'beautiful' Countess of (Maria Gunning), 45, 177
Coxcomb (horse), hunted at *eighteen* years of age, 61
Coxe (or Cox), Mr. Richard Hippisley (J. C.), 12, 112, 113
Craigmillar (horse), 300
Craven (sixth Baron), (J. C.), 12, 51
— (first Earl of), 51
— Lady (Margravine of Anspach), 51, 242
— Messrs. (J. C.), 266, 278, 310, 337
— (sporting writer's *nom de guerre*) 3
— Stakes, the (Newmarket), 51, 160, 310
'— La proposition,' 337
Crawfurd, Mr. W. Stirling (J. C.), 58, 266, 300
Crawley, Mr. Ambrose (Alderman), 41, 310
— Mr. J. S. (J. C.), 41, 266, 310
Creampot (*dun* horse), 91
Creeper (horse), 174, 311
Cremorne (horse), 302
Crescent (horse), 282
Cricket, 6, 301; (and gambling), 353
Cricketer (horse), 202
Crimea, travels in the, 241, 242
Cripple (horse), (sire of Gimcrack), 52
'Cripplegate' (nickname of an Earl of Barrymore), 42, 44, 154 275
Crockford, Mr. (fishmonger and hell-keeper), 361
Crofts (or Croft), Mr. William (of West Harling, Norfolk), (J. C.), 12, 113
— Mr. John (of Barforth, Yorkshire), 113

CRO

Crompton, Mr. G., 75
Cromwell, Oliver, 205
Cronie (horse), 33
Crossing and Jostling (allowed unless barred by agreement), 251
Crucifix (horse), 272
'Cub at Newmarket, The,' by J. Boswell, 22, 91
Cumberland, William, Duke of ('Culloden'), (J. C.), 12, 18, 41, 119, 344
— Henry Frederick, Duke of (J. C.), 12, 18, 20, 23, 30, 53, 172, 175
— Richard (the author), 176
— Stakes, 21
Curiosity (horse), 39
Curragh, the Whip at the, 184
Currency (horse), 270
Curwen, the family of (C.'s Bay Barb), 150, 311
Curzon, Mr. and Sir Nathaniel (first Baron Scarsdale), (J. C.), 12, 80
— name of, 312
Cussans, Mr. (J. C.), 173, 223
Cuthbert, Captain (duel with Sir J. Lowther), 88
Cwrw (horse), 191, 332
— Admiral Rous's story about, 191, 331, 332
Cypron (horse), (dam of King Herod), 20
Cyprus Arabian, 36
Czarewitch, the Grand Duke (J. C.), 263
Czarina (horse), (runs at 2 years of age), 76

DACRE, Lord, 107
— the Baroness (Hon. Gertrude Roper, afterwards Mrs. Brand), 107
Dædalus (horse), 55
Dainty Davy (horse), 192

DEL

Dalrymple, Mr., Col., and Gen. (? J. C.), 173, 178
Danby Lodge (Yorks), 310
Danebury (Hants), 282
Daniel O'Rourke (horse), 299
Darley, Messrs. (and their Arabian), 150
Darlington, Earl of (J. C.), 172, 191, 331
Daru, Vicomte, 326
'Dashington, Henry,' 128
D'Aubigny, Duchess of Portsmouth and, 133
Davers, Sir Charles (J. C.), 172, 215
— Sir Robert, 215
Davis, Mr. William (the original 'Leviathan' of the 'Ring'), 330
Dawson, Mr. Francis (J. C.), 173, 220, 223
— Daniel (horse-poisoner), 179
— Mr. J. (trainer), 361
Day, Mr. William, 78, 250, 282, 322, 329, 361
— Mr. John, 272, 361
Deard, Mr. (a 'judge' at Newmarket), 166, 167
Deard's Coffee-house (Newmarket), 167
Death of a Subscriber (voidance of nomination by), 322–326
— — — French Rule, 322–326
— — — German Rule, 322–326
— — — Austro-Hungarian Rule, 322–326
— — — Australian Rule, 322–326
December (horse), 322
'Declaring to win,' 331, 365
Defence (horse), 284
Defiance (horse), 224
Delamere (Wilbrahams of), v. Wilbraham
Delancey, Colonel (American), 138
'Delenda est Corona,' 365
Delmé, Mr. (J. C.), 173, 223

DEL

Delmé-Radcliffe or Radclyffe (J. C.), Mr., 107, 173, 223, 294
Delpini (he-dancer), 43
— (horse), 43, 146
'Deluge,' The (Mme. de Pompadour's), 188
De Mauley, Lord (J. C.), 265
Demirep (horse), 112
Denby Grange (Yorks), 86
Denmark (horse), 124
'Derby,' The (race), the Queen and Prince Albert at (1840), 283
— Earls of (J. C.), 67, 68, 79, 132, 172, 199, 200, 264, 271, 321, 329
— the fourteenth Earl and the J. C., 321, 347
Dervise (horse), 193
Desdemona (h. b. American mare, in the Stud Book), 302
Despair (horse, two years old), 77
Despencer, Baroness le, 291
Destiny (horse), 301
Des Vœux, Sir H. (J. C.), 265
'Devil on Two Sticks,' the (sporting writer's *nom de guerre*), 3
Devon, Earl of (ex-J. C.), 111
Devonshire, Georgiana, Duchess of, 29
— Dukes of (J. C.), 12, 19, 28, 196
Diamond (horse), 78, 221
Dick Andrews (horse), 207
Dictator (horse), 277
Didelot (horse), 220
Dilettanti Club, The, 107
Dilly, Mr., 192
Dimple (horse), (winner of the Whip), 20, 29
Diomed (horse), 74, 80, 244
Diophantus (horse), 102, 103, 277, 288
Ditto (horse), (won the Derby in a 'trot'), 221
Dobito, Mr. (breeder of roadsters 'up to ' 23 st.), 241
Doctor Syntax (horse), 284
Doddeshall (Bucks), 96

DUC

Doddington Hall (Gloucester), 110
Don Cossack (horse), 227
— John (horse), 198
Doncaster (horse), 280
Donovan (horse), 221, 308
Dorchester, Countess of (James the Second's mistress), 92
— Lord (J. C.), 3, 265, 310
Dorimant (horse), 60, 61
Dormer, Sir Cottrell, 125
— Lady (his widow), 125
Dorrimond (or Dorimond), (horse), 115, 119
Dorset, Dukes of (J. C. and others), 172, 175, 206, 207, 264
Douglas, Mr. Thomas (J. C.), 17 223, 233, 235, 266
— Hon. John, 314
— The Rev. Mr., 235
Downe, Viscountess, 130
— Viscount (J. C.), 265, 310
Downton, the Lords Feversham of, 114
Doyle, Sir F. H., Professor of Poetry at Oxford, 59, 75, 287
Dragon (horse), 189, 218
Drake, Mr. T. T. ('Squire'), (J.C.), 266, 300
Driveler (or Driver), (horse), 121
Driver (horse), ('Ancaster'), 25
— (*Little*), (horse), 49
Driving-feat, 218
Drogheda, Marquess of (J. C.), 264, 311
— Lord, 311
Dromedary (horse), 224
Dromo (horse), 29
Dromore, Bishop of, 53
Drone (horse), 181, 228
Drudge (Young), (horse), 116
Drumhead (horse), (Sir J. D. Astley's), 189, 298
Dubarry (or Dubarri), Madame, 44
Dublin, a ride up the steps of the Bank of, 293
Duchess (horse), 115, 157

Duchess (of Leven or Lieven), (horse), 243, 295
Dudley, Earl of (J. C.), 147
Dudwick (Aberdeen), 227
Duenna (horse), 204
Duke, The (horse), 275
'Duke's Course,' the, 208
Dumplin (horse), 19
Duncombe, Mr. Thomas (ancestor of the Earls of Feversham), 12, 113, 114, 300, 311
— Mr. Charles Slingsby, 114, 300
— Park, 114
Dundas, Sir Lawrance (or Laurance), (J. C.), 12, 80, 81, 148, 290, 316
— Sir Thomas (first Baron), 81
— Mr. and Baron, 81
— — (? J. C.), 173, 178, 231
Dundee (horse), 277
Dunn, Mr. Salisbury, 247
Dupplin, Lord (Viscount), (J. C.), 265
Durdans (estate), 296
— (Stakes), 269
Durham, Earls of (J. C.), 16, 248, 264, 306, 307, 311, 328, 361
Dutch Oven (horse), 291
Dutton, Mr. Ralph (J. C.), 75, 173, 181, 190, 223, 235, 236
— family of (ex-Naper), 137, 208, 236
Dutton's Course (at Newmarket), 208
Dux (horse), 39, 77, 116
Duxbury (Lancashire), 220

Eager (horse), 190
'Eagle' Tavern (City Road), 210
Eaglescliff (or Egglescliff), (Yarm), 146
Earl, The (horse), 111, 275
Earl's Court (Kensington), 54
— (Lambourne), 116
Eastwood, Mr. R., 303, 304
Ebor (horse), 304
Echidna (horse), (dam of The Baron), 304

Eclipse (horse), 20, 21, 139, 150, 187, 197, 350, 354
'— Foot,' the (trophy), 5, 186, 187, 197, 234, 300
— skeleton of, 187
Economist (horse), (sire of Echidna), 304
Eden, Sir Robert, 176
— Right Hon. W. (Lord Auckland), 176
— Castle (Durham), 176
Edinburgh, Duke of (J. C.), 263
Edmundsbury (Bury St. Edmund's), 215
Edwards, Messrs. (jockeys), 205
Effingham, Earl of, 121
'Égalité,' Philippe (Duc d'Orléans), 49, 172, 174, 182, 188
Egglescliff (Yarm; Yorks), v. Eaglescliff
Egham (Surrey), 218
— (horse), 216
Eglinton, Earls of (J. C.), 12, 52, 106, 174, 264, 284, 311, 315, 366
— the Tournament at, 284
Egremont, Earl of (J. C.), 35, 69, 79, 172, 190, 201, 202, 209, 227, 239, 264, 366
'Egyptian' (horse), The Ancaster, v. Ancaster
Eleanor (horse), 74, 244
Election (horse), 202
Elemore Hall (Yorks), 238
Elephant (horse), 141, 142
Elis (horse), 286
— Lord G. Bentinck and the backers of, 333
Elizabeth (horse; a twin), 209; (another horse), 300
Ellesmere, Earl of (J. C.), 264, 311
Elthiron (horse), 293
Elwes, Mr. ('Miser,') 39, 40
— Mr. R. C. (J. C.), 266
Ely (horse, 'the beautiful'), 285
Emetic (horse, by Chillaby), 233, 234

Emigrant (horse), 141
Emilius (horse), 227
Emma (horse), 65
Emperor, The (horse), 284
Emperor's Plate, 268, 284
Enamel (horse), 203
Enfield, Viscount (second Earl of Strafford), (J. C.), 265, 288
Engineer (horse), 115
England, Mr. or Captain, 'Dick' ('blackleg'), 344, 345, 360
Enguerrande (horse), 270
Enterprise (horse), 308
Enthusiast (horse), 308
Ephemera (horse), 202
Epsom, 167, 175, 179
— Comte de Mirabeau at, 175
Erratt, Messrs. (of Newmarket), 153, 246
Errington, Sir J. M. (J. C.), 265
Erroll, Earl of (J. C.), 264
Erskine, Lord Chancellor (? J. C.), 173, 178
Escape (horse, the Prince of Wales's—George IV.), 75, 181, 223
Essedarius (horse), 62
Essex, Earl of, 100
— Lady (horse), 100
Esterre (Mrs.), 193
Etwall, Mr. R. (J. C.), 266
Euston (seat of the Duke of Grafton), 30, 152
Evelyn, Sir Frederick (J. C.), 172, 216
— Mr. John (the celebrated), 9
— Sir John, 216
Everlasting (horse), 93, 190
Exeter, Marquess (second) of (J. C.), 172, 202–204, 264, 307, 311
Exning (near Newmarket), 247, 248
Exotic (horse), 286
Expectation (horse), 207
Extempore (horse), 240
Eye (Herefordshire), 118
— Court (Herefordshire), 118

FAGNIANI, Maria (Lady Hertford), 57, 132
Fairfield (estate, Yorks), 304
Fairplay (horse), 143
Faith (horse), 55
Falmouth, Viscounts, 216
— Viscount (J. C.), 216, 265, 278, 282, 291, 305, 326, 328, 334, 349
Falstaff, Sir John, 153
Fandango (horse), 290
Fanny (horse), 112
Farewell (horse), 308
Farnham, Lord (J. C.), 12, 50, 52, 53
Farren, Miss Ellen (actress and Countess of Derby), 200
Favonius (horse), 269, 302
Fawconer, Mr. (Tuting and F.), 164, 165
Fawkener, Mr. (Clerk of the Privy Council; duel with Lord John Townshend), 178
Fawley Court (Berks), 89, 90
Fazzoletto (horse), 271
Fearnought (horse), 145
Featherstonhaugh (family of), Fetherstonhaugh (J. C), 12, 81, Fetherston 217
Feenow (horse), 43
Fenton, Mr. William (J. C.), 12, 20, 65, 115
Fenwick, Mr. William (J. C.), 12, 115
— Sir John (very ancient racer), 116
Fermor, Miss Arabella (heroine of Pope's 'Rape of the Lock'), 280
Ferrers, Earls, 134, 135
Festetics, Count Tasselo (J. C.), 264, 268
Fetherston, Sir H. (J. C.), 53, 172, 183, 216, 366
Fettyplace, Mr. Robert (J. C.), 12, 116
— Hon. Mrs. (Charlotte Howe), 116
Feversham, Earl of (J. C.), 115, 264, 311

FEV

Feversham, Lords, 114, 300
— (of Downton), 114
Fidget (horse), 190
Fiennes, Messrs. (Lords Saye and Sele), 293
Filho da Puta (horse), 226, 301, 312
Fille de l'Air (horse), 268
Finches, 'the black funereal,' 275
Firebrand (horse), 272
Fire-tail (horse), (a mile in 1 min. $4\frac{1}{2}$ sec.), 59, 101–103
Fitzjames, Marquis de, 174
Fitzpatrick, Col. and Gen., the accomplished Hon. Sir Richard (brother of Lord Ossory), (? J. C.), 60, 173, 178
FitzRoland (horse), 296
Fitzroy, family of, 192
— Lord John (J. C.), 265
Fitzwilliam, Earl (J. C.), 66, 147, 243, 264, 312
— Messrs. (J. C.), 147, 266, 312
Flambe (horse), 116
Flatman (jockey), 284
Flayer, Mr. Charles, 62
Fleur-de-lis (horse), 183, 185
Fly (horse), 109
Flying Dutchman, The (horse), 148, 284, 290, 311
— Childers (horse), *v.* Childers
Foaty Island (County Clare, Ireland), 136
Foley, Mr. (afterwards second Lord), (J. C.), 12, 78, 79, 101, 116, 118, 124, 137, 172, 204, 256
— Lord (third), (J. C.), 172, 204
Folkestone, Viscount (Earl of Radnor), (ex-J. C.), 265
Fontainebleau (Forest of), 108
Foot's Cray (Kent), 241
Fop (horse), 56
Fordham, Mr. George (the 'demon' jockey), 299
Forester, Col. Hon. H. (J. C.), 266, 312
— (horse), 136, 141, 142
Formosa (horse), 295, 300

GAR

Fort George (Madras), 61
Fortescue, family of, *v.* Clermont
Forth, Mr. (trainer and jockey), 361
Fortune-hunter (horse), 107
Fox, Hon. and Rt. Hon. Charles James (the famous), (J. C.), 12, 79, 116–118, 124, 178, 182, 230, 279, 313, 318
— (horse), 86
— Strangways, name of, 312
Foxes, a 'leash' of (killed by a tripartite pack of hounds), 215
Foxhall (horse, bred in America), 334
Fox-hunting, the Father of, *v.* Meynell
Frampton, Mr. Tregonwell, 23, 28, 80, 148, 210, 345
Frank, the family of (of Campsall, Yorks), 220
Frenchmen at Newmarket, 174, 175
Frenzy (horse), (dam of Phænomenon), 86
Friary (Lewes, Sussex), the, 219
Frith, Miss (Lady Sedley), 92
Furbisher (horse), 196
Fynes (or Fines), Messrs., *v.* Fiennes

GALATA (horse), 203
Gallant (horse), 216
Galliard (horse), 291
Galopade (horse), 300
Galopin (horse), 268, 290, 354
Gambling (Society for the Propagation of), 353, 365
Gaming Acts Discontinuance Bill, 320
Gamos (horse), 295
Gangforward (horse), 300
Gaper (horse), Lord G. Bentinck and, 285
Gardiner, Mr. (J. C.), 12, 118
— Messrs. (of Roche Court and Beaurepair), 118

GAR

Gardnor, Mr. T. (J. C.), 266
Garforth, Mr., 76
Gascoigne, Sir Thomas (J. C.) and Mr., 12, 83–85, 96, 137, 215, 216, 223, 224
— foreign horse, the, 84
Gascoyne (Mr. Joseph), (J. C.), 83, 173, 223
Gatton (Surrey), 222
Gay, the poet, 57
Geheimniss (horse), 288
General Baudbox (horse), 175
— Peel (horse), 285
Geneva (place), 127, 276
Gentleman (horse), ('Ancaster'), 25
Gentlemen-jockeys, 319
George I. (King), 8
— II. (King), 8, 9, 18, 120, 246
— III. (King), 18, 20, 69
— IV. (King), (J. C.), 129, 172, 184, 185, 223
Gerard, Sir W. (? J. C.), 294
— Hon. W. (Lord), (J. C.), 266, 295, 312
— Sir J. (J. C.), 265, 294
Germaine, Lord George (Sackville), 207
Germany, the Crown Prince of (J. C.), 263
Giantess (horse), 62
Gift (horse), 67
Gilling (Yorks), 313
Gimcrack (horse), 52, 55, 174
Gisburn Park (Yorks), 276
'Give-and-take' Plates, 192, 216, 372
Gladiateur (horse), 268, 275
Gladiator (horse), 289
Glancer (horse), 26
Glasgow, Earl of (Lord Kelburne), (J. C.), 264, 274, 284, 285, 347
Glass-house (Leeds, Yorks), 115
Glaucus (horse), 197, 198
Glenartney (horse), ('pulled'. in the Derby), 205
Glencoe (horse), (exported and a great sire in America), 206, 302

GRA

Gloucester, City of, 133
— Duke of (? J. C.), 12, 21–23, 172
— Duchess of, 21, 69
Glow-worm (horse), 106
Goddard, Mr. Ambrose (J. C.), 266, 301
Godolphin, (second) Earl of, 69, 242
— — — (his Arabian), 150
Gogmagog (Cambs), 150
Gohanna (horse), 202, 210, 220, 228
Golden Leg (horse, bay with one leg chestnut), 209
Goldfinder (horse), 89
Goodricke, the Reverend Henry (breeder and runner of race-horses), 75–78, 129, 162
Goodwood, 35, 195, 314, 366
— House, 132
— Cup, a notable race for the, 185
Goose-race, a (at Newmarket), 59, 64
Gordon, Lord William (immediate cause of the divorce of Lady Sarah Bunbury), 73
Gorges (or Gorge), Mr. Richard (J. C.), 12, 20, 118
Gorham, Robert de, 212
— — — (horse), 212, 213
Gorhambury (Park), 212, 213
— (races), 212, 213, 366
Gower, Earls (J. C.), 12, 53, 271, 310
— Mr. or General or Field-Marshal Leveson Gower (J. C.), 173, 224, 236
— stallion, the, 53, 271
Græme, Mr., 314
Grafton, third ('Nancy Parsons') Duke of, 12, 13, 30, 111, 152, 192, 220, 221, 223
— fourth Duke of, 69, 172, 192, 264
— Duchess of (divorced and married Lord Ossory), 30, 60
— — — (Maria Waldegrave), 69
Graham (Marquess of), (J. C.), 175, 264
— Sir Bellingham, 243, 295, 312

GRA

Graham, Sir Sandford (J. C.), 265, 295
—— Reginald (J. C.), 265, 295, 312
— Messrs. (of Yardley Stud), 295, 361
Granby, Marquess of (the famous), (? J. C.), 36
'Grand Duke Michæl' Stakes, the, 268
— Prix, institution of the, 326
— Seignior (horse), 125
Grantham (Lincolnshire), 235, 309
— (horse), 121
Granville, Earl (J. C.), 53, 54, 264, 270, 298
Grasshopper (horse), 26, 138
Great Barton (Mildenhall), 72
— Eastern Railway, 355
Green, Mr. J. R. (historian), 13
— Mr. B. ('bagman' and 'bookmaker'), 361
— Mantle (horse), 203
— Sleeve (horse), 296
Grenville, Lord (? J. C.), 172, 177
Greville, Mr. Fulke (J. C.), 12, 115, 119
— Mrs. Fulke, 119
— Mr. C. C. F. (J. C.), 119, 197, 266, 286, 311, 329–331
Grey, Sir Henry (of Howick), (J. C.), 12, 85, 86
— Earl, 86
— Hautboy (horse), 191
— Momus (horse), 272
Grimston, Messrs. (Lords Verulam), 212
— Hon. Robert (President of M.C.C.), 213
— De, 212
— Miss, 224
— Sir Harbottle (or 'Airbottle'), 212
Grimthorpe (Yorks), 130
Grossley, Mr. or M. (Mirabeau), 175
Grosvenor, Sir Richard (J. C.), 12, 54, 55, 315

HAM

Grosvenor, Earls of (J. C.), 12, 21, 38–40, 54, 79, 97, 196, 204, 233, 282
— General and F. M., 173, 224, 236, 266
Gubbins, Miss 'Honor' ('virtutis præmia'), 236
Guerchy, Comte de, 174
Guernsey, Lord (J. C.), 276
'Guesses at Truth,' 58
Guildford, Earl of (? J. C.), 172, 177
— (horse), 199
Gulley, Mr. (pugilist and bookmaker), M.P., 361
Gulnare (horse), 195
Gunning (the beautiful Misses), 27, 177
Gunpowder (horse), 52, 183
Gustavus (*grey* horse), 302
Gwydyr, Lord (of the 'lucky' Burrells), 131

HABAKKUK (the Prophet), 209
Habena (horse), 281
Habit (horse), 143
Hale, Mr. William (J. C.), 173, 224
Halifax, Lords, 310
Hallett, Mr. (J. C.), 173, 224, 266
Halston (Salop), 313
Hambleton (Yorks), 76, 278
Hambletonian (horse), 75, 78, 96, 220, 221, 241, 313
Hamilton, Dukes of, 32, 200, 312
—— — (J. C.), 12, 31, 172, 193, 200, 264, 268, 307, 312, 336
— Lady Elizabeth (Countess of Derby), 200
— Lord Archibald (ninth Duke of), 32, 56, 193, 312
— Duchess of, 27, 193
— Lord Spencer (J. C.), 12, 55
— Street (Park Lane), 165
Hammond, Mr. John ('weigher of jockeys'), 167
— Mr., 129

HAM

Hammond, Miss, 129
Hampden, Mr. John (the 'Patriot'), 107
— Lord (ex-'Speaker,' Mr. Brand), 107
Hampton Court, 8
— — Royal Stud at, 8, 212, 294
Hanger, Col. Hon. George (J. C.), (Lord Coleraine), 154, 173, 224, 235, 237
Hannah (horse), 269
Hannibal (horse), 202
Hanoverian Kings, 8
Harbord, Hon. Mr., 211
Harcourt, Admiral, 186
Hardwicke, Earl of (J. C.), 264, 278, 307, 334
Hare, Mr. James (the 'Hare of many friends'), (? J. C.), 173, 178
— (Bishop of Chichester), 122
— Park (Newmarket), the, 222, 305
Haringbrook (Essex), 81
Harleigh (manor of), 92
Harling (West, Norfolk), 113
Harpham Lass (horse), 108
Harrington, Earl of (? J. C.), 172, 177
Harrison, Mr. John, 120
Hartington, Marquesses of (J. C.), 12, 28, 29, 264, 280, 307, 308, 312
Hartley, Mr. or Capt. Leonard, 121
— (horse), 94
— Mauduit (Hants), 94
Harvey, Rev. Mr. ('Parson'), 162
Hastings, Mr. Warren (? J. C.), 131, 173, 179
— (the last) Marquess of (J. C.), 111, 117, 239, 243, 256, 274, 275
— Lord (J. C.), 264, 265, 308, 312
Hautboy (Grey), (horse, sire of Bay Bolton), 191
Hawke, Admiral (Lord), 186
Hawkesbury, Lord (? J. C.), 172, 177
Hawkins, Mr. ('warned off'), 227, 258

HEW

Hawkins, Sir Henry (Mr. Justice), (J. C.), 180, 265, 307
Hawley, Sir Joseph (J. C.), 16, 211, 265, 281, 295, 296, 303, 328, 361
Hayford (manor of), 92
Hazlitt, Mr. (the essayist), 142
Heart of Oak (horse), 135
Heathcote, Sir Gilbert (J. C.), 265, 269, 296
Heaton Park (Lord Wilton's), 289, 300
— — races at, 289, 300, 366
Heats, first abolition of, 156
— renunciation of, 156
Heber, Mr. Reginald (and his Calendar), 163
— Bishop, 163
Helen (Lord John Scott's charger), 293
Hell Fire (horse), 311
'Hell-gate' (nickname of a brother of the seventh Earl of Barrymore), 42, 44
Helmsley (Yorks), (seat of the Duke of Buckingham and of the Duncombes), 114, 205
Hengrave (horse), 125
Henricus (horse), 82
Henry the Eighth (the clergy and horse-breeding), 162
Hercules (horse), 193
Hermione (horse), 109, 199
— (Young), 109
Hermit (horse), 182, 183, 274, 308
Hernandez (horse), 288
Herod (King Herod), (horse), 20, 90, 148
Herrick, Mr., 226
Hertford, Marquess of (J. C.), 49, 264, 272
— Marchioness of (Maria Fagniani), 57, 132
Hesperithusa (horse, h. b.), 304
Hewes, Mr., 248
Hewgill, Rev. Mr. (breeder of Priestess), 138, 162

HIG

Highflyer (horse), 45, 74, 150, 360
Highlander (horse), (14 hands 1 in.), 63
Hilton, Mr. John (official 'judge' to the J. C.), 167
— Park (Wolverhampton), (Mr. H. Vernon's), 241
Hippia (horse), (won the Oaks for Baron M. de Rothschild, but accidentally omitted), 269
Hippisley, Mr. J. Coxe, 113
Hippodrome (Bayswater), 249, 356
Hippolyta (horse), 190
Hirsch, Baron, 223
'Historical Memoirs' (Lord Waldegrave's), 68
'History of the British Turf' (Mr. Whyte's), 39
Hobbie Noble (horse), 293
Hocuspocus (horse), 207
Hogarth (painter), 74
Holcroft, Mr. Thomas (dramatist, ex-stableboy), 141, 142
Holderness (Yorks), 130
Holland, Lord (the first, father of C. J. Fox), 131, 132
— Lady, 112
— Kings of (J. C.), 18, 263, 267
Hollandaise (horse), 84, 125
Holmes (or Holme), Mr. (of Carlisle), (? J. C.), 12, 119, 120
Holyhock (or Hollyhock), (horse), 121
Homily (horse), 290
'Honor virtutis præmia' (Miss H. Gubbins), 236
Honywood, General Philip, 147, 298, 316
Hoo, The, Hertfordshire, 107, 366
Hoomes, Mr. or Colonel (American), 40
Hope (horse), (race between Hope and Despair, 2 yrs. old), 77
Horatius (horse), 112
Horizon (horse, the first of the 'Eclipses'), 197

HYD

Hornby Grange (Northallerton), 138
Hornsea (horse), 198
Horse-racing and the Clergy, 162
Horsley Park (Hunts), 121
Horton, Mrs. (Duke of Cumberland's), 20, 23
— — (Nancy Parsons), 20, 31, 238
Hotspur (horse, h. b.), 284
'Hotspur' (*nom de guerre*), 3
Houghton (horse), 60
Houldsworth, Mr. T. (J. C.), 226, 266, 301
— Mr. J. H. (J. C.), 266, 301, 302, 312
Hove (near Brighton), 241
Howard, Hon. Bernard, 9, 47, 315
— Hon. Richard (Sec. to Queen Charlotte), 121
— Mrs. (Countess of Suffolk), 274
Howe, Earl (J. C.), 264, 307, 312, 315
— Mr. H. F. (Baron Chedworth), 48
— Miss, 148
— — Charlotte, 116
— Admiral, 186
Howorth, Mr. (J. C.), 173, 224, 297
Howth, Earl of (J. C.), 264, 285
Hugh Capet (or Caput), (horse), 223
Hughes, Mr. (the circus-keeper, owner of Chillaby), 233, 234
Hume, Mr. David (the philosopher), 60
Huncamunca (horse), 112
Hunter, Sir John (the great surgeon), 66
— Mr. J. (J. C.), 266, 302
Hurricane (horse), 291
Hurstmonceux (Sussex), 122
Hutchinson, Mr. John (of Shipton, near York, ex-stableboy), 75–78, 95, 120, 147, 360
— Mr. (J. C.), 12, 120
Hydrophobia (death of a Duke of Richmond from), *v.* Richmond

I'ANSON, Messrs. (trainers and jockeys, of Malton), 139, 350 361
Ibrahim (horse), 206
Idas (horse), 211
Ilchester, Earl of (J. C.), 264, 307, 312
Iliffe, Miss ('Mrs. Wyndham'), 201
Iliona (horse), 272, 292
Imogen (horse), 138
Imperatrix (horse), 129
Impérieuse (horse), 290
Incantator (horse), 209
Inclosure Acts (of George II.), The, 246
Indicus (horse), 115
'Indifference,' Ode to or Prayer for (by Mrs. Fulke Greville), 119
Industry (horse), 198
'Infant,' The (Col. Hanger's club), 237
Inskip, the family of (Lade), 217
Ipswich (place), 211
Irby, Mr. W. H. (J. C.), 266
Iris (horse), 271
Irish Turf Club, 184
Ixworth Abbey (Suffolk), 140
Izinson, Mr., 123

JACKSON, Mr. John ('Jock o' Fairfield'), ('bookmaker'), 304
Jacksonborough (S. Carolina), 145
Jamaica, 98, 139
James II., King, 174
Jannette (horse), 291
Jardine, Sir Robert (J. C.), 266, 307
Jason (horse), 80, 88
— Young, 80
Jekyll, Mr. (celebrated 'wit'), (? J. C.), 173, 179
Jenison (or Jennison), Mr. Ralph (J. C.), 12, 13, 120
Jenkinson, Charles, Earl of Liverpool, 177

Jennings, Mr. 'Chillaby' (J. C.), 57, 111, 173, 225, 228, 231–234
— Mr. Tom, 258
Jenny (horse), 67
— (Yorkshire), 81
Jerboa (horse), 210
Jerker (horse), 53
Jerkin (horse), 148
Jerome Park (New York racecourse), 335
Jerry (horse), 84
Jersey, Earls of, 206
— Earl of (J. C.), 204, 206, 223, 264, 297
Jerusalem (horse), 46
Jesse (author), 7
Jewison, Mr. Leonard (jockey), 147
'Jock o' Fairfield' (Mr. J. Jackson, 'bookmaker'), 304
'Jockey, Receipt to make a,' 72
— Club, The, *passim*
— — threatened by the Legislature, 326
— — (and the 'Calendar'), 161–166, 255, 256
— — (and its officials), 166, 167
— — members of (1751–1773), 12, 13
— — — (1773–1835), 172, 173
— — — (1835–1890), 263–267
— — — first published list of, 171
— — (Challenge Cup of 1768), 5, 20, 30, 158
— — Stewards of, 259
— — (Plates), 4–6, 11
— — (rules and orders of the), 157–160, 255, 256, 318–340
— — Master of the Buckhounds *ex-officio* member of, 327
— — (the French), 7, 362–364
— — — — President, V.-P., and Stewards of the (J. C.), 264
'— —' publication so called, 22, 230
— — 'shocking examples' of, 111, 117, 228–234, 274–280
— — American and Australian (J. C.), 264, 333

JOC

Jockeys, the betting among, 337
— the fees of, 337, 347
John Bull (horse), 55
Johnson, Dr. Samuel, 5, 43, 45, 105, 217
Johnstone, Sir Frederick (J. C.), 265, 308, 313
— Sir F., 294
— Mr. J. ('Pretender'), 308
Jolly Bacchus (horse), 112
Jouvence (French horse). 270
Judge Jefferies (horse), 175
Julius (horse), 274
Juniper (horse), 20, 118
'Junius' (the famous writer), 30, 87

KALEIDOSCOPE (horse), 277
Kangaroo (horse, impostor), 275
Kaye, Sir John (? Lister), (J. C.), 12, 86
— Very Rev. Sir Richard, 86
— Mr. Lister (Sir John P. L.), 86
Keddlestone (Derbyshire), 80
Kelburne, Viscount (Earl of Glasgow), (J. C.), 265, 284
Kempton Park, 310, 333, 353
Kensal Green (cemetery), 273
Kentucky, 40
Kenyon, Lord (? J. C.), 172, 177
Kerenhappuch (horse), 219
Kesteven (Duke and Lord), 25
Kettledrum (horse), 277, 303
Kildonan (horse), 277
Kilwarlin (horse), 308
King, Rev. Mr. ('Launde'), 162
— Henry VIII. (the clergy and horse-breeding), 162
— Herod (horse), 20, 90
— Lud (horse), 286
— Pepin (horse), 107, 174
— Tom (horse), 269
Kingcraft (horse), 291
King's Bench, Rules of the, 231
— Walden (Herts), 224
Kingsbury, suburban races at, 336
Kingsclere (Hants), 253
Kingsman, Mr. (J. C.), 173, 225

LAM

Kingston, the ('infamous') Duchess of), 32, 33
— the (last) Duke of (J. C.), 12, 32, 107, 146
Kinnoul, Earls of, 277. 278
Kippax Park (Skipton, Yorks), 130
Kirkby Baber (Leicestershire), 92
Kirkleatham (Yorks), 94, 241
Kirkstall (Yorks), 295
Kitt Carr (horse), 207
Kitty (horse), 67
Klarikoff (horse), 277
Knaresborough, 178

LA FLÈCHE, 294
Labrador (horse), 196, 204
Ladbroke, Mr. (the banker, intimate with Frederick, Duke of York), 79
Lade, Mr. ' Counsellor,' 217
— Sir John (J. C.), 43, 82, 105, 172, 183, 189, 217–219, 230
Lady Augusta (horse), 288
— Catherine (horse), Gen. Grosvenor's charger, 237
— Elizabeth (horse), 111, 275, 296
— Evelyn (horse), 198
— Grey (horse), 302
— of the Lake (horse), 293
— Orford (horse), 286
— Teazle (dramatic character), 200
Lagrange, Comte F. de (J. C.), 264, 268, 324, 327
Lake, Mr. Warwick (third and last Viscount), (J. C.), 173, 224, 225
— General (Lord), 225
Lamb, Hon. J. Peniston (J. C.), 173, 225
— family of, 312, 366
Lambkin, The (horse), 304
'Lambourne,' Mr. (Gen. M. Wood), (J. C.), 305
— (Berks), 116
Lambton, Messrs. (Earls of Durham), (J. C.), v. Durham

INDEX

LAN

Landscape (horse), 236
Lane, Capt. Douglas (J. C.), 266, 313, 322
— Col. John (friend of Charles II.), 313
Langham Hall (Suffolk), 100
Langton Wold (Yorks), 249, 299
Lansdowne, Marquess of (the celebrated Lord Shelburne), (? J. C.), 172, 177
Lapdog (horse), 202
Lardon (horse), 36
Lascelles, Viscount (J. C.), 265, 313
— Rev. Mr., 313
Lasingcroft (Yorks), 83
Launcelot (horse), 283
Lauraguais, Comte de (owner of Gimcrack), 174
Lauzun, Duc de, 174
Lawn, The (estate, Swindon, Wilts), 301
Le Beau (horse), (the beautiful Duchess of Devonshire's), 29
— Despencer, Baroness (Viscountess Falmouth), 291
— Maréchal (horse, bred in France), 288
— Sang (horse), 116
Leander (horse), 318
— Case, the, 318
Leaping-match, Sir C. (Mr.) Turner's, 95
Lecturer (horse), 275
Ledstone Hall (Yorks), 243
Leedes, Mr. (Yorkshire breeder), 139
Leeds, Duke of (? J. C.), 172, 175
— — (J. C.), 194, 264
Lees Court (Kent), 67
Leeway (horse), 212
Lefèvre, Monsieur C. J. (of Chamant), 287
Legard, Sir Charles (ex-J. C.), 265
Legge, Messrs. Bilson (and Lord Stawell), 209
Legh, Mr. W. J. (J. C.), 266, 313
— Mr., 313

LON

Leicester, Earl of (Marquess Townshend), (? J. C.), 172, 177
Leigh, Colonel, 302
Lenox (or Lennox), Lady Sarah, 72, 73
— — Charles, first Duke of Richmond, 36
— Col. and Gen. (Duke of Richmond), 195
— (horse), 112
— Lord H. G. (J. C.), 265
Leominster, 118
Leonidas (horse), 53
Lepicq (horse), 220
Lethbridge, Sir W. A. (J. C.), 265, 313
Letter of Lord Derby to the J. C., an admonitory, 321, 339
Leviathan (horse), 38
— (of the Ring, Mr. Davis, the), 330
— a, 360
Lewes (Sussex), 219
Lexington (American horse), 80
Leybourne Grange (Kent), 295, 296
Lichfield, Earl of (J. C.), 264, 286
Lightfoot, Mr. (of Virginia, U.S.), 239
Lime Kilns, The (Newmarket), 248
Lincoln, Earl of (J. C.), 264
Lindsey, Earls of, 25, 274
Linkboy (horse), 195
Lister, family name of, 276
Little Driver (horse), 49
— Duck (French horse), 324
— Wonder (horse), 283
Liverpool, Earl of (? J. C.), 177
Livy (Roman historian), 50
Lloyd, Mr. Cynric (J. C.), 266
Locust (horse), 120
Londesborough, Lord (J. C.), 265, 291
— Lodge, 292
Londonderry, Marquess of (J. C.), 220, 264, 307, 313
Lonely (horse), 308

D D

LON

Longchamps, 273
Longford, Earls of, 112
Long Witton (Northumberland), 138
Lonsdale (first Viscount), 87
— (third Viscount), 87
— Earls of (J. C.), 87, 88, 206, 264, 266, 286
Lord Clifden (horse), 277
— Lyon (horse), 280, 303
Loughborough, Lord (St. Clair-Erskine), (? J. C.), 231, 287
Louis the XV., King, 174
— the XVI., 188
Lowther (place in Westmorland), 88
— Lord (J. C.), 172, 206, 265, 286
— Sir J. (the 'bad' Lord Lonsdale), (J. C.), 12, 87, 119, 206
— the Rev. Sir W., 88
— Right Hon. J. (J. C.), 266, 306, 307, 313
— Hon. Margaret, 87
— Mr. Robert (of Barbados), 87
— Col. (third Earl of Lonsdale), (J. C.), 266, 286
Lucetta (horse), 222, 223
Luck's All (horse), 193
'Lucky Baronet,' The (Sir J. Hawley), (J. C.), 295
'— Burrells,' The, 131
Ludgershall, borough of, 133
'Ludlow' Year, The, 332
Lumley, Mr. R. G. (breeder of Musjid), 296
Lupin, Monsieur A. (J. C.), 236, 266, 270, 327
Luss (horse), 223
Luttrell, Colonel, 20
— Miss (Mrs. Horton), 20
Lyme Park (Cheshire), (Messrs. Legh, of), 313
Lymington, Viscount, 314

MACARONI (horse), 289
Macclesfield, second Earl of, 125

MAR

Macdonald (jockey), 283
Macedon, 47
Mackay, Mr. George, 62
Magic (horse), 207
Magog (horse), 83–85
Maid of Orleans (horse), 236
— — the Oaks (horse), 55
Maidstone, Lord (Earl of Winchilsea), (J. C.), 265, 292
Mainstone (horse), 272
Malton (place), a dispute at, 157
— (Bay, horse), v. Bay Malton
Maltzahn, Barons (well established on the English Turf), 312
Mambrino (horse), 55, 84, 115, 235
Mameluke (horse), 205
Manfred (horse), 303
Manners, Lord William (J. C.), 12, 36, 37, 41, 56
— Lord George (J. C.), 253, 265
— Lord C. (J. C.), 265; family of, 312
Mansfield, Lord (the great), (decision of), 126, 228
Maple, Mr. Blundell ('Childwick'), 223
Marble Hill (Twickenham), Gen. Peel's, 274
Marbury Hall (Belmont, Cheshire), 136
Marc Antony (or Mark Anthony), (horse), 50, 139
Marcellus (horse), 192
March (and Ruglen), the Earl of ('old Q.'), (J. C.), 12, 27, 31, 56, 58, 113, 114, 121, 126, 131, 132, 148, 310
— Earl of (J. C.), 264, 314
— Mr. John (J. C.), 13, 121
Maresfield Park (Sussex), 93
Maria (horse), 216
— Fagniani (Marchioness of Hertford), 57
Marie Antoine (horse), 33
-- Antoinette, Queen, 49
Marigold (dam of Doncaster), 280

INDEX 403

MAR

Market Weighton (Yorks), 130
Marlborough, (fourth) Duke of (J. C.), 12, 33, 309
— Henrietta, Duchess of, 33
Marlow (jockey), 284
Marmier, Marquis de, 363
Maroon (horse), ('pulled' for the St. Leger), 283
Marquis (horse), 141
Marske (horse), (sire of Eclipse), 18, 139
Marston, Mrs. Frances (afterwards Burlton), 108
Martin, Mr. Baron (Samuel), (J.C.), 180, 265, 272
Martindale, Mr. (saddler), 49, 150, 360
Match Book (keeper of the, at Newmarket), 164-166
Matchem (horse), 20, 35, 115
Matches, notable, 133, 134, 238, 242
Matilda (horse), 280
Matson (Gloucestershire), 133
Mauley, de, Lord (J. C.), *v.* De Mauley
'Maxims and Characters,' by Fulke Greville (J. C.), 119
Maynard, Lord, 31, 237
— Mr. (J. C.), 173, 225, 237, 238
Mayonnaise (horse), 300
Meaburn (horse), 192
Meath, Bishop of, 53
Medea (horse), 112
Medora (horse), 195
Melbourne, Lords, 225, 312, 366
— (horse), 139
— (place), 292
Mellish, Col. (J. C.), 54, 173, 224, 225, 238
Melton (horse), 308
Melville, Viscount (? J. C.), 178
Memnon (horse), 192, 304
Memoir (horse), 294, 308, 329
Mentmore (estate), 269
— Lass (horse), 269
Merlin (Old), (horse), 345
— Lord Lindsey's, 24

MIR

Merry, Mr. James ('Thormanby'), 55, 293, 361
— Hampton (horse), 148
— Hart (horse), 280
Messenger (horse), the 'Father of Trotters,' 55, 115, 223, 235
Meteor (horse), 299
Metropolitan Racecourse Bill (Mr. Anderson's), 336
Meynell, Mr. Hugo ('Father of Fox-hunting'), (J. C.), 13, 105, 121, 133, 154, 174, 295
— Mr. Littleton Poyntz, 121
Miami (horse), 296
Michel Grove (Sussex), 93
Mickleham (Surrey), 242
Middle Park, 361
— — Plate, 277
Middleton, Sir William (J. C.), 12, 64, 89
— Sir John Lambert, 89
— — W. (the hero of Minden), 89
— (Bay), (horse), 205, 206
— (Chestnut), (horse), 205, 297
— Stony (estate, Oxon), (Lord Jersey's), 204
Midge (horse), 89
Mildenhall (Suffolk), 72
Milford (North), (Yorks), 139
Mills, Mr. J. (J. C.), 266
Milltown, Earls of (J. C.), 264
Milner, Mr. W. M. (Sir W.), (J C.), 266
Milsington, Viscount (J. C.), 63
— — 63
Milton, Viscount (Earl Fitzwilliam), (J. C.), 265
Minden, battle of, 89
Minos (the 'infernal' judge), 116
Minstead Manor (Hants), 111
Minthe (horse), 304
Minting (horse), 304
Minuet (horse), 193, 220
Mira (horse), 216
Mirabeau, Comte de (Mr. Grossley), 174

D L 2

MIR

Miramon, Marquis de, 363
Miranda (horse), 44
Mirza (horse), 89, 119
Misfortune (horse), 40, 73
Miss Belsea (Belsay), (horse), 89
— Craven (horse), 195
— Elis (horse), 272
— Fortune (horse), 112
— Jummy (horse), 308
— Osmer (horse), 53
— Ramsden (horse), 215
— South (horse), 63
— Spindleshanks (horse), 52
— Western (horse), 77
Mixbury (Regulus), (horse), 68
Molecatcher (horse), 92
Molyneux, Sir Francis (? J. C.), 173, 178
— Viscount (first Earl of Sefton), (J. C.), 12, 58
Monaco, Prince of, 23
Monarque (French horse), 284
Moncreiffe, Sir David, 309
Monmouth, James, Duke of, 9; (place), 47
Monson, Mr. Lewis (first Baron Sondes), v. Sondes
— Lord, 222
Montagu, Lord (of Cawdry) 19; (his mares), 19
— Mr. Wortley (gambler), M.P., vii
Montalbo (or Mentalba), Comtesse de (Mrs. Bowes), 299
Monte Carlo (place), 277
Montgregon, Comte Edouard de, 363
Montrose, Dukes of (? J. C.), 172, 175, 314
— Duke of (J. C.), 264, 300
Moon, Mr. Washington, 48
Moore, Sir John (owner of King Herod), (J. C.), 12, 63, 89, 90
Morel (horse), 31
Morion (horse), 29
Morley, Earls of, 239
Morny, Comte de (purchaser of West Australian), 292
Moses (horse), 49; (another), 185

NET

Moslem (horse), 300
Mostyn, Mr. and Lord (J. C.), 55, 265, 266, 290, 292
Mouravieff (horse), 289
Mouse (Young), (horse), 197
Mulcaster, Capt., 242
Mulgrave, Earl of (J. C.), 264
Mündig (horse), 299
'Musæ Anglicanæ,' The, 110
Musgrave, Mr. Christopher, 310
Music (horse), 193, 220
Mu-jid (horse), 296
Mustachio (horse), 185
Mustard (horse), (Queen Anne's), 311, 314
Myrtle (horse), 113; (Mr. Wentworth's), 115
Mytton, Mr. 'Jack' (of Halston), 313

NABOB (*alias* Flambé), (horse), 116
Naburn (place near York), 129
'Nænia Britannica' (author of), 235
Nanny (Wynn), the Rev. Mr., 162
Nantwich (Cheshire), 149
Naper, Messrs. (original family name of the Duttons, Lords Sherborne), 208, 236
Napier, Col. (second husband of Lady Sarah Lenox), the Hon., 73
— Sir Charles and Sir William, 73
Narcissus (horse), 35
Nassau Stakes, the, 267
'Nat' (Elnathan Flatman, jockey), 284
Naylor, Mr. Francis (J. C.), 13, 122
— Mr. R. C., 122, 292
Nectar (horse), 197
Nelson, Mr. John (and his 'Calendar'), 161
Netherfield (horse), 192
Netherlands, King of the, 263, 267
'Nethermost Hell,' definition of, 231

INDEX

NEV

Neva (horse), 243
Nevill, Mr. R. H. (J. C.), 266
Neville, Mr. (Lord Braybrooke, editor of 'Pepys's Diary'), (J. C.), 173, 225
Nevison (highwayman, and his black mare), 85
Newbyth (Haddingtonshire), 294
Newcastle, Duke of (J. C.), 264, 274
— Dukes of, 28, 57, 67
Newcomen, Sir W. (banker), 95
'Newgate' (nickname of an Earl of Barrymore), 42, 44, 275
— Market, 150
Newmarket, *passim*
— (meetings at), 158–160, 320
— Coffee Room, admission to the, 158
— Heath, right of 'warning off,' 194
— Rooms, the, 17, 157
— Whip, The, 9, 19
' — The Cub at ' (poem), 22, 153
Newminster (horse), 222, 354
Newport, Viscount (Earl of Bradford), (J. C.), 265
Newspapers and betting, the, 352, 359
Newton (place), 313
— Gold Cup at, 313
Nicholas, the Emperor, 268
'Nicholson's Gin,' 361
Nicolls, Lady (Duchess of Ancaster), 23
Nicolo (or Niccolo), (horse, a twin), 209
Nightshade (horse), 202
Niké (horse), 55
Ninon de l'Énclos, 132
'Nobbling,' 85, 319
Noble (horse), 125
Nobody (horse), 52
Nogent, le Chevalier, 363
Nominations (voidance of, by death), 322–326
Norfolk, Duke of (? J. C.), 172, 175

OLD

Normanby, Marquess of (J. C.), 264, 311
Norris, Mr., Captain, and Admiral (Henry). (J. C.), 13, 122, 123
North, Lord (? J. C.), 177
— Colonel, 223
— Milford (Yorks), 139
Northampton, Earls of, 111
Northey, Mr. (? J. C.), 173, 179
— Messrs., 179
Northfleet (estate), 92
Northumberland (Sir Hugh Smithson), Duke of (J. C.), 12, 33, 154, 243
— Countess of, 33, 34
Norton Conyers (Yorks), 295
Nottingham (horse), 218
Now or Never (horse), 120
Nuncio (horse), 226
Nunnykirk (horse), 222
Nuttall (Notts), 92
Nymphina (horse), 224, 225

'OAKS,' The (race), 199; (estate), 199
Oatlands (estate belonging to the Duke of York), 93, 185, 187
Oberon (horse), 76, 96, 220, 241
Octavian (horse), 194
'Ode to Indifference,' by Mrs. Fulke Greville, 119
Odine (horse), 108
Offley, Mr. (J. C.), 13, 122
Ofley, Mr. (very ancient 'racer'), 123, 124
Ogilvy, Mr. Charles (J. C.), 13, 123
Okehampton (place), 142
O'Kelly, Mr. (senior), ('blackleg,' and owner of Eclipse), 33, 150, 183, 226, 238, 313, 344, 345, 350, 360
— — (junior), (J. C.), 173, 226, 238
— — (senior), on 'crossing and jostling,' 251
Old Burlington Street, 165
— England (horse), 75; (another) 319

OLD

'Old England Case,' the, 319, 322
(Old) Merlin (horse), 345
'Old Q' (last Duke of Queensberry), (J. C.), 31, 56–58, 310
'— Rowley' (Charles the Second), 8
— Sarum (Wilts), 100
'Old' White's Club, vii, 143
Olive (horse), 225, 244
Oliver, Mr. Richard (afterwards Gascoigne), 84
— Cromwell (horse), 199
Omar (horse), 52
Onslow, Hon. Mr. 'Tommy' (second Earl of), (? J. C.), 173, 179
Oppidan (horse), 195
Orange, Princes of (J. C.), 263, 267
— Plate, the (at Ascot), 267
Orde, Mr. T. (Powlett), 190
Orford, Earls of (J. C.), 12, 58, 59, 64, 78, 111, 264, 286
— Lady (horse), 286
Oriana (horse), 295
Orion (horse), 120
Orlando (horse), 273
Orléans, Duc d' ('Égalité'), 108, 172, 182, 188
— (horse), 188
Ormonde (horse), 48, 148, 221, 280, 308, 354
— Marquess of, 61
Oroonoko (horse), 114
Orton, Mr. John (and his 'Annals'), 75, 77, 148
Osborne, Mr. John (senior, trainer), 79
Osnaburgh, Prince-bishop of (Duke of York), (J. C.), 184
Ossian (horse), 308
Ossory (Upper), Earl of (J. C.), 12, 31, 60, 61, 154
— — Dowager Countess of, 143
Othello (horse), 63
Otheothea (horse), 61
Otho (horse), 49, 60
Ottley, Messrs. William (senior and junior), (J. C.), 13, 124, 125
Oulston (horse), 222

PAR

Oxenden Street (Haymarket), 165
Oxford (Corporation of), 40
— (races at), 40
Oxton Hall (Yorks), 243
Oxygen (horse), 193

PADWICK (or Padwicke), Mr. (usurer), 242, 275, 277
Paget, Mr. G. E. (J. C.), 266, 307, 314
Paine, Mr. 'Tom' (the notorious), 188
Pall Mall, 6
Palmer, W. (the poisoner), 322
Palmerston, Lord (J. C.), 265, 272, 320
Pan (horse), 221, 222
Pantaloon (horse), 139
Panton, Mr. Thomas (junior), (J.C.), 13, 24, 75, 79, 119, 125, 131, 181, 183, 250
— Miss Mary (Duchess of Ancaster), 23, 125
Papist (horse), 135
Paragon (horse), 138
Parasol (horse), 31, 221, 223
Parisot (horse), 220
— (she-dancer), 220
Park Hill (Doncaster), 63
Parker, Col. and Gen. Hon. George Lane (J. C.), 13, 125
— Mr. (Lord Boringdon), (J. C.), 126, 173, 181, 183, 226, 239
Parlington (Yorks), 83, 137
— (horse), 137
Parmesan (horse), 302
Parrot, a (that whistles the 104th Psalm), 238
Parsons, Nancy (Mrs. Horton), 13, 31, 237
— Mr. Henry, 108
— Mr. Humphry (Alderman), 108
Parthian (horse, two years old) 78
Partisan (horse), 222
Partner (horse), (Mr. Grisewood's), 63

PAS

Pastille (horse), 193
Patrician (horse), 174
Patron (horse), 203
Patshull (near Wolverhampton), 61, 62
'Pavo' (sporting writer's *nom de guerre*), 3
Paymaster (horse), 45, 65, 138
Payne, Messrs., 135
— (J. C.), 266, 279
Pearson, General (J. C.), 266, 303, 306, 307, 314
— Mr. Anthony, 314
Pedley, Mr. ('book-maker'; son-in-law of Gully), 361
Peel, Col. and Gen. (J. C.), 214, 266, 273, 347
— (General), (horse), 285
Peirson, Sir Matthew, 190
Pelham, Miss (and 'Old Q.'), 27, 28, 57
— 'Tommy,' 123
Pelisse (horse), 31, 224
Pelter (horse), 219
Pemberton, Mr. C, 247
Pembroke College (Cambridge), 247
Penelope (horse), 31, 193
Pennington, Sir Joseph, 87
— Miss Catherine, 87
Penrhyn, Lord (J. C.), 265, 314
Pepys, Samuel, 9
Percy, Lady Elizabeth, 33
Perdita (horse), (dam of the Yellow Mare), 86, 220
Perion (horse), 241
Pero (horse), 33
— Gomez (horse), 296
Peter (horse), 274
— (nickname of Lord Glasgow), 274, 285
'— Pindar' (Dr. Walcot), 88
Petit Gris (French horse), (Duc d'Orléans's), 188
Petrarch (horse), 277
Petre, Hon. Mr. Edward (J. C.), 266, 280

PIQ

Petre, Mr. (and the 'Rape of the Lock'), 280
Petronel (horse), 308
Petruchio (horse), 223
Petworth (seat of Lord Egremont), 35, 202
— races at, 35, 202, 366
Phænomenon (horse), 86, 87
Phantom (horse), 93, 204, 205, 224, 297
Phillimore, Mr. W. R. (J. C.), 266
Phillips, Mr. (horse-buyer for the Duke of Northumberland), 34
Phosphorus (horse), 243, 294
Phryne (horse), 293
Piccadilly (horse), 226
— (Street), the gentleman who owned, 303
Pick, Mr. William (and his 'Register'), 314 (and elsewhere)
Pickwick Club, 10
Pic-nic (mare), 195
Pigot, Admiral (? J. C.), 173, 179
— — Sir Hugh, 62
— General Sir Robert, 62
— Lord, 12, 61, 179
— Sir George, 61, 62
— — Robert, 62
Pigott, Mr. Robert (senior), (of Chetwynd), 126, 228
— — — (junior), (of Chetwynd), (J. C.), 13, 110, 126, 127, 228
— — Charles ('Louse'), (of Chetwynd), (J. C.), 60, 111, 127, 173, 226, 228-231
— Rev. W., 228, 229
— 'Black' (of Chetwynd), 127, 229
— Mr. W. (of Doddeshall), 96
Pilgrimage (horse), 206
Pincher (horse), 124
Pindar (the famous Greek poet), 287
Pindarrie (horse), 193
Piper (horse), 60
Pique (Admiral Rous's ship), 210, 274

PIT

Pitt, Right Hon. W. (? J. C.), 87, 173, 179, 231
Place, Mr. (Cromwell's studmaster), 205
Plaisanterie (French horse), 334, 337
Plantagenet (horse), 224
Plasto (horse), 29
Platina (horse), 202
Pleader (horse), 88
Plenipotentiary (horse), 186, 235
Pléville, Monsieur Couret, 363
Plunder (horse), 108
Poisoning (of horses), 179
Poland, King of (bids 2,000 gs. for the famous sire (King) Herod), 90
Pole Star (horse), (property of the murdered Mr. Cooke), 322
'Political Dictionary,' Mr. C. Pigott's, 230, 231
Poltimore, Lords (Bampfylde), 107, 178
Pompadour, Madame de, 97, 188
Pond, Mr. John (and his Calendar), 5, 127, 134, 156, 163, 253, 254, 309, 357, and v. Appendix
— Miss (and her match), 5
— Mrs. 163
Pontac (horse), 81
Poole, Sir Ferdinando (J. C.), 173, 219, 220, 224
— Sir Henry, 219
— the Rev. Sir Henry, 220
— (estate, Wirrall, Cheshire), 219
Pope, Alexander (the poet), 114
— (horse), 31, 220 (called 'Waxy' P. to distinguish him from P. by Shuttle)
Poppet (horse), (brother to Chuff), 56
'Porch,' the Father of the, 19
Porter, Mr. John (trainer), 253
— on taking the age of racehorses, 253
Portia (horse), 190
Portius (horse, by Cato), 124, 125
Portland, Duchess of, 130

PUL

Portland, Dukes of (J. C.), 172, 176, 194, 221, 246, 264, 271, 306, 307, 311, 314, 329, 349
— Duke of v. Hawkins, 258
Portmore, Earl of (J. C.), 12, 62, 63
Portsmouth, Earl of (J. C.), 264, 310, 314, 316
— Duchess of (de la Querouaille), 132, 133
Pot8os (famous horse), 38, 55, 145
Powers, Mr. (American), 26
Powerscourt, Lord, 207
Powlett, Lord W. (J. C.), 265, 292, 322
Pratt, Mr. John (of Askrigg), (J. C.), 13, 101, 128–130, 146
Precarious (horse ; first-recorded two-year-old runner at Newmarket), 78
Premier (horse), 53
Preston, Mr., breeder of Sampson, 64, 65
Pretender (horse), 308
Priam (horse), 186, 198
Price, 'Charley,' 140
Priestess (horse), 138, 162
Prince Charlie (horse), 101
— Leopold (horse), 185
Princess, The (horse), 273
Privateer (horse), 157
Prize (horse), 216
Problem (horse), 193
Professor, The (horse), 300
Propagation of Gambling, Society for the, 353, 358
— of the Gospel, Society for the, 140
Property of the J. C. at Newmarket, 246–248
Proserpine (horse), 82
Prospero (horse), 119
Protest (by the stewards of J. C. against a reported decision of a J. C. committee), 254
Prunella (horse), 31, 193
Pulteney, William (Earl of Bath), 140

Pumpkin (horse), (a mile in four and a half minutes !!), 101-103
Punch (horse, imported into America), 26
Pussy (horse), 300
Pyrrhus (horse), 118, 124, 139

QUEEN ANNE, *v.* Anne
— Bertha (horse), 291
— Charlotte, *v.* Charlotte
— Mab (the famous brood mare), 313
— Marie Antoinette, *v.* Marie Antoinette
— Mary (famous brood mare), 139, 350
— of Trumps (horse), (her peculiarity), 292
— Victoria (and horse-racing), *v.* Victoria
Queensberry (last Duke of, 'Old Q.'), (J. C.), 12, 27, 31, 56, 58, 113, 121, 126, 131, 148, 232
Querouaille, Madame de la (Duchess of Portsmouth), 132
'Qui tam' actions, 320
Quick (and Castle), Messrs. ('blacklegs'), 344, 360
Quick-sand (horse), 215
Quits (horse), 300
Quiz (horse), 220, 223
'Quorn,' The, 122
Quorndon Hall, 122

RABY, Lord (Duke of Cleveland), (J. C.), 191
— (horse), 192
— (place), 191
Racecourse Bill (Mr. Anderson's Metropolitan), 336
'Racehorse in Training,' Mr. W. Day's, 78, 329
Radcliffe (Delmé), Mr., 183, 186
Ragamuffin (horse), 136
Raglan, Lord, 280
Ralph (horse), (poisoned), 283, 284

Rama (horse), 280
'Rape of the Lock' (Pope's), 280
Ratan (horse), 318
— Case, the, 318
Ratoni (horse), 227
Read, Mr. (? Wilberforce), (J. C.), 13, 130
— — Rudston, 272
'Receipt to make a Jockey,' 72, 146, 188
'Reciprocity' (from France), demand for, 278, 282, 288, 334
'Red Lion,' The (tavern at Newmarket), 153
— — Square (Holborn), 188
Red-deer, a four-in-hand of, 59
Redrose (horse), 114
Reform Bill, the (effect of), 222
Refraction (horse), 195
Regalia (horse), 295, 361
Reginald (horse), 193
Regulus (horse), 48, 49, 120, 150
Remembrancer (horse), 331
Remus (horse), 95, 289
Rendlesham, Lord (J. C.), 265, 314
Repeal of racing statutes, 320
Repulse (horse), 275
Restitution (horse), 269
Rêve d'Or (horse), 308
Reveller (horse), 222
Rhadamanthus (horse), 55
— the 'infernal' judge, 116
Rhoda (horse), 195
Ribblesdale, Lord (suicide of), (J. C.), 265, 276
Richmond, Dukes of, 35, 36, 194, 211, 366
— — (J. C.), 12, 35, 172, 194, 211, 246, 264, 307, 314, 315, 320
— Bay, 81
— (horse), 112
— (Yorks), (Gold Cup won five years running), 192
Riddle (horse), 97
Riddlesworth (horse), 206, 240
— (place), 226, 240
Ridicule (horse), 226

RID

Riding in with the leading horses, 318
Ridsdale, Mr. ('bookmaker'), 241, 361
'Ring,' The, 306, 345–347, 351–353, 358
— attempt of a noble lord to 'do,' v. Cwrw (horse)
'Ringworm,' The, 359
Ripponden (Yorks), 302
Risby (Suffolk), (or ? near Beverley, Yorks), 146
Rise (in Holderness, Yorks), 130
Robert de Gorham (man), 212
— (horse), 212
Roberts, Mr. W. A. (J. C.), 266
Robin Hood (horse), (by Wild Dayrell), 298
— — — (by North Lincoln), 298
Robinson, Mr. ('Judge to the J. C.'), 167
— — (owner of the famous Sampson), 64
— Rt. Hon. John (Sec. to the Treasury), (? J. C.), 173, 179
— Sir Hercules (J. C.), 265, 307
Rockingham, Marquess of (J. C.), 12, 59, 63, 65, 69, 89, 95, 227, 243, 312
— — — sister of, 65, 66
— (horse), 42, 147; (another), 304
'Rolliad,' The, 175
Romeo (horse), 135
Roper, Hon. Gertrude (Baroness Dacre), 107
Rosaletta (horse), 136
Rose, Mr. C. D. (J. C.), 266, 355
Rosebery, Earl of (J. C.), 264, 296, 307, 315
— Hannah, Countess of, 269
Rosebud (horse), 115
Rosicrucian (horse), 296
Rosslyn, Earl of (J. C.), 264, 287
— — (son of the former), 147
Rothschild, Baron Meyer (J. C.), 264, 269, 315

RUS

Rothschild, Baron Lionel, 270, 31
— Miss (Hannah, Countess of Rosebery), 269
— Mr. Leopold (J. C.), 266
Rouge (horse), (bred in France), 108, 188
Rougham (Suffolk), 215
Rous, Lord (Sir John), (J. C.), v. Stradbroke
— Admiral (J. C.), 9, 173, 186, 226, and *passim*
— — continuous re-election of, 326
— Major, 210
— Mr. (of the 'Eagle' Tavern), 210
'— Bravo !' (whence derived), 210
Rowena (horse), 193
Rowton (horse), 280
Royal College of Veterinary Surgeons, 188
— Hunt Cup (Ascot), 303, 321
— mares, 19
— Stud (Hampton Court), 186
Royston, Viscount (Earl of Hardwicke), (J. C.), 265
Rubens (horse), 40, 226
Ruffler (horse), 120
Rufford Abbey (Notts), 302
Rugeley (Staffs), 322
Ruler (horse), 130
Rules and Orders of the J. C., 157–160, 256, 318–340
— Concerning Horse-racing, 156, 254–256, 318–340, and v. Appendix
Run (of more than fifty miles after a fox), 95
'Running Rein' (horse), (the notorious case), 259, 318, 347, 356
Rupee (horse), 288
'Rupert of Debate,' The (J. C.), 271
Rush, Mr. George (J. C.), 173, 226, 266
Rushout, Sir Charles (J. C.), 265, 314

INDEX

RUS

Russia, Empress of, 59
Russias, Emperor of all the (J. C.), 263
Rutland, Dukes of, 36, 37, 56, 69
— — (J. C.), 36, 37, 172, 185, 195, 264
Ryshworth (Yorks), 302

SABLONS (France), the plain of, 97
Saccharometer (horse), 289
Sackville, Viscounts (J. C.), 172, 206, 207
— Lord George, 207
Sadler, Mr. (ex-ostler), 361
Sagitta (horse), 271
Sailor (horse), 240, 241
St. Albans, Duke of (J. C.), 264, 307, 315
— — (horse), 282
— — (place), 212
— Albin, Monsieur A. de, 362
— Blaise (horse), 308
— Christopher, island of (St. Kitt's), 124
— Donat's (Glamorganshire), 301
— George (horse), 191, 206, 226, 227
— George's Fields, 233
— Giles (horse), 241
— John, Colonel, 100
— — Hon. John (? J. C.), (a 'macaroni' and author), 173, 179
— Lawrence (horse, and name of the Earls of Howth), 285
— Leger, Colonel, 63
— — (race), 63, 125
— Marguerite (horse), 300
— Patrick (horse), 112, 222
— Peter's (Isle of Thanet), 103
— Quintin, Sir. W., 20
— Simon (horse), 48, 268
— Vincent, Lord (Viscount), (J.C.), 265, 276, 277
Salisbury, race for Silver Bowl at, 116
— Lord, 138

SCR

Salisbury, Countess of (beheaded), 231
Sally (horse), 122
Salterley Common, 47
Saltram (horse), (so-called from the seat of the Earls of Morley, Devon), 226, 239
Sam (horse), 240, 241
Sampson (horse), (15 hands, 2 in.), 64, 65
Sancho (horse), 239
Sanderson, the Rev. T., 92
Sandown Park, 333, 353
Sarpedon (horse), 81
Satirist (horse), 283
Saturn (horse), 61
Saucebox (horse), 286
Savernake (horse), 282
Savile, Mr. H. (J. C.), 266, 302
Saye and Sele, Lord (J. C.), 265, 293
Scales, tampering with the, 280
Scaramouch (horse), 33
Scarf (horse), 63
Scarsdale (Lord, first Baron),(J.C.), 80
Scipio (Roman general), 50
— (and tooth-picks), 50
— (horse), 50, 89
Scotia (horse), 146
Scott, Mr. (? Capt., Major, Col., and Gen.), (J. C.), 13, 58, 130, 131
— the three Misses (Duchess of Portland, Viscountess Downe, and Viscountess Canning), 130, 131
— Lord J. (J. C.), 265, 293
— Mr. J. (trainer), 248, 249, 272, 291, 299, 310, 361
— Mrs., 291
— Mr. W. (jockey), 361
Scottish Queen (horse), 308
Scrimsher ⎫
Scrymsher ⎬ Mr. Boothby, 13, 104, 134, 135
Scrymshire ⎪
Skrymsher ⎭
Scriven (Yorks), 114

Scud (horse), 240
Seabreeze (horse), 308
Sebright, Sir Thomas Saunders (J. C.), 12, 91
— Lieut.-Gen. Sir John S. (? J. C.), 91
Sedley (or Sidley), Sir Charles (J. C.), 12, 91–93
See-saw (horse), 289
Sefton, Earls of (J. C.), 58, 122, 303
— (horse), 58, 300
— House (Newmarket), 58, 300
Selim (horse), 40
Selima (horse), 61
Selwyn, Mr. George (the wit), 7, 13, 14, 57, 117, 131–133, 201, 229
Semolina (horse), 308, 329
Senlis (horse), 41
Seringapatam (siege of), 294
Sevastopol (fortress), 268
Seymour, Lady Elizabeth, 33
— Capt. H. (J. C.), 266
— Lord Henry, 272
— Sir Hamilton, 268
Shafto, Messrs., or Capts. J. and R. (J. C.), 13, 89, 111, 132–134, 141, 159, 215
— Mr. J. (matches), 133, 134
Shakespeare, William, 212, 239, 240
Shakspear, Mr. Arthur (J. C.), 173, 226, 239
Shardeloes (Amersham, Bucks), 300
Shark (horse), 127, 229, 230
Sheerness, curious horse-wager at, 186
Shelburne, Lord (Lansdowne), (? J. C.), 177
Shelley, Sir John (fifth Baronet), (J. C.), 12, 93, 190
— — — (sixth Baronet), (J. C.), 93, 204, 224, 265, 297
— — — (seventh Baronet), (J. C.), 265, 266, 297
Sherborne, Lord (J. C.), 137, 172, 208, 209, 236

Sherborne (place), 208
Sheridan, Right Hon. R. B. (? J. C.), 173, 180
Shiplake (Oxon), 231
Shipton (near York), 75, 120, 360
Shirley, Hon. Messrs., 134, 135
Shoemaker (horse), 112
Shorthand-writers, the J. C. and, 320, 321
Shotover (horse), 308
Shottesbrook, 241
Shoveller (or Shoveler), (horse), 240, 241
Siberia (horse), 308
'Sick Man,' The (Turkey), 268
Siderolite (horse), 296
Signal (horse), 216
Signorina (horse), 162
Silver (horse), 207
— Bowl (at Salisbury), 116
Silvertail (horse), 145
Silvio (horse), 291
Sim Tappertit, 73
Singleton, Mr. John, senior (jockey), 130
Sir Archy (American horse), 80
— Bevys (horse), 270, 315
— Harry (horse), 235
— Joshua (horse), 226, 301
— Oliver (horse), 244
— Peter Teazle (more commonly Sir Peter), 67, 68, 200
— Thomas (horse), 81, 183
— — Jellybag (horse), 175
Sister to Pharamond (horse), 190
Six Mile Bottom Stud Farm (Newmarket, the Prince Regent's), 302
Skelmersdale, Lord, 149
Skim (horse), 63
Skipton (Yorks), 130
Skirmisher (horse), 93
Skrymsher, &c., v. Scrimsher, &c.
Skyscraper (horse), 190, 236
Slane (horse), 286
Slingsby, Miss Sarah (maid of honour to Queen Anne, Mrs. Duncombe), 114

SLI

Slingsby, Sir C., 148
Slipby (horse), (bay), 120
— — (brown), 120
Smart (afterwards Claret), (horse), 217
Smiling Betty (horse), 278
— Molly (horse), 310
— Nanny (horse), 309
Smith, Mr. or General (J. C.), 13, 135, 136
— (the Young General), (? J. C.), 136
— Mr. Hugh (millionaire, whose daughters married into the Barrymore and Derby families), 68, 136, 199
— — and Mrs. Robert Percy, 143
— the Right Hon. Mr. Vernon, 143
— the Rev. Sidney, 122
— Mr. T. Assheton (J. C.), 266
— Mrs. (Lady Lade), 218
Smith-Barry, Mr. (J. C.), v. Barry
Smithson, Sir Hugh (Duke of Northumberland), 33, 34
Smolensko (horse), 74, 224, 244, 278
Smyrna (place), 150
Snap (horse), 20, 89, 216
Snapdragon (horse), 61
Snewing, Mr. ('vet.' and 'bookmaker'), 361
Snip (horse), (maternal grandsire of Pyrrhus), 139
'Snipe' (*alias* W. Taylor), (earliest published case of 'warning off' by the J. C.), 257, 258, 282
Sober Robin (horse), 206
Société d Encourgement. 7, 362
Society for the Propagation of Gambling, 353, 358
— — — — of the Gospel, 140
— a Turf, 363
Sog (horse), 82
Soldier (horse), 52
Solon (horse), 65

SQU

Soltykoff, Prince D. (J. C.), 264, 268
Somerset, Dukes of, 33
— Edward (Earl of Worcester), 309
— the proud Duke of, 33, 36
Sondes, Lord (J. C), 12, 66, 67
Songstress (horse), 270
Soothsayer (horse), 84
Sorcery (mare), 195
Sotterley (Suffolk), 298
Sourface (horse), 118
South, Mr., 78
— East (horse), 63
— West (horse), 63
Southampton, Duke of Cleveland and, 192
— Lord (J. C.), 265
Southfleet (estate), 92
Southwark (place), 217
Spain (toothpicks introduced from), 50
Spalding, Mr. (J. C.), 266
Spaniel (horse), 206, 286
'Speaker,' Mr., vii
Spectator (horse), 89, 148, 156
Spectre (horse), 26, 137, 208
Speculum (horse), 274
Spencer, Lady Diana, 44
— Earl (J. C.), 264
— Hon. Capt. (J. C.), 266
'Spider and Fly,' 275, 277
Spiletta (horse), 20
Spinaway (horse), 291
Spitfire (horse), 60
'Sporting Kalendar,' The (Mr. J. Pond's), 5
'— Magazine,' a writer in the, 229
Sportsman (horse), 67, 145
Sportsmistress (horse), 145
Spot (horse), 61, 194
Spread Eagle (horse), 207, 220
Sprightly (horse), 139
Squerries (Kent), 143
Squirrel (first called Surly), (horse), 89
Squirt (horse), (grandsire of Eclipse), 139

STA

Stafford, Marquess of (the first, grandfather of Lord Granville), (J. C.), 53
Stamford (and Warrington), Earl of (J. C.), 250, 258, 264, 287, 335, 355
— (place), 309
Standard (horse), 80
Standby (horse), 139
— Young, 80
Standish, Sir Frank (J. C.), 207, 220
Stanhope, Philip, Earl of Chesterfield (J. C.), 172, 177
— Amelia, Countess of Barrymore, 177
— Dormer, Earl of Chesterfield (? J. C.), 172, 177
— Earl of Harrington (? J. C.), 172, 177
Stanley, Lord (Earl of Derby), (J. C.), 265, 271, 329–331
— — and Canezou, 330
— — — Mr. Greville's Cariboo, 330
— Messrs. (J. C.), 265, 266, 295, 303
— Sir M. (J. C.), 266
— the family of, 199
Stapleford (Notts), 145
Stapleton, Mr. (ancestor of Lord Beaumont), (J. C.), 13, 83, 84, 137
Star (Queen Anne's horse), 24, 311
' — and Garter,' The (Pall Mall), 6, 7, 152
— Davis (American horse), 302
Stargazer (horse), 71
Starling (horse), (the Ancaster S.), 24
— (Bay), 120
— (Brown), 120
Statira (horse), 108
Staveley (horse), 239
Stawell, Lord (? J. C.), 172, 208, 209

STU

Stawell, Baroness, 209
Stella (horse), 108
Stephenson, Mr. (Alderman of Newcastle), 120
Steyne, the (Brighton), 49
— — (match on), 219
— (Thackeray's), Marquess of, 49
Steyning, 100
Stickler (horse), 224
Stilton (churchyard), 47
Sting (mare), 223; (horse), 270
Stockton (Wilts), 299
Stockwell (horse), 203, 292, 304, 354, 361
Stoic (horse), 123
Stonehewer, Mr. Scott (J. C.), 266, 303
Stow (place), 123
Stowell, Lord, 209
Strabally Hall (Ireland), 300
Stradbroke, Earls of (J. C.), 172, 209–211, 264
Stradling, the family of, 301
Strafford, Earls of (J. C.), 214, 264, 265, 288
Strange, Lord (so self-styled, father of the twelfth Lord Derby), (J. C.), 12, 67, 68, 199
Strangways (not Strangeways), Fox- (name of the Earl of Ilchester), 312
Strathmore, Earls of (J. C.), 265, 288, 299
Stratton, Mr. George (and Lord Pigot), 62
Strawberry Hill, 51, 242
Streatlam Castle (Durham), 248, 288, 299
Strickland, Sir William, 147
Stripling (horse), 26
Strode ⎱ Mr. or Captain Edward
Stroud ⎰ (J. C.), 12, 137, 138
Stuart, Sir Simeon (J. C.), 12, 94
Stuart-Wortley, v. Wortley
Stud Companies, 361
' — Book,' the, 165, 234, 237, 303
Stumbler (horse), 112

INDEX 415

STU

Stumps (horse), 202
Sturgeon, William or John (a groom), 65, 66
Sturt, Mr. Humphry, 309
—— Gerard (Lord Alington), (J. C.), 267, 296
Subscribers to the J. C. Challenge Cup, 30, and *passim*
Subscription Rooms (Newmarket), 358
Sudbury (Suffolk), 113
Suffield, Lords (J. C.), 172, 207, 211, 293, 294, 307
Suffolk and Berkshire, Earl of (J. C.), 9, 248, 265, 315, 346, 356, 366
Sultan (horse), 205, 282
Summerside (horse), (winner of the Oaks), 291
Sunshade (horse), 300
Surly (horse), 89
Surplice (horse), 272, 290
Surprise (horse), 183
Surrey, Earl of, 175
Surveyor (horse), 112
Sutton, Mr. R. (Sir Richard), (J. C.), 267, 303
Swaffham (Bulbeck), 246, 247
— (Prior), 247
Sweepstakes (horse), 54
Sweet Briar (horse), 55
— William (horse), 55; (Mr. Barker's), 313
Sweetsauce (horse), 284
Swillington (place, the Rev. Sir W. Lowther's), 88
Swinburne, Mr. William (J. C.), 13, 89, 134, 138, 139
Swindon (Wilts), 301
Swymmer, Mr. Anthony Langley (J. C.), 13, 119, 139, 140, 315
Symme, Colonel (American), 119
Symmetry (horse), 84
Synge, Colonel (J. C.), 267
Syntax, Doctor (horse), 284
Syphon (horse), 139, 190

THA

TAAFFE, Mr. Theobald, M.P. (gambler), vii
— Count, vii
Tadcaster (Yorks), 242, 243
Tag (horse), 202
Takamahaka (horse), 40
Tampering with the scales, 280
Tan gallops, 249, 299
Tandem (horse), 43, 134, 220
Tankerville, Countess of, 140
Tappertit, Sim, 73
Tarleton, Mr., Colonel, and General Banastre (? J. C.), 173, 180
Tarragona (horse), 258
— Case, the, 258
Tarran, Rev. Mr. (his 'Black Barb'), 162
Tartar Mare, the fabulous, 313
— (horse), 313
Tattersall, Messrs., 7, 45, 74, 144, 150, 327, 360
'Tattersall's,' 162, 256, 327, 359
Tavistock (place), 142
— Marquess of (J. C.), 172, 212, 264, 281
—— 189
Tawney (horse), 56, 121
Taylor, Mr. (*alias* Snipe), 257
—— C. (J. C.), 173
Teazle, Sir Peter (horse), 200
'— (Lady),' 200
Teddington (horse), 295, 296, 303
Teddy the Grinder (horse), 71
Teissier, Barons de, 269
— Baron de (J. C.), 264, 268, 269, 296
——— Lewis, 269
Tempest, Sir H. Vane (J. C.), *v.* Vane
Ténébreuse (French horse), 335, 338
Tetotum (horse), 235
Texas (country), 275
Thanet, Isle of, St. Peter's, 103
Tharp, Mr. W. M. (J. C.), 267, 315
— Mr. John, 315

THA

'Thatched House,' the (tavern), 7, 152
Thebais (horse), 300
Thelusson, Messrs. (Lords Rendlesham), 314
'— Act,' the, 314
Theobald, Mr. (hosier and breeder of Stockwell), 203, 361
Theodore (horse), (extraordinary winner of the St. Leger), 280
Theophania (horse), 84
Thesiger, Sir F. (Lord Chancellor), 178
Thetford (horse), 223
Thirty Stone, a match at, 77, 238
Thomond, Lords (Earls of), 201, 202
— — (their stud in Charles II.'s time), 201
— House (Newmarket), 201
Thompson, 'Bet,' 140
Thornhill, Mr. (of Riddlesworth), (J. C.), 173, 226, 240, 241, 267, 301
Thornton, Colonel (the famous), 148
Thornville (horse), 148
Thoulouse (or Toulouse), (place), 127
Thrale, Mr. Henry (eminent brewer), 217
— Mrs. (Dr. Johnson's friend), 217
'Three D.'s v. three K.'s,' 277
Thucydides, 48
Thumper (horse), 112
Thurlow, Lord (Chancellor), (? J. C.), 172, 177
Thwackum (horse), (*alias* Scipio), 89
Thynne, family of, 309
Tigress (horse), 112
Tigris (horse), 210
Tim Whiffler (horse), 292
Timoleon (American horse), 80
Tipping, Mr, 90
Tiresias (horse), 194, 271
Titchfield, Marquess of (J. C.), 172, 194

TRU

Tolstone ⎫
Toulston ⎬ Hall (Yorks), 147
Towlestone ⎭
Tomato (horse), 269
Tomlinson, Mr. (breeder of Teddington), 295
Tommy (horse), 84, 137
Tomtit (or Tom Tit), (horse), 311
Tooley Park (Leicester), 122
Toothpicks (Scipio and), 50
Topham, Capt., Major, and Col. (the celebrated), (? J. C.), 173, 180
Tortoise (horse), 53
Tot (horse), 206
Touchstone (horse), 139, 219, 282, 283, 354
Toulouse, v. Thoulouse
'Touts,' the J. C. and the, 346
Towneley (place, Lancashire), 303
— Col. Charles (J. C.), 267, 303
— Marbles, the, 303
Townshend, Lord John (? J. C.), 172, 177
— George, Earl of Leicester and Marquess T. (? J. C.), 177
— Hon. Charles (a joker), 74
Toxophilite (horse), 271
Toy (horse), 314
Training 'Reports' (in the newspapers), 334
Trajan (horse), 55
Tramp (horse), 304
Transit (horse). 38
Tregony (place), 126
Trentham, Viscount (J. C.), 53, 116, 118, 124
— (horse), 92, 137
Trials, 346
Trifle (horse), 50
Tristan (horse), 287
Trollope (Lord Kesteven), 25
Trotinda (horse), 221
Trousers (first wearer in public of), (J. C.), 218
True Blues (horses), the two, 147, 298
Trumpator (horse), 50

LAN

Landscape (horse), 236
Lane, Capt. Douglas (J. C.), 266, 313, 322
— Col. John (friend of Charles II.), 313
Langham Hall (Suffolk), 100
Langton Wold (Yorks), 249, 299
Lansdowne, Marquess of (the celebrated Lord Shelburne), (? J. C.), 172, 177
Lapdog (horse), 202
Lardon (horse), 36
Lascelles, Viscount (J. C.), 265, 313
— Rev. Mr., 313
Lasingcroft (Yorks), 83
Launcelot (horse), 283
Lauraguais, Comte de (owner of Gimcrack), 174
Lauzun, Duc de, 174
Lawn, The (estate, Swindon, Wilts), 301
Le Beau (horse), (the beautiful Duchess of Devonshire's), 29
— Despencer, Baroness (Viscountess Falmouth), 291
— Maréchal (horse, bred in France), 288
— Sang (horse), 116
Leander (horse), 318
— Case, the, 318
Leaping-match, Sir C. (Mr.) Turner's, 95
Lecturer (horse), 275
Ledstone Hall (Yorks), 243
Leedes, Mr. (Yorkshire breeder), 139
Leeds, Duke of (? J. C.), 172, 175
— — (J. C.), 194, 264
Lees Court (Kent), 67
Leeway (horse), 212
Lefèvre, Monsieur C. J. (of Chamant), 287
Legard, Sir Charles (ex-J. C.), 265
Legge, Messrs. Bilson (and Lord Stawell), 209
Legh, Mr. W. J. (J. C.), 266, 313
— Mr., 313

LON

Leicester, Earl of (Marquess Townshend), (? J. C.), 172, 177
Leigh, Colonel, 302
Lenox (or Lennox), Lady Sarah, 72, 73
— — Charles, first Duke of Richmond, 36
— Col. and Gen. (Duke of Richmond), 195
— (horse), 112
— Lord H. G. (J. C.), 265
Leominster, 118
Leonidas (horse), 53
Lepicq (horse), 220
Lethbridge, Sir W. A. (J. C.), 265, 313
Letter of Lord Derby to the J. C., an admonitory, 321, 339
Leviathan (horse), 38
— (of the Ring, Mr. Davis, the), 330
— a, 360
Lewes (Sussex), 219
Lexington (American horse), 80
Leybourne Grange (Kent), 295, 296
Lichfield, Earl of (J. C.), 264, 286
Lightfoot, Mr. (of Virginia, U.S.), 239
Lime Kilns, The (Newmarket), 248
Lincoln, Earl of (J. C.), 264
Lindsey, Earls of, 25, 274
Linkboy (horse), 195
Lister, family name of, 276
Little Driver (horse), 49
— Duck (French horse), 324
— Wonder (horse), 283
Liverpool, Earl of (? J. C.), 177
Livy (Roman historian), 50
Lloyd, Mr. Cynric (J. C.), 266
Locust (horse), 120
Londesborough, Lord (J. C.), 265, 291
— Lodge, 292
Londonderry, Marquess of (J. C.), 220, 264, 307, 313
Lonely (horse), 308

D D

LON

Longchamps, 273
Longford, Earls of, 112
Long Witton (Northumberland), 138
Lonsdale (first Viscount), 87
— (third Viscount), 87
— Earls of (J. C.), 87, 88, 206, 264, 266, 286
Lord Clifden (horse), 277
— Lyon (horse), 280, 303
Loughborough, Lord (St. Clair-Erskine), (? J. C.), 231, 287
Louis the XV., King, 174
— the XVI., 188
Lowther (place in Westmorland), 88
— Lord (J. C.), 172, 206, 265, 286
— Sir J. (the 'bad' Lord Lonsdale), (J. C.), 12, 87, 119, 206
— the Rev. Sir W., 88
— Right Hon. J. (J. C.), 266, 306, 307, 313
— Hon. Margaret, 87
— Mr. Robert (of Barbados), 87
— Col. (third Earl of Lonsdale), (J. C.), 266, 286
Lucetta (horse), 222, 223
Luck's All (horse), 193
'Lucky Baronet,' The (Sir J. Hawley), (J. C.), 295
'— Burrells,' The, 131
Ludgershall, borough of, 133
'Ludlow' Year, The, 332
Lumley, Mr. R. G. (breeder of Musjid), 296
Lupin, Monsieur A. (J. C.), 236, 266, 270, 327
Luss (horse), 223
Luttrell, Colonel, 20
— Miss (Mrs. Horton), 20
Lyme Park (Cheshire), (Messrs. Legh, of), 313
Lymington, Viscount, 314

MACARONI (horse), 289
Macclesfield, second Earl of, 125

MAR

Macdonald (jockey), 283
Macedon, 47
Mackay, Mr. George, 62
Magic (horse), 207
Magog (horse), 83-85
Maid of Orleans (horse), 236
— — the Oaks (horse), 55
Maidstone, Lord (Earl of Winchilsea), (J. C.), 265, 292
Mainstone (horse), 272
Malton (place), a dispute at, 157
— (Bay, horse), v. Bay Malton
Maltzahn, Barons (well established on the English Turf), 312
Mambrino (horse), 55, 84, 115, 235
Mameluke (horse), 205
Manfred (horse), 303
Manners, Lord William (J. C.), 12, 36, 37, 41, 56
— Lord George (J. C.), 253, 265
— Lord C. (J. C.), 265; family of, 312
Mansfield, Lord (the great), (decision of), 126, 228
Maple, Mr. Blundell ('Childwick'), 223
Marble Hill (Twickenham), Gen. Peel's, 274
Marbury Hall (Belmont, Cheshire), 136
Marc Antony (or Mark Anthony), (horse), 50, 139
Marcellus (horse), 192
March (and Ruglen), the Earl of ('old Q.'), (J. C.), 12, 27, 31, 56, 58, 113, 114, 121, 126, 131, 132, 148, 310
— Earl of (J. C.), 264, 314
— Mr. John (J. C.), 13, 121
Maresfield Park (Sussex), 93
Maria (horse), 216
— Fagniani (Marchioness of Hertford), 57
Marie Antoine (horse), 33
-- Antoinette, Queen, 49
Marigold (dam of Doncaster), 280

MAR

Market Weighton (Yorks), 130
Marlborough, (fourth) Duke of (J. C.), 12, 33, 309
— Henrietta, Duchess of, 33
Marlow (jockey), 284
Marmier, Marquis de, 363
Maroon (horse), ('pulled' for the St. Leger), 283
Marquis (horse), 141
Marske (horse), (sire of Eclipse), 18, 139
Marston, Mrs. Frances (afterwards Burlton), 108
Martin, Mr. Baron (Samuel), (J.C.), 180, 265, 272
Martindale, Mr. (saddler), 49, 150, 360
Match Book (keeper of the, at Newmarket), 164-166
Matchem (horse), 20, 35, 115
Matches, notable, 133, 134, 238, 242
Matilda (horse), 280
Matson (Gloucestershire), 133
Mauley, de, Lord (J. C.), *v.* De Mauley
'Maxims and Characters,' by Fulke Greville (J. C.), 119
Maynard, Lord, 31, 237
— Mr. (J. C.), 173, 225, 237, 238
Mayonnaise (horse), 300
Meaburn (horse), 192
Meath, Bishop of, 53
Medea (horse), 112
Medora (horse), 195
Melbourne, Lords, 225, 312, 366
— (horse), 139
— (place), 292
Mellish, Col. (J. C.), 54, 173, 224, 225, 238
Melton (horse), 308
Melville, Viscount (? J. C.), 178
Memnon (horse), 192, 304
Memoir (horse), 294, 308, 329
Mentmore (estate), 269
— Lass (horse), 269
Merlin (Old), (horse), 345
— Lord Lindsey's, 24

MER

Merry, Mr. James ('Thormanby'), 55, 293, 361
— Hampton (horse), 148
— Hart (horse), 280
Messenger (horse), the 'Father of Trotters,' 55, 115, 223, 235
Meteor (horse), 299
Metropolitan Racecourse Bill (Mr. Anderson's), 336
Meynell, Mr. Hugo ('Father of Fox-hunting'), (J. C.), 13, 105, 121, 133, 154, 174, 295
— Mr. Littleton Poyntz, 121
Miami (horse), 296
Michel Grove (Sussex), 93
Mickleham (Surrey), 242
Middle Park, 361
— — Plate, 277
Middleton, Sir William (J. C.), 12, 64, 89
— Sir John Lambert, 89
— — W. (the hero of Minden), 89
— (Bay), (horse), 205, 206
— (Chestnut), (horse), 205, 297
— Stony (estate, Oxon), (Lord Jersey's), 204
Midge (horse), 89
Mildenhall (Suffolk), 72
Milford (North), (Yorks), 139
Mills, Mr. J. (J. C.), 266
Milltown, Earls of (J. C.), 264
Milner, Mr. W. M. (Sir W.), (J C.), 266
Milsington, Viscount (J. C.), 63
— — 63
Milton, Viscount (Earl Fitzwilliam), (J. C.), 265
Minden, battle of, 89
Minos (the 'infernal' judge), 116
Minstead Manor (Hants), 111
Minthe (horse), 304
Minting (horse), 304
Minuet (horse), 193, 220
Mira (horse), 216
Mirabeau, Comte de (Mr. Grossley), 174

D D 2

MIR

Miramon, Marquis de, 363
Miranda (horse), 44
Mirza (horse), 89, 119
Misfortune (horse), 40, 73
Miss Belsca (Belsay), (horse), 89
— Craven (horse), 195
— Elis (horse), 272
— Fortune (horse), 112
— Jummy (horse), 308
— Osmer (horse), 53
— Ramsden (horse), 215
— South (horse), 63
— Spindleshanks (horse), 52
— Western (horse), 77
Mixbury (Regulus), (horse), 68
Molecatcher (horse), 92
Molyneux, Sir Francis (? J. C.), 173, 178
— Viscount (first Earl of Sefton), (J. C.), 12, 58
Monaco, Prince of, 23
Monarque (French horse), 284
Moncreiffe, Sir David, 309
Monmouth, James, Duke of, 9; (place), 47
Monson, Mr. Lewis (first Baron Sondes), *v.* Sondes
— Lord, 222
Montagu, Lord (of Cawdry) 19; (his mares), 19
— Mr. Wortley (gambler), M.P., vii
Montalbo (or Mentalba), Comtesse de (Mrs. Bowes), 299
Monte Carlo (place), 277
Montgregon, Comte Edouard de, 363
Montrose, Dukes of (? J. C.), 172, 175, 314
— Duke of (J. C.), 264, 300
Moon, Mr. Washington, 48
Moore, Sir John (owner of King Herod), (J. C.), 12, 63, 89, 90
Morel (horse), 31
Morion (horse), 29
Morley, Earls of, 239
Morny, Comte de (purchaser of West Australian), 292
Moses (horse), 49; (another), 185

NET

Moslem (horse), 300
Mostyn, Mr. and Lord (J. C.), 55, 265, 266, 290, 292
Mouravieff (horse), 289
Mouse (Young), (horse), 197
Mulcaster, Capt., 242
Mulgrave, Earl of (J. C.), 264
Mündig (horse), 299
'Musæ Anglicanæ,' The, 110
Musgrave, Mr. Christopher, 310
Music (horse), 193, 220
Musjid (horse), 296
Mustachio (horse), 185
Mustard (horse), (Queen Anne's), 311, 314
Myrtle (horse), 113; (Mr. Wentworth's), 115
Mytton, Mr. 'Jack' (of Halston), 313

NABOB (*alias* Flambé), (horse), 116
Naburn (place near York), 129
'Nænia Britannica' (author of), 235
Nanny (Wynn), the Rev. Mr., 162
Nantwich (Cheshire), 149
Naper, Messrs. (original family name of the Duttons, Lords Sherborne), 208, 236
Napier, Col. (second husband of Lady Sarah Lenox), the Hon., 73
— Sir Charles and Sir William, 73
Narcissus (horse), 35
Nassau Stakes, the, 267
'Nat' (Elnathan Flatman, jockey), 284
Naylor, Mr. Francis (J. C.), 13, 122
— Mr. R. C., 122, 292
Nectar (horse), 197
Nelson, Mr. John (and his 'Calendar'), 161
Netherfield (horse), 192
Netherlands, King of the, 263, 267
'Nethermost Hell,' definition of, 231

NEV

Neva (horse), 243
Nevill, Mr. R. H. (J. C.), 266
Neville, Mr. (Lord Braybrooke, editor of 'Pepys's Diary'), (J. C.), 173, 225
Nevison (highwayman, and his black mare), 85
Newbyth (Haddingtonshire), 294
Newcastle, Duke of (J. C.), 264, 274
— Dukes of, 28, 57, 67
Newcomen, Sir W. (banker), 95
'Newgate' (nickname of an Earl of Barrymore), 42, 44, 275
— Market, 150
Newmarket, *passim*
— (meetings at), 158–160, 320
— Coffee Room, admission to the, 158
— Heath, right of 'warning off,' 194
— Rooms, the, 17, 157
— Whip, The, 9, 19
'— The Cub at' (poem), 22, 153
Newminster (horse), 222, 354
Newport, Viscount (Earl of Bradford), (J. C.), 265
Newspapers and betting, the, 352, 359
Newton (place), 313
— Gold Cup at, 313
Nicholas, the Emperor, 268
'Nicholson's Gin,' 361
Nicolls, Lady (Duchess of Ancaster), 23
Nicolo (or Niccolo), (horse, a twin), 209
Nightshade (horse), 202
Niké (horse), 55
Ninon de l'Enclos, 132
'Nobbling,' 85, 319
Noble (horse), 125
Nobody (horse), 52
Nogent, le Chevalier, 363
Nominations (voidance of, by death), 322–326
Norfolk, Duke of (? J. C.), 172, 175

OLD

Normanby, Marquess of (J.C.), 264, 311
Norris, Mr., Captain, and Admiral (Henry), (J. C.), 13, 122, 123
North, Lord (? J.C.), 177
— Colonel, 223
— Milford (Yorks), 139
Northampton, Earls of, 111
Northey, Mr. (? J. C.), 173, 179
— Messrs., 179
Northfleet (estate), 92
Northumberland (Sir Hugh Smithson), Duke of (J. C.), 12, 33, 154, 243
— Countess of, 33, 34
Norton Conyers (Yorks), 295
Nottingham (horse), 218
Now or Never (horse), 120
Nuncio (horse), 226
Nunnykirk (horse), 222
Nuttall (Notts), 92
Nymphina (horse), 224, 225

'OAKS,' The (race), 199; (estate), 199
Oatlands (estate belonging to the Duke of York), 93, 185, 187
Oberon (horse), 76, 96, 220, 241
Octavian (horse), 194
'Ode to Indifference,' by Mrs. Fulke Greville, 119
Odine (horse), 108
Offley, Mr. (J. C.), 13, 122
Ofley, Mr. (very ancient 'racer'), 123, 124
Ogilvy, Mr. Charles (J. C.), 13, 123
Okehampton (place), 142
O'Kelly, Mr. (senior), ('blackleg,' and owner of Eclipse), 33, 150, 183, 226, 238, 313, 344, 345, 350, 360
— — (junior), (J. C.), 173, 226, 238
— — (senior), on 'crossing and jostling,' 251
Old Burlington Street, 165
— England (horse), 75; (another) 319

OLD

'Old England Case,' the, 319, 322
(Old) Merlin (horse), 345
'Old Q' (last Duke of Queensberry), (J. C.), 31, 56–58, 310
— Rowley' (Charles the Second), 8
— Sarum (Wilts), 100
'Old' White's Club, vii, 143
Olive (horse), 225, 244
Oliver, Mr. Richard (afterwards Gascoigne), 84
— Cromwell (horse), 199
Omar (horse), 52
Onslow, Hon. Mr. 'Tommy' (second Earl of), (? J. C.), 173, 179
Oppidan (horse), 195
Orange, Princes of (J. C.), 263, 267
— Plate, the (at Ascot), 267
Orde, Mr. T. (Powlett), 190
Orford, Earls of (J. C.), 12, 58, 59, 64, 78, 111, 264, 286
— Lady (horse), 286
Oriana (horse), 295
Orion (horse), 120
Orlando (horse), 273
Orléans, Duc d' ('Égalité'), 108, 172, 182, 188
— (horse), 188
Ormonde (horse), 48, 148, 221, 280, 308, 354
— Marquess of, 61
Oroonoko (horse), 114
Orton, Mr. John (and his 'Annals'), 75, 77, 148
Osborne, Mr. John (senior, trainer), 79
Osnaburgh, Prince-bishop of (Duke of York), (J. C.), 184
Ossian (horse), 308
Ossory (Upper), Earl of (J. C.), 12, 31, 60, 61, 154
— — Dowager Countess of, 143
Othello (horse), 63
Otheothea (horse), 61
Otho (horse), 49, 60
Ottley, Messrs. William (senior and junior), (J. C.), 13, 124, 125
Oulston (horse), 222

PAR

Oxenden Street (Haymarket), 165
Oxford (Corporation of), 40
— (races at), 40
Oxton Hall (Yorks), 243
Oxygen (horse), 193

PADWICK (or Padwicke), Mr. (usurer), 242, 275, 277
Paget, Mr. G. E. (J. C.), 266, 307, 314
Paine, Mr. 'Tom' (the notorious), 188
Pall Mall, 6
Palmer, W. (the poisoner), 322
Palmerston, Lord (J. C.), 265, 272, 320
Pan (horse), 221, 222
Pantaloon (horse), 139
Panton, Mr. Thomas (junior), (J.C.), 13, 24, 75, 79, 119, 125, 131, 181, 183, 250
— Miss Mary (Duchess of Ancaster), 23, 125
Papist (horse), 135
Paragon (horse), 138
Parasol (horse), 31, 221, 223
Parisot (horse), 220
— (she-dancer), 220
Park Hill (Doncaster), 63
Parker, Col. and Gen. Hon. George Lane (J. C.), 13, 125
— Mr. (Lord Boringdon), (J. C.), 126, 173, 181, 183, 226, 239
Parlington (Yorks), 83, 137
— (horse), 137
Parmesan (horse), 302
Parrot, a (that whistles the 104th Psalm), 238
Parsons, Nancy (Mrs. Horton), 13, 31, 237
— Mr. Henry, 108
— Mr. Humphry (Alderman), 108
Parthian (horse, two years old) 78
Partisan (horse), 222
Partner (horse), (Mr. Grisewood's), 63

INDEX

PAS

Pastille (horse), 193
Patrician (horse), 174
Patron (horse), 203
Patshull (near Wolverhampton), 61, 62
'Pavo' (sporting writer's *nom de guerre*), 3
Paymaster (horse), 45, 65, 138
Payne, Messrs., 135
— (J. C.), 266, 279
Pearson, General (J. C.), 266, 303, 306, 307, 314
— Mr. Anthony, 314
Pedley, Mr. ('book-maker'; son-in-law of Gully), 361
Peel, Col. and Gen. (J. C.), 214, 266, 273, 347
— (General), (horse), 285
Peirson, Sir Matthew, 190
Pelham, Miss (and 'Old Q.'), 27, 28, 57
— 'Tommy,' 123
Pelisse (horse), 31, 224
Pelter (horse), 219
Pemberton, Mr. C., 247
Pembroke College (Cambridge), 247
Penelope (horse), 31, 193
Pennington, Sir Joseph, 87
— Miss Catherine, 87
Penrhyn, Lord (J. C.), 265, 314
Pepys, Samuel, 9
Percy, Lady Elizabeth, 33
Perdita (horse), (dam of the Yellow Mare), 86, 220
Perion (horse), 241
Pero (horse), 33
— Gomez (horse), 296
Peter (horse), 274
— (nickname of Lord Glasgow), 274, 285
'— Pindar' (Dr. Walcot), 88
Petit Gris (French horse), (Duc d'Orléans's), 188
Petrarch (horse), 277
Petre, Hon. Mr. Edward (J. C.), 266, 280

PIQ

Petre, Mr. (and the 'Rape of the Lock'), 280
Petronel (horse), 308
Petruchio (horse), 223
Petworth (seat of Lord Egremont), 35, 202
— races at, 35, 202, 366
Phænomenon (horse), 86, 87
Phantom (horse), 93, 204, 205, 224, 297
Phillimore, Mr. W. R. (J. C.), 266
Phillips, Mr. (horse-buyer for the Duke of Northumberland), 34
Phosphorus (horse), 243, 294
Phryne (horse), 293
Piccadilly (horse), 226
— (Street), the gentleman who owned, 303
Pick, Mr. William (and his 'Register'), 314 (and elsewhere)
Pickwick Club, 10
Pic-nic (mare), 195
Pigot, Admiral (? J. C.), 173, 179
— — Sir Hugh, 62
— General Sir Robert, 62
— Lord, 12, 61, 179
— Sir George, 61, 62
— — Robert, 62
Pigott, Mr. Robert (senior), (of Chetwynd), 126, 228
— — — (junior), (of Chetwynd), (J. C.), 13, 110, 126, 127, 228
— — Charles ('Louse'), (of Chetwynd), (J. C.), 60, 111, 127, 173, 226, 228–231
— Rev. W., 228, 229
— 'Black' (of Chetwynd), 127, 229
— Mr. W. (of Doddeshall), 96
Pilgrimage (horse), 206
Pincher (horse), 124
Pindar (the famous Greek poet), 287
Pindarrie (horse), 193
Piper (horse), 60
Pique (Admiral Rous's ship), 210, 274

PIT

Pitt, Right Hon. W. (? J. C.), 87, 173, 179, 231
Place, Mr. (Cromwell's studmaster), 205
Plaisanterie (French horse), 334, 337
Plantagenet (horse), 224
Plasto (horse), 29
Platina (horse), 202
Pleader (horse), 88
Plenipotentiary (horse), 186, 235
Plóville, Monsieur Couret, 363
Plunder (horse), 108
Poisoning (of horses), 179
Poland, King of (bids 2,000 gs. for the famous sire (King) Herod), 90
Pole Star (horse), (property of the murdered Mr. Cooke), 322
'Political Dictionary,' Mr. C. Pigott's, 230, 231
Poltimore, Lords (Bampfylde), 107, 178
Pompadour, Madame de, 97, 188
Pond, Mr. John (and his Calendar), 5, 127, 134, 156, 163, 253, 254, 309, 357, and v. Appendix
— Miss (and her match), 5
— Mrs. 163
Pontac (horse), 81
Poole, Sir Ferdinando (J. C.), 173, 219, 220, 224
— Sir Henry, 219
— the Rev. Sir Henry, 220
— (estate, Wirrall, Cheshire), 219
Pope, Alexander (the poet), 114
— (horse), 31, 220 (called 'Waxy' P. to distinguish him from P. by Shuttle)
Poppet (horse), (brother to Chuff), 56
'Porch,' the Father of the, 19
Porter, Mr. John (trainer), 253
— on taking the age of racehorses, 253
Portia (horse), 190
Portius (horse, by Cato), 124, 125
Portland, Duchess of, 130

PUL

Portland, Dukes of (J. C.), 172, 176, 194, 221, 246, 264, 271, 306, 307, 311, 314, 329, 349
— Duke of v. Hawkins, 258
Portmore, Earl of (J. C.), 12, 62, 63
Portsmouth, Earl of (J. C.), 264, 310, 314, 316
— Duchess of (de la Querouaille), 132, 133
Pot8os (famous horse), 38, 55, 145
Powers, Mr. (American), 26
Powerscourt, Lord, 207
Powlett, Lord W. (J. C.), 265, 292, 322
Pratt, Mr. John (of Askrigg), (J. C.), 13, 101, 128-130, 146
Precarious (horse; first-recorded two-year-old runner at Newmarket), 78
Premier (horse), 53
Preston, Mr., breeder of Sampson, 64, 65
Pretender (horse), 308
Priam (horse), 186, 198
Price, 'Charley,' 140
Priestess (horse), 138, 162
Prince Charlie (horse), 101
— Leopold (horse), 185
Princess, The (horse), 273
Privateer (horse), 157
Prize (horse), 216
Problem (horse), 193
Professor, The (horse), 300
Propagation of Gambling, Society for the, 353, 358
— of the Gospel, Society for the, 140
Property of the J. C. at Newmarket, 246-248
Proserpine (horse), 82
Prospero (horse), 119
Protest (by the stewards of J. C. against a reported decision of a J. C. committee), 254
Prunella (horse), 31, 193
Pulteney, William (Earl of Bath), 140

Pumpkin (horse), (a mile in four and a half minutes !!), 101-103
Punch (horse, imported into America), 26
Pussy (horse), 300
Pyrrhus (horse), 118, 124, 139

QUEEN ANNE, *v.* Anne
— Bertha (horse), 291
— Charlotte, *v.* Charlotte
— Mab (the famous brood mare), 313
— Marie Antoinette, *v.* Marie Antoinette
— Mary (famous brood mare), 139, 350
— of Trumps (horse), (her peculiarity), 292
— Victoria (and horse-racing), *v.* Victoria
Queensberry (last Duke of, 'Old Q.'), (J. C.), 12, 27, 31, 56, 58, 113, 121, 126, 131, 148, 232
Querouaille, Madame de la (Duchess of Portsmouth), 132
'Qui tam' actions, 320
Quick (and Castle), Messrs. ('blacklegs'), 344, 360
Quick-sand (horse), 215
Quits (horse), 300
Quiz (horse), 220, 223
'Quorn,' The, 122
Quorndon Hall, 122

RABY, Lord (Duke of Cleveland), (J. C.), 191
— (horse), 192
— (place), 191
Racecourse Bill (Mr. Anderson's Metropolitan), 336
'Racehorse in Training,' Mr. W. Day's, 78, 329
Radcliffe (Delmé), Mr., 183, 186
Ragamuffin (horse), 136
Raglan, Lord, 280
Ralph (horse), (poisoned), 283, 284

Rama (horse), 280
'Rape of the Lock' (Pope's), 280
Ratan (horse), 318
— Case, the, 318
Ratoni (horse), 227
Read, Mr. (? Wilberforce), (J. C.), 13, 130
— — Rudston, 272
'Receipt to make a Jockey,' 72, 146, 188
'Reciprocity' (from France), demand for, 278, 282, 288, 334
'Red Lion,' The (tavern at Newmarket), 153
— — Square (Holborn), 188
Red-deer, a four-in-hand of, 59
Redrose (horse), 114
Reform Bill, the (effect of), 222
Refraction (horse), 195
Regalia (horse), 295, 361
Reginald (horse), 193
Regulus (horse), 48, 49, 120, 150
Remembrancer (horse), 331
Remus (horse), 95, 289
Rendlesham, Lord (J. C.), 265, 314
Repeal of racing statutes, 320
Repulse (horse), 275
Restitution (horse), 269
Rêve d'Or (horse), 308
Reveller (horse), 222
Rhadamanthus (horse), 55
— the 'infernal' judge, 116
Rhoda (horse), 195
Ribblesdale, Lord (suicide of), (J. C.), 265, 276
Richmond, Dukes of, 35, 36, 194, 211, 366
— — (J. C.), 12, 35, 172, 194, 211, 246, 264, 307, 314, 315, 320
— Bay, 81
— (horse), 112
— (Yorks), (Gold Cup won five years running), 192
Riddle (horse), 97
Riddlesworth (horse), 206, 240
— (place), 226, 240
Ridicule (horse), 226

Riding in with the leading horses, 318
Ridsdale, Mr. ('bookmaker'), 241, 361
'Ring,' The, 306, 345-347, 351-353, 358
— attempt of a noble lord to 'do,' v. Cwrw (horse)
'Ringworm,' The, 359
Ripponden (Yorks), 302
Risby (Suffolk), (or ? near Beverley, Yorks), 146
Rise (in Holderness, Yorks), 130
Robert de Gorham (man), 212
— (horse), 212
Roberts, Mr. W. A. (J. C.), 266
Robin Hood (horse), (by Wild Dayrell), 298
— — — (by North Lincoln), 298
Robinson, Mr. ('Judge to the J. C.'), 167
— — (owner of the famous Sampson), 64
— Rt. Hon. John (Sec. to the Treasury), (? J. C.), 173, 179
— Sir Hercules (J. C.), 265, 307
Rockingham, Marquess of (J. C.), 12, 59, 63, 65, 69, 89, 95, 227, 243, 312
— — — sister of, 65, 66
— (horse), 42, 147; (another), 304
'Rolliad,' The, 175
Romeo (horse), 135
Roper, Hon. Gertrude (Baroness Dacre), 107
Rosaletta (horse), 136
Rose, Mr. C. D. (J. C.), 266, 355
Rosebery, Earl of (J. C.), 264, 296, 307, 315
— Hannah, Countess of, 269
Rosebud (horse), 115
Rosicrucian (horse), 296
Rosslyn, Earl of (J. C.), 264, 287
— — (son of the former), 147
Rothschild, Baron Meyer (J. C.), 264, 269, 315

Rothschild, Baron Lionel, 270, 31
— Miss (Hannah, Countess of Rosebery), 269
— Mr. Leopold (J. C.), 266
Rouge (horse), (bred in France), 108, 188
Rougham (Suffolk), 215
Rous, Lord (Sir John), (J. C.), v. Stradbroke
— Admiral (J. C.), 9, 173, 186, 226, and *passim*
— — continuous re-election of, 326
— Major, 210
— Mr. (of the 'Eagle' Tavern), 210
'— Bravo !' (whence derived), 210
Rowena (horse), 193
Rowton (horse), 280
Royal College of Veterinary Surgeons, 188
— Hunt Cup (Ascot), 303, 321
— mares, 19
— Stud (Hampton Court), 186
Royston, Viscount (Earl of Hardwicke), (J. C.), 265
Rubens (horse), 40, 226
Ruffler (horse), 120
Rufford Abbey (Notts), 302
Rugeley (Staffs), 322
Ruler (horse), 130
Rules and Orders of the J. C., 157-160, 256, 318-340
— Concerning Horse-racing, 156, 254-256, 318-340, and v. Appendix
Run (of more than fifty miles after a fox), 95
'Running Rein' (horse), (the notorious case), 259, 318, 347, 356
Rupee (horse), 288
'Rupert of Debate,' The (J. C.), 271
Rush, Mr. George (J. C.), 173, 226, 266
Rushout, Sir Charles (J. C.), 265, 314

INDEX 411

RUS

Russia, Empress of, 59
Russias, Emperor of all the (J. C.), 263
Rutland, Dukes of, 36, 37, 56, 69
— — (J. C.), 36, 37, 172, 185, 195, 264
Ryshworth (Yorks), 302

SABLONS (France), the plain of, 97
Saccharometer (horse), 289
Sackville, Viscounts (J. C.), 172, 206, 207
— Lord George, 207
Sadler, Mr. (ex-ostler), 361
Sagitta (horse), 271
Sailor (horse), 240, 241
St. Albans, Duke of (J. C.), 264, 307, 315
— — (horse), 282
— — (place), 212
— Albin, Monsieur A. de, 362
— Blaise (horse), 308
— Christopher, island of (St. Kitt's), 124
— Donat's (Glamorganshire), 301
— George (horse), 191, 206, 226, 227
— George's Fields, 233
— Giles (horse), 241
— John, Colonel, 100
— — Hon. John (? J. C.), (a 'macaroni' and author), 173, 179
— Lawrence (horse, and name of the Earls of Howth), 285
— Leger, Colonel, 63
— — (race), 63, 125
— Marguerite (horse), 300
— Patrick (horse), 112, 222
— Peter's (Isle of Thanet), 103
— Quintin, Sir. W., 20
— Simon (horse), 48, 268
— Vincent, Lord (Viscount), (J.C.), 265, 276, 277
Salisbury, race for Silver Bowl at, 116
— Lord, 138

SCR

Salisbury, Countess of (beheaded), 231
Sally (horse), 122
Salterley Common, 47
Saltram (horse), (so-called from the seat of the Earls of Morley, Devon), 226, 239
Sam (horse), 240, 241
Sampson (horse), (15 hands, 2 in.), 64, 65
Sancho (horse), 239
Sanderson, the Rev. T., 92
Sandown Park, 333, 353
Sarpedon (horse), 81
Satirist (horse), 283
Saturn (horse), 61
Saucebox (horse), 286
Savernake (horse), 282
Savile, Mr. H. (J. C.), 266, 302
Saye and Sele, Lord (J. C.), 265, 293
Scales, tampering with the, 280
Scaramouch (horse), 33
Scarf (horse), 63
Scarsdale (Lord, first Baron), (J.C.), 80
Scipio (Roman general), 50
— (and tooth-picks), 50
— (horse), 50, 89
Scotia (horse), 146
Scott, Mr. (? Capt., Major, Col., and Gen.), (J. C.); 13, 58, 130, 131
— the three Misses (Duchess of Portland, Viscountess Downe, and Viscountess Canning), 130, 131
— Lord J. (J. C.), 265, 293
— Mr. J. (trainer), 248, 249, 272, 291, 299, 310, 361
— Mrs., 291
— Mr. W. (jockey), 361
Scottish Queen (horse), 308
Scrimsher ⎫
Scrymsher ⎬ Mr. Boothby, 13, 104, 134, 135
Scrymshire ⎨
Skrymsher ⎭
Scriven (Yorks), 114

SCU

Scud (horse), 240
Seabreeze (horse), 308
Sebright, Sir Thomas Saunders (J. C.), 12, 91
— Lieut.-Gen. Sir John S. (? J. C.), 91
Sedley (or Sidley), Sir Charles (J. C.), 12, 91–93
See-saw (horse), 289
Sefton, Earls of (J. C.), 58, 122, 303
— (horse), 58, 300
— House (Newmarket), 58, 300
Selim (horse), 40
Selima (horse), 61
Selwyn, Mr. George (the wit), 7, 13, 14, 57, 117, 131–133, 201, 229
Semolina (horse), 308, 329
Senlis (horse), 41
Seringapatam (siege of), 294
Sevastopol (fortress), 268
Seymour, Lady Elizabeth, 33
— Capt. H. (J. C.), 266
— Lord Henry, 272
— Sir Hamilton, 268
Shafto, Messrs., or Capts. J. and R. (J. C.), 13, 89, 111, 132–134, 141, 159, 215
— Mr. J. (matches), 133, 134
Shakespeare, William, 212, 239, 240
Shakspear, Mr. Arthur (J. C.), 173, 226, 239
Shardeloes (Amersham, Bucks), 300
Shark (horse), 127, 229, 230
Sheerness, curious horse-wager at, 186
Shelburne, Lord (Lansdowne), (? J. C.), 177
Shelley, Sir John (fifth Baronet), (J. C.), 12, 93, 190
— — — (sixth Baronet), (J. C.), 93, 204, 224, 265, 297
— — — (seventh Baronet), (J. C.), 265, 266, 297
Sherborne, Lord (J. C.), 137, 172, 208, 209, 236

SLI

Sherborne (place), 208
Sheridan, Right Hon. R. B. (? J. C.), 173, 180
Shiplake (Oxon), 231
Shipton (near York), 75, 120, 360
Shirley, Hon. Messrs., 134, 135
Shoemaker (horse), 112
Shorthand-writers, the J. C. and, 320, 321
Shotover (horse), 308
Shottesbrook, 241
Shoveller (or Shoveler), (horse), 240, 241
Siberia (horse), 308
'Sick Man,' The (Turkey), 268
Siderolite (horse), 296
Signal (horse), 216
Signorina (horse), 162
Silver (horse), 207
— Bowl (at Salisbury), 116
Silvertail (horse), 145
Silvio (horse), 291
Sim Tappertit, 73
Singleton, Mr. John, senior (jockey), 130
Sir Archy (American horse), 80
— Bevys (horse), 270, 315
— Harry (horse), 235
— Joshua (horse), 226, 301
— Oliver (horse), 244
— Peter Teazle (more commonly Sir Peter), 67, 68, 200
— Thomas (horse), 81, 183
— — Jellybag (horse), 175
Sister to Pharamond (horse), 190
Six Mile Bottom Stud Farm (Newmarket, the Prince Regent's), 302
Skelmersdale, Lord, 149
Skim (horse), 63
Skipton (Yorks), 130
Skirmisher (horse), 93
Skrymsher, &c., v. Scrimsher, &c.
Skyscraper (horse), 190, 236
Slane (horse), 286
Slingsby, Miss Sarah (maid of honour to Queen Anne, Mrs. Duncombe), 114

SLI

Slingsby, Sir C., 148
Slipby (horse), (bay), 120
—— —— (brown), 120
Smart (afterwards Claret), (horse), 217
Smiling Betty (horse), 278
—— Molly (horse), 310
—— Nanny (horse), 309
Smith, Mr. or General (J. C.), 13, 135, 136
—— (the Young General), (? J. C.), 136
—— Mr. Hugh (millionaire, whose daughters married into the Barrymore and Derby families), 68, 136, 199
—— —— and Mrs. Robert Percy, 143
—— the Right Hon. Mr. Vernon, 143
—— the Rev. Sidney, 122
—— Mr. T. Assheton (J. C.), 266
—— Mrs. (Lady Lade), 218
Smith-Barry, Mr. (J. C.), r. Barry
Smithson, Sir Hugh (Duke of Northumberland), 33, 34
Smolensko (horse), 74, 224, 244, 278
Smyrna (place), 150
Snap (horse), 20, 89, 216
Snapdragon (horse), 61
Snewing, Mr. ('vet.' and 'bookmaker'), 361
Snip (horse), (maternal grandsire of Pyrrhus), 139
'Snipe' (*alias* W. Taylor), (earliest published case of 'warning off' by the J. C.), 257, 258, 282
Sober Robin (horse), 206
Société d Encouragement, 7, 362
Society for the Propagation of Gambling, 353, 358
—— —— —— —— of the Gospel, 140
—— a Turf, 363
Sog (horse), 82
Soldier (horse), 52
Solon (horse), 65

SQU

Soltykoff, Prince D. (J. C.), 264, 268
Somerset, Dukes of, 33
—— Edward (Earl of Worcester), 309
—— the proud Duke of, 33, 36
Sondes, Lord (J. C), 12, 66, 67
Songstress (horse), 270
Soothsayer (horse), 84
Sorcery (mare), 195
Sotterley (Suffolk), 298
Sourface (horse), 118
South, Mr., 78
—— East (horse), 63
—— West (horse), 63
Southampton, Duke of Cleveland and, 192
—— Lord (J. C.), 265
Southfleet (estate), 92
Southwark (place), 217
Spain (toothpicks introduced from), 50
Spalding, Mr. (J. C.), 266
Spaniel (horse), 206, 286
'Speaker,' Mr., vii
Spectator (horse), 89, 148, 156
Spectre (horse), 26, 137, 208
Speculum (horse), 274
Spencer, Lady Diana, 44
—— Earl (J. C.), 264
—— Hon. Capt. (J. C.), 266
'Spider and Fly,' 275, 277
Spiletta (horse), 20
Spinaway (horse), 291
Spitfire (horse), 60
'Sporting Kalendar,' The (Mr. J. Pond's), 5
'—— Magazine,' a writer in the, 229
Sportsman (horse), 67, 145
Sportsmistress (horse), 145
Spot (horse), 61, 194
Spread Eagle (horse), 207, 220
Sprightly (horse), 139
Squerries (Kent), 143
Squirrel (first called Surly), (horse), 89
Squirt (horse), (grandsire of Eclipse), 139

STA

Stafford, Marquess of (the first, grandfather of Lord Granville), (J. C.), 53
Stamford (and Warrington), Earl of (J. C.), 250, 258, 264, 287, 335, 355
— (place), 309
Standard (horse), 80
Standby (horse), 139
— Young, 80
Standish, Sir Frank (J. C.), 207, 220
Stanhope, Philip, Earl of Chesterfield (J. C.), 172, 177
— Amelia, Countess of Barrymore, 177
— Dormer, Earl of Chesterfield (? J. C.), 172, 177
— Earl of Harrington (? J. C.), 172, 177
Stanley, Lord (Earl of Derby), (J. C.), 265, 271, 329-331
— — and Canezou, 330
— — — Mr. Greville's Cariboo, 330
— Messrs. (J. C.), 265, 266, 295, 303
— Sir M. (J. C.), 266
— the family of, 199
Stapleford (Notts), 145
Stapleton, Mr. (ancestor of Lord Beaumont), (J. C.), 13, 83, 84, 137
Star (Queen Anne's horse), 24, 311
' — and Garter,' The (Pall Mall), 6, 7, 152
— Davis (American horse), 302
Stargazer (horse), 71
Starling (horse), (the Ancaster S.), 24
— (Bay), 120
— (Brown), 120
Statira (horse), 108
Staveley (horse), 239
Stawell, Lord (? J. C.), 172, 208, 209

STU

Stawell, Baroness, 209
Stella (horse), 108
Stephenson, Mr. (Alderman of Newcastle), 120
Steyne, the (Brighton), 49
— — (match on), 219
— (Thackeray's), Marquess of, 49
Steyning, 100
Stickler (horse), 224
Stilton (churchyard), 47
Sting (mare), 223 ; (horse), 270
Stockton (Wilts), 299
Stockwell (horse), 203, 292, 304, 354, 361
Stoic (horse), 123
Stonehewer, Mr. Scott (J. C.), 266, 303
Stow (place), 123
Stowell, Lord, 209
Strabally Hall (Ireland), 300
Stradbroke, Earls of (J. C.), 172, 209-211, 264
Stradling, the family of, 301
Strafford, Earls of (J. C.), 214, 264, 265, 288
Strange, Lord (so self-styled, father of the twelfth Lord Derby), (J. C.), 12, 67, 68, 199
Strangways (not Strangeways), Fox- (name of the Earl of Ilchester), 312
Strathmore, Earls of (J. C.), 265, 288, 299
Stratton, Mr. George (and Lord Pigot), 62
Strawberry Hill, 51, 242
Streatlam Castle (Durham), 248, 288, 299
Strickland, Sir William, 147
Stripling (horse), 26
Strode) Mr. or Captain Edward
Stroud) (J. C.), 12, 137, 138
Stuart, Sir Simeon (J. C.), 12, 94
Stuart-Wortley, v. Wortley
Stud Companies, 361
' — Book,' the, 165, 234, 237, 303
Stumbler (horse), 112

INDEX   415

STU

Stumps (horse), 202
Sturgeon, William or John (a groom), 65, 66
Sturt, Mr. Humphry, 309
— — Gerard (Lord Alington), (J. C.), 267, 296
Subscribers to the J. C. Challenge Cup, 30, and *passim*
Subscription Rooms (Newmarket), 358
Sudbury (Suffolk), 113
Suffield, Lords (J. C.), 172, 207, 211, 293, 294, 307
Suffolk and Berkshire, Earl of (J. C.), 9, 248, 265, 315, 346, 356, 366
Sultan (horse), 205, 282
Summerside (horse), (winner of the Oaks), 291
Sunshade (horse), 300
Surly (horse), 89
Surplice (horse), 272, 290
Surprise (horse), 183
Surrey, Earl of, 175
Surveyor (horse), 112
Sutton, Mr. R. (Sir Richard), (J. C.), 267, 303
Swaffham (Bulbeck), 246, 247
— (Prior), 247
Sweepstakes (horse), 54
Sweet Briar (horse), 55
— William (horse), 55; (Mr. Barker's), 313
Sweetsauce (horse), 284
Swillington (place, the Rev. Sir W. Lowther's), 88
Swinburne, Mr. William (J. C.), 13, 89, 134, 138, 139
Swindon (Wilts), 301
Swymmer, Mr. Anthony Langley (J. C.), 13, 119, 139, 140, 315
Symme, Colonel (American), 119
Symmetry (horse), 84
Synge, Colonel (J. C.), 267
Syntax, Doctor (horse), 284
Syphon (horse), 139, 190

THA

TAAFFE, Mr. Theobald, M.P. (gambler), vii
— Count, vii
Tadcaster (Yorks), 242, 243
Tag (horse), 202
Takamahaka (horse), 40
Tampering with the scales, 280
Tan gallops, 249, 299
Tandem (horse), 43, 134, 220
Tankerville, Countess of, 140
Tappertit, Sim, 73
Tarleton, Mr., Colonel, and General Banastre (? J. C.), 173, 180
Tarragona (horse), 258
— Case, the, 258
Tarran, Rev. Mr. (his 'Black Barb'), 162
Tartar Mare, the fabulous, 313
— (horse), 313
Tattersall, Messrs., 7, 45, 74, 144, 150, 327, 360
'Tattersall's,' 162, 256, 327, 359
Tavistock (place), 142
— Marquess of (J. C.), 172, 212, 264, 281
— — 189
Tawney (horse), 56, 121
Taylor, Mr. (*alias* Snipe), 257
— — C. (J. C.), 173
Teazle, Sir Peter (horse), 200
' — (Lady),' 200
Teddington (horse), 295, 296, 303
Teddy the Grinder (horse), 71
Teissier, Barons de, 269
— Baron de (J. C.), 264, 268, 269, 296
— — Lewis, 269
Tempest, Sir H. Vane (J. C.), *v.* Vane
Ténébreuse (French horse), 335, 338
Tetotum (horse), 235
Texas (country), 275
Thanet, Isle of, St. Peter's, 103
Tharp, Mr. W. M. (J. C.), 267, 315
— Mr. John, 315

THA

'Thatched House,' the (tavern), 7, 152
Thebais (horse), 300
Thelusson, Messrs. (Lords Rendlesham), 314
'— Act,' the, 314
Theobald, Mr. (hosier and breeder of Stockwell), 203, 361
Theodore (horse), (extraordinary winner of the St. Leger), 280
Theophania (horse), 84
Thesiger, Sir F. (Lord Chancellor), 178
Thetford (horse), 223
Thirty Stone, a match at, 77, 238
Thomond, Lords (Earls of), 201, 202
— — (their stud in Charles II.'s time), 201
— House (Newmarket), 201
Thompson, 'Bet,' 140
Thornhill, Mr. (of Riddlesworth), (J. C.), 173, 226, 240, 241, 267, 301
Thornton, Colonel (the famous), 148
Thornville (horse), 148
Thoulouse (or Toulouse), (place), 127
Thrale, Mr. Henry (eminent brewer), 217
— Mrs. (Dr. Johnson's friend), 217
'Three D.'s v. three K.'s,' 277
Thucydides, 48
Thumper (horse), 112
Thurlow, Lord (Chancellor), (? J. C.), 172, 177
Thwackum (horse), (*alias* Scipio), 89
Thynne, family of, 309
Tigress (horse), 112
Tigris (horse), 210
Tim Whiffler (horse), 292
Timoleon (American horse), 80
Tipping, Mr. ,90
Tiresias (horse), 194, 271
Titchfield, Marquess of (J. C.), 172, 194

TRU

Tolstone ⎫
Toulston   ⎬ Hall (Yorks), 147
Towlestone ⎭
Tomato (horse), 269
Tomlinson, Mr. (breeder of Teddington), 295
Tommy (horse), 84, 137
Tomtit (or Tom Tit), (horse), 311
Tooley Park (Leicester), 122
Toothpicks (Scipio and), 50
Topham, Capt., Major, and Col. (the celebrated), (? J. C.), 173, 180
Tortoise (horse), 53
Tot (horse), 206
Touchstone (horse), 139, 219, 282, 283, 354
Toulouse, v. Thoulouse
'Touts,' the J. C. and the, 346
Towneley (place, Lancashire), 303
— Col. Charles (J. C.), 267, 303
— Marbles, the, 303
Townshend, Lord John (? J. C.), 172, 177
— George, Earl of Leicester and Marquess T. (? J. C.), 177
— Hon. Charles (a joker), 74
Toxophilite (horse), 271
Toy (horse), 314
Training 'Reports' (in the newspapers), 334
Trajan (horse), 55
Tramp (horse), 304
Transit (horse), 38
Tregony (place), 126
Trentham, Viscount (J. C.), 53, 116, 118, 124
— (horse), 92, 137
Trials, 346
Trifle (horse), 50
Tristan (horse), 287
Trollope (Lord Kesteven), 25
Trotinda (horse), 221
Trousers (first wearer in public of), (J. C.), 218
True Blues (horses), the two, 147, 298
Trumpator (horse), 50

INDEX

TRU

Trumpetta (horse), 51
Trustee (horse), 241
Turcoman (horse), 193
'Turf Society' (a proposed), 364
Turner, Sir Charles (? J. C.), 95, 96, 241
— Teresa (Lady), 241
— Mr. and Sir C. (J. C.), 12, 84, 94, 147
— — — — (his leaping-match), 95
Turnus (horse), 61
Turpin, Dick (highwayman), 85, 242
Turquoise (horse), 193
Tuting (and Fawconer), Messrs., 164, 165, 360
— — — —'s Calendar, 164
Twickenham, Marble Hall at, 274
Two-year-old Racing, who began, 76–80
— — — — sanctioned by the J. C., 51, 365
Two Thousand (the race), 331
— — Cwrw's (sharp practice by a noble member of the J. C.), 331
Tyrant (horse), 31

UDNEY, Mr. or Col. John Robert Fullarton (J. C.), 173, 226, 227, 267
— Castle (Aberdeen), 227
Uffington, Viscount (first Earl of Craven), 51
Ulick (horse), 193
Uppark (Sussex), 81 ; races at, 82, 366
Upper Ossory, Earl of (J. C.), 12, 31, 60, 61, 178
— — Dowager Countess of, 143
Uxbridge, Earl of (J. C.), 265

VACCINATION ACT, a compulsory, 239
Vaharina (horse), 212

VIN

'Valentine,' Mr. (Lord Falmouth), 291
Vampire (horse), 26
Van Tromp (horse), 284
Vandyke (Junior), (horse), 162, 211
Vane, Sir H. T. (J. C.), 173, 220, 313
— family of, 192
Vansittart, Messrs., 90
— Mr. Henry (J. C.), 96, 173, 227, 241, 267
Varey, Mr. William (J. C), 13, 140
Variation (horse), 303
Vauban (horse), 308
Vauxhall Snap (horse), 216
Vavasour, Sir W., 77
Vedette (horse), 290
Velocipede (horse), 346
Velocity (horse), 53
Vengeance (horse), (property of the 'Rugeley poisoner'), 322
Ventilator (horse ; yearling), 250
Ventre-Saint-Gris (horse), 109
Vernon, Henrietta (Lady Grosvenor), 54
— Mr. H. (J. C.), 13, 173, 227, 241, 250
— — R. (J. C.), 13, 41, 54, 55, 60, 79, 111, 140–143, 153, 241, 246
— Lord, 92
— Place, 142
— Smith, Rt. Hon. Mr., 143
Vert (French horse), (Duke of Orléans's), (bred in France), 108, 188
Verulam, Lords (J. C.), 172, 196, 212, 213, 224, 246, 265, 366
Victoria, Queen, 18, 283, 293
Villiers (Duke of Buckingham), 114, 204
— Viscount (Earl of Jersey), (J. C.), 265
— Rt. Hon. J. C. (third Earl of Clarendon), (J. C.), 173, 227
— Hon. A. and F. (J. C.), 267
Vincent, Sir F., 140
'Vintner mare,' the, 113

E E

Violante (horse), 55, 220
— (she-rope-dancer), 220
Virago (horse), 125, 239
Viret (horse), 194
Virginia (U. S. of America), 119, 230, 239
Viscount (horse), 234, v. Young Chillaby
Vitellina (horse), 196, 212
Vivian (Lord), (J. C.), 265, 278, 334
Vladimir, Prince and Grand Duke (of Russia), 263
Volante (horse), 51
Vole (horse), 224
Voltaire (the famous Arouet de), 209
Voltigeur (horse), 284, 290
Vyner, Mr. H. F. Clare (J. C.), 267, 304
— — R. C. (declines the J. C.), 304

WADDINGTON, Mr. H. S. (J. C.), 267
Waldegrave, Earl of (J. C.), 12, 68, 69
— — — (John), 69
— Countess of (Duchess of Gloucester), 21, 23, 69
— Lady Maria (Duchess of Grafton), 69, 201
Wales, Prince of (George the Fourth), (J. C.), 4, 49, 75, 79, 81, 129, 172, 181–184, 223
— — — (Albert Edward), (J. C.), 184, 263
' — — — ' (Sir Watkin Wynn), 297
Walker, Mr. Thomas (J. C.), 173, 227, 230, 242
— Mr. B. (and his Calendar), 164
— 'Old Tom,' 242
— Mr. T. E., 300 [v. Case-Walker (J. C.)]
Wallace, Sir Richard (J. C.), 265, 272
Wallop (Viscount Lymington), 314

Walpole, Horace, vii, 7, 14, 286 and *passim*
— Sir Robert, 13, 59, 242
— — Edward, 69
— Maria (Countess Waldegrave and Duchess of Gloucester), 21, 69
Walton, Mr. (American 'plunger'), 348
— (horse), 221, 222
Walworth (Durham), 120
Warde (or Ward), Mr. John (of Squarries, Kent), (J. C.), 13, 143
— Mr. John ('glorious John'), (? J. C.), 143, 144
Warhawke (horse), 121
Warren, Admiral Sir P., 40
— Captain J. B., 145
— Mr. John Borlase (J. C.), 13, 145
— Admiral Borlase, 145
— Hill (Newmarket), 248
Warwick, Earls of, 143
Wastell, Mr. John (J. C.), 145–147
— Miss, 146
Waterford, Marquess of (J. C.), 264
Waterloo, battle of, 195, 236
Watson, Hon. George (J. C.), 173, 227, 243
Watt, Mr. Richard (J. C.), 192, 267, 304
Watts, Mr. (of Ireland), 304
Waxy (horse), 38, 202, 209, 219, 220
Weald House (Essex), 68
Weatherby, Messrs., 11, 161, 164–167, 245, 249, 253, 257
Weights and Scales Plate, 99, 157
Welbeck (estate of Dukes of Portland), 272
Wellington, the Duke of, 236, 238
Wenlock (horse), 289
Wentworth (Charles Watson, second and last Marquess of Rockingham), (J. C.), 64–66
— Mr. Peregrine (J. C.), 13, 81, 147, 227, 243

WEN

Wentworth, Lady Henrietta Alicia (married her groom), 65, 66
West Australian (horse), 148, 291, 292, 299
— Harling (Norfolk), 113
— Wratting (Cambs), 132-134
Westminster (Dean and Chapter of), 176
— Abbey, 162
— school, 189
— Marquess of (J. C.), 55, 176, 196, 264, 282, 283
— Duke of (J. C.), 55, 221, 264, 283, 307, 315, 326
Westmorland, Earl of (J. C.), 265, 279, 280, 315, 316
— Earls of, 315
Weybridge (place), 185, 187
Whalebone (horse), 38, 220
Wharncliffe, Lord (J. C.), 227, 258, 265
Wharton, Philip, Duke of, 42
— Lord, 28
Wheel of Fortune (horse), 291
Whip, The (Newmarket Challenge), 19, and *passim*
— Royal, The (at the Curragh), 184
Whipcord (horse), 215
Whipper In (horse), 114
Whisker (horse), 38, 193, 220
Whistlejacket (horse), Lord Rockingham's, 64
White, Mr. (of Australia), 324
White's Club ('Old'), vii, 143
Whitenose (horse), 145
Whitewall (Yorks), (famous training place at), 248, 272, 277
Whitworth (Durham), 120, 133, 134
Whizgig (horse), 193
Why Not (horse), 120
Whyte, Mr. Christie, 39, 75, 142
— Mr. John (hippodrome), 249, 356
Wickham Mills (Essex), 108
— (horse), 108, 180
Wigram, Mr. W. (J. C.), 267

WOO

Wilbraham, Mr. Roger (J. C.), 13, 148, 149
— Bootle, Mr. Richard, 149
Wildair (horse, by Cade), 138
Wildman, Mr. (meat-salesman), 21, 150, 360
Wilkes, Mr. John W. (and Liberty), 21
Willes, Mr. Irwin ('Argus'), ('warned off'), 258
William III., King, 8, 19, 150
— IV., King, 172, 184, 223, 263
Williams, Mr. 'Gilly,' 14
— Gen. Owen (J. C.), 267, 307, 315
— Sir J., 316
Williamson, Sir Hedworth (J. C.), 173, 221
Williamson's Ditto (horse), 220, 221
Wilmington (Lord), 58
Wilson, Mr. Christopher (J. C.), 173, 227, 243, 267
— Rt. Rev. Christopher, 243
— Mr. or Col. Robert (Lord Berners), 243
— — Richard, 243
— — William, 243
Wilton, Earl of (J. C.), 107, 265, 289, 290, 294, 366
Windhound (horse), 293
Windsor (place), 314
Wings (horse), 236, 270
Wirrall (Cheshire), 219
Witton (Long), (place), 138
Wizard (horse), (by Sorcerer), 244
Wolseley, Sir William (J. C.), 12 96
— — Charles, 96
— — Henry, 96
— Lord, 96
— Mount (Ireland), 96
Wood, Sir Mark (J. C.), 173, 222, 265, 305
— General Mark (J. C.), 267, 305
Woodcock, Mr. (great rider), 133, 134

WOO

Woodcote (estate of), 269
— (Stakes), 269
Woodpecker (horse), 215
Worcester, Earl of (Edward Somerset), 309
'World, The' (publication), 180
Worley, Mr. W., 187
Wormwood (horse), 215
Wortley, Rt. Hon. J. Stuart W. (Lord Wharncliffe), (J. C.), 173, 227, 258
Wotton (horse), 216
Wouvermans (horse), 223
Wowski (horse), (dam of Smolensko), 224
Wratting, West (Cambs), 133, 134
Wraxall, Sir N., 66
Wroughton, the Rev. Philip, 90
Wyke House (Middlesex), 179
Wyndham, Hon. C. (J. C.), 173, 181, 196, 225, 227, 244
— Mrs. (Miss Iliffe), 201
— Col. G. (J. C.), 267
Wynn, Sir W. W. (J. C.), 265, 297
Wynne (or Wynn), Rev. Mr. Nanney, 162
Wyvill, Sir M., 29

ZOR

XAINTRAILLES (French horse), 270

YARDLEY STUD, the, 295
Yarm (Yorks), 146
Yates, General (J. C.), 267
Yearling races, 79, 250, 365
Yellow Filly, The (or Y. Mare), 87, 220
York, Edward Augustus, Duke of (brother of George III.), 12, 22, 23
— Frederick, Duke of, 71, 172, 184, 185, 187, 195, 225
'— and Ainsty' (accident), 148
Yorkshire Jenny (horse), 81
Young Chillaby (*alias* Viscount), (horse), 234
— Drudge (horse), 116
— Mouse (horse), 197
— Vandyke (horse), 162

ZEAL (horse), 193, 316
Zetland, Earls of (J. C.), 81, 148, 265, 284, 290, 307
Zinc (horse), 193
Zinganee (horse), 185, 197
Zoraïda (horse), 221

www.ingramcontent.com/pod-product-compliance
Lightning Source LLC
Chambersburg PA
CBHW032138010526
44111CB00035B/610